SEVERELY HANDICAPPED STUDENTS

SEVERELY HANDICAPPED STUDENTS
An Instructional Design

WAYNE SAILOR

San Francisco State University

DOUG GUESS

University of Kansas

HOUGHTON MIFFLIN COMPANY BOSTON

Dallas Geneva, Illinois Hopewell, New Jersey Palo Alto London

*To the parents of children
with severe disabilities*

Cover design by Jerry Wilke.

Photographs by Marvin Silverman and Patricia Weissman.

Design and Production by Phil Carver & Friends, Inc.

Printed in U.S.A.

Library of Congress Catalog Card Number: 82-83289

ISBN: 0-395-32788-1

CONTENTS

PREFACE

It is our intent, with this book, to present a comprehensive system that may serve as a basis for organizing instructional programs for severely handicapped students. The system we present is an outgrowth of nearly a decade of research into the learning processes and response styles of a wide range of handicapped children and young adults who are, for the first time in their lives, receiving an intensive educational effort.

Conceptually, the system is strongly behavioral, but in a pragmatic sense rather than in the sense of a philosophical or theoretical bias. The system combines behavioral techniques of instruction with curricular considerations from cognitive theory and developmental psychology as well as from a newer and rapidly growing model of environmental adaptation.

Most importantly, the book is designed to present an *adaptable* system, one that can be altered, bent, twisted, and manipulated to conform to each reader's specific circumstances and service delivery realities. It is not a "cookbook." Rather, it is intended to be a foundation on which to build, a starting place, and an organizational framework.

AUDIENCE

This book has been written for present and future teachers, therapists, and other professionals who are preparing to work with moderately to severely disabled students, whether in public school, community, or institutional settings. In addition, it can serve parents seeking background information.

COVERAGE

Severely Handicapped Students: An Instructional Design begins with an overview of the subject and a discussion of basic concepts and categories.

It then traces the recent legal and historical developments related to the provision of educational services to severely handicapped persons. Later chapters examine curriculum development, evaluation, and sequencing and cover the spectrum from assessment, goal setting, and IEP planning through instructional design, measurement, and data-based decisions for change. Among the topics discussed are parent involvement, organization of staff and class schedules, selection of special furniture and equipment, and the range and nature of appropriate educational environments. Throughout, the text seeks to convey the system through careful illustration and example. Applications of the system to different age groups (from infants and preschoolers to secondary-level students and adults) and with disability-specific considerations are noted as well.

ACKNOWLEDGMENTS

The system that we present has developed (and continues to develop) as the framework for teacher training programs at the University of Kansas and at San Francisco State University since 1976. Our former students in school districts from Anchorage, Alaska, to Portland, Maine, use this system. As teacher trainers, it has been our continuing contact with and feedback from our former students, practicing in the field, that has most influenced the system in its present form.

So many people have contributed in so many ways to this text that adequate acknowledgment would require a separate text in itself. There are, however, two individuals in particular to whom we owe a great deal. Education of severely handicapped students is one area of national endeavor for which leadership at the federal level has been of major and significant import. In particular, there is little represented in this book that would have been possible without the dedication and direction provided by Ed Sontag of the United States Department of Education. Additionally, the reader will be struck early in the text with the enormous extent to which the system presented here relies upon the creative thought, energy and direction in curriculum development that emanates from Madison, Wisconsin, under the tutelage of Lou Brown.

We also wish to acknowledge the significant contributions made by John Filler, Jr., California State University at Hayward, Sharon Freagon, Northern Illinois University, and Greg Frith, Jacksonville State University, in providing comprehensive and helpful reviews of the developing manuscript. R. Don Horner, University of Kansas, contributed significantly to Chapter 2, and Mary Noonan, University of Hawaii, and Cynthia Janssen, Philadelphia School District, assisted directly in the preparation of Chapters 9 and 11. The critical reviews and analyses provided by Marci Hanson, San Francisco State University, of Chapter 9 and Owen White,

University of Washington, of Chapter 8, were particularly helpful in the final revision. Many of our students supplied us with examples, as well as original and innovative applications of the system. These include Catherine Breen, Fredda Brown, David Esquith, Joyce Forte, Robert Haas, Mary Frances Hanline, Jennifer Holvoet, Richard Hopper, Ann LaLonde-Berg, Sue Langford, Judith Looby, Marilyn Mulligan, Nena Murphy-Herd, and Jane Rues. Ann Halvorsen helped us with our library work and Kathy Doering with photograph selection, placement, and permissions. Marv Silverman and Patricia Weissman took the photographs.

Finally, Sue Elkins and Nancy Dodd provided technical editing assistance and Barbara Brautigam together with Jim Nance got us through our deadline crises with technical management and manuscript preparation. Many others helped us in many ways and we hope they will forgive us the omission of recognition. In the end, the responsibility for errors and failures is ours alone for, we confess, we did not always take the good advice that was offered to us.

Wayne Sailor   Doug Guess
San Francisco State   *University of*
University   *Kansas*

CHAPTER 1

The Severely Handicapped Student

Who are the students for whom this book is written? Every reader will have some idea of the characteristics of a severely, multiply handicapped child. For some, the image will be that of a Down's Syndrome child, ambulatory, sociable, and with limited speech and dressing skills. For others, the image may be that of a large, aggressive, twenty-year-old with little or no ability to communicate expressively. For still others, the image may be that of a small, nonambulatory child with little muscle control and no communication or self-help skills. All these images are correct, as are many others. Severely handicapped individuals have in common only their degree of dependence. Do these diverse characteristics form an identifiable category? The answer is no. We cannot reliably define our target population in terms of common characteristics of its members. Fortunately, that is not the only approach to definition that is available to us. Before we present the solution we favor, let us review the problem of educational categorization in general.

EDUCATIONAL CATEGORIZATION

Human beings have a strong organizational tendency. That is a statement about our essential nature that few would dispute. We are neither as organizationally meticulous as, for example, the ant nor as organizationally sloppy as the dog, but we are closer to the ant. We deal with the complexities of our social existence by conceptualizing categorical boundaries. We typically associate certain behavioral characteristics with each example of our categorical structure and then behave toward others in large part on the basis of the category to which we assign each new person we meet. There are categories that serve an obvious function for our survival as a species, for example, male-female, young-old. Other categories seem to have no function and are therefore arbitrary, for example, black-white, Protestant-Jew.

In no single institution of our complex societies is that organizational tendency more obvious than in our educational structures. In earlier periods, schools were organized first by socioeconomic class and second by the nature of the subject matter to be taught. Schools for the rich offered programs in medicine; schools for the poor, programs in farming and carpentry. Writing, according to available evidence, seems to have emerged as curricular preparation for the middle-class occupation of warehouseman. The tendency to organize public education along economic lines persisted into more recent times with middle-class schools further stratifying along sex and, later, racial lines as the transmigration of various

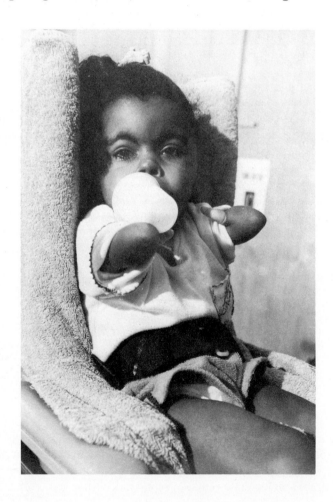

ethnic groups increased. Black children in the United States were originally denied access to public schools on the grounds that literacy might make them discontented with their role as slaves. Later, black children were relegated to separate schools on the basis that there was a need to prevent "miscegenation," or despoilment of the purity of the "white race." Sadly enough, acknowledgment of the attribute of blackness is as necessary to the integrated system as to the segregated one. Schools must report the number of black children in white classes (or vice versa) in order to prove compliance with integration guidelines.

CATEGORIZING THE HANDICAPPED

The education of people with handicaps, which developed primarily in the 1950s, gave rise to the concept of *special education*. With its advent, the process toward integration with nonhandicapped persons followed a well-worn path trod by several generations of handicapped persons in nearly the same sequence of graduated steps experienced by several generations of black students. The process seems to be: identify, categorize, separate, equalize, integrate. The process for blacks was called desegregation; for handicapped people, it is called *mainstreaming*. The process is the same and the forces propelling it are the same (federal legislation, for example), but the process for handicapped persons is proceeding much more rapidly.

Handicapped people come with different handicaps, so naturally the tendency to categorize has prevailed. As a result, there are today classifications within special education that cover nearly the entire spectrum of possible handicaps. For example, Table 1.1 presents a list of categorical programs within special education that have been used in the past decade within the state of California, yet this list is not exhaustive.

TABLE 1.1
Disability Categories in the State of California

Trainable mentally retarded	Hard of hearing
Educable mentally retarded	Seriously emotionally disturbed
Communication disordered	Orthopedically impaired
Aphasic	Other health impaired
Autistic	Emotionally handicapped
Learning disabilities	Multiply handicapped
Deaf/blind	Handicapped infant
Deaf	Handicapped preschool
Visually handicapped	Gifted

Institutionalizing Disability Categories.   When the U.S. Congress passed legislation in 1975 to fund educational programs for the handicapped (Public Law 94–142), it specified that funds be apportioned across disability areas according to the prevalence of a disability in society at large. With only so many dollars available, each disability group or its advocates apply pressure to ensure that its group receives its fair share. Pressure is applied through mailings, lobbying, and so on. The U.S. Office of Special Education is responsible for making sure that programs it funds are neither over- nor underspent within one identified disability area. The result of this is a strong tendency toward the institutionalization of categorical disabilities in the educational structure.

Take what we will call Syndrome X as a case in point. Certain behavioral and physical characteristics of the handicapped are identified in common across a number of children. Theoretical arguments are put forward to explain the phenomena. A catchword is chosen to communicate the syndrome. Grants are applied for and received. Parents of the identified group form an association and apply pressure for increased funds and local specialized services. Colleges see an expanding market for new personnel and establish a new training program for which they request state and federal funds to support instructional staff. Special classes are established at the local school district level. Incidence figures are compiled (frequently inflated) and are used to justify rapidly expanding yearly budgets. Pressure mounts to create a new division of the Council for Exceptional Children (CEC), the division of Syndrome X. When sufficient votes are obtained, new division statutes are granted, and the process of institutionalization is nearly complete. Yearly business meetings are held, officers are elected, and a journal is launched: *The American Journal of Syndrome X.*

Is this process evil, the product of selfish, ambitious, and uncaring people? Not at all. Usually the opposite is true. The question for us and for all severely handicapped students should be, is this process necessary and in the *best* interests of the handicapped individual's long-range progress toward independence?

With the categorical issue in mind, what are we now to do about severely handicapped students? To a degree, we are locked into a categorical definition simply because the other categories already exist and our population, too, needs its fair share of shrinking dollar resources. Ideally, with this consideration in mind, we should develop a check list that will reliably identify all members of our categorical disability, develop incidence figures, and proceed to institutionalize our category within the field of education.

There are two problems, however. First, this procedure would extend and perpetuate an already nonfunctional system (Sontag, Smith, and Sailor, 1977); and second, as we shall see when we discuss assessment (Chapter 5), it probably cannot be done. One major difference exists between the factors that lead to the establishment of Syndrome X and those that are identified with the severely, multiply handicapped. The difference is that the former is a potentially discrete category, whereas the latter is open ended. The severely, multiply handicapped population has the troublesome distinction of being "everybody who is not someone else." In the absence of defining characteristics, incidence figures cannot be adequately compiled.

Defining Disability Characteristics.   Sontag et al. analyzed the efforts to define the severely, multiply handicapped population immediately following passage of the Education of All Handicapped Act in 1975. The authors presented two approaches to the definition problem that were in use up to 1977. The first approach consisted of identifying and defining a new disability category to add to the existing list. This category would be called something like SPH (severely/profoundly handicapped) or SMH (severely, multiply handicapped). Sontag, Burke, and York (1973) were the first to list characteristics for identifying severely handicapped students.

> Now that the exclusion privilege is becoming no longer a legal option, school administrators will have to provide educational services for all children in their districts. This includes students who are not toilet trained; aggressive toward others; do not attend to even the most pronounced social stimuli; self mutilate; ruminate; self stimulate; do not walk, speak, hear, or see; manifest durable and intense temper tantrums; are not under even the most rudimentary forms of verbal control; do not imitate; manifest minimally controlled seizures; and/or have extremely brittle medical existences. (p. 21)

The Bureau of the Education of the Handicapped (USOE/BEH, 1974; now U.S. Department of Education, Office of Special Education Programs) provided the next logical extension of this effort with a much more detailed informal description.

> A severely handicapped child is one who because of the intensity of physical, mental, or emotional problems, or a combination of such problems, needs educational, social, psychological, and medical services beyond those which have been offered by traditional regular and special educational programs, in order to maximize his full potential for useful and meaningful participation in society and for self-fulfillment. Such children include those classified as seriously emotionally disturbed (schizophrenic and autistic), profoundly and severely mentally retarded, and those with two or more serious handicapping conditions such as the mentally retarded deaf, and the mentally retarded blind.
> Such severely handicapped children may possess severe language and/or perceptual-cognitive deprivations, and evidence a number of abnormal

behaviors including: failure to attend to even the most pronounced social stimuli, self-mutilation, self-stimulation, manifestation of durable and intense temper tantrums, and the absence of even the most rudimentary forms of verbal control, and may also have an extremely fragile physiological condition. (RFP 74–10: pp. 2–3)

Defining the population in terms of specifiable characteristics such as the above proves in practice to be nearly impossible. With a set of, at best, subjective parameters with which to characterize a discrete population and with no standardized assessment device or check list, statements including the phrases "must be characterized by" or "may be characterized by" become necessary. The "must" statement greatly increases the probability of an error in identification of the false-negative type: a child who is in fact severely, multiply handicapped may not be identified and served educationally because that child failed to show one or more of the "must have" characteristics. The "may be" statement equally increases the chance of an error of the false-positive type: a child of a different disability group is identified and served inappropriately as if the child were severely, multiply handicapped because one or more of the identifying characteristics is present.

A second approach to the definition problem has been to include the most disabled persons with *all other* categories to comprise a population known as severely handicapped. One state, for example, provided the following definition in its state plan for educational services: "The severely handicapped are those children who are profoundly retarded, seriously emotionally disturbed, deaf, blind, and deaf/blind." The problem here is that almost no one would put a typical deaf student into the same classroom with a typical profoundly retarded student. Attempting to define the severely handicapped in terms of existing disability categories only compounds the problem created by the existence of the multiplicity of disability categories in the first place. Yet tremendous pressure exists for the states to provide definitions and plans for service geared to their definitions (Justen and Brown, 1977).

The implications of this approach can be examined from the multitiered perspectives of the school, the state department of education, the university, and the U.S. Office of Special Education. Under the existing categorical system, the school must: (1) create a class for the severely, multiply handicapped; (2) determine criteria for placement; and (3) recruit and hire a teacher competent to teach the severely handicapped. The state department must decide upon the competencies required of teachers of the severely handicapped and set certification standards. It must then adopt a definition of the category and collect incidence data to report to the U.S. Office of Special Education. The university must create a program within a department of special education to prepare teachers of the severely handicapped and must recruit and hire a qualified instructor to develop the program. Finally, the Office of Special Education must create branches for the severely handicapped within its various divisions in order to disperse funds to the consumers of the new categorical program. The most obvious element common to each of the tiers is the expansion of the existing bureaucracy. Meanwhile, let us steal a look at what is waiting in the wings. Advocates for children with "critical listening deficiency" are steadily applying pressure for the institutionalization of a categorical disability of that name. The same is true for the "mentally gifted" and the "minimal brain dysfunction" and "hyperactive" groups. There is no end to the possibilities for expansion with a categorical disability model.

DEFINITION BY SERVICE NEEDS

A potential solution to the problem was suggested in Sontag, Smith, and Sailor (1977) and elaborated on in Sailor and Haring (1977). It requires a shift away from categorization by disability characteristics to the educational service *needs* of the population under consideration.

EDUCATING DISABLED STUDENTS: SERVICE-NEED MODEL

In this solution, a child is considered severely handicapped if the child requires instruction primarily in basic skills, regardless of the characteristics of the handicapping condition. Conversely, if a child, regardless of handicap, requires primarily academic instruction, then that child belongs in a program of general special education. Children in need of both types of service would spend time in a split program of both types.

Sailor and Haring discussed the concept in terms of referral.

If the diagnosis and assessment process determines that a child with multiple handicaps needs academic instruction, that child should not be referred to the severely/multiply handicapped program. If the child's service need is basic skill development, the referral to the severely/multiply handicapped program is appropriate. Basic skill development consists of: (1) self-help skills, (2) fine and gross motor skills, (3) beginning communication development, (4) beginning social skill development, and (5) beginning cognitive or preacademic skills.

Obviously, this solution to the problems of program referral and placement is not perfect. Some children may be found who require both basic skill training and academic instruction. Perhaps these children should divide their school time between two separate programs. The placement decision will continue to pose problems, in many cases, but we hope that the referral process has been simplified – that children can be referred to the severely/multiply handicapped program on the basis of service need.

In general, the lower incidence population of children who are most severely impaired are the children for whom this program designation pertains. Retardation is the underlying factor – not mental retardation as primary diagnostic consideration, but functional retardation resulting from severity of handicap. Most severely/multiply handicapped children are functionally severely retarded (and, hence, untestable by standardized measures of intelligence). The issue, again, is that regardless of handicapping conditions, the factor determining a child's placement in a class for severely/multiply handicapped children is basic skill development needs. (p. 4)

With a service-need model, the entire superstructure of education of the disabled population would be organized around four components: handicapped early education, elementary and secondary remedial programs, elementary and secondary functional life skills programs, and handicapped career education. The first and last categories are defined by age, handicapped early education being birth to school age and career education being post–school age. Within the two school-age categories, programs are distinguished by the type of instruction offered.

In this model, the public school would offer, in addition to its classes for nonhandicapped students (which would include children with mild disabilities under the mainstreaming concept), classes of remedial special education, basic special education, and a program for handicapped infants and preschool toddlers. Referrals to the basic and remedial special classes would be on the basis of the extent of instructional need as determined by assessment and program plan. Students who are blind, deaf, deaf/blind, orthopedically impaired, behaviorally disordered, functionally retarded, or any combination of these and other handicapping conditions could be assigned to a class of either type or assigned to spend part of the day in one class and part in another. Similarly, a student with academic special needs in particular areas could spend time in both the remedial education class and the appropriate regular-age nonhandicapped class. Children who benefit from intensive instruction, as most do regardless of handicap, could "graduate" from one program to another without leaving the neighborhood school. Therapy services could be concentrated at the district level and made available to a wider range of students. Special education district directors would need to worry about recruitment and selection of only four types of teachers instead of up to sixteen, some of whom are quite "rare and exotic."

What problems are encountered with the four-part service-need model? Advocates associated with categorical disability groups are fond of pointing to the unique characteristics of a particular disability. Syndrome X, for example, requires certain compensatory responses to be established by the child and certain specific kinds of equipment to be employed which only a specialist trained in the nuances of Syndrome X would know how to use properly. Mixing a Syndrome-X child with nonhandicapped children would potentially expose the child to cruel ridicule. Mixing the child with other non-Syndrome-X handicapped children, by the usual logic, would deprive the child of the special resources, equipment, and understanding needed to deal properly with the syndrome. The shift to a service-need model may also pose some specific problems at the level of the state department of education.

TRAINING TEACHERS: DISABILITY CATEGORIES
VERSUS EDUCATIONAL NEEDS

The standards for certification of teachers set by the state department of education (or its affiliates) determine hiring practices, and thus service delivery, at the level of the school district. These standards consequently determine the training programs offered at the university. California, for example, up to 1982 offered four specialist credentials for teachers of handicapped children. These categories were communicative disorders, learning handicapped, severely handicapped, and physically handicapped. Particular categorical programs were ordered within categories. For example, a teacher of the "trainable mentally retarded" had to earn a "severely handicapped" credential, and a teacher of the "deaf/blind" had to earn a "communicative disorders" credential. The result in California was that large university departments of special education offered a wide range of categorical programs for teachers with relatively little crossover and exchange of courses. Smaller college departments tended to have the same personnel offering courses that applied to all credential programs. One program had the potential for expensive overspecialization and narrowness, the other for a watered-down curriculum and insufficient specialization. At this writing, California was developing new credential standards designed to reflect its noncategorical special education legislation passed in 1981.

The state of Oregon earlier adopted a dual specialist credential program that certifies teachers for serving either the severely handicapped (stressing basic skill development competencies) or the mildly handicapped (stressing academic skill competencies). The result in Oregon has been a greatly simplified personnel training and selection system. Teachers are prepared to work with a broader range of children, and schools focus more on the needs of the child in program placement rather than on quasi-medical "diagnosis," with its emphasis on disability characteristics.

Debate over Specialized Training. The issue of specialized training for teachers of a particular disability group is hotly contested and often debated. Any survey of area curricula for teachers in a large university department of special education would likely show a high degree of similarity in the competencies required at completion of training. Teachers of the deaf, blind, orthopedically impaired, and retarded are all taught to become competent in assessment, derivation of goals, specification of objectives, task analysis, evaluation, instructional technique, and environmental programming. Differences exist in the content of the curriculum for the student but usually only between academic and basic skills or between chronological age distinctions. The teacher of the orthopedically impaired student must indeed have specialized training in the motor development area and must have an understanding of the competencies associated with physical and occupational therapy. Similarly, the teacher of the blind student must be competent in specialized sensory and communication-skill approaches and equipment as well as orientation and mobility training; the teacher of the deaf child must be skilled in nonverbal communication modes; and so on. Of course, the teacher of the severely, multiply handicapped child must possess a mix of skills necessary to serve all the child's disabilities. Similarly, if we are committed to the civil rights of handicapped children and to the philosophy of mainstreaming, then we must see that teachers of mildly handicapped students (and eventually regular teachers) acquire some of these competencies, too. There is no longer justification for creating a separate class for children whose only educational problem is that they are confined to wheelchairs.

The Problems of Transition.   Nicholas Hobbs (1975) raises the important issue of how to bring about a transition from categorical labels to programs based on more generic educational needs. School district directors of special education, for example, have expressed concern that the removal of categorized labels would reduce levels of special program funding and thus result in a deterioration of services (Gallagher, 1972). Similarly, parents of children with a categorical disability often fear that amalgamation of educational services with other disabilities will result in a lessening of the extent of expertise brought to bear on the particular disability of their child. Parents, however, often find greater satisfaction in working with teaching personnel with a more broadly based educational preparation (as in Oregon, for example) than that which is current under the specific disability system. And the problem faced by the special education directors might be solved by shifting determinants of funding support away from categorical types to those services necessary to meet the educational needs of students regardless of handicap. The result might well increase the levels of available support simply from the savings produced by the elimination of redundancies in the system. Hobbs (1975) cites an earlier report by Reynolds (undated) in which one state, Minnesota, moved to alleviate the problems posed by the categorical model.

The state of Minnesota has had experience with a state support system for special education programs which has solved many of the problems.... Before 1957, the state financial aid system was similar to that still followed in most of the nation; that is, special state financial aids were paid to local districts for every handicapped child identified by category and placed in a separate program of some form, mostly in special classes. The system rewarded educators for labeling children as retarded or emotionally disturbed, etc., and for displacing them from regular classroom settings into special classes.

In 1957, the support in terms of child "categories" was recognized as being dysfunctional and a new plan was instituted. Instead of dispensing funds according to the labels that were attached to children, the state began to pay two thirds of the salary costs of the personnel who were needed to serve the children with special needs. Thus, the attention was shifted from the child's handicap to the quality of the personnel and the programs that fulfilled his educational needs. The communities receiving the funds were able to develop more and better options to serve the children involved. (pp. 100–101)

Other states, according to Hobbs, that have moved away from conventional categories and have adopted legislation reimbursing school districts on the basis of services required include Massachusetts and Tennessee. Finally, in summarizing the work of the Project on Classification of Exceptional Children, Hobbs concluded that

what is needed is a classification system that provides, on the one hand, increased understanding of the complex character and etiology of handicapping conditions and increased information for purposes of program planning, for providing services, and for determining accountability, and, on the other hand, decreased possibilities of inappropriate treatment and stigmatization by labeling or by experiences provided the labeled child. These seemingly disparate goals can be achieved through the development of a classification system that takes into account (for individual children in particular settings) assets and liabilities, strengths and weaknesses, linked to specified services required to increase the former and decrease the latter. Gross categories and stigmatizing labels are a product of a period when diagnostic formulations were crude and the processing of information sharply limited. Increased precision in describing children and increased capacity for handling data make obsolete the familiar and limiting categories of exceptionality. Improvement in classification procedures must be sought not as an end in itself but as a means to deeper understanding and to improved programming for children. (pp. 281–282)*

---

*Nicholas Hobbs, *The Futures of Children: Categories, Labels, & Their Consequences* (San Francisco, Calif.: Jossey-Bass, 1975), pp. 100–101, pp. 281–282. Used by permission.

We concur with that summary and propose the four-level service-need model as a realistic approach to meet, at the very least, the educational needs of severely handicapped children.

There are encouraging developments throughout the country toward declassification in education. The state of California recently passed a law to implement the state's educational programs emphasizing noncategorical service models. Similarly, progress in deinstitutionalization litigation and the movement toward placement of handicapped students in regular public schools in many states has greatly reduced the barriers that weaken programs for disabled children and youth.

FUNCTIONAL RETARDATION

As Guess and Mulligan (1982) have pointed out, the severely handicapped student is primarily characterized by *functional retardation*. This is a different concept than that described traditionally under the rubric *mental retardation*. It is not intended to be a descriptor by which we can categorize children. In fact, the extreme differences in the behavior and constitution of severely handicapped children probably far outweigh their similarities. Functional retardation implies more than missed milestones of development. It implies a failure of the environment to provide for the needs of the individual (Gold, 1976) and a failure of the system, family or community, of which the child is a part, to function as an integrated unit (Hobbs, 1975). Finally, it suggests that a definition of *severely handicapped* must be based on goals of programmatic instruction and environmental modification and adaptation.

Children who are severely handicapped are significantly delayed in their development relative to their nonhandicapped peers. They learn, under the most ideal conditions, at a significantly slower rate than nonhandicapped students or students in remedial special education programs. Their learning impairment is usually associated with significant delay in several critical aspects of development.

RETARDATION OF LIVING-SKILLS DEVELOPMENT

One form of functional retardation or delay associated with severely handicapped persons is in the realm of independent *self-care skills*. Many of these children are either not toilet trained at all or are only partly so. Urinary and fecal incontinence with severely handicapped students is often an initial target of educational programming, particularly because incontinence is aversive to a teaching staff and may impair progress toward other goals requiring a close relationship with the student. In some cases, neurological considerations may modify this goal, however. *Spina bifida* is an example of a syndrome sometimes encountered with severely handicapped children in which bowel and bladder control may not be possible, and a prosthetic device may be required.

Failure to feed themselves, to perform hygienic activities like washing and toothbrushing, to groom themselves, and so on, is characteristic to some degree of severely handicapped children. The common thread underlying these manifestations of functional retardation in adaptive behavior is a very high degree of dependence on caretakers and instructional personnel.

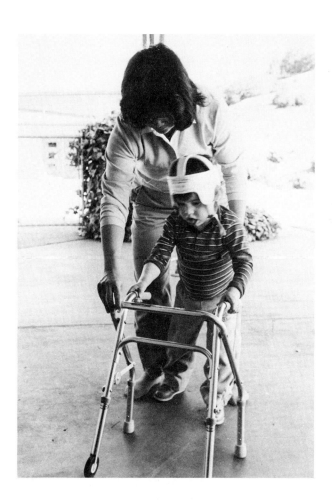

RETARDATION OF SOCIAL DEVELOPMENT

Functional retardation in the sociobehavioral sphere can take the form of bizarre and inappropriate actions. Severely handicapped students may avoid eye contact and seek to remove themselves from others, as in the case of the autistic child. More frequently they will be found to exhibit inappropriate behavior, such as undressing or masturbating in public, displaying random aggression toward others, smearing and eating feces or paper objects, and so on. In an infant, these behaviors are not usually as socially appalling as they are in a twelve-year-old. The difference is that the older child has failed to acquire socially adapted responses and must learn them at the later age.

Stereotyped Behavior. Stereotyped behavior is often associated with severely handicapped persons. Rocking, finger stimulation in front of the face, teeth-grinding, and so on, are examples of stereotyped behavior that is seemingly random and purposeless. Stereotypical bizarre behavior has been linked to arousal (Berkson and Mason, 1963), to reaction to frustrating situations (Baumeister and Forehand, 1972), and to learned patterns of responding in an earlier social context (Spradlin and Girardeau, 1966). Berkson and Davenport (1962) found that some form of stereotyped behavior characterized up to two-thirds of the residents of state institutions for the retarded and that the longer the child's stay at the institution, the more likely that stereotyped behaviors would emerge.

One of the most puzzling and certainly the most serious of the stereotyped behaviors found among severely handicapped children is the cluster of responses called *self-injurious behavior.* Corbett (1975) found that self-injurious behavior characterizes up to 15 percent of severely mentally retarded individuals. This kind of behavior often is manifested by head banging, with hands or against objects, and biting, usually hands, arms, or lips. In most cases, the origin of the onset and maintenance of these behavior patterns is as puzzling as are other forms of stereotyped behavior, although two rare syndromes, the *Cornelia de Lange Syndrome* and the *Lesch-Nyhan Syndrome,* have both been reported to be accompanied by high rates of self-injurious behavior (Guess and Mulligan, 1982).

Some hypotheses offered to explain self-injurious behavior have included a high state of arousal (Berkson and Davenport, 1962); an attempt to reduce or terminate adult contact in a demanding situation (Frankel and Simmons, 1976); or simply a learned response within a deviant social context (Lovaas, Schaeffer, and Simmons, 1965). There has recently been a growing body of evidence supporting the operant interpretation of self-destructive behavior. Within this interpretation, the behavior functions as an operant to terminate or reduce the level of adult contact in some cases and, in others, to increase and maintain the level of adult contact. In some instances, self-injurious behavior has been controlled with operant conditioning procedures, such as "time out from positive reinforcement" (Murphy, Nunes, and Hutchings-Ruprecht, 1977; Frankel and Simmons, 1976). The implications of these studies for the management of stereotyped and self-destructive behavior will be discussed in Chapter 3.

Relationships with the Handicapped Child. Functional retardation of social development characteristics of the severely handicapped is reflected also in the child's relationships with peers and adults. It is usually wrong to consider the severely handicapped child incapable of significant social relationships, for characteristically, relationships almost always exist with one or two adults and with the child's parent or primary caretaker, although almost never with the child's peers. Even children who are so profoundly impaired as to be almost devoid of functional or expressive behavior will reveal differential social recognition in the presence of a significant and meaningful adult with whom they have a continuing relationship. This recognition may take the form of a smile, increased eye movements, reflexive extension, or even a response as subtle as a flush in skin coloring. The importance of these relationships for the child's education is immense. The establishment of a close, meaningful relationship with the severely handicapped child by the teaching staff acts as a catalyst to the instruction process. The absence of a relationship to other children, however, is likely a significant detriment to the child's later social development. The reasons for the imbalance are clear. Severely handicapped children are highly dependent upon adults for care, attention, and affection. Other dependent children may not display these attributes, and when they are present in large numbers such as in the wards of large state institutions, they can come to be perceived as objects of competition to be avoided and pushed away. Educational programming for peer sociability, cooperative play, and problem solving are all important aspects of educational programming for the severely handicapped student.

Because the child's parent or primary caretaker is likely to have an established relationship with the child, educational programming that is cooperative with and includes parents takes on more importance in the education of the severely handicapped than in any other area of special education. Initially, the relationship between parent and child can facilitate the establishment of a significant relationship between child and teacher. Later, the parent-child relationship can be used to strengthen and generalize newly acquired skills by effecting transfer from classroom to home and community.

The Autistic Child.   Autism, while occurring at a very low rate among the general population, presents an identifiable but unique and difficult problem in social retardation. The child who is labeled autistic is likely not only to have well-developed stereotyped behaviors, such as the twirling of objects, finger movements, and so on, but also to be devoid of significant relationships with others, including the child's parents (Rimland, 1971). There have been numerous reports of successful efforts to establish meaningful social relationships with autistic children (for example, Wing, 1972; Bettelheim, 1967), but the picture remains clouded although certainly more optimistic (Koegel, Rincover, and Egel, 1982).

Lovaas and his associates have postulated an impairment characteristic of autistic children – called *stimulus overselectivity* – that may account for their extreme level of social and developmental retardation. This hypothesis is based on the assumption that the autistic child, relative to nonautistic, severely handicapped peers, cannot respond consistently to a mix of stimuli from several sensory modalities. Lovaas, Schreibman, Koegel, and Rehm (1971) trained autistic and nonhandicapped children to make a consistent response to a stimulus "package" consisting of visual, auditory, and tactile components. By subtracting modality-specific components one at a time, they were able to determine the relative contribution of each sensory modality by noting whether responses decreased following the deletion of each component. It was found that nonhandicapped children utilized all three components, whereas the autistic children displayed stimulus overselectivity; that is, autistic children's responses tended to depend upon a single component of the three-stimulus package. This finding has since been replicated several times. Lovaas and Schreibman (1971) produced the same result in a two-cue situation, as did Koegel and Wilhelm (1973) within the visual modality, and Reynolds, Newsom, and Lovaas (1974) within the auditory modality. Evidence has begun to mount that the stimulus-overselectivity phenomenon adversely effects the results of instructional efforts in the classroom (Koegel, Egel, and Dunlap, 1980).

Does the stimulus-overselectivity hypothesis provide us with a basis for the diagnosis and prescriptive treatment of autistic children? Indeed not, although other studies have shown stimulus overselectivity to be related also to IQ levels (Wilhelm and Lovaas, 1976).

These data strongly suggest that a relationship may exist between IQ and the number of cues utilized in a discrimination learning situation. It appears that the degree of stimulus overselectivity may be correlated with degree of retardation. Thus, we may be able to think of intellectually retarded functioning as being related to problems in overselective attention; the lower a person's IQ level, the less of the environment becomes functional in controlling his behavior. (p. 28)

Further in the article, the authors say,

This finding confirms our hypothesis (or suggestion) that stimulus overselectivity is not an exclusive feature of early autism but of mental retardation in general. (p. 30)

What are the direct implications of this research for classroom instruction of severely handicapped children? A typical prompt-fade teaching procedure, wherein the student is physically guided through the required behavior and the teacher's degree of physical involvement is systematically reduced with each trial, may well fail with certain students since they tend to become stimulus-bound. The term *stimulus-binding* refers to selectively overattending to the prompt, for example, waiting for the teacher to guide the student's hand before responding. The prompt simply cannot be faded out as a cue. Schriebman (1975) examined a successful procedure for what she called *within-stimulus fading,* a technique that reduced the attentional demands made upon the child. Koegel and Schriebman (1977), for example, taught a discriminated response by training simultaneous multiple cues, singly and combined. The results of this ongoing program of research into the stimulus-overselectivity hypothesis has recently been described in detail by Koegel et al. (1982).

The issue of self-stimulatory behavior is also receiving increased attention in systematic research. According to the *sensory-stimulation hypothesis* (Rincover, Newsom, Lovaas, and Koegel, 1977), simple sensory events, such as motion in the visual field (for example, windshield wipers), have been shown to have reinforcing properties when made contingent upon desirable behaviors (Bailey and Meyerson, 1969; Freeman and Ritvo, 1976). Rincover and Koegel (1977) demonstrated a reinforcing property of sensory stimulation with autistic children. If sensory reinforcers can be hypothesized to maintain self-stimulatory behaviors, then programmed extinction of sensory consequences for self-stimulatory behavior should eliminate those behaviors. This process, called *sensory extinction,* is now being examined experimentally by Rincover, Koegel, and associates (Koegel et al., 1982). Sensory reinforcers may or may not provide clues to the management of self-stimulatory behavior in autistic children, but as a potential solution to the search for reinforcers with which to build educational skills with these children, some recent successes have been encouraging (Rincover et al., 1977).

Generalization of Learned Skills. The problem of generalization of learned-skill components continues to be of major concern. Severely handicapped children often fail to display skills learned in one situation in another situation. A child, for example, who learns in the classroom to sign "want to drink" as a request for liquid may well not provide the same request for the parents at home. Warren, Rogers-Warren, Baer, and Guess (1980) have been engaged in research to determine the functional parameters of generalization, findings that may translate into better educational procedures for all handicapped children. Severely handicapped children may need to be taught in each case systematically across settings and persons those skills for which generalization is requisite. Specialized parent-training efforts (for example, Lovaas, Koegel, Simmons, and Long, 1973) may be needed to facilitate these efforts.

Language Development in Handicapped Children. Finally, the area of language development with severely handicapped children has a relatively long history of intensive research efforts (Guess, 1980). Much of this effort began with attempts to teach autistic children to imitate speech sounds (for example, Lovaas, 1977) and to learn to produce functional syntactic structures (for example, Sailor and Taman, 1972). This evaluation proceeded through the emergence of simultaneous communication approaches (for example, total communication) and then to current approaches that tend to place additional stress on physical aids, such as communication boards, pictured stimuli in booklets, and so on (Sailor, Guess, Goetz, Schuler, Utley, and Baldwin, 1980).

RETARDATION OF PHYSICAL DEVELOPMENT

When the image of a moderately retarded, or Trainable Mentally Retarded (TMR), youngster comes to mind, it is usually that of a little Down's Syndrome child. When the image of a severely, multiply handicapped child is visualized, it is usually of a much less attractive child with severe physical deformity, possibly in an adapted wheelchair or other mobile positioning device. Many severely handicapped children are characterized by *abnormal physical development* and/or *delayed physical development*.

Bigge (1982) and Bleck and Nagel (1975) have provided excellent textbooks with comprehensive treatments of educational considerations in physical disability, so we will not deal extensively with the topic in this text. Suffice it to say that severe impairment of physical development combined with functional social, communicative, and sensory disability is often a defining characteristic pattern of severely, multiply handicapped children. Delayed or abnormal physical development sometimes originates in drug-induced birth defects, birth trauma, genetic abnormalities, or improper or inadequate developmental care. Many of the extreme deformities of bone structure that characterize teen-age and older severely handicapped persons, for example, might have been prevented if alternatives had been provided to constant side-lying positions during the early years of growth and development.

Types of Physical Abnormalities.   Some of the more common patterns of physical abnormality include:

Spasticity: extreme tightness of limb muscles often characterized by contractures following attempted movement.

Athetosis: involuntary, purposeless movement of the limbs, such as that which characterizes some persons described as cerebral palsied.

Rigidity: extreme spasticity that overrides even the stretch reflex; a characteristic of some persons described as quadriplegic (no use of all four limbs).

Ataxia: uncoordinated movement from lack of sensation of balance. An ataxic child may be expected to fall frequently.

Hypotonia: a condition of flacid muscles, lacking tone. A hypotonic child may be floppy when positioned and need much support.

Scoliosis: lateral curvature of the spine; a spinal deformity, often developmental in origin, and often resulting from incorrect positioning.

Severely, multiply handicapped children frequently exhibit epileptic seizures, including the familiar petit mal and grand mal types, as well as other types characterized by projectile vomiting and involuntary defecation and urination. Abnormal reflex patterns frequently can be found in these children, such as the asymmetrical tonic neck reflex which resembles the swordsman's stance.

Treating Physical Abnormalities.   Many of the more striking educational gains that are being made with severely, multiply handicapped children evolved from strong inputs from the fields of physical and occupational therapy. Educationally oriented treatment techniques have been derived from the work of the Bobaths (Bobath and Bobath, 1975) and from the sensory integration conceptions of Ayres (1972). The Bobath approach to therapy of physically handicapped individuals is based upon techniques designed to inhibit abnormal (for example, tonic) reflexes. A child who under certain patterns of stimulation will "go into extension" (that is, will exhibit an abnormal reflex pattern) may be presented with alternative stimulation designed to inhibit the expression of the reflex. The child learns to respond in new ways to situations that were inhibiting normal motoric development. By engaging in proper positioning techniques, a teacher may facilitate normal motoric development and movement by inhibiting the abnormal reflexive pattern.

One of the most intense and striking developments in the field of education of the severely handicapped has been an outgrowth of the recent shift in education of the severely handicapped toward a functional life-skills model. The implications of this shift have nowhere been expressed more dramatically than in applications to problems of severe physical and perceptual abnormality. Under older models, physical abnormalities were considered to be lifelong *modifying* characteristics for which any educational approach must be *compensatory*. A child with cerebral palsy, for example, when the "disease was diagnosed" might be considered to be permanently nonambulatory and incapable of articulated expressive speech. The current model, on the other hand, assumes that normal physical posture and ambulation are susceptible to educational remediation in the same way that a reading disability is remediable in a mildly impaired child. That some children may have been variously diagnosed as cerebral palsied, quadriplegic, and blind are not factors that restrict the possibilities for remediation through educational intervention.

RETARDATION OF SENSORY DEVELOPMENT

Severely handicapped students frequently seem to have *sensory impairments*. Often one hears something like, "We think that he's deaf but we're not sure." Because severely handicapped students cannot communicate effectively, they cannot reveal through the usual means the extent to which they rely on various sensory modalities in responding to their world. It is an unfortunate fact that many sensory impairments in these students go undetected for years. Worse, sensory impairments are often assumed, when in fact there are none!

Audiological information, for example, is extremely difficult to obtain by conventional methods in the low-functioning population. These children's audiological reports usually read "untestable," "will not wear aids," or "no improvement with aids." At this point, the child has received no auditory training, the aids are returned, and the child and teacher are back where they started.

A review of curriculum guides for the severely handicapped "deaf/blind" child emphasizing visual impairment reveals very few educational programs designed for implementation with severely/profoundly handicapped deaf/blind students (Lowell and Rouin, 1977). Very few activities intended to improve development in the areas described can be used with this population, usually because such activities assume or require a high degree of gross and fine motor ability, receptive and expressive language, and higher

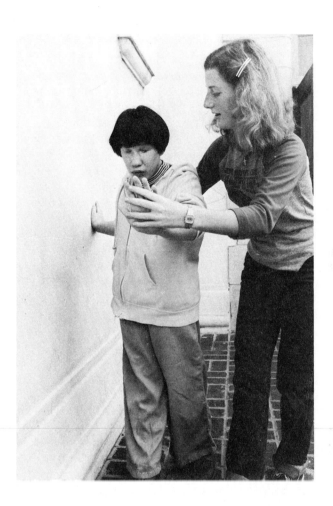

degrees of visual and auditory functioning upon program entry. Most programs discussed in presently available curriculum guides for the visually impaired, deaf/blind child are indeed important to the SMH deaf/blind child's total growth and development (body image, motor coordination, sensory modalities, mobility, daily living skills, and language). However, it would appear that many of the specific activities designed to improve functioning within these areas cannot be used with this special population of children, at least without further adaptations.

Visual impairment with most children is determined by ophthalmological or optometric procedures. But because severely handicapped children suspected to be deaf/blind cannot give the necessary subjective responses needed for assessment by these techniques, the determination of extent of visual loss by standard ophthalmology is difficult. As Langley and DuBose (1976) have pointed out, when examining these children in traditional multidisciplinary treatment and education settings, the vision expert tends to rely on anecdotal visual information from teaching staff. Among other problems, severely handicapped children are often easily distracted, lose interest in testing procedures, fear the test situation, fail to discriminate the response requirements, and provide inconsistent and hence unreliable responses. More recently, innovative procedures have been developed to help assess the visual acuity of young handicapped children, including the severely handicapped (Cress, Spellman, DeBriere, Sizemore, Northam, and Johnson, 1981). These and more recent procedures offer the promise that more exacting assessments can be made of visual acuity among severely handicapped children (Utley, Goetz, Gee, Baldwin, Sailor, and Peterson, Note 1).

In addition to problems of visual acuity, severely handicapped children also exhibit other visual abnormalities. They include: rubella retinopathy (pigment deposits on the retina), congenital cataracts (clouding of the lens), microthalma (abnormally small eyeballs which can affect the total refractive status of the eye), glaucoma (an increase of pressure in the eye which kills retinal cells and optic nerve fibers and can lead to total blindness), and strabismus and nystagmus (which interfere with proper focusing).

Many children in this population who are examined are found to have healthy eyes, yet exhibit no visual response. Because of their inability to give subjective responses, the examiners tend to label these children as untestable and/or cortically blind. Vaughn and Asbury (1974) define *cortical blindness* as "bilateral, widespread destruction of the visual cortex."

Since definite knowledge of cortical damage with these children cannot be ascertained, cortical blindness should not be assumed. Because of the severity of their handicaps, it is possible that they have not "learned" to use their vision, and the possibility for training their vision exists.

SUMMARY

Early attempts to define the term *severely handicapped* centered on efforts to identify common physical and behavioral characteristics or to extend downward existing categorical labels. A more current approach is based upon the identification of educational needs that reflect the major sensory, motor, or cognitive disorders of these children; these disorders, whether singly or in combination, require special instructional adaptations and approaches to enable the children to interact better with their environment.

To return to the question posed earlier: who are the students for whom this book is written? The answer is that this book is written for students in need of basic rather than remedial or academic skill development. It is designed to enable teachers and others to foster increased independence in persons who are *functionally* retarded in their living skills and their physical, social, and/or sensory development, and who are in need of transition to less restrictive, more integrated, and increasingly complex social environments.

CHAPTER 2

The Legal Imperative for Education

We have argued in Chapter 1 that severely handicapped students neither constitute a new disability category nor represent downward extensions of existing disability categories. They are students whose educational needs are specialized, necessitating special classrooms. There is no convincing argument that these students should be educated apart from the mainstream of American youngsters.

As this chapter is being written, classes for severely handicapped children are being conducted increasingly in regular public school buildings. Young, nonhandicapped children, in the lunchroom and on the playground, are playing and interacting with children who appear to be very different from themselves. We have insufficient data to tell us definitely whether this interaction is beneficial to either group. We know from observations, *anecdotally*, that the mix is a joy to behold. Third-grade children run to assist in pulling a young multihandicapped child around in a wagon. Sixth-grade students help feed severely handicapped children in their corner of the lunchroom. We see young severely handicapped children smile and track the movements of their normal age peers in a social context, instead of attending only to similar movements provided by an adult teacher.

On the less positive side, we see indications of severe problems among responsible adults in integrated situations. Teachers of severely handicapped students sometimes find themselves socially ostracized in the public school by local school administrators and other teachers. In some cases, services like recreation facilities are denied to a class of severely handicapped students. Why? It is a sad fact that in our society there is constant pressure to separate groups of people from one another on the basis of their distinctive characteristics. When one group at any one time controls a disproportionate share of the nation's economy, the other groups suffer from a systematic denial of opportunity and must necessarily settle for less while waging a constant uphill battle to attain a more equitable share. Handicapped persons are only just beginning to press their efforts, and the

severely handicapped are in the position of caboose on the train. Pressures to prevent the integration of severely handicapped children into the mainstream of American society, although often quite subtle, are nevertheless intense. Teachers, as advocates for the civil rights of severely handicapped children and as agents of the integration imperative provided by public law, often experience these pressures in uncomfortable ways (Frith, 1981). In this chapter, we will examine the key historical and legal landmarks that have moved severely handicapped students to their current position in the educational spectrum.

ORIGINS OF THE RIGHT-TO-EDUCATION CONCEPT

ZERO REJECTION

The concept of "zero rejection," and expansions of it, played an early and major role in procuring the legal rights of severely handicapped children to appropriate educational opportunities. The phrase *zero rejection* was coined by Stephen Lilly (1971) who used it to describe a particular service-delivery model for special education: one in which it is impossible to separate administratively for *any* reason a child enrolled in a regular education program. Lilly proposed a training-based model in which special educators become teacher educators and in the process abandon their present child-centered service function. The goal of this model would be self-sufficient teachers in the regular classroom who would be able to solve problems presented by students, rather than having to resort to referring them to a support service.

Goldberg (1971), Gilhool (1973), and Lippman and Goldberg (1973) then expanded the concept of zero rejection to mean access to a free public education for all handicapped children. Lilly had limited the proposed application of the zero-reject model to retention in the regular classroom of children traditionally labeled mildly handicapped; it would not apply to children, "who have been called trainable mentally retarded, severely emotionally disturbed, multiply handicapped, or to children who are so obviously deviant that they have never been enrolled in any kind of normal school program" (Lilly, 1971). Apparently Lilly considered special class placement or other direct support services to be more appropriate for children so categorized. He probably would not quarrel, however, with those who have expanded the application of the concept of zero rejection in order to prevent administrative separation or denial of access to a free public education for all handicapped children.

Zero rejection is perhaps best defined today as follows: the right of an individual to be "deviant" (Segal, 1972) and an affirmation of that right by society through its schools, requiring them to accommodate to the child rather than requiring the child to either accommodate to the school or be excluded (Lippman and Goldberg, 1973).

FROM EXCUSED TO EXCLUDED

How have certain handicapped individuals come to be excluded from public education? When parents of nonhandicapped children find that they have reached school age, they simply enroll them in the local public school. Why then have school-attendance laws not also required that all handicapped children be enrolled in school? The reason is that in the past the compulsory education statutes of most states provided officials of the school district (or board) the option of *excusing* an individual from school attendance if the individual was considered to be unable to profit from the instruction offered by the schools. These statutes were designed to permit parents of handicapped children either not to enroll their child or to remove their child from public schools without legal liability if local school officials agreed that the child was unable to profit from the instruction offered by the schools. Unfortunately the statutes, rather than excusing a child from a public education, have been used to exclude children from public education. Teachers who believed certain children too handicapped for their classes could request that local school officials excuse the child from any further attendance. If local school officials concurred, the parents were notified that their child could no longer participate in the public school program. School officials sometimes recommended that the parents enroll their child in the nearest "state school" that was equipped and staffed to provide the type of educational services needed by their child.

FROM LEGISLATION TO LITIGATION

The means of obtaining social change in the provision of services for the handicapped has shifted from a focus on *legislation* to an intensified focus on *litigation*. In the past, individuals and groups advocating the initiation, improvement, or expansion of services for the handicapped relied on lobbying efforts designed to influence legislators and other public officials to pass new laws, revise existing statutes, and reallocate funds. The frustration generated by political powerlessness, endless delays, and inadequate action led many such individuals and groups to form their own services, largely outside the public sector. Only then was consideration given to going to the courts, a move that had its roots in the labor movements of the thirties and forties, the civil rights movements of the fifties and sixties, and now the movements to secure equal rights for women, the elderly, and the poor, as well as the handicapped.

Some initial success was achieved through legislative action prior to the moves to obtain action through judicial means. Equal access to education was the original rationale for establishing state training schools as a means for creating education resources for the handicapped. However, this goal has not been realized in most state training schools, so that full educational opportunities for all residents in these settings have not been accomplished. Equal access to education was also partly obtained through the enactment of local special education legislation by many states.

The Legal Background.   The judicial origins of the right-to-education concept lie in the historical decision of *Brown* vs. *Board of Education* (1954) in which the Supreme Court stated:

> In these days, it is doubtful that any child may reasonably be expected to succeed in life if he is denied the opportunity of an education. Such an opportunity, where the state has undertaken to provide it, is a right which must be made available to all on equal terms.

Although this decision concerned the segregation of black children in separate schools, it served as well as a precedent in establishing the rights of the handicapped to the opportunity for an education. This right was officially affirmed when the United States District Court in *Pennsylvania Association for Retarded Children, Nancy Beth Bowman et al.* vs. *Commonwealth of Pennsylvania, David H. Kurtzman* (1972) stated that

> the Commonwealth of Pennsylvania has undertaken to provide a free public education for all its children between the ages of six and twenty-one years. It is the Commonwealth's obligation to place each mentally retarded child in a free, public program of education and training appropriate to the child's capacity.

Constitutional Provisions.   The attorneys representing the plaintiffs in suits concerning the right to treatment and education have largely based their cases on violations of rights guaranteed by the U.S. Constitution.

There are three basic constitutional provisions that may be interpreted as establishing a right to *treatment*. The first is *due process*. The Fifth and Fourteenth Amendments both state that no person can be deprived of liberty without due process of law. This provision through various court decisions has been interpreted to require that governmental action affecting individual liberties be consistent with "fundamental fairness". In the case of a mentally handicapped person who has been involuntarily confined, "fundamental fairness" would require that the nature and duration of confinement bear a reasonable relationship to the purpose of that commitment. A mentally handicapped person subject to civil commitment is denied the full range of procedural safeguards made available to criminal defendants. Since the mentally handicapped person can be confined for an indefinite term even though he or she has committed no criminal act, fundamental fairness requires that treatment and not mere custody be the necessary quid pro quo for this loss of liberty.

The second constitutional provision is *equal protection of the laws*. The Fourteen Amendment also prohibits denial to any citizen or group of citizens equal protection of the laws. Under this constitutional provision, courts may be asked to scrutinize classifications of citizens to ensure that the classifications are reasonable. Classifying certain persons as mentally handicapped and subsequently depriving them of their liberty is reasonable only if treatment is provided. The third constitutional provision is the *prohibition of cruel and unusual punishment* provided by the Eighth Amendment. The Supreme Court has held that punishing a "sickness" as if it were a criminal offense violates this prohibition. Since civil commitment of mentally handicapped persons without treatment amounts to punishing them for their "sickness," such a commitment violates the Eighth Amendment. Conditions such as physical deprivation, lack of basic sanitation, overcrowding, lack of physical exercise, inadequate diet, unchecked violence, lack of adequate medical and psychiatric care, and the abuse of solitary confinement and restraint would also constitute cruel and unusual punishment.

Even though education is not mentioned in the U.S. Constitution, some court decisions indicate that the due process and equal protection of the laws provision of the Constitution may apply to education as well as to treatment. The interpretation of due process as requiring that governmental action affecting individual liberties be consistent with "fundamental fairness" (labeled *substantive* due process) has been applied where handicapped individuals have been excluded from public education on the basis of vague and unjustifiable criteria. Another interpretation of the process (labeled *procedural* due process) requires that government procedures be conducted in a fair manner. Thus, in cases of exclusion from educational opportunity, of transfers from one educational situation to another, and of placement in special education classes, procedural due process usually requires that an individual be allowed a hearing, be notified of this hearing, be represented by an attorney, be given the opportunity to present evidence, and be able to confront and cross-examine witnesses.

The equal protection of the laws provision of the Fourteenth Amendment has also been used in right to education cases. The application of this provision has established that if the government undertakes to provide education at all, it must do so for everyone.

Class Action versus Private Action.   The attorneys representing the plaintiffs in landmark right to education cases have largely filed class action rather than private action suits. In a *private action suit,* the plaintiff is a single individual or organization seeking a judgment against another single individual or organization. In a *class action suit,* the plaintiffs represent the "class" of all individuals or organizations for whom a judgment is sought, and the defendants represent the "class" of all individuals or organizations against whom a judgment is sought. In the Pennsylvania case, the plaintiffs were all retarded persons excluded from schooling, and the defendants were the educational and other public agencies obligated to provide services.

There are several advantages to a class action suit. If the named plaintiff is dropped from the case, the whole action is not necessarily dropped. Any judgment granted by the court is for all members of the class and is not limited to the named plaintiff. Any member of the class can initiate contempt proceedings if the order is not carried out with respect to that member.

Concurrently with legal interpretations and decisions pertaining to constitutional provisions for equal educational opportunities, specific – indeed *landmark* – federal legislation has been enacted to strengthen and expand these provisions and to identify more clearly the processes by which they should be implemented. These two pieces of legislation, which were conceived and enacted very closely together in time, are: (1) the Education for All Handicapped Children Act of 1975 and (2) the Rehabilitation Act of 1973. We will discuss the former first in order to clarify some of the concepts in the earlier act by showing how they were extended in the Education Act.

EDUCATION FOR ALL HANDICAPPED CHILDREN ACT

The Education for All Handicapped Children Act of 1975 (PL 94–142) was designed "(1) to assure that all handicapped children have available to them a free appropriate public education; (2) to assure that the rights of handicapped children and their parents are protected; (3) to assist States and localities to provide for the education of handicapped children; and (4) to assess and assure the effectiveness of efforts to educate such children" (Federal Register, August 23, 1977).

PUBLIC PARTICIPATION

Implementation of the Education for All Handicapped Children Act necessarily requires consideration of two sets of written material. The first is the *statutory language* contained within the act itself, and the second is the *rules and regulations* for implementation of the act. In general, the use of statutory language is restricted to providing a basis both for the development of rules and regulations for implementation and for *litigation* when interpretation of the intent of the act or any of its parts is in dispute. Regulations are *policy* and do not have a legal basis apart from the statutory language upon which they are based. Regulations usually extend beyond the specifics of statutory language and thus can become a basis for dispute over the intent of the original statutory language. Because regulations are policy, and because policy is implemented by agencies of the federal government charged with the disbursal of public funds appropriated by Congress to implement an act, the policy and its implementation is subject to scrutiny and modification by the executive branch which oversees government agencies.

At this writing, President Reagan, for example, has commissioned the vice president, George Bush, to convene a special task force to review and recommend changes in extant government regulations. This task force recently reviewed the regulations of PL 94–142, and as an outgrowth of this review, new proposed regulations were released by the Department of Education sometime in August of 1982.

Because PL 94–142 was predicted to have a strong impact on the education of handicapped children and on state and local educational agencies, the Office of Education arranged for intensive public participation in the development of the original regulations guiding implementation of the act. The Office of Education arranged meetings concerning the law in specific geographic areas and with special interest groups. These meetings, attended by over 2,000 persons, produced several hundred comments concerning the implementation of the law. A national group of over 150 persons was convened in June of 1976 to develop "concept papers" for use in writing the regulations. In December of 1976, the proposed regulations were first published in the *Federal Register*. Comments and recommendations were invited for a sixty-day period, and public hearings concerning the proposed regulations were held in several major cities. Over 1,600 written comments were received, reviewed, and considered for inclusion in the final regulations, which went into effect October 1, 1977.

A large number of comments expressed reservations about implementation of the act. Concerns were voiced about the timelines; the anticipated cost; the inconsistencies between state, local, and federal priorities; the provision of individualized educational plans for *each* handicapped child; and the costs involved in providing prior notice of a change in educational status and due process hearings, the supervision by the state education agency of *all* special education programs in the state including those portions provided by other state agencies, and compiling figures on the number and type of handicapped children in a state.

INCENTIVE GRANTS

The act provides incentive grants to states that develop educational programs for handicapped children three to five years of age. The rationale is that with early education "(1) benefits are maximized, (2) additional or more severe handicaps may be prevented, and (3) greater long-term effectiveness is realized."

ANNUAL STATE PROGRAM PLAN

The act requires that an annual program plan for education of all handicapped children in the state be submitted by the highest organizational unit for education in the state (for example, a state department of education). The plan must include procedures for identifying, locating, and evaluating all children who are handicapped regardless of the severity of their handicap. This includes all children served by public and private agencies or institutions in the state. The plan must also show that each public agency in the state maintains records of the individualized educational plans for each handicapped child, how the state regulates the development of the individualized educational plans, how the plans are implemented, reviewed, revised, and monitored, and how progress is evaluated. The procedures for evaluating the effectiveness of programs designed to meet the objectives of the individualized educational plans must be conducted at least annually.

The state education agency submits the annual program plan to the U.S. Commissioner of Education. The plan must document the procedures by which public participation in its development (through public hearings) is provided, a list of any revisions made as a result of public input, and the means by which the plan will be made public after approval by the Commissioner. The plan must also include procedures that will ensure a free appropriate public education for all handicapped children aged three through twenty-one.

Additionally, each annual program plan must include a comprehensive system of personnel development that includes inservice training of general and special education personnel; procedures to ensure that personnel will be trained to fulfill the purpose of the act and the schedule of activities to implement the personnel development plan; and procedures for acquiring and disseminating information derived from educational research, demonstration, and similar projects, and for implementing appropriate educational practices and materials developed as a result of such projects. The annual program plan must ensure the opportunity for all public and private institutions of higher education in the state, as well as other agencies and organizations interested in personnel preparation (including representatives of handicapped, parent, and other advocacy organizations), to participate in the development, review, and annual updating of the personnel development plan.

An annual needs assessment must be conducted to determine if a sufficient number of qualified personnel are available in the state. The inservice personnel development program must be based on the assessed need. The act permits the state educational agency to enter into contracts with institutions of higher education, local educational agencies, and others (including parent, handicapped, or other advocacy organizations) to carry out experimental or innovative personnel development programs, to develop or modify instructional materials, and to disseminate information derived from education research and demonstration projects.

DEFINITIONS CONTAINED IN THE ACT

The term *free appropriate public education* means special education and related services that are: (1) provided at public expense, under public supervision and direction, and without charge; (2) consistent with the standards of the state educational agency; (3) inclusive of preschool, elementary school, and secondary school education in the state; and (4) provided in conformity with an individualized educational plan for each handicapped student.

The term *handicapped children* means children who have been diagnosed as mentally retarded, hard of hearing, deaf, speech impaired, visually handicapped, seriously emotionally disturbed, orthopedically impaired, health impaired, deaf-blind, multihandicapped, or as having specific learning disabilities and who because of these impairments need special education and related services.

Special education, as defined by the act, means specially designed instruction, at no cost to the parent, to meet the unique needs of a handicapped child including classroom instruction, instruction in physical education, home instruction, and instruction in hospitals and institutions. The term includes speech pathology, vocational education, or any other related service if that service consists of specially designed instruction and is considered special education under state standards. This definition of special education is particularly important since a child is not considered handicapped (and thus would not be covered by the act) unless he or she needs special education services.

RESPONSIBILITIES OF LOCAL EDUCATIONAL AGENCIES

In order to receive payments under the act, a local educational agency (a county school district, for example) must submit an application to the state educational agency. This application must include procedures that ensure that all handicapped children residing within the jurisdiction of the local educational agency are identified, located, and evaluated, including a practical method of determining which children are currently receiving needed special education and related services and which children are not. It must also provide procedures for involving the public in the plan and, in general, provide the type of information required in the overall state plan. In addition, it must ensure that the local educational agency provides special services to enable handicapped children to participate in the regular educational programs. It must describe the types of alternative placements currently available to handicapped children, and the number of handicapped children within each disability category served in each type of placement.

Each public agency must ensure that handicapped children have available to them the variety of educational programs and services available to nonhandicapped children. These may include, for example, art, music, industrial arts, consumer and homemaking education, and so on. They must also include vocational education and physical education by statute. In addition, nonacademic and extracurricular activities available to the nonhandicapped should be available to the handicapped student. If placement in a public or private residential program is necessary to provide special education and related services to a handicapped child, the program must be provided at no cost to the parents of the child.

INDIVIDUALIZED EDUCATIONAL PLAN (IEP)

The public agency is required to conduct a meeting at least once a year to develop or review and/or revise each child's individualized educational plan (IEP). This meeting is to include: (1) a representative of the public agency, other than the child's teacher, qualified to provide or supervise a specially designed program of instruction; (2) the child's teacher; (3) one or both of the child's parents, guardian, or advocate; (4) the child, when appropriate; and (5) other individuals at the discretion of the parents or agency. When a handicapped child is being evaluated for the first time, the public agency must ensure either that a member of the evaluation team participates in the meeting or that a representative of the public agency, the child's teacher, or some other person is present who knows the evaluation procedures used with the child and is familiar with the results of the evaluation.

The importance of parental participation in the development of the child's IEP is underscored by the steps each public agency must take to include them. These are: (1) providing parents with sufficient advance notice of the meeting to ensure that they will have an opportunity to attend, and (2) scheduling the meeting at a mutually agreed upon time and place. The notice must indicate the location, time, and purpose of the meeting and who will attend. If neither parent can attend, the public agency must arrange another method for parent participation, such as a conference telephone call. The meeting may be conducted without a parent in attendance if the public agency is unable to convince the parents that they should be there. In this case, the agency must maintain a record of attempts to arrange a mutually agreed upon time and place, such as telephone calls made or attempted and the results of the calls, copies of correspondence sent to the parents and any responses received, and visits made to the parent's home or place of employment and the results of those visits. The public agency must also ensure that the parent understands the proceedings of the meeting, such as arranging for an interpreter for parents who are deaf or whose native language is other than English.

Each child's IEP must include:

1. The child's present levels of educational performance
2. Annual goals
3. Short-term instructional objectives
4. The specific special education and related services to be provided
5. The extent of participation in regular educational programs

6. The projected dates for initiation of services
7. The anticipated duration of the services
8. Appropriate objective criteria and evaluation procedures
9. A schedule for determining, on at least an annual basis, whether the short-term instructional objectives are being achieved.

The act does not require that anyone be held accountable if a child does not achieve the growth projected in the annual goals and objectives. This provision was intended to relieve concerns that an IEP might be viewed as a guarantee that a child will progress at a specified rate. This does not, however, relieve agencies and teachers from making good-faith efforts to help the child achieve the objectives and goals listed in the IEP. Further, the section does not limit a parent's right to complain and ask for revisions of the child's program, or to invoke due process procedures, if the parent feels that these efforts are not being made.

PROVISION FOR DUE PROCESS

The due process procedures of the act require that the parents of a handicapped child be afforded the opportunity to review all educational records with respect to the identification, evaluation, and educational placement of the child, and the provision of a free appropriate public education to the child.

A parent has the right to independent educational evaluation at public expense if the parent disagrees with an evaluation obtained by the public agency. However, the public agency may initiate a hearing to show that its evaluation is appropriate. If the hearing results in a finding that the evaluation is appropriate, the parent still has the right to an independent evaluation, but not at public expense. If the parent obtains an independent evaluation at private expense, the results of the evaluation must be considered by the public agency in any educational decision pertaining to the child and may be presented as evidence at a future hearing regarding that child.

The act requires that a *written notice* be sent to parents of each special education child in the case of a hearing and that it must include: (1) a full explanation of all the procedural safeguards available to the parent; (2) a description of the action proposed or refused by the agency; (3) an explanation of why the agency proposes or refuses to take the action; (4) a description of any options the agency considered; (5) the reasons why those options were rejected; (6) a description of each evaluation procedure, test, record, or report the agency used as a basis for the proposal or refusal; and (7) a description of any other factors relevant to the agency's proposal or refusal. The written notice must be in language understandable to the general public, and in the *native language* or other mode of communication used by the parents.

The parent, state, or local public educational agency may initiate a hearing to resolve any disagreements related to the education of the handicapped child. Mediation may be attempted prior to conducting a formal due process hearing, although the process of mediation is not required by statute or regulation. Mediation conducted by someone not previously involved in the case may lead to resolution of differences between parents and agencies and avoid the adversarial nature of a due process hearing. Mediation may not be used as an attempt to deny or delay a parent's rights.

The hearing may not be conducted either by an employee of the public agency involved in the education or care of the child, or by any person whose personal or professional interest might conflict with his or her objectivity. Any party to a hearing has the right (1) to be accompanied and advised by counsel and/or individuals with special knowledge or training in the problems of handicapped children; (2) to present evidence and cross-examine witnesses; (3) to prohibit the introduction of any evidence not disclosed at least five days before the hearing; (4) to obtain a verbatim record of the hearing; and (5) to obtain a written copy of the findings. In addition, parents have the right to the child's presence at the hearing and to open the hearing to the public.

A decision made in a hearing is final, unless one party appeals the decision. If there is an appeal, the state educational agency must conduct an impartial review of the hearing. The official conducting the review must examine the entire record of the hearing; must ensure that the procedures at the hearing were consistent with the requirements of due process; must seek additional evidence, if necessary; must provide the parties an opportunity for oral or written argument, or both, at the discretion of the review; and must provide a written copy of the findings and the decision to the parties. The decision made by the reviewing official is final, unless a party brings civil action.

Civil action as an outgrowth of due process hearings can result in litigation that ultimately restricts or extends statutory language and its policy for implementation through regulations. Each state, to qualify for federal funding through PL 94–142, must have *enabling legislation* on its statutory books. Interpretation of this statute, the *local* special education act, is usually the basis for the first round of civil litigation. If, for example, a court finds for a school district in a case involving a parent dispute of the outcome of a hearing, the state statute is left unchallenged. If the court finds for the parent and the district appeals the decision, a higher court may interpret the state statute in such a way as to modify local policy and procedure. A challenge to a state statute may find its way ultimately through appeals to a federal court interpretation of federal statute, which in turn can ultimately restrict or extend the federal law, and so on.

While proceedings regarding a complaint are pending, the child involved must remain in his or her present educational placement, unless the public agency and the parents of the child agree otherwise. If the complaint involves an application for initial admission to a public school program, the child, with the consent of the parents, must be placed in the program until the completion of all proceedings. This does not preclude the agency from implementing appropriate procedures for dealing with children who are endangering themselves or others. Parents have the right to refuse to agree to any part of a proposed program, and due process may be invoked when such disputes occur.

The public agency must arrange for an individual to act as a parent-surrogate when (1) no parent can be identified, (2) the whereabouts of a parent are completely unknown, or (3) the child is a ward of the state.

EDUCATIONAL EVALUATION

The testing and evaluation materials used for evaluation and placement of handicapped children must not be racially or culturally discriminatory. State and local educational agencies must ensure that tests and other evaluation materials are administered in the child's native language or other form of communication (manual signing for a deaf child, for example), are validated for the specific purpose used, and are administered by trained personnel. Tests and other evaluation procedures include those tailored to assess specific areas of educational needs. They cannot be limited to those designed to provide a single general intelligence quotient. Tests are selected that accurately reflect the child's aptitude or achievement level (or other factors the test purports to measure) rather than impaired sensory, manual, or speaking skills (except when those skills are the factors that the test is designed to measure). No single procedure may serve as the exclusive criterion for determining the educational program to be provided for a child. The evaluation is made by a multidisciplinary team that includes at least one person with specialized knowledge in the area of the *suspected disability,* and the child is assigned in all areas related to this suspected disability. This assessment could include health, vision, hearing, social and emotional status, and motor abilities. Children with certain impairments (like speech) may not need a complete battery of assessments (for example, psychological, physical, or adaptive behavior). However, a person qualified to assess the extent of impairment should evaluate the child, using procedures appropriate for the diagnosis and appraisal of the impairment, and make any necessary referrals for additional assessments required for an appropriate placement.

In interpreting evaluation data and in making placement decisions, each public agency must draw information from additional nontesting sources, including teacher recommendations, physical condition, social or cultural background, and adaptive behavior; must carefully consider the information obtained from these sources; must ensure that the placement decision is made by persons who know the child, the meaning of the evaluation data, and the placement options; and must provide an educational placement in the *least restrictive environment*. Evaluations must be conducted at least every three years, but may be more frequent than this if a parent or teacher requests an evaluation or if conditions affecting the child change.

CONFIDENTIALITY OF INFORMATION

Each public agency must permit parents to inspect and review any of their child's educational records maintained by the agency. Access to these records must be provided within forty-five days, and five days before any meeting regarding an IEP or a hearing concerning the child. The right to inspect and review educational records includes the right to a reasonable request for an explanation and interpretation of the records; the right to copies of the records (at parental expense unless this would prevent access); and the right to have a representative of the parent inspect and review the records.

If information contained in the record is believed inaccurate, misleading, or in violation of the privacy or other rights of the child, a parent may request that the information be amended. If the agency refuses to amend the information, the parents must be informed and advised of their right to a hearing. If the agency rules against the parents, it must inform the parents of their right to place in the records a statement commenting on the information and the reasons for disagreeing with the decision of the agency. Any explanation placed in the child's records must remain as long as the contested portion is maintained by the agency. If the agency discloses the contested portion of the record to any party, the explanation must be included.

One official at each participating agency must be responsible for the confidentiality of any personally identifiable information. Parental consent must be obtained before such information is disclosed to anyone other than officials of another public agency. The public agency must inform the parents if personally identifiable information is no longer needed to support educational services to the child and must destroy the information, if requested by the parents. However, a permanent record containing a student's name, address, phone number, grades, attendance record, classes attended, grade level completed, and year completed may be maintained by the agency without a time limitation.

REFLECTIONS ON PL 94–142

PL 94–142 represents a comprehensive and monumental effort to guarantee the right to education for all handicapped children within a context that judiciously specifies, in detail, fundamental processes and safeguards for both the children who receive these services and their parents. This federal legislation is especially important to severely handicapped children, those who care for them, and those who provide them with needed educational and treatment services. However, as we are writing this book, we are aware of the fact that governmental philosophies periodically change in this country—a fact that is neither good nor bad, but simply a matter of reality.

The present shift in philosophy away from concentration at the federal level toward state responsibility for the education of children represents the first serious challenge to PL 94–142. President Reagan has sought recently to repeal the act and replace it with block-grant legislation coupled with a drastically reduced federal budget. It is our hope that the substantive provisions of PL 94–142 will remain intact and that the act will not in the foreseeable future come to be viewed as an extinct but well-intentioned historical document.

There are reasons for assuming this will not happen. First, PL 94–142 does represent an equal education effort agreed upon by persons from both ends of the political and philosophical spectrums. It is, in essence, a mechanism for safeguarding a recognized fundamental and cherished right to education and a higher quality of life. Second, the act has been in place long enough for most states to recognize its importance and potential value. This is stressed by strong advocacy groups, including parents, who strongly support PL 94–142 and who are willing to actively lobby for its continuation.

There will, of course, always be some who oppose the act. Some opposition has been there from the beginning. The extent to which supporters of PL 94–142 will prevail depends heavily on the ultimate success of the act in realizing its intended purpose and objectives.

Finally, in this context, we would like to comment on an implication of PL 94–142. Questions have again been raised recently about the value of *education* as opposed to treatment for severely handicapped individuals (cf., Burton and Hirshoren, 1979). Related questions have been asked, some in recent congressional hearings, about the value of public school placement of special day classes for severely handicapped children and youth. Will severely handicapped persons ultimately repay society for its educational "loan" by becoming "productive" citizens who contribute to the gross national product? For some, perhaps; for others, perhaps not. But more important is the question, what is the true value of an education? We believe that the improvement in one's *quality of life* that results from education is its major value. Liberty and the pursuit of happiness are constitutional rights.

If research continues to show demonstrable gains from public school educational placement for severely handicapped children, as it already has by our quality of life criterion (cf., Voeltz, 1980), then the protection of PL

94–142 should, we believe, be a legacy for all of us acquainted with the many individual citizens/human beings that make up the population of people with severe handicaps.

THE REHABILITATION ACT

As part of the Rehabilitation Act of 1973 (PL 93–112), Congress enacted Section 504 to provide that "no otherwise qualified handicapped individual in the United States shall, solely by reason of his handicap, be excluded from participation in, denied the benefits of, or be subjected to discrimination under any program or activity receiving federal financial assistance." The act originally referred to those eligible for vocational rehabilitation services, but the Rehabilitation Act amendments of 1974 extended the act to forbid discrimination against any handicapped individual.

Subpart D is concerned with preschool, elementary, and secondary education. Many of the provisions are identical to those of PL 94–142. The 1975 act required that recipients operating public education programs provide a free appropriate education to each qualified handicapped child in the most normal setting possible. The regulations governing implementation of both acts are designed to ensure the proper classification and placement of handicapped children and to provide due process procedures for resolving disputes arising from this activity. The intent of the regulations is to ensure that appropriate testing and evaluation procedures are implemented and that a mechanism is available by which parents can challenge and seek review of any decisions concerning their children.

The Rehabilitation Act defines a *handicapped person* as being any person who has a physical or mental impairment (including mental retardation, organic brain syndrome, emotional or mental illness, and specific learning disabilities) that substantially limits one or more major life activities (such as caring for one's self, performing manual tasks, seeing, hearing, speaking, working, and so on).

Subpart D requires that a recipient of federal assistance operating a public education program must identify and locate every qualified handicapped person residing in the recipient's jurisdiction who is not receiving a public education and then notify them and their parents or guardians of their rights and the recipient's obligations under the act.

THE "LEAST RESTRICTIVE ALTERNATIVE" PRINCIPLE

The phrase *least restrictive alternative* (Chambers, 1974) has been used to summarize the specific method of establishing alternative educational programs for the handicapped, originally ordered by judicial decision in the

Pennsylvania case. In this case, the consent agreement stated that placement in a regular public school class is preferable to placement in a special
public school class and that placement in a special public school class is
preferable to placement in any other type of education and training program. Thus, the principle of the least restrictive alternative would require
that a handicapped individual be educated in a regular public school class
and placed in a special class only if there is a "compelling state interest" to
do so, if there are specific and justifiable criteria against placement in a
regular public school class, and if any arguments against such a placement
are allowed in a public hearing. Under this principle high priority must be
given to placing the child as close to home as possible. The parents have the
right not only to challenge the placement of their child in special classes or
separate schools but also to challenge placement in a distant school and, in
particular, to residential placement.

When providing nonacademic and extracurricular services and activities
(meals, recess periods, and so on), a recipient of federal assistance must en-

sure that handicapped individuals have the opportunity to participate in face-to-face contacts with nonhandicapped individuals. This is especially important for children whose educational program limits their interaction with nonhandicapped children most of the day.

EVALUATION AND PLACEMENT

A recipient of public funds who operates a public education program must conduct an evaluation of any person believed to need special education services before taking any action with respect to the placement of the person in any educational program and any subsequent change in placement. The phrase *any action* includes denial of placement. The Rehabilitation Act, like the Education for All Handicapped Children Act, requires that a recipient of federal funds establish standards and procedures for the evaluation and placement of persons that ensure: (1) that evaluation materials have been validated for the specific purpose for which they are used and are administered by trained personnel; (2) that tests and other evaluation materials are tailored to assess specific areas of educational need and are not merely designed to provide a single general intelligence quotient; and (3) that the test results accurately measure the student's aptitude, achievement level, or other factors the tests purport to measure, rather than reflect the student's impaired sensory, manual, or speaking skills (except when those skills are the factors to be measured).

The failure to provide handicapped persons with an appropriate education is frequently the result of misclassification or misplacement. Thus, placement procedures should be designed to ensure that children are not misclassified, unnecessarily labeled handicapped, or incorrectly placed as a result of inappropriate selection, administration, or interpretation of evaluation materials. The procedures used should prevent misinterpretation of test scores and, in particular, should avoid excessive reliance on tests of general intelligence. A recipient is required to draw upon a variety of sources in the evaluation process to minimize the possibility of error in classification. All significant factors relating to the learning process, including adaptive behavior (the individual's effectiveness in meeting the standards of personal independence and social responsibility characteristic of his or her age and cultural group), must be considered.

PROCEDURAL SAFEGUARDS

The Rehabilitation Act, like the Education of All Handicapped Children Act, also requires that a recipient operating a public education program establish and implement a system of procedural safeguards with respect to actions regarding the identification, evaluation, or educational placement of handicapped persons. The safeguards must include the right to prior notice, examination of relevant records, an impartial hearing with participation by parents or guardian and representation by counsel, and a review procedure.

NONACADEMIC SERVICES

A recipient must provide nonacademic and extracurricular services and activities that afford handicapped students an opportunity for participation equal to that of nonhandicapped students. These services and activities include counseling services, recreational athletics and activities, transportation, health services, and so on.

A recipient of federal funds providing personal, academic, or vocational counseling, guidance, or placement services to nonhandicapped students must provide the same services to handicapped students without discrimination. The recipient must also ensure that handicapped students are not counseled toward more restrictive career objectives than nonhandicapped students with similar interests and abilities.

A recipient who offers physical education courses or who operates or sponsors interscholastic, club, or intramural athletics must provide qualified handicapped students an equal opportunity to participate in such activities. A recipient may offer physical education and athletic activities that are separate or different from those offered to nonhandicapped students only if this is in the best interest of the handicapped student and only if the handicapped student has the opportunity to compete for teams or to participate in courses that are not separate or different.

Some handicapped students will be able to participate in regular physical education and athletic activities. For example, a student in a wheelchair might be able to participate in regular physical education and athletic activity, including a regular archery course; a deaf student might be able to participate in a wrestling course. Thus, this section requires a recipient to provide nonacademic and extracurricular services and activities in such a manner as is necessary to afford handicapped students an equal opportunity for participation. Because these services and activities are part of the recipient's education program, they must be provided in the most appropriate integrated setting.

PRESCHOOL AND ADULT EDUCATION PROGRAMS

A recipient of federal funds who operates a preschool, day care, or adult education program cannot exclude qualified handicapped persons from the program. The recipient must take into account the needs of handicapped persons in determining what services will be provided.

PRIVATE EDUCATION PROGRAMS

A recipient who operates a private education program cannot exclude a qualified handicapped person from any program, provided that the person can, with minor adjustments, participate in the program. Handicapped persons may not be charged more than nonhandicapped persons unless the additional charge is justified by substantially increased costs to the recipient.

It is clear that recipients of federal funds who operate private education programs are required to provide an appropriate education to handicapped students with special educational needs. A private school that does not provide a program for mentally retarded persons is not required to admit such a person into its program or to pay for the person's education in another program. However, a private recipient of federal funds would not, for example, be able to exclude a blind student if that student required only minor adjustments in the manner in which the program is offered.

Subpart D of the Rehabilitation Act generally conforms to the standards established for the education of handicapped persons in *Mills* vs. *Board of Education of the District of Columbia* (1972) and *Pennsylvania Association for Retarded Citizens* vs. *Commonwealth of Pennsylvania* (1972), as well as in PL 94–142.

The basic requirements common to these cases and legislative acts are: (1) handicapped persons, however severe their handicap is, must be provided a free appropriate public education; (2) handicapped students must be educated with nonhandicapped students unless this would result in an inappropriate education; (3) educational agencies must identify and locate all unserved handicapped children; (4) evaluation procedures must be improved to avoid inappropriate education resulting from misclassification of students; and (5) procedural safeguards must be established to enable parents and guardians to actively participate in decisions concerning the school's evaluation of the handicapped. If a recipient of federal funds demonstrates that placement in a regular educational setting cannot be achieved satisfactorily, then the student must be provided with an adequate alternative service without additional cost to the student's parents or guardian. Thus, a recipient who operates a public school system must either educate handicapped children in the regular program or provide an appropriate alternative program at public expense.

THE INTEGRATION IMPERATIVE

Let us examine more closely the issue of the least restrictive environment (LRE) which we discussed in the previous section.

PL 94–142 requires the states to establish:

procedures to *assure* that, *to the maximum extent appropriate, handicapped* children, including children in public or private institutions, *are educated with children who are not handicapped.* (20 U.S. Code, sect. 1412 [5] [B])

A public agency that is a recipient of federal funds must maximize the extent to which handicapped children, including those in public or private institutions or other care facilities, are educated with children who are not handicapped. The removal of handicapped children from the regular educational environment can occur only if the nature or severity of the handicap is such that even with supplementary aid, education in regular classes cannot be achieved satisfactorily. When education of handicapped children cannot be best accomplished in a regular classroom, as in the case of most severely handicapped children, that education must be imparted in the *least restrictive* (alternative) *environment* available. In the case of severely handicapped students, the issue becomes, is a special class within a regular public school the most appropriate educational alternative, or should a segregated facility be established for this purpose?

The problem seems to center upon two key questions. First, is the public school the most *appropriate* educational setting for the severely handicapped student? Second, is public service a *legal imperative* as specified under the least restrictive environment clause of PL 94–142?

The issue of the appropriateness of the public school facility has been positively stated by Brown, Wilcox, Sontag, Vincent, Dodd, and Gruenewald (1977), who have called for total participation and integration within the larger society for the handicapped. They state:

Long-term, heterogeneous interactions between severely handicapped and nonhandicapped students facilitate the development of the skills, attitudes, and values that will prepare both groups to be sharing, participating, contributing members of complex, postschool communities. Stated another way, separate education *is not* equal education.

Segregated service delivery models have at least the following disadvantages:

1. Exposure to nonhandicapped student models is absent or minimal;
2. Severely handicapped students tend to learn "handicapped" skills, attitudes and values;
3. Teachers tend to strive for the resolution of handicapped problems at the expense of developing functional community-referenced skills;
4. Most comparisons between students are made in relation to degrees of handicap rather than to the criteria of nonhandicapped performance;

5. Lack of exposure to severely handicapped students limits the probability that the skills, attitudes, and values of *nonhandicapped* students
   will become more constructive, tolerant, and appropriate.

Certainly, it is possible that interaction may not take place even if severely
handicapped students are in the physical presence of nonhandicapped
students. However, unless severely handicapped and nonhandicapped
students occupy the same physical space, interaction is impossible. ... In the
future, severely handicapped students, upon the completion of formal schooling, will live in public, minimally segregated, heterogeneous communities,
where they will constantly interact with nonhandicapped citizens. Thus, the
educational experience should be representative and help prepare both
severely handicapped students and nonhandicapped students to function
adaptively in integrated communities. (p. 198)

More recently, this Madison, Wisconsin group, has provided an in-depth
analysis of the arguments for and against regular school placement (Brown,
Ford, Nisbet, Sweet, Donnellan, and Gruenewald, Note 1).

What of the legality issue? Does the current legal structure bearing on
education of the severely handicapped *mandate* public school service
delivery? Gilhool and Stutman (Note 2), in a comprehensive review of the
legal issues and precedents that bear on the question, conclude emphat-
ically *yes*. The authors conclude that an integration imperative is consistent
with historical and concurrent civil rights legislation in this country. The
issue today, according to Gilhool and Stutman, is not whether severely
handicapped students should be served in the public school but rather how
to define criteria to measure compliance at the public school (LEA) level
with the imperative.

Reviewing the historical context of PL 94–142, the authors also draw a
strong case that the *intent* of the legislation is to guarantee that all handicapped children shall be educated in an environment that ensures social
contact with nonhandicapped peers. They conclude:

To trade the institution for segregated facilities operated by school systems
was not the Congressional intention. A component of the stereotype and pre-
judice which historically attends disabled people is, of course, the view that
disabled people cannot learn or function productively. The responding, and
piercing, legislative fact found by the Congress in the 1974 and 1975 Education Acts is that "developments in the training of teachers and in diagnostic
and instructional procedures and methods have advanced to the point that,
given appropriate funding, State and local agencies can and will provide effective special education to meet the needs of handicapped children." P.L.
91–230, Section 601; P.L. 94–142, Section 3b(7); 20 U.S.C.A. Section 1401

note "Congressional Findings." In short, the Congress found that all disabled children, however severely disabled, can learn and can function in society. (pp. 19–20)

And further on:

Under the statutes any degree of segregation can be maintained only if it is *necessary* to the appropriate education of a child. There is not cognizable reason under the statues – that is, no *learning* reason and no *disability* – for handicapped-only centers, certainly not on the scale they now exist. If a child can come to a school at all, even to a self-contained class in a handicapped-only center, he can come to a self-contained class in a normal school. Any teaching technique that can be used in a self-contained class can be used in a self-contained class located in a regular school building. There are few if any legitimate teaching strategies which require the complete isolation of a child from interaction with other children, and the few such strategies that there may be apply to very few children and for very short periods of time. Such strategies do not require massive segregated centers or massive institutions. The "continuum" of school settings permissible under the statutes thus includes regular class (and all its variations) and special classes (and all their variations) located in school buildings where nonhandicapped children are also schooled and, for those few children whose disability precludes their moving for the short period of time that will be true, instruction in the home (whether the family home or an institution "home"). (pp. 22–23)*

Gilhool and Stutman (Note 2) made specific recommendations to the U.S. Office of Special Education for the formulation of enforcement guidelines for Section 504 (least restrictive environment) of the Rehabilitation Act of 1973. The authors suggested that state plans for service delivery include goals and timetables for a phased achievement of the integration imperative, that is, for the flow of handicapped students from educational programs in segregated environments to programs in the public schools. Finally, a test through litigation of the interpretation of least restrictive environment as regular school, special class placement, occurred recently in the state of Alabama. In *Joseph C.* vs. *Talladega County Board of Education* (1981), Judge Vance refused to accept a "comparable" but segregated placement for Joseph and ordered that he be returned to the local high school.

It is clearly time that most or all handicapped children coexist with age peers in a regular education setting, and that the state (as represented by

_____

*Gilhool and Stutman (Note 2). Used by permission.

individual school districts) bear the burden of proof when making placements or when applying treatments that involve partial or complete removal of handicapped children from regular school.

SUMMARY

This chapter has reviewed the concepts and legal and legislative actions that support the basic right of students with severely handicapping conditions to full educational opportunities in the least restrictive environments. Collectively, these actions have dramatically altered the educational services now available to these students, and our rationale for them.

The main conclusion that can be drawn from the legislative, judicial, and professional sources presented above is that all members of our society should have the same rights. In the past, individuals who were different from the American norm, whether culturally, intellectually, emotionally, or physically, lost rights that are now in the process of gradually being regained.

The relevance of this restoration of rights to the field of education is apparent, and it is just beginning to bring about change. One of the most significant changes is in the philosophy of education. Educators can no longer design a program and expect students to respond to the program or be failed. The field of education is being forced to recognize the social, cultural, intellectual, emotional, and physical histories that students bring into the system. This perhaps places too much responsibility on the educational system. Teachers should not be expected to remedy all the deficits created by society's lack of knowledge, or failure to apply knowledge, in the fields of government, medicine, psychology, sociology, and so on. The educational system, however, has its own past deficiencies to remedy. The system should begin by providing all school-age persons in our society, including the severely handicapped, an equal education as is their right.

Beginning in Chapter 5, we will present an educational model for severely handicapped students that is consistent with the integration imperative and is designed to maximize the student's progress toward independence in multiple, normal environments.

CHAPTER 3

Instructional Design:
Motivation

In order to learn a skill, the severely handicapped student must perform the various components of the skill in sequence, experiencing its benefits. Severely handicapped students sometimes evidence no intrinsic desire to learn the skills that would decrease their dependence on others. If left to their own desires, they will often choose not to engage in means activity, but rather to defer to the tendency of the adult caretaker to provide for their needs. This chapter and those that follow are intended to convey a teaching process that is reflected in a model that borrows extensively from behavioral psychology. The model, however, is eclectic in that its instructional techniques and procedures are applicable to a variety of approaches and theories pertaining to teaching severely handicapped students. We are not offering the behavioral model as an explanation of human behavior, but only as a collection of well-investigated *procedures that can assist* in the education and treatment of severely handicapped students, regardless of one's theoretical approach. (The interested reader should refer to Guess and Noonan [1982] for a critical review of the behavioral model when it is perceived as a total approach to educating severely handicapped students, and for its caution to view strict behaviorism as only one of many useful orientations for working with this population.)

The eclecticism of the model and its flexibility lie in the combination of its parts: a system grounded in developmental and environmental considerations, task analysis, and processes for creating the motivation to perform learned actions and for managing aberrant behavior.

A perfect strategy to achieve shoe tying will consistently fail if the child is not provided with a good reason for practicing the sequence. The process is the same as that at work in your own case. If you must take a written examination on the contents of this chapter, you will need to rehearse its contents in some *meaningful* way. Putting the book under your pillow the night before will not do nor will simply reading it over several times. A better strategy would be to rehearse the key points in your mind; the best would be to understand the contents, compare them with your own experience, and then rehearse the key points. It all involves work on your part. Instructional technique is concerned with providing a reason to per-form what is to be learned. The instructional technique used in your case has probably consisted largely of awarding grades for performance on assigned material. Your students will need other reasons, other sources of motivation to perform.

CASE: A MOTIVATIONAL MODEL

The simplest and most efficient way to motivate severely handicapped students is to *schedule systematic effects to follow actions that occur in the presence of recognizable cues.* A schedule of cued actions and their effects which is rewarding or pleasurable for the student will increase the tendency to act again. A schedule that is aversive to the student will decrease the tendency to perform the act and thus promote learning of a different sort, that is, learning *not* to do something.

The motivational paradigm is presented in this chapter in terms of the four components comprising the system: *cues* (stimuli), *actions* (responses), *schedules* (of reinforcement), and *effects* (reinforcers and punishers). The letters *C, A, S,* and *E* are used throughout to illustrate the relationship among the four parts and to describe the function and properties of each.*

The principle relationship among the four parts may be stated as follows: *An action (A) that is performed in the presence of a discriminated cue (C) that produces a contingent effect (E) according to a specific schedule (S) will tend to be repeated in future occurrences of the cue if the effect is positive or rewarding for the person and will tend not to be repeated if the effect is aversive.*

MOTIVATIONAL EFFECTS (E)

Effects that are available to the teacher of severely handicapped students take three forms: *objects, events,* and *actions.* Each of these three classes of effects may be manipulated in a student-environment relationship to pro-

---

*The notation system described in this chapter is based on the earlier work of Ogden R. Lindsley, "Direct measurement and protheses of retarded behavior," *Journal of Education,* 1964, *147,* 60–82.

mote learning. One of the most important skills of a good teacher is the ability to select and tailor appropriate motivational effects to actions required of the student.

EFFECTS AS OBJECTS

Experimental psychology has provided educators with insights into animal learning and behavior through experiments using tangible consequences immediately following discrete responses. In a typical experiment, a rat enclosed in a small, lighted box will learn to press a bar when it is rewarded with a food pellet. A hungry rat will learn to press a bar at a very high and stable rate in order to gain access to food. Food is the *effect* of the act of pressing the bar in this example.

Educators are usually quick to apply the results of laboratory studies of experimental psychology to the classroom. It was not long after the demonstration of learning in laboratory animals using food as an effect for discrete actions that we began to see food appear in the classroom as a consequence for discrete human responses. Laboratory animals, pigeons, and rats nearly always received food reinforcement in the form of tiny pellets. Can you think of a tiny pellet that will provide food reinforcement to a

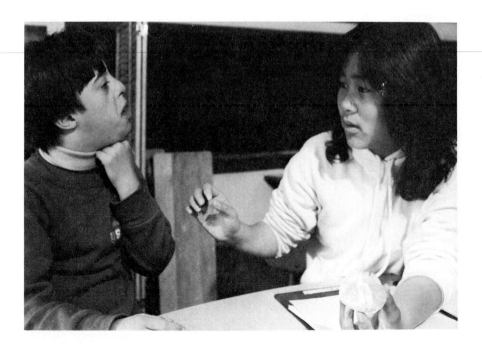

child? If so, you have probably correctly guessed the name of the nation's largest selling classroom candy, the one that melts in your mouth and not in your hand. In this case, the extrapolation from laboratory to classroom was very direct. One wonders if children somewhere were taught to press bars. Several enterprising companies even introduced automatic candy-dispensing machines for classroom use.

We have come a long way in a short time from the days of candy in the classroom as the prime learning motivator. In the education of severely handicapped children, items of food still play a role as programmed effects of actions performed by the student, *but,* as we shall see, the circumstances are much more carefully controlled.

Effects as *objects* can, of course, include much more than food items. Any tangible item that follows specifiable, discrete actions on the part of a student, according to some schedule programmed by teaching staff, can serve as an effect. Examples of tangible effects for learned actions with severely handicapped students can include food, toys, tokens, and functional objects like cups, pens, and money.

EFFECTS AS EVENTS

Early in the development of operant conditioning, it became clear that the establishment of motivation in laboratory animals was not limited to the provision of tangible reinforcing consequences. Certain events, such as sounds, when associated with tangible effects over repeated performance trials, would themselves become effects for which the animal would work. The principle of *secondary reinforcement* was conceptualized to account for the process by which *neutral* object or event effects could themselves become positive reinforcers in a learning situation, and the exact process of secondary reinforcement remains a subject of intense theoretical and research interest. The current accepted notion of the process of secondary reinforcement, however, poses some problems for education of the severely handicapped; thus some discussion of the issue is warranted.

In the prevailing view, motivating effects (reinforcers) are of two varieties: primary and secondary. *Primary reinforcers* arranged *contingent* upon, that is, immediately following, discrete actions will cause those actions *(responses)* to increase. According to Bijou and Baer (1965), primary reinforcers are food items for a hungry child and liquid for a thirsty child. If a previously neutral object or event is continuously presented to the child at the same time as the primary reinforcer, the neutral object or event will come to have motivating properties and will stand on its own, in time, as a *secondary reinforcer.* All that is required to maintain this relationship is that the primary reinforcer be paired *occasionally* with the secondary reinforcer in order for the secondary reinforcer to continue to increase responses it follows in a contingent arrangement.

As an example, imagine a child with little motor control undergoing instruction on visual tracking of an object. Initially, the movement of a brightly colored toy in the child's visual field will not be enough to cause the child to reliably track the object from center position to 45° left or right of center. There is no surprise so far, since only a cue is presented and no effect has been scheduled to motivate the child to act, which would require work and energy expenditure on the part of the child. Suppose the toy is rigged to make a pleasant sound and light up when a button is pushed by the teacher. A schedule is established so that when the child tracks the object, an event effect (sound, light) immediately follows. The child fails to exhibit an increase in the strength of the tracking act. For a number of instructional sessions, a bit of apple juice, previously determined to motivate the child, is now paired with the colored toy. Reliable tracking is established, the action increases satisfactorily, and the apple juice is withdrawn for 90 percent of the teaching trials. The child continues to progress toward criterion on the tracking objective, motivated now by the secondary reinforcer of light and sound provided by the toy. A previously neutral consequence, paired with a positive consequence, has itself become positive for the child and will now motivate actions required for learning.

The example above falls easily within the tenets of secondary reinforcement theory. But what if the simple addition of the sound and light had reliably increased the required action of tracking without the pairing with apple juice? We would now have to speculate that at some time in this child's history, light and/or sound of the type supplied by the toy had been paired with a primary reinforcer, food or water, a sufficient number of times to have lent the sound and/or light secondary reinforcing powers. The fact is there is a growing body of evidence for the existence of highly motivating event effects that had no prior association of any systematic type with "primary reinforcers," as we shall see. One very interesting and promising current line of research into this phenomenon is *sensory reinforcement* (Kish, 1966; Fowler, 1971; Rincover, Newsom, Lovaas, and Koegel, 1977). It is becoming commonplace for instructional designs with severely handicapped children to include motivational effects of the event type which in all likelihood have never undergone systematic or even casual association with primary reinforcers. Some recent examples of event effects of the sensory reinforcer type with severely handicapped children include the use of vibratory stimulation (Bailey and Myerson, 1969; Murphy and Doughty, 1977); music (Rincover and Koegel, 1977); and tactile stimulation (Hewett, 1965). Some other possibilities for event effects include praise, hugging, and other forms of demonstrated affection; sounds such as music; lights, sound and light combinations; vibratory stimulation; tactile effects such as soft brushlike stroking; olfactory stimulation; stimulation of taste buds by honey, lemon, or powdered sugar; and vestibular stimulation (such as that produced by swinging).

The concern with whether sensory event effects attain their reinforcing properties through the conditioned (or secondary) reinforcement process as suggested by Kelleher and Gollub (1962) or simply exist as a separate class of reinforcers of the primary type (Kish, 1966) is important, because it offers teachers of the severely handicapped some very useful alternatives to excessive reliance upon object effects, especially food. Whether teachers should in the main attempt to create new reinforcers (secondary reinforcement) or search for a wider range of existing reinforcing phenomena must await further research for a definite answer. Present evidence suggests the latter to be a more fruitful strategy.

EFFECTS AS ACTIONS

David Premack, about a decade ago, provided yet another problem for secondary reinforcement theory in the form of some rather impressive experimental evidence that an organism's own responses can be employed to strengthen still other responses if the relative opportunities to respond are arranged in a contiguous relationship (Premack, 1965; 1971). Known instantly as the *Premack principle*, the relationship was discovered during an effort to examine more carefully how animals learn in their natural environment, that is, when no experimenter is present to provide tiny compressed food pellets. It takes little familiarity with rodents to realize that pressing a bar to earn food pellets constitutes, for the rat, an *unnatural act*. Similarly, the act of pressing an illuminated key to gain access to bird seed is a very unlikely event in the life of nonexperimental pigeons.

Premack created an environment that would at least simulate some aspects of natural rat life. He calculated the frequencies with which the animals would engage in various behaviors as their opportunities were made available. He thus was able to compute the relative probabilities of certain rat performances under certain conditions. He noted, for example, that wheel running of the type found in childrens' hamster cages constituted a very high-probability behavior. Rats obviously enjoy running in cage wheels and will do so for surprisingly long periods of time. Premack found that, conversely, rats would engage in bar pressing with a very low degree of probability. It occurred to him that perhaps a rat would learn to do something it did not readily take to, such as bar pressing, if the act of bar pressing were immediately followed by access to wheel running. An experiment was designed to test this hypothesis and the results were dramatic.

The Premack principle may be stated simply, albeit somewhat awkwardly, as follows: if the opportunity to engage in a high-probability response is made contingent upon the occurrence of a low-probability response, the former will increase the probability of the latter with repeated trials. In other words, the rat *learned* to press the bar at a very high and stable rate, with the only reinforcer being the opportunity to wheel-run. Again, we have a finding that does not fit easily into a secondary reinforcement paradigm.

Extrapolation from the animal laboratory to the classroom was once again swift and premature. The Premack principle came to mean: have the child do arithmetic problems in order to gain access to recess and the playground. The relationship in terms of probabilities for a child is essentially the same as is bar pressing to wheel running for the rat.

On a more positive note, the experimental findings from Premack's laboratory led to the application of a whole new class of motivational effects, namely, the child's own tendencies to engage in certain preferred actions. Some problems, however, came with overuse of the principle by special educators, coupled with a misunderstanding of some of the implications of Premack's findings. There is a second aspect of the Premack principle that is less well known and almost never cited in educational reports. To return to probabilities for the moment, the total principle based on the research findings is restated thus: if the opportunity to engage in a high-probability response is made contingent upon the occurrence of a low-probability response, the former will increase the probability of the latter with repeated trials. *Conversely, the high-probability response will be observed to decrease in probability as an outgrowth of the relationship.*

Now we have a potential explanation for an often observed phenomenon when the Premack principle is misapplied. Take the case of the child who loves to ring a hand-held bell. The bell is placed in different locations during a period of instruction, say on a sensorimotor objective, four-point creeping. The child is showing dramatic increases in average distances creeped when opportunity to seize and ring the bell (high-probability activity) is made contingent upon increases in creeping (a difficult and hence low-probability activity). Success with the bell-as-reinforcer is so striking that the teacher decides to arrange another relationship. A communication objective – manipulation of a communication board to indicate a yes response – is now followed by the opportunity to seize and ring the bell for a while. The bell-ring activity has now been made contingent upon two separate, difficult, and low-strength activities. What happens? First, the teacher notices that an increase in the performance on the communication board is disappointingly slow and not what was expected; second, the child is showing less enthusiasm for creeping; and third, the child no longer seems to enjoy ringing the bell as much as before. So while arranging relationships such that more rewarding actions increase less rewarding actions, the process takes its toll on the reinforcer. The contingent action becomes less rewarding for having strengthened some other actions.

It is beginning to look as if there is an *economy* to be considered in the scheduling of effects to follow actions. Although there is at present experimental evidence only for action effects weakening in reinforcement potential following the arrangement of more than one contingent relationship, it is reasonable to assume that a similar reduction will be found to occur with the reward value of *object* and *event* effects. Reinforcers wear out (as in satiation, for example). A good reinforcer cannot be made contingent upon multiple activities and be expected to remain a good reinforcer. Although the experimental analysis of actions as motivating effects of other actions is only just beginning with humans, there are sufficient examples of the employment of the principle with mildly handicapped individuals in a contingency-contracting paradigm (Homme, 1970) to warrant serious consideration by teachers of severely handicapped students.

To summarize thus far, we are considering one aspect of instructional design as a systematic method for motivating students to perform the difficult actions that are necessary to learn new skills and to progress from dependence to relative independence. We have considered learned actions to be a function of their effects on the environment. By way of classifying motivational effects, we have considered objects, events, and actions, all of which are available to the classroom teacher to schedule programmatically and systematically in order to increase motivation.

Students of behavior analysis and behavior management will recognize these principles as identical to the tenets of the operant conditioning reinforcement paradigm. Operant behavior, considered as discrete responses, may be strengthened or weakened in tendency as a function of contingent stimuli which may be in one of two forms: *reinforcers,* where the effect on the response tendency is to increase it, and *punishers,* where the effect on the response tendency is to decrease it.

EFFECT VALENCE (+, –)

Motivational effects (E), whether objects, events, or actions, may be characterized both by what happens to the behavior that produces them and by whether the behavior added the effect or subtracted one that was already in place. These effects on behavior may be described in terms of *valence:* positive (+) or negative (–). The valence of an effect is communicated in this chapter by a *superscript* (E^+ or E^-). Whether an effect is added or subtracted by the behavior that produced it is communicated by a *subscript* (E_+ or E_-).

POSITIVE EFFECTS (E^+): SKILL BUILDING

There are two types of positive motivational effects: added effects (E_+^+) and subtracted effects (E_-^+). In the former, the child's action *produces* (or adds) a positive or rewarding object, event, or action. In the latter case, the

child's behavior *reduces* (or subtracts) a present or ongoing object, event, or action that is *aversive* to the child. An added effect or positive valence is pleasant for the child, and she or he will take action to produce it. A subtracted effect or positive valence is also pleasant, because it reduces or terminates something unpleasant. The child will therefore act to produce this effect as well. Remember, in the notation system, the superscript, denoting valence, refers to what happens to the preceding action (the action upon which the effect is *contingent*). The subscript refers to the effect of the action on the environment, whether it adds or subtracts an object, event, or action. The notation E_-^+ thus denotes an effect that increases behavior (E^+) but which does so by subtracting from an existing object, event, or action. In standard behavior analysis terminology, for example, E_+^+ is a *positive reinforcer*. E_-^+ is a *negative reinforcer*.

E_+^+ is a very common instructional strategy. Suppose a child is learning to talk. Upon seeing the teacher present a cup with some apple juice, the child attempts to articulate the verbal label *cup*. If the attempt is acceptable, the child is immediately provided with a sip of apple juice from the cup. If apple juice is rewarding for the child, the linguistic performance will improve under this arrangement. The articulated verbal label has added a positively valenced effect, juice.

E_-^+ is a much less common instructional strategy. A child must be in an uncomfortable situation and be required to perform some action that, as an effect, will reduce or terminate an aversive situation already in effect. Lovaas (1967) and his associates at the UCLA Neuropsychiatric Institute began a large-scale, intensive effort in the mid 1960s to develop speech and appropriate social behavior in very severely autistic children in state hospitals. These children had no speech, a great deal of bizarre stereotyped behavior, and a tendency to avoid social contact with adults. Early attempts to use positive reinforcement (E $\frac{+}{+}$) failed. The clinicians could find no positive reinforcers that would provide sufficient motivation to learn speech. It occurred to these clinicians that social reinforcers might be conditioned through repeated association with some other kind of reinforcer. If two effects are scheduled contingent upon some behavior, one neutral and the other positive, the neutral effect will itself, over repeated pairings, become rewarding and will attain a positive valence. The new positive effect will strengthen the action that produced it as long as it continues to be *occasionally* associated with established positive effects. This process was considered under the previous discussion of secondary reinforcement.

Lovaas and his associates elected to try supplying the motivation to learn by repeated pairings of a subtracted effect (E $^+$) of demonstrated motivational value with a previously neutral effect of no motivational value. The child was placed barefooted in a small room with an electric shock grid for a floor. A low-voltage, but nevertheless, painful shock would be delivered to the child's feet: an ongoing aversive stimulus. The child would run to the only available exit, a door, on the other side of which stood the speech trainer who would receive the fleeing child with a warm hug. The action of running to the person terminated contact with the grid and the aversive stimulus. Previously, a warm affectionate hug and pleasant words from a trainer had no motivational value for the child's behavior. Termination of the painful stimulus (E $^+$) was a strong motivator. Repeated pairings soon led to a condition in which the child would run to be hugged by the trainer in the absence of the shock grid (E $\frac{+}{+}$). Hugging had become a rewarding event through repeated association. A previously neutral effect, in other words, had gained positive valence. Hugging and affectionate speech from the trainer would now serve as a positive, added effect for behavior other than running to the trainer, and the process of speech instruction had begun. The results were striking and dramatic. A breakthrough had been achieved with very-difficult-to-reach children, although the breakthrough was short-lived.

Suppose we have a quadraplegic student, characterized by spastic rigidity, who finds the supine position to be quite aversive. Typically, when positioned supine, this student would cry and fuss and so be shifted to prone or side-lying. But now the student is undergoing systematic instruction to accomplish the objective of rolling from supine to prone. Motivation to acquire this remedial skill may be effected by the mechanism of the positive subtracted effect. By gradually removing himself from an ongoing aversive stimulus (supine position), certain discrete actions by the student become strengthened by terminating that stimulus (subtracting an ongoing aversive event) and attaining comfort ($E^{\pm}$). The discomfort in one position is used to strengthen behavior that is educationally significant, that is, that increases the student's motoric independence.

Suppose a neutral effect is paired repeatedly with an $E^{\pm}$. Perhaps, for example, our student is not much affected by social praise. Repeated pairings of social praise with the completed act of rolling from supine to prone may well act to increase the attractiveness of social praise. Social praise may in time, for this student, through pairings of this type with identified, positive effects become available to the teacher to strengthen other educationally relevant actions.

NEGATIVE EFFECTS (E⁻): BEHAVIOR MANAGEMENT

Where positive valenced effects are useful to teach a child what to do, negative valenced effects are useful in teaching what not to do. E^+ strengthens the actions that produce them; E^- weakens actions. In operant terminology, the term for E^- is punishment and typically is denoted as S^{R-}. The effect of E^- on the behavior that produces it is to weaken its tendency to occur in similar situations. Again, as with positive effects, E^- exists in two forms: added effects (E^-_+) and subtracted effects (E^-_-).

Negative Added Effects (E^-_+).   If an action on the part of a child produces an *aversive* object, event, or action effect, that action will tend not to occur again in that situation; its tendency will have been weakened. The use of aversive effects (punishment) in special education is not new, but in recent years, it has been decreasing somewhat in favor of skillful manipulations of positive effects to achieve the same ends (c.f., Gaylord-Ross, 1980). Historically, the emphasis on punishment procedures in a learning context has been identified more with the field of psychology than with education. The term *behavior modification* has tended to be largely associated with efforts to reduce the occurrence of behaviors defined as aberrant or undesirable. The association of behavior modification with psychology and its reliance upon negative effects is tied to the predominant service needs typically provided by the psychologist. Except when they are asked to conduct evaluations, psychologists are almost always called in to deal with the *problems* children present to teachers and parents. They are expected to help get rid of bad behavior. Educators are usually faced with a different task—helping students learn new skills.

Among proponents of the behavioral model in special education, there are two contrasting views of the role of negative effects. One position, represented, for example, by Browning and Stover (1971) and Gardner

(1971), assumes that a child is not likely to benefit from systematic instruction until he or she is free from aberrant behaviors that might distract the child's attention from learning tasks or that might compete with other actions needed for positive learning. For example, a child who bangs her head or bites her hand will need this behavior to be greatly reduced or eliminated as an early educational objective. Under this application of the model, a program of behavior modification often precedes educational skill-building activities in the child's educational plan. Occasionally, a special education school program, if sufficiently large, will include a special classroom exclusively for behavior modification activity. Classes of this type usually come to be called the behavior-shaping class, and so on; they tend to concentrate severely handicapped students who have bothersome, aberrant behaviors in one room with a structured program of behavior management activity, much of which will be of the negative-effect type.

There are some problems with the behavior modification approach in special education. First, heavy reliance on negative added effects (punishment) as a management procedure often leads to a phenomenon that resembles the classic symptom substitution of psychoanalytic theory. For example, a child is punished each time he strikes another child (aggressive behavior). The rate of hitting is reduced substantially by this procedure over time, but soon an increase in the child's rate of head banging is observed. Punishment is now applied to head banging and the rate is reduced, but now the child's rate of knocking over furniture is observed to increase. Is the problem in management here a failure to eliminate a deep-seated, underlying cause, common to all these behaviors? Maybe, but whatever the reason, one is likely witnessing an artifact of the application of punishment as a behavior control technique. In the absence of positive effects for behaviors other than those punished, the punishment procedures will only suppress those actions they follow, not eliminate them (Azrin and Holz, 1966). Other environmental events that have supported the aberrant actions will tend to increase the rate of those actions that are not followed by punishment when those actions are "dormant"; that is, they occur, but at a lower rate. The child who has learned not to strike other children (very often) begins to return to that behavior when some other behavior is being punished, particularly if the child is stimulated positively by the signs of distress these actions produce on the part of teaching staff or the child who was struck. Behavior-problem children in a situation of this type can seem to "invent" an incredible number of ways to get into trouble as more and more punishment is employed.

Is punishment ($E \bar{+}$) always inappropriate in education of the severely handicapped? No. Children learn by aversive as well as positive effects. Punishment is appropriate when employed carefully and under the right conditions. Contingent aversive effects can be mild, as in the case of a verbal reprimand, or severe, as in the case of electric shock. An aversive effect does not have to be *painful* to reduce the frequency of an action that produces it; it needs merely to be aversive. For some children, evidence of social disapproval, such as frowning, can reduce behavior when made contingent. When nonpainful objects, actions, or events act as successful punishing effects, it may be because they have been paired with painful events in past learning. Previously neutral effects can take on punishing characteristics, through conditioning, by association with other punishing effects, just as neutral events can become positively valenced through repeated association with reinforcers.

One special application of the general class of E_+^- effects merits some separate consideration, and that is the procedure called *overcorrection* (Foxx and Azrin, 1972). This technique calls for identifying a socially acceptable and appropriate behavior to substitute for an aberrant behavior, and then to require the student to repeatedly practice the socially acceptable behavior contingent upon each occurrence of the aberrant behavior. Two types of overcorrection have been discussed and researched in various studies by Foxx, Azrin, and others. The first, called *restitutional overcorrection,* calls for the student who disrupts the physical environment to make repeated efforts at restitution, that is, to restore and perhaps improve upon the damaged environment. Thus, a student who has a tantrum and tips over a chair would be required to pick up and restore the chair to an upright position and then perhaps in addition to carefully arrange each chair in the room. The second type called *positive-practice overcorrection* calls simply for repeated practice of an appropriate behavior. For example, a child who slaps her head might be required to experience the effect each time of repeatedly raising her arms to some specified number of repetitions. In terms of our analysis of motivational effects, restitutional overcorrection is a negative added effect (E_+^-) of the *event* type, and positive-practice overcorrection is E_+^- of the *action* type.

Although overcorrection has been cited as a successful teaching procedure in many recent publications, Axelrod, Brautner, and Meddock (1978) have raised several serious questions about the validity of the concept as something different from other punishment techniques. According to Axelrod and his colleagues, the studies reported by Foxx and Azrin (for example, 1973), in which they presented comparisons of overcorrection with other behavior modification procedures, are methodologically inadequate to support their claims for the technique. Overcorrection also requires an extensive amount of close, one-to-one supervision which may well place more demands on teaching staff time than simpler behavior management techniques. Finally, it should be noted that overcorrection does not always proceed as smoothly as some reports of its application have suggested. Axelrod et al. (1978) referred to reports of "great physical resistance" for several clients who experienced the procedures and also reported a number of cases of discontinued use of overcorrection because of inconvenience or other objections by personnel. In short, an analysis of research into the overcorrection phenomenon seems to warrant a conclusion that the phenomenon should best be described as a particular application of mild punishment, of E^- manipulation, and not "the miracle cure" (Azrin, Note 1; cited by Sunner, Meuser, Hsu and Morales, 1974) for behavior-disordered persons.

Studies of punishment as a method of behavior management indicate that, contrary to expectations, it is not the reverse of positive reinforcement. There are at least two important differences in the effects on behavior of E^+ compared to E^- consequences. First, positive effects can establish lasting behaviors and are sufficient alone to accomplish this. Usually, negative effects can only reduce the frequency of behaviors they follow, not eliminate them. Second, E^+ becomes more effective as the arrangement by which it follows discrete actions becomes more intermittent. Punishment is more effective when *continuous* – that is, when it follows each discrete action – rather than when it is intermittent. For these reasons, punishment is not usually regarded as a behavior management technique of choice. Gaylord-Ross (1980), for example, has presented a survey of techniques to reduce the frequency of aberrant behaviors. The contingent use of aversive effects ranks *last* among the techniques discussed as methods of choice.

Is punishment of a severely handicapped child a morally and ethically justifiable technique when employed by educators? The issue is a difficult one and in some cases may be decided by legal statute. Thompson and Grabowski (1972), considering residents of state institutions, present the issue succinctly:

Most commonly, punishment procedures are justified in terms of the nature of the behavioral problem and the possible consequences of failure to implement the procedures. For example, it is neither reasonable nor humane to permit self-destructive or aggressive behavior to continue while awaiting the discovery of procedures which do not involve aversive methods. The magnitude of the injustice in failing to apply appropriate punishment procedures is especially great when the usual regime of nursing-custodial alternatives is employed. In an effort to prevent harm to the client or others, chemical restraint is used. That is, the resident's physician prescribes high doses of behaviorally active drugs to keep him out of harm's way or prevent harm to others. While the prescription may provide security, the resident may be essentially immobilized. He may be asleep, grossly ataxic, or extremely lethargic most of the time. He may be awake but incapable of participating in training experiences because of the drug. Furthermore, chemical restraint may have to be supplemented. When medication is only partially effective, the client may be exposed to other forms of containment, i.e., he may be placed in a seclusion room.

In summary, some of the accepted alternatives to the use of punishment procedures can destine some clients to a life of deprivation which will insure their continued status as severe behavior problems and drastically curtail any chance of enhancing their humanity. (pp. 470–471)

To summarize, negative added effects (E_+^-) are those objects, events, or actions that decrease actions that produce them and upon which they are contingent. Their application in an educational program constitutes punishment and may be a necessary and effective form of behavior management when used carefully and appropriately in the context of positive effects for skill-building activities. Particular care should be taken in the programming of any aversive effects that may be painful or potentially harmful to the severely handicapped student. No program of this type should be undertaken without the consent and agreement of the child's parents or caretakers, the school administration, and appropriate educational support staff. Particular attention should also be given to the legality of classroom punishment procedures in any given locale. Finally, a dependent student's comfort and well-being is the first consideration in the design of any educational program.

Negative Subtracted Effects (E^-).   Effects of this type decrease actions upon which they are contingent by reducing (or subtracting) an ongoing object, action, or event that is rewarding or pleasing to the child. On the punishment side of the ledger, the paradigm is much like negative reinforcement (the positive subtracted effect).

Using sensory stimulation as an example, Murphy, Nunes, and Hutchings-Ruprecht (1977) successfully eliminated stereotyped behavior in two profoundly retarded students by interrupting ongoing vibratory stimulation. In this study, a student who exhibited hyperventilation was placed in a chair with a vibrator attached to one leg for periods of time each day. The student had previously given signs of enjoyment when subjected to the vibration produced by this arrangement. During the experimental periods, the vibrator was activated and left on until hyperventilation began. The effect produced by each instance of this action was contingent termination of vibration for a period of time. Following cessation of the hyperventilation and a time delay, the vibrator was reactivated. The arrangement was continued at various periods of the day and in various settings. The result was a significant reduction in hyperventilation which remained reduced, even following the fading out and ultimate removal of the vibrator.

The behavior management procedure called *timeout* is a subtracted effect of this type. A teacher, for example, who is providing positive effects

(E^+) during a skill-building period may control the occurrence of aberrant behavior during the instructional period by this technique. Following the dispensing of a sufficient number of positive effects, the teacher and teaching situation in combination will *become* an ongoing positive stimulus for the child, a situation the child will be motivated to maintain. An aberrant behavior can now be followed by the teacher turning away or even leaving the situation for a brief period of time. If an action by the child has the effect of repeatedly terminating (subtracting) the rewarding situation, even for brief periods of time, the action will tend to decrease and may even stop altogether. The child's aberrant action has produced, in this instance, a condition of timeout from ongoing positive reinforcement. It is important to note here that timeout is *only* a brief interruption of ongoing reinforcement. It manages aberrant behavior by briefly terminating an ongoing positive stimulus, the reinforcement situation. It costs the child the ability to continue to earn the positive effects he or she has been enjoying in the situation.

The term *timeout* has been often misused as a euphemism for a punishment (E^-) procedure. The most frequent misuse of timeout is in the context of physical removal and subsequent isolation of a child following an episode of aberrant behavior. If a child is physically removed and isolated in a quiet room for a period of time as a scheduled effect of displaying aberrant behavior during a program of ongoing positive effects for skill-building actions, the procedure is not E^- but rather a form of punishment ($E\overline{+}$) called *contingent isolation*. The fact that the quiet room in this procedure is often labeled the timeout room does not justify its consideration as anything other than production of a particular type of contingent aversive effect ($E\overline{+}$) of the event variety. In general, if the procedure includes only the teacher's behavior (temporary withdrawal), the procedure is timeout (E^-). If the procedure includes a physical manipulation of the child, such as placement in isolation, it is more like $E\overline{+}$, or punishment. The distinction is useful because the behavior managed by contingent isolation, a drastic and unpleasant procedure, may, in many cases, be managed equally well by a simple timeout procedure that will not result in the shortcomings of the application of punishment detailed above.

Another example of E^- is given in the procedure called *response cost*. In this paradigm, a child has earned a number of *objects* that have positive effect valence. For example, in a skill-building program, a child has accumulated a number of *tokens* which are later to be exchanged for a favorite toy on the playground. The tokens have provided the motivational force in the instructional period, and their accumulation has become an ongoing positive stimulus for the child. With each new token earned, the child discriminates the increasing probability of the favored long-range effect of toy play. *Subtraction* of a token during this instructional period reduces the ongoing positive stimulus value of the accumulating tokens. If this subtraction (removal) is made contingent upon an aberrant action, the arrangement will tend to reduce the frequency of these actions. Removal of a token provides a response cost for the occasion of the aberrant behavior. The mechanism is $E\,\bar{}$.

The final class of subtracted effects of the negative type is shown by the procedure called *extinction*. Extinction is the reduction in the frequency of a behavior by terminating ongoing positive effects that are maintaining that behavior. It is the process of managing aberrant behavior by removing the motivation to engage in it. As a procedure, it is therefore dependent upon knowledge of those effects that are supporting an ongoing behavior. As an example, a child bites his hand periodically throughout the day, and members of the teaching staff attempt to correct the aberrant behavior by verbal reprimand and pulling the child's hand down. It is noticed that the procedure seems to be ineffective and, if anything, the child's rate of hand biting seems to be on the increase. At this point, it may be reasonable to hypothesize that the efforts to control the aberrant act are actually motivating it. The verbal reprimand and pulling down of the hand may actually constitute positive effects of the event type for the child: teacher attention! If this hypothesis is correct, cessation of this activity on the part of the teaching staff may ultimately reduce the aberrant behavior by the process of $E\,\bar{}$. An ongoing rewarding situation (reinforcement by teacher's attention) is terminated as an effect of the aberrant behavior. The child is ignored now when he bites his hand, rather than attended to. This procedure, of course, would not be attempted if it were likely to result in self-injury to the child through a period of uncontrolled hand biting. If the hypothesis is *incorrect,* the action will neither increase nor decrease, but remain the same. What if the hypothesis is correct? Since extinction is a behavior-reduction procedure, we might well expect to see an *immediate* decrease in the frequency of the aberrant behavior. But this, paradoxically, is not the case. If the hypothesis is correct and extinction will occur, the evidence is usually in an immediate *increase* in the frequency of the response.

One of the problems with extinction as a behavior management procedure is that it results in just such an initial increase in the action that it is employed to control, followed by a gradual decrease. It is as if the child is trying harder to reproduce the previously available positive situation that has been terminated.

Another problem with extinction is a phenomenon called *spontaneous recovery.* An action for which motivating effects have been removed will tend to flare up in frequency each time the child is in the same setting or situation in which that action had previously been reinforced. The hand biting, for example, although steadily decreasing over a period of weeks on a daily basis, may suddenly occur at a high rate each morning when the child comes into the classroom. This spontaneous recovery phenomenon is apt to occur throughout the course of extinction. Extinction as a method to reduce aberrant behavior is very effective when the following conditions are present:

1. Motivating positive effects of the behavior are known (or correctly surmised).
2. An increase in the frequency of the aberrant behavior can be initially tolerated by the teaching staff following the initiation of the procedure.
3. The initial increase in frequency of the behavior over the course of extinction will not result in personal injury to the child or to others.
4. Spontaneous recovery at various times during extinction is tolerable by the teaching staff.

Extinction has the advantage over punishment, for example, of usually leading over time to permanent elimination of an aberrant act. It has the disadvantage of allowing the behavior to "get worse" before getting better. It is not uncommon for a teacher to discontinue a program of extinction immediately after it begins because the problem seems to be intensifying. This is often all the more a shame since, unknown to the teacher, the intensification was a signal of ultimate success!

In some cases, extinction can be employed to eliminate an aberrant behavior even when the maintaining effects of the behavior are unknown. One of the authors was able to eliminate echolalic responses on the part of a severely handicapped child by first *increasing* the rate of the echolalia by programming positive effects and then terminating the reinforcement procedure. In this procedure, a girl who was observed to be echolalic about 60 percent of the time was brought to about 90 percent verbal imitation, or echolalia, during two half-hour periods each day. The frequency of echolalia was increased by providing a sip of the girl's favorite juice (E $\ddagger$) contingent upon each echolalic response during the specified time period (continuous reinforcement for verbal imitation). Following the criterion of 90 percent imitation, extinction was programmed (E $^-$) and echolalic acts produced no juice during the experimental sessions. The frequency of echolalic behavior increased briefly to 100 percent during the initial sessions following the onset of extinction and then decreased to 0 percent in a matter of days. The frequency of echolalic responses *outside* the experimental setting was also observed to have decreased to zero following the experimental extinction procedure. In the meantime, socially appropriate verbalizations were responded to with enhanced teacher attention and praise.

Finally, one further behavior management technique worthy of attention is the *differential reinforcement of other behavior (DRO)*. This procedure is actually classed as a type of schedule of reinforcement and is thus more closely associated with the S factor in CASE (to be described in Chapter 4) than it is with effect (E) manipulation, but we discuss it here for convenience. The DRO procedure is in actuality a program of positive effects for any behavior that occurs during a fixed interval of time *other* than the aberrant behavior that we wish to decrease or eliminate.

Suppose a student has wanderlust. She cannot remain in any one area for a period of time but must wander the classroom. Suppose we are interested in maintaining the child's presence in a designated area during down time when no teaching staff members are scheduled to work with the student. A DRO-2 program is put into effect, so that after every two-minute period that passes in which the child has *not* left the holding area, she achieves a positive effect. It doesn't matter if the student is self-stimulating, sleeping, or whatever; as long as she has not exhibited the target behavior, she is reinforced. If the procedure proves successful at the two-minute interval, the interval is gradually increased to, say, DRO-5, then DRO-10, and so on, until the child is able to remain in the holding area for the duration of the required period. Favell (1977) has pointed out some of the limitations of the DRO procedure. One, the procedure is heavily dependent upon the strength of a very powerful positive effect. If no such effect can be scheduled, the procedure will probably fail. Two, the procedure can tie up the teaching staff who have to watch the time and deliver effects. For low DRO schedules (DRO-2), the program may simply be too demanding. Three, the effect is achieved at the end of the interval, no matter what the student is doing, as long as specified aberrant actions such as self-stimulation are not occurring.

In general, the DRO behavior management technique has shown some promise for those students who are able to discriminate the particular action that causes the effect to be subtracted, a necessary discrimination in DRO. Most severely handicapped children will not easily make this discrimination and cannot have the rules explained to them in the form, say, of a *contingency contract* (Homme, 1970).

To summarize, a class of negative effects of the subtraction type ($E\bar{\ }$) can be employed to manage or eliminate aberrant behaviors that produce them, as alternatives to punishment ($E\bar{+}$). These procedures include:

1. The cessation of ongoing rewarding sensory stimulation
2. The use of timeout, or interruption of a situation, wherein positive effects are produced by desirable actions
3. Response cost, or the subtraction from a supply of already-earned objects (such as tokens)
4. Extinction, or the cessation of ongoing positive effects supporting an aberrant behavior

A fifth behavior management procedure, differential reinforcement of other behavior (DRO), was discussed in this section on behavior management for convenience but is based on scheduling considerations rather than on negative effects.

A CONSEQUENCE-CLASSIFICATION SYSTEM

Figure 3.1 presents a schematic diagram that illustrates the relationship of valence superscripts to the type of effect denoted (subscripts) and the typical function served in motivational and behavior management terminology.

Table 3.1 is provided as a system to examine the possibilities for the systematic manipulation of motivating effects in the education of severely handicapped students. The skill-building side of the chart is intended to help provide a mechanism for a solution to an old problem in classroom education of SH children: "Nothing seems to reinforce this child." It is a fact that *all* students, no matter how severely handicapped, can be motivated to acquire new, more independent skills through the careful arrangement of effects. Our problem in the past has been that we have been too tied to the experimental analogues of our colleagues in animal research psychology to search for more appropriate effects for our human "subjects." Small can-

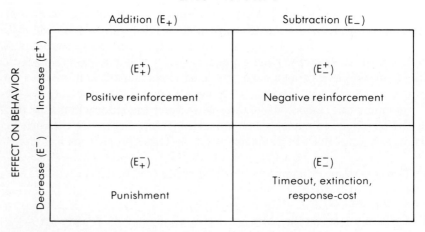

FIGURE 3.1
Schematic of the relationship between added or subtracted effects and corresponding decreases or increases in behavior

TABLE 3.1
Effect Classification System

	Skill Building: Positive Effects of		Behavior Management: Negative Effects of	
	ADDITION TYPE (E‡)	SUBTRACTION TYPE (E±)	ADDITION TYPE (E∓)	SUBTRACTION TYPE (E=)
OBJECTS	Food bits Juice Milk Candy Cereal Tokens Toys	Removal of penalty tokens	Aversive liquids Aversive foods Penalty tokens	Response cost Removal of tokens
EVENTS	Attention Social praise Sensory verbal-tactile reinforcers: Tongue stimulation: Honey Powdered sugar Music-TV Vibration Tactile stimulation Olfactory stimulation	Terminate aversive stimulation: Noise Uncomfortable position	Disapproval cues: Verbal reprimand, frowns, etc. Contingent isolation Physical punishment Restitutional over-correction	Removal of sensory stimulation: Music Vibration Tactile Timeout Extinction
ACTIONS	Play Self-stimulation opportunity Privileges	Escape from hard work Switch to easier activity	Hard work Aversive actions: Stand in corner Hands outstretched Positive-practice overcorrection	Termination of play Cancelation of privilege Interruption of favored activity: Sitting Lying Rocking Self-stimulation

dies and peanuts once provided the only options for reinforcement, and when they failed, education failed. Special educators are now just beginning to explore other sources of motivation for severely handicapped students, sources that provide us with much more powerful tools in our efforts to teach effectively in multiple, normalized environments.

SUMMARY

The first of a two-part instructional model, CASE, was discussed, in which C is cue, A is action, S is schedule (of reinforcement), and E is effect. The first part of the model was concerned with E, and we presented a framework for analyzing the *motivational* requirements of an educational program for severely handicapped students.

In this analysis, there are three classes of motivational effects: objects, events, and actions. These effects, in turn, can be positive, in which case they strengthen the actions they follow, or negative, in which case they weaken the actions they follow. The effects, whether positive or negative, can occur by adding to ongoing stimulation or by subtracting from it. A notational system of superscripts and subscripts was presented to aid in identifying the type of effect discussed in the analysis. Various procedures used in behavior management were discussed in the context of the CASE analysis of motivation, including overcorrection and other forms of punishment, timeout, extinction, response cost, and DRO, the differential reinforcement of other behavior. The second part of the CASE analysis continues with a discussion of stimulus control in Chapter 4.

Instructional Design:
Stimulus Control

In Chapter 3, we discussed motivation in terms of the effects of a severely handicapped student's actions on the environment, the E in our CASE model. We also considered the management of aberrant behavior as the programming of effects that teach a student either not to engage in a given behavior or to engage in alternative, socially acceptable behaviors. In this chapter, we discuss the cluster of teaching strategies known as *stimulus control,* the skillful arrangement(s) by which different cues (C) provided by the teaching staff can mold generalized, increasingly independent behaviors (A) in multiple, normalized environments.

ACTIONS (A)

Organisms' behavior may be viewed as an ongoing flow of discrete actions on their environment. Actions, for our purposes, are bits of behavior that may be examined particularly in terms of the effects they produce on the environment. The locus of causation in learning is as follows: An action (A) produces an effect (E) in the environment and is thus changed in terms of future repetitions. What happens *after* the action is what causes an action to occur.

The definition of an *action,* for our purposes, is *any behavior that has a discrete beginning and end and that can be measured.* Obviously, this definition allows a very broad range of behavior to be examined in the context of this learning model. A group of students, for example, may exhibit a common behavior that can be affected by a single, scheduled effect provided to the entire group. A college student wishing to improve his study habits may elect to schedule motivational effects for improved study habits. In this case, *study habit* is first defined as an action. Since our student usually studies while seated at his desk at home, he defines the action as "number of minutes per day" spent at his desk. He assumes that increasing

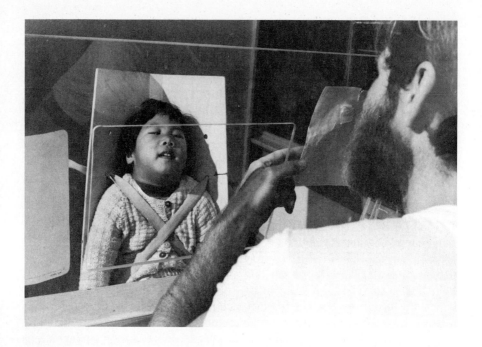

the amount of the action will be tantamount to improving his study habits. As a positive effect, he "rewards" himself with a glass of beer on Friday afternoon for specifiable increases above the average of the previous weeks' study time at his desk. Over the course of the semester, his chart of time spent per day at his desk shows a steady increase. His study habits have improved (but he now must manage a burgeoning weight problem). In this case, the action, although very large in scope, met the criteria of delimitability (time at desk) and measurability (by stopwatch). What about the smaller end of the behavioral scale?

A severely handicapped student is characterized by spastic rigidity. An educational goal of increased range of motion in the upper extremities has been set for her. The instructional objective is to increase forearm reach from the elbow. Initially, the student's muscles must be relaxed by tapping and gentle rubbing around the elbow in order to promote a slight forward, bending movement of the arm. Because no voluntary reach is exhibited, an instructional technique is begun to *facilitate* forward reach. The action in this case is so small that it cannot be observed but may be *transduced* with the aid of an electromyelograph (EMG). With electrical leads placed above and below the elbow, a change in electrical potential of the muscle may be registered as movement on the equipment's gauge and may also be employed to activate a switch. In this case, the change in potential is used to activate a vibrator attached to the student's wheelchair. Vibration of the wheelchair in short bursts has been determined to be a positive added effect of the event variety and will motivate other actions to be learned. In the instructional procedure, the student is cued to move her arm, "reach." A change in muscle potential following the cue produces contingent vibration. The action is initially prompted physically, and the prompt is rapidly *faded out* as a supplementary cue. *Fade* is a term that refers to the procedure of gradually reducing the intensity of a physical prompt [visual or auditory cue, and so on] across repeated instructional trials through successive approximations. As the action becomes stable in occurrence (learned), the amount of change in potential required to activate the vibrator is increased. The definition of the action in this example, has now changed as a function of the electrical potential required to activate the vibrator. As each new action is learned and redefined to enhance further progress, the behavior soon can be observed. First, a muscle jump at the elbow becomes noticeable, later a slight movement preparatory to a reach; finally, a definite reach is obtained that can be strengthened by requiring increased distance of forearm from bicep. In this example, the initial action was very small, yet it was *delimitable* and *measurable*.

Actions, in this model, are partly characterized by the method in which they are measured. If a particular action that is selected as a target for instruction varies as a function of the passage of time, then it is apt to be measured by *duration*. In the example of the study habit improvement above, the action was defined as time spent at desk and the measure was duration as timed by a stopwatch. Other actions are of interest in terms of their discrete occurrences over time, as measured by their *rate* (number per minute) or *frequency* (number per some other specifiable unit of time). Still others are measured by their correctness against a standard criterion, such as *trials to criterion* or *percentage*. Some actions may be measured by the *latency* of occurrence following a cue. A more comprehensive treatment of the measurement of actions will be presented in Chapter 7.

Finally, actions are characterized by *elasticity*. If only discrete, uniform actions could be taught, the process of learning simple functions would take forever. A child who learns to put on a shirt learns at the same time to put on all shirts of that type, shirts varying in size, color, shape, and fabric. In many cases, elasticity of action may be taught to the student in a process called *generalization*.

In summary, *actions* (A), defined as behaviors that are discrete (have a definite start and finish) and are measurable, will increase in occurrence if followed by positive effects (E$^+$) or will decrease in occurrence if followed by negative effects (E$^-$).

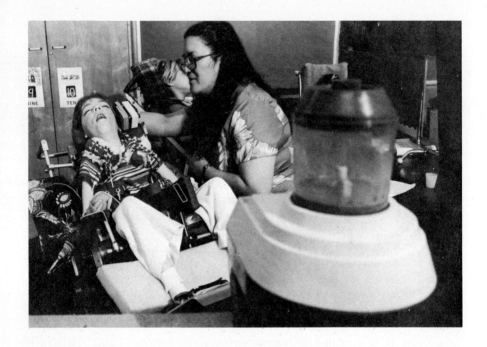

CUES

To understand the present motivational framework, it is necessary to grasp the relationship between what happens *prior* to an action and what occurs following it. The locus of causation is at the *end* of the CASE chain. The effect of the action determines whether or not it will reoccur in the presence of similar cues. It *causes* the learning to occur. Whether or not an action will occur, however, depends on a key ingredient, the cue (C). A rat in a Skinner box learns to run to a bar and press it to earn reinforcement when a light in the box comes on. It learns to stop pressing when the light goes off. To the casual observer, it seems that the light *causes* the bar press to occur (S ⟶ R). The phenomenon is called *stimulus control*. Actually, the light signals the hungry rat that bar pressing will result in food. The food causes the rat to perform the action, but the light signals the availability of the food. The learned action will not be performed in the absence of the cue because the cue has become a part of what was learned. The rat learns not just to press a bar, but to press when the light comes on. Severely handicapped children similarly learn not just to wash their hands, but to wash (1) when they are dirty; (2) when they are asked to; and/or (3) when it is time to eat.

CUES AS DISCRIMINATIVE STIMULI

The cue is the single most powerful variable of the four components to be manipulated by a teacher in carrying out an instructional program. In operant terminology, the cue is called a *discriminative stimulus*. In order for stimulus control to occur, the cue must be discriminated. The discrimination need not be conscious. Much of what we have learned to do is performed in the presence of discriminated cues of which we are unconscious. Most drivers, for example, have the occasional, somewhat disconcerting experience of suddenly realizing that they have driven from point A to point B with no memory of a large portion of the trip. They will have changed lanes, stopped and started for traffic lights, turned corners at appropriate intersections, and so on, all with no conscious awareness of the cues that are normally relied upon. It is as if they were on "automatic pilot."

The term *stimulus* is avoided here in favor of the term *cue,* because we wish to stress the locus of causality at the end of the chain. The terms *stimulus* and *response* have become associated with the S $\longrightarrow$ R classical conditioning model, wherein a stimulus *evokes* a response and a response occurs in *reaction* to a stimulus. In the operant paradigm, on the other hand, an action in the presence of a discriminated cue produces some effect which will determine whether the action will tend to be repeated or not in future cue situations.

The definition of *cue* (C) for our purposes is: *any environmental occurrence that can be discriminated by the child as a signal that some action or chain of actions may produce some specifiable effect.* The term *environmental* is used to differentiate an instructional cue from an internal state. A hunger pang, for example, may be discriminated by a severely handicapped child, but is not available to a teacher for arranging an instructional program. The term *may* refers to the fact that actions performed in the presence of cues produce effects only in accordance with some arrangement or schedule (S) and not necessarily each time.

Because a cue must be discriminated to have the function of C in our system, it is important to consider each student's sensory efficiency *in each modality* in the selection of a cue. A child with little or no efficiency in the visual modality (blind), for example, cannot discriminate visual components of presented cues. Similarly, functional cues can be masked in verbiage and necessitate many more training trials than if kept simple. A child learning to wash his hands, for example, may initiate a chain of actions to the cue, "Okay, Tommy, it's time now to go and wash your hands to get ready for lunch," but may well require many more training trials than if the cue at this stage of instruction were simply "Tommy, wash hands," particularly if the student's level of receptive speech is quite low.

STIMULUS CONTROL PROCEDURES

Teachers engage in *stimulus control* procedures constantly during instructional programs. When motivation (reinforcement) is constant, the precise shifting of the control of an action from one cue to the next comprises a powerful education technology. Three examples are presented below to illustrate stimulus control in terms of the CASE model.

Example 1: Reach and Grasp.   Suppose you are teaching a young child to grasp, raise, and squeeze a soft, spongy object (such as a squeaky toy) as one objective in a series designed to facilitate self-care activities requiring fine motor hand control. Let us say that the first step in your program is "extend hand 12 inches to touch object." If your student is severely, motorically impaired and nonimitative, you will likely select a *physical prompt-fade* teaching strategy; that is, you will physically guide the student through the act initially, allowing the positive effect to be experienced (squeaky sound), and gradually "fading" on successive teaching trials your physical involvement, the "prompt." What are the cues available to you? If the child is auditorially efficient and learning receptive speech, then a spoken instruction or a combination of speech and sign is one cue ("touch squeaky"). If the child is visually efficient, sight of the object is one cue. Perhaps you will decide to begin instruction with a plan to shift across two physical prompt cues: a complete, guided putting-through of the required action initially leading up to a light touch on the elbow. We now have a chain of potential controlling cues: C_1 – object; C_2 – object plus instruction; C_3 – object, instruction, plus partial prompt; and C_4 – object, instruction, partial prompt, plus full prompt.

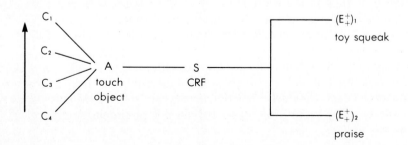

The schematic illustrates the *functional operant* represented by step 1 of the hypothetical learning task. The instructional procedure requires a shift of control of A across cues C_4 to C_1 where the sound made by the toy and the teacher praise, given each time the toy is touched, represent sufficient motivation with which to power the instructional task. The trick is to get from C_4 to C_1 as rapidly as possible and in such a manner as to permit the student as few failures as possible. CRF means *continuous reinforcement* and will be discussed a little later in the chapter.

There is currently a surge in experimental research aimed at determining the most efficient cue shift techniques (see particularly Koegel et al., 1982, for a review of these procedures). Touchette (1971), for example, found that a *time delay* technique between C components during fading from one C to another was effective with some children in accomplishing stimulus shift. For example, if our student above has reached the stage of C_3, partial prompt, and we are hoping to rapidly achieve control with C_2, instruction, the Touchette procedure would call for the gradual increasing of small amounts of time between C_2 and C_3 with successive trials in the teaching session. The first few trials consist of saying "touch squeaky" and prompting the elbow simultaneously. Soon "touch squeaky" is followed by a short delay before touching the elbow. Gradually, the delay is increased until the fade from C_3 to C_2 is accomplished. The child in this situation is given very few opportunities to err and be denied reinforcers, thus keeping the motivation to act high and constant.

When the student no longer requires a physical prompt, the delay procedure can be instituted to move from C_2 to C_1. The toy and instruction are first presented simultaneously, then the toy alone followed after a short delay by the instruction, and so on, until a simple discrimination of the presence of the toy produces a reach and touch response. Instruction is now concentrated on the next step in the task, and a new cue shift strategy is designed and employed. The arrangement of small steps leading toward the successful learning of a larger training objective will be discussed more completely in Chapter 6, which pertains to task analysis. At the end of the training objective, the student will have learned to reach out, grasp, and squeeze a toy that brings him pleasure. The child will have done so with few errors en route, if the cue shift procedure has been effective.

Example 2: A Self-feed Cycle.   Bricker and Campbell (1980) have suggested that curriculum sequences for the severely handicapped child be structured, where possible, in a *chain of actions* that begin with, and ultimately lead to, an action the student enjoys performing. Mealtime training provides an excellent example of this type of instructional chain. Learning to self-feed is difficult. For many students who have been force-fed in the past, food will be aversive rather than rewarding. Beginning an instructional chain with a food the child enjoys will increase the efficiency of instruction. Teach the student to complete a self-feeding chain on a favored meal dessert, and you are in a position to *chain backwards* from the favored food (dessert). Success at this point leads to further *backward chaining* through the entire meal. (Specific procedures for forward and backward chaining will be discussed more fully in Chapter 6.) At the completion of the instructional chain, the student is self-feeding a meal in order to enjoy the dessert. How many of us grew up with essentially the same principle?

Suppose we are working with a student who has successfully learned to eat with a spoon when assisted. At this point, the child has achieved a degree of head control and upper extremity use, can chew and swallow, has some tongue control, and is motivated to eat certain foods. We have discovered that our student loves chocolate pudding desserts, and conveniently, this food is available at the conclusion of the meal.

We may now construct a program for teaching the first objective in our chain: completion of a self-feeding cycle with a dish of dessert and a spoon. Our utensil is *prosthetic,* that is, its handle has been built up with a cone (small end toward bowl of spoon) and masking tape to facilitate grasp. As we succeed with instruction on self-feeding, we will gradually remove the tape through a series of *successive approximations* to decrease the handle size. When we are down to the cone, we will replace it with tape wrapped around the spoon handle to further decrease its size. Ultimately, we will unwind the tape and the child will use the regular spoon.

Step 1 of our hypothetical teaching program has us instruct our student to return the empty spoon from mouth to bowl. We have selected physical prompt and fade as our instructional technique. We can describe the procedure with this schematic diagram.

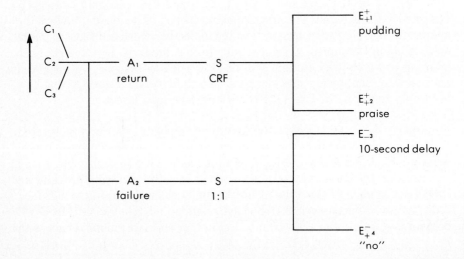

C_1 is the pudding itself, C_2 the instruction "eat some pudding," and C_3 is a full prompt with the teacher's hand over the child's hand from mouth to bowl. The early instructional procedure calls for shifting stimulus control from C_3 to C_2. A combination time delay and distance fade technique is used. The full physical prompt is initially employed from mouth to bowl, then part way, then only initially, then only after a slight delay, then after increasing delay, and so on.

Suppose our student has recently completed a shift from C_3 to C_2 but slips up and misses the bowl. With some (but not all) students, a correction procedure of the timeout variety (paired with mild verbal punishment) will speed up the process. In this case, the occasional error results in a removal of the spoon and dish for a few seconds. Note that the S factor, the arrangement between the effect and the action, is labeled CRF when positive reinforcement is in effect $(E{\ddagger})_1$, $(E{\ddagger})_2$ and 1:1 when E^{-}_{3}, E^{-}_{+4} is in effect. This is simply a customary difference in notation. The term CRF (continuous reinforcement) refers only to the employment of positive reinforcement. Both terms mean that each time the action is performed (whether under C_3 or C_2 instruction), an effect will be produced. The S factor is discussed in detail further in this chapter. In this example, a teacher would ordinarily provide $E{\ddagger}$ for each action except for an occasional miss, which would simply be restarted. If failures showed signs of increasing following a cue shift, the correction procedure, E^{-}, might be begun. Every student will perform differently with respect to an optimal cue shift technique. Part of the skill of creative teaching lies in discovering the combination that succeeds most effectively with each student.

When the cue shift is complete from prompt to instruction, the student is ready to undergo instruction on the next step of the task. When the child has learned to spoon feed without physical assistance on dessert, dessert can continue to motivate learning to spoon feed the main course. Initially, spoonfuls of dessert may be interspersed with initial teaching steps of main-course feeding, then gradually be faded out until self-feeding of the main course is complete.

Example 3: Expressive Speech Instruction.   Our first two examples have concerned physical prompt and fade as the instructional technique. Let's examine the stimulus control paradigm with the use of *imitation* as an instructional technique. Teaching expressive communicative actions, whether speech or manual, can often be accomplished by teaching the child to imitate en route to the desired objective, and then to use the imitative skill as a vehicle for instruction with more complex objectives.

Suppose we constructed a program to teach a nonverbal student to expressively label the object "bell." A bell was selected to begin speech training for two reasons: (1) the student had occasionally demonstrated the "ĕ" phoneme in random babbling, and (2) the student loved to grasp and shake a toy bell.

In this example, the cue shift occurs across, rather than within, steps in the task. Suppose we diagram the entire objective as shown in the schematic.

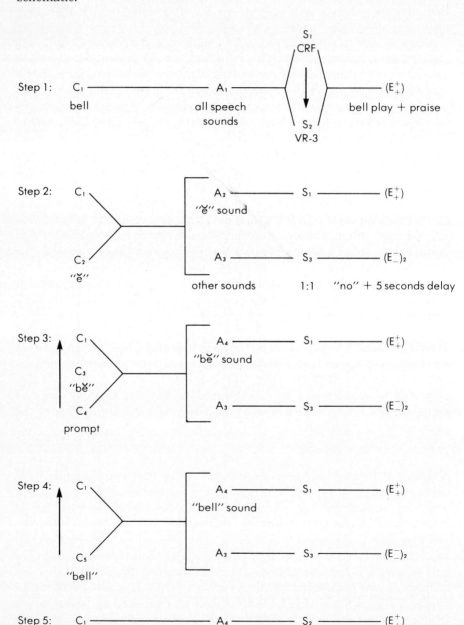

Combinations of three cues were presented across steps to teach the word *bell*. The first task was to increase the student's rate of babbling, or speech-sound production. The child learned that when the teacher presented the toy bell, speech sounds would earn the privilege of ringing the bell (initially after each sound [S_1] and later an average of every three sounds [S_2]). The VR-3 (or variable ratio-three) notation will be described in the next section.

When the student's sound rate reached a suitable level, stimulus control was begun. The teacher paired presentation of the object with the spoken word *bell* and began to *differentially reinforce,* that is, to *shape* the "ĕ" sound and to extinguish all other sounds. This is the first step in teaching *sound imitation* in addition to teaching the specific sound "ĕ". The child is learning, across the sequence of steps, to *match* (A_2) the sound presented by the teacher. Once the student begins to match the "ĕ" sound, occasional lapses into other sounds (A_3) result in a brief timeout. The correction procedure is used for lapses following learning, not for errors during acquisition, and for many students, might not be used at all. By beginning to reinforce only the matched sound across trials, cue control from object alone to object plus *modeled* sound is accomplished. The action in step 2, "ĕ" is called an *echoic* response; it echoes the teacher's modeled sound.

Step 3 requires a physical prompt with this particular student in addition to the modeled and object cues. As the action is about to be given, the teacher gently pinches off the child's lips, catching the voiced flow of the sound and beginning the "b" sound. C_4 is gradually faded with a time delay procedure. The "ĕl" sound proves difficult or impossible to physically prompt with this child, and so a match to the modeled sound is patiently, differentially reinforced until accomplished. The objective is completed when the time delay between C_1 and C_5 results in a shift of stimulus control from echoic stimuli to the object alone. Accordingly, the action shifts (is differentiated) from echoic to object labeling. The child, now having learned to say the first word with echoic stimulus control, should learn subsequent words more rapidly *because imitation has been learned as well.*

SUMMARIZING C, A, AND E

Our instructional design model for teaching severely handicapped students has examined three of the four interrelated components, the four parts of the learning cycle. *Effects* provide the reason for learning. As a motivational variable, the effects of the students' actions power the learning system. Effects, whether negative or positive, can be arranged to systematically shift across different actions in a learning sequence to manage aberrant behavior or to teach a skill as in shaping.

Actions are the behaviors that are learned in the system. In the presence of discriminated cues, actions followed by effects of positive or negative valence will tend to increase or decrease accordingly when the cues are discriminated in later trials or situations. Actions may be arranged to occur in sequences which themselves enhance learning through the process called chaining. The systematic arrangement of a forward or backward chain (see Chapter 6) in a learning task illustrates the close interaction that exists between motivation and instructional technique.

Cues are the crux of the instructional design. Selective sequencing and arrangement of cues, where motivation is high, comprise a strong educational technology. In the examples of stimulus control called prompting and fading, with the fading process often accomplished by a time delay procedure, a student may be gently guided with few errors through a chain of actions leading to gradually increasing independence.

SCHEDULES OF REINFORCEMENT (S)

The schedule, or S factor, is the last of the four variables to be considered in the model. The *contingency,* or *schedule of reinforcement,* in an educational program is *the arrangement by which effects are programmed to follow specified actions.*

CONTINUOUS REINFORCEMENT (CRF) OR 1:1

If the effect is positive and if each (correct) action occurring during instruction is to be immediately followed by the effect, the schedule is designated CRF, or continuous reinforcement. If the effect is negative, but occurs for each action, the designation is 1:1. Continuous reinforcement (or punishment) is the best way to initially establish the learning of a new action. It is the worst way to promote a durable, long-term behavior that has generality outside of the immediate learning context.

The best way to understand the relationship of continuous reinforcement to other possible schedules is to consider the process of *extinction.* This process, as pointed out earlier, is the reduction in the frequency of a behavior by terminating ongoing positive effects that are maintaining that behavior. If extinction is employed as a technique to manage aberrant behaviors, it is a consequence of E^- type, as we have seen. But extinction can be examined in another context. Apart from behavior management where extinction is programmed, the incidental weakening of a learned action upon withdrawal of its maintaining positive effect is another example of extinction.

To return to an earlier example, suppose we wish to begin a student on an expressive speech development program. During our assessment of this student in the communication domain, we collect a few days of *baseline* data, that is, a sample of data points from natural observation; no effects are programmed. We determine that, on the average, for a fixed twenty-minute period each day, the child emits six speech sounds. At this point we begin step 1 of our program. We seek to establish an increase in speech sounds by delivering a positive effect (bell ring) immediately following each sound. Our schedule is CRF. We find an immediate and steady increase in the frequency of speech sounds emitted by the student in this period.

But suppose another teacher examines our graph of progress and expresses grave doubt that bell ringing can cause more speech sounds. This person offers the counterexplanation that the child is simply becoming happier in her home life and is expressing her joy at school with more babbling. Can we test, in a simple fashion, the hypothesis that our instructional program is increasing the student's speech-sound frequency? The answer is yes. We can simply suspend the bell-ringing effect for a few sessions and note the effect on the graphed data; when it reaches a low (but not vanished) point, reinstate the effect. Figure 4.1 presents the typical results one would expect from such an operation. In the baseline condition, the fre-

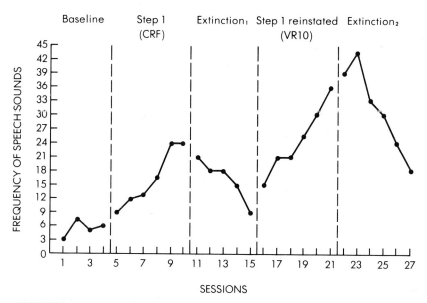

FIGURE 4.1
Reduction in speech-sound production when bell ringing is removed as a reinforcer (hypothetical data)

quency is relatively constant. It increases steadily under the first teaching condition, decreases just as steadily following the onset of *extinction,* and is reinstated in the second teaching condition. The effect on the action of withdrawing the positive effect was a trend toward extinction. If it had been carried out to its final end point, the speech-sound behavior might not only have returned to the baseline level but might even have gone to a frequency of zero. Notice that in this example, the trend downward of the learning curve occurred during the first session of the extinction condition. The learned action began to weaken immediately when an action that was continuously reinforced (CRF) was placed on extinction. If the action had been reinforced *intermittently,* the action would show the characteristic increase before turning down that we noted in Chapter 3 in the discussion on the use of programmatic extinction as a behavior management procedure.

Now suppose that we have progressed further along in step 1 of the same instructional program. We soon find that the student's speech sounds are increasing so rapidly that there is not time to allow ringing of the bell between sounds. At this point, we begin to *thin* the schedule of reinforcement, that is, we arrange the relationship of the effect following the action to become more *intermittent.* Suppose over the next few sessions, we thin the schedule (S) to a point where on the average, every tenth speech sound (denoted VR-10 for variable ratio-ten) is followed by the opportunity to ring the bell. Suppose also that now we decide to test the hypothesis that our program is increasing the frequency of speech sounds. Figure 1 again presents results of the kind one would expect from such a test. Notice that it required three sessions under extinction following this S factor for the action to begin to weaken. Its strength actually increased briefly under the onset of extinction. Why did this occur? If we examine the data from each individual session looking at the frequency of speech as a function of four 5-minute blocks per session, we would expect the data to look about like this.

Session	0–5′	6–10′	11–15′	16–20′
22	95	105	90	110
23	115	275	100	10
24	250	100	75	5
25	100	75	25	0

Under baseline, the student's vocalizations are spaced fairly evenly across the time span of the session. Under extinction, responses increase briefly and then begin to decrease within sessions. The first few sessions will hold enough sustained initial bursts of activity to actually show an increase relative to baseline sessions. Why? From the student's point of view, her vocalizations produced the effect of an opportunity to play briefly with her favorite toy, initially each time, and then, every now and then as long as she continued to vocalize. When the bell was no longer presented, the student took awhile to discriminate the schedule, that is, to notice the absence of the vocalization-bell relationship. When it became clear the bell ringing was not forthcoming, the action dropped off rapidly. During the next session, the action spontaneously reoccurs until again, the absence of a contingent relationship is discriminated. It is *as if* the student begins a new session hoping that more actions will reinstate the favored effect, but then loses hope as the session progresses with no effect. In general, the thinner the schedule of reinforcement (the greater the S factor differs from CRF or 1:1), the more resistant to initial extinction an action becomes.

If we now want to establish a durable behavior that will occur in different places in the presence of other persons at different times than during instruction, we will need to arrange a schedule of programmed effects that will allow for occasional strings of actions to occur in the absence of effects and yet still occur in the presence of cues.

There are four principal methods to use to thin a schedule of reinforcement. Two of these methods are response-dependent (FR-VR), and two are dependent upon the passage of time (FI and VI).

RATIO SCHEDULES

Response-dependent Schedules (FR-VR).   Response-dependent ratio schedules of reinforcement or punishment accomplish the thinning procedure by delivering an effect for either a fixed or variable number of actions. In the earlier speech-acquisition example, the student began to emit vocalizations at an increasing frequency per session under CRF. We might now begin to reinforce every other vocalization instead of each one. If so, we have established a *fixed-ratio* schedule, or FR-2. In the FR-2 schedule, a ratio of 2 actions to one effect is programmed. We could carry this fixed ratio up to 3, 5, 10 and FR-20 if we wished, but there is a problem with *fixed* schedules.

The problem is that the student can learn, quite rapidly sometimes, what schedule is in effect when it is fixed. A child vocalizing under, say, FR-10 typically will, upon discriminating the schedule, emit rapid bursts of vocalizations up to 10 and then wait for a period after the effect is delivered to resume the action. In some cases, a student who has not been formally taught to count will eventually under FR-10 begin to deliver precisely 10 actions and then stop to await reinforcement. It may be that the greatest value of the fixed-ratio schedule in education of severely handicapped students is instruction in counting. In any event, the aim of most educational programming is to provide a smooth, steady acquisition of new skills that are resistant to extinction, not bursts of activity followed by long pauses.

The *variable-ratio* schedule accomplishes just that by making the schedule of reinforcement impossible for the child to accurately discriminate. For example, by moving the student from CRF to FR-2 and then to VR-3, we increase the frequency of vocalizations, yet maintain a stable, constant overall flow of actions. The VR-3 schedule presents an E *on the average* every 3 vocalizations. Sometimes under this arrangement of S, 2 actions in a row will be reinforced; sometimes it will require 4 or 5 vocalizations before the bell is presented. If, for example, at the end of the twenty-minute session, the number of vocalizations are summated and the number of effects achieved are also summated, the total of the latter will equal one-third the total of the former.

In general, low fixed-ratio schedules and CRF are used only to begin the establishment of new skills. These schedules are found usually only at the beginning of each step, or even only during the initial step, in a teaching program. Typically, low VR schedules are present when criterion is reached on a step and instruction is ready to begin on a new step or on a new objective. Higher VR ratios are found when it is deemed necessary to produce very high rates of some behaviors. A VR-20, for example, may require strings of up to 50 actions before an effect is earned. Most educational programming for severely handicapped students typically requires maximum rates that can be achieved with VR-3 or VR-4 schedules.

Time-dependent Schedules (FI and VI).   There are occasions when thinning S should be made time-dependent rather than action-dependent. *Fixed-interval* (FI) and *variable-interval* (VI) schedules program effects as a function of the passage of intervals of time following an action. FI-2, for example signifies that an effect will follow the next action that occurs following the lapse of a two-minute time interval. The effect of this schedule on actions is analogous to its response-dependent counterpart. The schedule is discriminated and actions are forthcoming in bursts only at the end of each interval. Axelrod (1977) describes the effect from a phenomenon of everyday life:

> A situation analogous to the pattern of responding on a FI schedule is the amount of activity exhibited by election officials at various times of the election cycle. Immediately after the election, the victor often seems to have disappeared. A few months before the next election, however, the incumbent reemerges to raid pornographic book stores, kiss babies, and eat soul food. (p. 13)

Just as the FR schedule may prove to be an untapped resource in the instruction of counting, the FI schedule may prove beneficial to teaching the ability to read clocks and tell time. Where this behavior is undesirable, however, the VI schedule can be put into effect and the interval following which a programmed effect will occur cannot be discriminated. The acquisition curve under this schedule will smooth out just as it did under VR. A student who is working quietly on a task, say in a workbook, may be motivated to remain in his seat and work by delivering a positive effect on a VI-5 schedule. On the average, for every five minutes (S) that passes while the student is working in the workbook (A), he will receive reinforcement (E^+). Sometimes he will be reinforced after only a minute or two, and sometimes after ten or twelve minutes. He continues to work steadily because he cannot tell which "work response" will achieve an effect. If he is not working when his time for reinforcement comes up, he "misses the boat" and foregoes the positive effect.

The advantages of VI schedules over VR are twofold. First, the teacher need not be engaged on a face-to-face basis with the student and can work with other students during the time intervals between effects; second, the VI schedule will often produce smooth, steady, on-task behavior without the dramatic push for increased action rates that is associated with the VR schedule.

A good rule of thumb for teachers of severely handicapped students is to employ a CRF $\longrightarrow$ VI (2–10) when the action calls for steady work on task, when teaching staff need not be present, and when a high speed of action is not particularly desirable. Should a teacher be precise in the construction of VR and VI schedules for classroom instruction? Surprisingly, the answer is no. The best variable schedules are based upon teachers' hunches about the action averages and the passage of time. For one thing, it would require access to a computer to precisely calculate variable schedules. For another, the process works whether or not averaging is sloppy or precise. Use the ratios and intervals as rules of thumb rather than as precise guidelines.

TWO SPECIAL-CASE SCHEDULES

The DRO schedule as a special case of fixed-interval scheduling to accomplish a behavior management goal was discussed earlier under effects (E) in Chapter 3. Two other special-case schedules, or examples of S factors to meet special circumstances, are given by the procedures called DRL and noncontingent reinforcement.

Differential Reinforcement of Low-Rate Behavior DRL. The DRL, or *differential reinforcement of low-rate behavior,* was designed to meet a special need of reducing the rate of a behavior without allowing it to extinguish. There are times when you can have too much of a good thing from your students. Suppose you have just taught Gwen the sign for "potty." This is her sixth functional sign and she is becoming ecstatic over the new possibilities that expressive communication are opening up for her. Now, when she signs "potty," she is taken to the toilet, where she may or may not eliminate because she is not yet fully toilet regulated. Gwen soon discovers that a great deal of highly motivating teacher attention and time may be monopolized by signing "potty." Trips to the bathroom are occurring with ever-increasing frequency. What a dilemma for Joe the teacher, who now feels he has created a monster. On the one hand, he cannot spend all his time in the classroom taking Gwen to the potty. On the other hand, he does not want to extinguish her newly acquired sign, especially when she is nearing the accomplishment of toilet regulation. The solution is DRL. Reinforcement for signing "potty" has begun with CRF. The teacher begins by going rapidly to FI-5. Under this fixed interval S, Gwen will not be taken to the potty when she signs until five minutes have elapsed. At the next sign, after the five-minute interval, she goes. When she has quit signing during the five-minute intervals, the teacher moves the schedule to FI-10. Then the schedule continues to increase in interval length gradually to the point where the sign comes into correspondence with bodily need and there is a reason for Gwen to sign "potty." The effect of the sliding DRL schedule has been to slow down, yet maintain stability, of a newly acquired action.

Noncontingent Reinforcement. Noncontingent reinforcement as a special case of contingency arrangement is designed to solve another test-of-hypothesis problem. Earlier we discussed the role of extinction in demonstrating that our bell effect was responsible for increasing our student's vocalization frequency. Suppose our skeptical friend from the classroom next door remained unimpressed by our little demonstration of the power of positive effects. Suppose this skeptic suggested that quite possibly our student's vocalizations were related to having a bell to ring, and that the process had nothing to do with contingencies of reinforcement. Rather, the child was simply expressing joy over being in a twenty-minute session that included occasional play with a favorite toy. To test our hypothesis that *contingent* bell ringing causes an increase in vocalization in light of this new and disturbing attack on our method, we shall need to repeat the experiment conducted earlier (that is, eliminate the bell for a few sessions) but control for the number of programmed positive effects delivered in each condition. Noncontingent reinforcement is a procedure for accomplishing this.

Using the vocalization example, the baseline condition remains the same (no effects are delivered). The first teaching condition also remains the same. The bell is presented contingent upon vocalization, and the frequency of vocalizations increases. Now, instead of extinction, we program noncontingent reinforcement. Under this procedure, the effect is delivered in exactly the same form and number as in the preceding condition except now it is presented just *before* each action rather than immediately following. Of course, now we have an *antecedent* rather than an effect, and as a procedure, it will be difficult to manage in the vocalization example. If done, however, the results would be about the same as shown in Figure 4.1 when extinction was in effect. We would have now shown that it is not only bell ringing that increased vocalizations but that it was *contingent* bell ringing, because absolute numbers of effects were constant across the teaching and test conditions. Noncontingent reinforcement has no known practical utility for the classroom teacher, but for the classroom teacher as *researcher,* the method offers possibilities for hypothesis testing that can assist in the process of curriculum validation.

GENERALIZATION OF LEARNED ACTIONS

We have thus far in this chapter outlined the motivational and stimulus control model as a basis for instructional design for severely handicapped students. We have examined its four working parts and have tried to show how each contributes to the learning process. What remains is to show how the parts effectively interact to produce stable and durable learned skills that lead to increased independent functioning.

The behavioral model was once criticized as being artificial and mechanistic. Critics said that it produces learned responses, but responses that quickly disappear outside the confines of the settings in which they were learned. The world, after all, does not provide continuous reinforcement in the form of small candies to its growing students. Of what service are we as educators if we prepare handicapped students to expect small rewards for their finest efforts in the next environment they encounter? The criticism is not unfounded. Past applications of the method have all too frequently developed behaviors that have not held up outside the original learning context. Skills have been established and have disappeared for want of reinforcement in a changed social context. In short, they have failed to *generalize* (cf., Guess and Noonan [1981] for a critique of the behavioral approach with respect to the issue of generalization).

Educators have become increasingly aware of this problem, and efforts have been made (partly successful) to increase the probability of generalization of newly acquired skills. In our discussion of task analysis, for example, in Chapter 6, we discuss strategies for programming generalization in the area of communication development.

What is generalization? Kazdin (1975) presented an analysis of generalization in terms of two dimensions: stimulus and response. *Stimulus generalization* is the "... *transfer of a response to situations other than those in which training takes place*" (p. 45). *Response generalization,* on the other hand, is the process by which "... *reinforcement of a response increases the probability of other responses which are similar* ..." (p. 47). In the one case, an action under reinforcement control will occur in different settings (stimulus conditions); in the other case, similar responses will tend to come under the control of a particular stimulus, or cue, when one of the responses has been under reinforcement. Similarly, Koegel and Rincover (1977) discussed areas that teachers designing educational programs should be familiar with: initial acquisition of treatment, and maintenance of change over time in the outside (of initial teaching) conditions. These authors and many more have begun to itemize parameters of generalization that need to be attended to in the instructional process. Parameters, however, are not all that we need to know to program effective generalization.

STRATEGIES TO PROMOTE GENERALIZATION

A great deal of research into the parameters of generalization has begun to emerge in the past few years. Stokes and Baer (1977), in surveying the published literature on generalization, identified nine strategies that have been employed by various educators and child trainers to promote generalization of learned actions. These are summarized below.

Strategy 1: *Train and hope.*   In this strategy, several persons engage in teaching a single action in hopes that the effect will transfer to other persons and the child will respond to them, although they (new persons) never reinforce the child.

Strategy 2: *Use sequential modification.*   An action is taught in one situation and tested in another. If not demonstrated in the second setting, it is trained there and tested in setting three and so on.

Strategy 3: *Introduce to natural maintaining contingencies.*   In this case, a student is specifically taught a skill that will elicit reinforcers from others in the environment. Certain social and communication skills can accomplish this effect.

Strategy 4: *Train sufficient exemplars.*   This is the most common technique. Teach an action with a sufficient number of persons, objects, settings, and so on, to increase the probability that the action will be exhibited in all settings and with all persons, objects, and so on. Gee (Note 1) reported a research study that examined the relative probability of generalization on three of these components with severely handicapped students.

Strategy 5: *Train loosely.* In this strategy, a teaching condition is created that reduces the likelihood of fine discriminations being made by the student. If students fail to discriminate fine features of various cue dimensions, then the likelihood is increased that they will "err" in future situations and generalize to new cues.

Strategy 6: *Use indiscriminable contingencies.* By using a thinner schedule of reinforcement, such as VR, in which it is difficult or impossible to predict which trial will be reinforced, the likelihood that an action will occur in other contexts is increased beyond what would be expected, for example, when the schedule (S) is CRF.

Strategy 7: *Program common stimuli.* If there are sufficient cues common to both the teaching and nonteaching settings, then the likelihood of generalization is increased. The strategy is to build in cues to new situations, a strategy that has been successfully employed by Koegel, Egel, and Dunlap (1980) with autistic children.

Strategy 8: *Mediate generalization.* In this technique, the teacher mediates generalization by teaching specific actions that can be utilized in other skill sequences, as well as in the particular skill being trained. An action, for example, like "grasp" may be taught using a door handle to gain exit to a playground, but it will find quick generalization to a desired toy or object the relative size of the door handle.

Strategy 9: *Train to generalize:* Specific steps in a teaching program are designed to promote generalization. Guess, Sailor, and Baer (1976a; 1977a; 1978a), for example, provide training steps for generalization at the end of each of the sixty steps in their language instruction program. This strategy assumes that generalization is a skill in itself and can be taught in the context of other skill instruction efforts.

GENERALIZATION STRATEGIES AND CASE

Suppose we examine in a general way these various strategies in terms of the four operant-cycle components: CASE. First, generalization (or stimulus generalization):

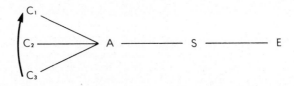

In this instance, a particular action that is being learned and is under some program of arranged effects is systematically shifted from an initial training cue across other cues. The procedure is similar to the stimulus-control paradigm discussed earlier. In this instance, rather than combining several cues (prompts, for example) and gradually shifting control to a single cue, control of the action is shifted from cue to cue where all the relevant cue stimuli have something in common. Strategy 7, for example, called for building similar cues in different settings to facilitate generalization. The most common foci of generalized actions are across persons, places, and objects. A child who learns to sign "potty" for the teacher may learn to generalize the sign to mother by having mother come into the school and accomplish the transfer to the bathroom together with the teacher. A shift to a third person and other settings may necessitate yet another person responding to the child's sign in both school and home, and so on. Severely handicapped students are often remarkably "stimulus bound" after learning a new skill. One of the principal reasons for the movement from an "isolated" model for speech therapy (the student is removed from the class and taken to a small room for communication instruction) to the "integrated" model (within class instruction) was to counteract the tendency toward stimulus binding. We have all too often seen students who learned to speak or sign words in the speech therapy room, but failed, even after months, to show the same skills in a classroom two doors away.

The second component is represented by the notion of action, or response generalization:

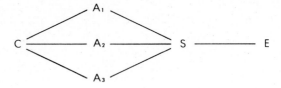

Here a single cue controls several closely related actions that are under some program of arranged effects. This operation is similar to strategy 8. A student is taught an action that is adaptable in different forms to meet slightly different situations. A student learning to draw, for example, is taught to draw with pen, chalk, crayon, and pencil, slightly different discrete actions that adapt across various media.

In the third component, contingency generalization, the schedule of reinforcement may be varied to allow the action to occur numerous times in succession in the absence of positive or negative effects.

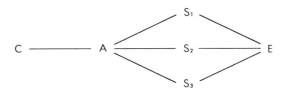

This procedure is identical to strategy 6 above. If a student cannot discriminate occasions when programmed effects will or will not be forthcoming, then a given action will become more resistant to extinction and is thus more likely to occur in situations other than those involving specific training.

Finally, the manipulation of effects can facilitate generalization:

In this instance, an action is established with a strong positive effect, for example, but then is shifted away from the training effect to other effects that may be less potent but more likely to occur in a broader environmental context. Actions established, for example, with food effects may be shifted with repeated pairings to social effects. A student taught to wave good-by as a social act may learn for tangible reinforcers, but the action may come to be maintained eventually by the reciprocal act on the part of other persons.

All four components of the operant cycle contribute to generalization, and all four should be considered when the goal of instruction is to produce generalization of learned skills.

Suppose we are interested in developing an independent social skill in a severely handicapped student. The objective is to teach a student to express "come here" to another student and to deliver a positive effect for compliance, thus helping to increase the reward value of students for each other and decreasing the strong dependence bond on adult teaching staff.

The program moves through a number of steps that can be represented schematically as:

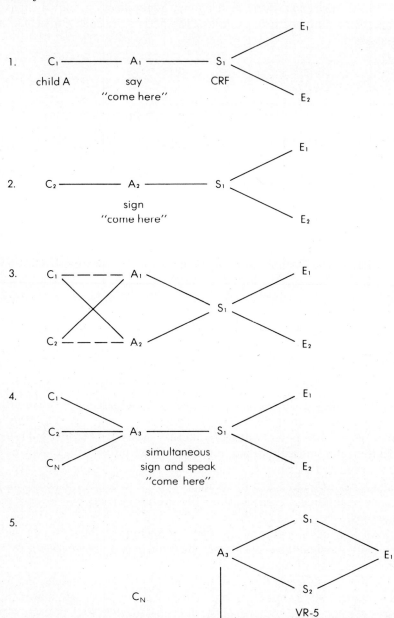

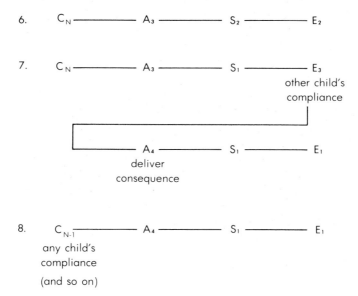

6. C_N ———————— A_3 ———————— S_2 ———————— E_2

7. C_N ———————— A_3 ———————— S_1 ———————— E_3
                                                    other child's
                                                    compliance

      ———————— A_4 ———————— S_1 ———————— E_1
                deliver
              consequence

8. C_{N-1} ———————— A_4 ———————— S_1 ———————— E_1
      any child's
      compliance
      (and so on)

SUMMARY

This chapter has presented the second part of a two-part instructional model that began with an analysis of motivation in Chapter 3. In this part, we discussed the first three letters in the CASE model and their implications for instruction. First, *actions* (A) were defined and discussed with some consideration of their measurement during instruction. (Measurement is discussed in greater detail in Chapter 8.) Cues (C) were then discussed as an analysis of stimulus-control techniques in teaching. A series of schematic designs illustrating case examples was presented. These procedures included prompting, fading, time delay, chaining, imitation, differential reinforcement (shaping), and direct verbal instruction. "Errorless" shaping techniques were emphasized with particular stress placed on using naturally occurring cues and prompting procedures in normal environments.

Schedules of reinforcement (S) were discussed and classified as time-based (interval) schedules or action-based (ratio) schedules. These two types can each be arranged in turn as fixed in time or number, or variable in time or number. The latter is preferred as a way to prevent a student from discriminating the type of schedule and adjusting actions accordingly. It was suggested in this analysis that the scheduling of effects should be continuous during initial instruction on a task but become intermittent as progress ensues in order to ensure transfer and generalization. Two special kinds of schedules were discussed, DRL, or *differential reinforcement of low-rate behavior,* for skill transfer, and *noncontingent reinforcement* for tests of effectiveness of instruction.

Finally an analysis of generalization was provided with some illustrations and suggestions for facilitating instruction.

We will present a system for devising an instructional plan in Chapters 5, 6, and 7.

CHAPTER 5

Curriculum Development:
Goals and Objectives

The preceding two chapters discussed some basic motivational and environmental programming principles in relation to teaching severely handicapped students. As cautioned earlier, these principles should be viewed as aids to the teaching process, not as uncompromising explanations of why and how human beings behave in all situations. This chapter, and the three that follow, will provide more specific information and suggestions on the identification of instructional goals for severely handicapped students, the process for breaking down these goals into obtainable, short-term objectives, methods of evaluating the progress of students, and some considerations for organizing and sequencing the content of what is to be taught. A logical starting point for the presentation of this information is the individualized educational plan (IEP).

THE IEP

As a concept, the IEP represents a turning point in the field of special education: a turning away from a group standard for assessment and program planning, and a turning toward a focus on the needs of the individual student. Specifically required by PL 94–142, the IEP has proved over the past years to be a major boon to the provision of service to severely handicapped students, for whom the concept seems to have been intended. Although the benefits of individualized program specification are clear in the case of our students, our colleagues in learning disabilities and other areas of milder impairment complain that the focus is burdensome and unrealistic. The process of IEP is the same, whether applied to a child with a minor, identified speech dysfluency, referred for limited speech therapy during the course of regular education, or to a severely retarded, multihandicapped child with extensive, highly individual needs. Clearly, the IEP was conceived with our students (and their parents) in mind, and its advantages are numerous.

The IEP is, in reality, two things: a committee meeting and a written plan to which parents and school district administrators affix their signatures. The meeting and the resultant plan must occur at the outset of the identification of a student for special education services, and then at least once each subsequent year that such services are provided. The group that meets must include the child's parents or referring teacher, a representative of the school district, and the child's parent or guardian. Other persons may be included as deemed appropriate by the parent or school district.

The program plan must include a statement of the child's present levels of educational performance, a statement of annual goals and short-term objectives, a statement of specific services (such as therapies) and educational programs to be made available to the child, the projected dates for initiation and the anticipated duration of the services, and evaluation procedures for determining progress toward completion of the short-term objectives. For an excellent and comprehensive analysis of the specific requirements and overall structure of the IEP process, the reader is referred to Haring (1977).

It is our belief that although the formal IEP represents a beginning point for the delivery of an educational program to a severely handicapped student, it is completely inadequate as a day-to-day program guide for the teacher. The primary reason for its inadequacy lies in the premise that short-term instructional objectives can be meaningfully drawn from a single "shotgun" assessment of a student's current functioning level. Experience with the severely handicapped population has taught us that many of our assumptions about developmental sequencing, drawn from observations of normal infant development, fail to hold up when applied to the handicapped. Yet nearly all the standardized assessment check lists available to teachers, therapists, psychologists, and others are simply "slices" of normal, average development across a number of dimensions deemed relevant for instructional intervention. What we know is that the assessment of functioning of a severely handicapped student is completely bound up in and part of the instructional process. The *ontogeny* of nonhandicapped child development is very different from that of the severely handicapped person. The direction of growth on any dimension can be revealed only in the context of attempted movement through the individual child's sequence of activities leading to an identified goal, *under optimal instructional conditions.*

A severely handicapped nonambulatory student, for example, for whom a goal of achieving walking has been established will likely not progress through the motoric stages of development that characterize the infant in achieving the same outcome. The short-term objectives leading to the goal may be different for each student and may be determined only from initial attempts to encourage, with assistance, the final target behavior. As we shall see, the actual sequence of objectives selected will be determined by characteristics of the student, the current and subsequent environments available to the student, and the function for the student that the goal activity serves. Often, the identified sequence of short-term objectives leading to a specified goal will change, following the completion of each short-term objective in progress! What then are the implications of this idiosyncratic learning pattern for the establishment of standardized assessment systems and fixed curricula for education of the severely handicapped? It suggests, in fact, that they cannot suffice as an educational program basis, but can ultimately serve only as supplementary sources of information.

The job of determining what to teach a severely handicapped student falls to the classroom teacher *with assistance* from parents and other professionals. The construction of an appropriate curriculum for an individual child will arise from the initial attempts to instruct the child over the course of a year. It is our intent in this chapter to provide the reader with a systematic framework from which to develop a working program plan that will be appropriate and functional for the movement toward independent functioning of a severely handicapped student. The system is developed on the assumption that the first IEP will necessarily be considered only as a framework for beginning instruction and not as a suitable, long-range program plan. Rather, our system views the *second* IEP as the outgrowth of information that will lead to the formulation of short-term objectives ideally suited to the progress of the individual student. Thus, the system is designed to provide a teacher with a single school year instructional format, the completion of which will constitute additional primary assessment data as well as a progress evaluation toward identified goals for beginning Year 2.

THE WORKING PROGRAM PLAN

Whereas the new student's first IEP provides a minimum set of educational goals and objectives established at the outset, the working program plan constitutes a daily working format for the actual delivery of instruction. It is the blueprint from which the teaching staff work, and as such it must be accessible and meaningful to its users. We will provide a framework for a program plan that we believe will apply to any severely handicapped classroom. It is not intended to be programmatic in the "cookbook" sense, but rather, a guiding structure that can be modified to fit the needs of each severely handicapped classroom and its teaching staff.

The program plan is usually kept on a clipboard on the wall of the classroom, but may also be stored in a file folder, notebook, and so on. We prefer the clipboard because of its accessibility and the ease with which material can be added or withdrawn from it. When the individual is not the focus of the educational program, program plans are built around curriculum components, for example, a reading instruction lesson plan, an art plan, and so on. The focus of individualized education for the severely handicapped student has led to program plans structured for the individual; thus in a classroom of eight students, one will find eight clipboards.

The content of each program plan should consist of *the minimum information necessary to enable knowledgeable substitute teaching personnel to carry out each student's program in the absence of regular teaching staff.* The purpose of this standard for program description is twofold. First, it provides a sufficient amount of detail to assist the regular teaching staff on a day-to-day basis in remembering each specific procedure and its updated changes for each student. In a dynamic, changing program, with students showing rapid progress, a reasonable standard of detail specifying program parameters will prove invaluable. The second reason for the standard is to ensure that persons other than the immediate teaching staff can examine a child's program plan and not only understand each instructional objective and the procedure for teaching it but be able to carry out the program in the absence of the teaching staff. Parents, therapists, substitute teaching staff, and others can then provide continuity of significant educational involvement with only a minimum of in-service training time on the part of regular teaching staff. This is most important to the curriculum-sequencing model to be presented in Chapter 8. Each component of the program plan, then, is detailed with this combination of mnemonic and instructional benefit in mind.

EDUCATIONAL GOALS

The first sheet of paper on the clipboard lists between four and six educational goals for the student. For our system, an *educational goal* is a specific functional skill or cluster of skills that the student should be able to attain in one year under existing instructional conditions and that will significantly enhance the student's progress toward reduced dependency upon adult caretakers. There are two aspects of this goal definition that are worthy of note. The first is the requirement of specificity in terms of a discrete skill. The second is the somewhat arbitrary selection of one year as the target range of time for attainment of the goal. The reason for the skill description is to enable the specification of a *sequence* of short-term instructional objectives that will culminate in some real act of greater independence. Remember that we have ruled out the sequences provided by standardized assessment check lists taken from observations of normal child development as our basis for curriculum development. The specification of a discrete goal enables us to assess the student's current ability to perform the act specified as the goal and then to determine an initial sequence of objectives that will guide the student from present functioning to completion of the act. The sequence specified in this manner will be tailored to the student and will reflect his or her unique characteristics that might contribute to or detract from progress along the dimensions represented by the goal.

The second specification, one year's time, enables the teacher to project a sequence of short-term objectives, each of equal length, that culminate in completion of the act specified in the goal. The arbitrary unit of time selected for completion of short-term instructional objectives is one month. Therefore, an educational program that operates ten months out of a calendar year will provide the framework for specification of ten objectives, arranged in a sequence, to attain each goal. If goals are established at midterm intervals, then they should be scaled down in scope to fit, realistically, the time period available for instruction. Goals should not be specified to include a break of one month or more, such as summer recess. A program that begins anew in the fall should provide the opportunity to redesign each student's working program plan.

SELECTION OF EDUCATIONAL GOALS

Thus far, we have determined that each student's working program plan should have from four to six educational goals that are specified in terms of discrete (observable) acts. Each of these acts represents a fantasy, a visualized projection of a discrete skill that we believe the student is capable of attaining in one year under our current instructional conditions.

Traditional Selection Methods. Educational goals have traditionally been vague and general, and have been stated in terms of conceptual development rather than in terms of specific behavioral acts. An educational goal might be specified, for example, that states "Joan will become more proficient at mealtime skills" or "Joan will exhibit less aggressive and self-destructive behavior." Obviously, goals of this type neither provide specifications for individualized curriculum sequences nor suggest guidelines for instructional content. They are open-ended and unmeasurable. By contrast, the goal "Joan will walk unassisted from the school bus to the classroom" fulfills all these requirements.

But how do we arrive at the conclusion that walking a fixed route is a reasonable goal for Joan over the next year? Obviously a kind of *assessment* system applicable to long-range programmatic specifications is called for. Existing assessment systems for severely handicapped students are too *personalized* and too *microscopic*. The child is considered as a person who exists in a vacuum. The skills addressed usually require only a minimum of attention to the child's environment and his or her interaction with that environment. The discrete skills assessed are typically small in scope, more geared to short-term objectives than goals. These systems almost universally are geared to personal domains, consisting of skills arranged vertically under communication, motor, self-help (survival), social, and cognitive development. Certainly a teacher can think up a year-long goal under each of these domains for a particular student, but what is there to tie the instructional design into a cohesive unit? We believe that recent information published by the Madison, Wisconsin, group provides a very workable solution to the problem (Brown, Branston-McClean, Baumgart, Vincent, Falvey, and Schroeder, 1979; Brown, Falvey, Vincent, Kaye, Johnson, Ferrara-Parrish, and Gruenewald, 1979; Falvey, Ferrara-Parrish, Johnson, Pumpian, Schroeder, and Brown, 1979).

Selection by Environmental Assessment.   These authors have rejected the standard child-assessment model as being too personalized and unlikely to result in skills being taught to the child that will maximize the child's success in future as well as present environments. They have similarly rejected a model that focuses exclusively upon the ecology of the student. They opt instead for a match-mismatch assessment model that analyzes the student's current abilities to function in all present as well as likely subsequent environments. Those aspects of environment-student match are used as the basis for strengthening the student's independence in that environment. Areas of mismatch are used as the basis for recommending placement in a more appropriate (and necessarily less restrictive) environment, or as a basis for modifying the environment to match the needs of a student. An autistic student, for example, is being taught to sign expressively and receptively in a current environment that is segregated (no nonhandicapped peers) and self-contained. A subsequent environment has been identified as a public school placement in a special class. Is there likely to be a match between the communication skills of the student and the persons to be communicated with in the public school environment? Probably not. Signing is not typically found among public school, nonhandicapped populations. To provide a match between the skills of the student and the demands of the subsequent environment, one of two things will follow: signing will be introduced into the nonhandicapped curriculum of the public school, or the autistic student will achieve a shift from sign communication to speech or symbol/picture systems. Similarly, a nonambulatory student will be taught to function more independently in a matched environmental context, an environment accessible to wheelchairs and mobility aids.

In our opinion, an adequate source of structured and detailed information about the various environments in which a severely handicapped student moves would be of far more value in determining specifically what to teach than are the standardized and nonstandardized check lists, but unfortunately, as of this writing, developments in this area are only just beginning to reach fruition. The first significant work to be done on this important effort was carried out by Lou Brown, Mary Falvey, and their colleagues at the University of Wisconsin in association with personnel at Madison Wisconsin Metropolitan School District. These efforts were published in Volume IX of the MAZE series (Madison Metropolitan School District, 1979), and in Falvey et al. (1979). In these works, the authors referred to the development of ecological inventories, which are conceived as individualized *processes* that educators can use to secure such information as:

1. A list of current and potential subsequent environments a student is apt to encounter
2. A list of specific subenvironments within each environment
3. A list of activities that occur in each subenvironment that a student may need to learn to increase independence
4. A list of specific skills or skill clusters required to participate in the activities

The specific skills can then be task analyzed into smaller behavioral units for instruction. Clearly, this is a different basis for the derivation of goals and objectives than the normal-developmental basis.

Haas and Hanline (Note 1), for example, have recently designed a prototype checklist for analyzing the requirements of independent functioning in a specific environment, the home. Table 5.1 lists areas under the environment designated "home," an activity list for the area designated "eating area," and a skill list for the activity designated "setting table." The authors suggest that in using any environmental assessment tool for the home environment, teachers should make home visits whenever possible for each student assessed. Parent interviews can provide useful secondary information. Specific skills, such as "carries plates to table," can be specified as short-term objectives (to be discussed) for students for whom this is an appropriate activity to be learned in one month. The same activity can be

TABLE 5.1

Domestic Environment (Home) Divided into Areas Showing Activities for Eating
Area with Further Breakdown of the Particular Skills for the Activity of Setting the Table

Environment: home

Subenvironments
  Food preparation area ⟶
  Dining/eating area ⟶
  Sleeping area
  Dressing area
  Hygiene area
  Family recreational area
  Laundry area
  Workshop
  Foyer/entrance area
  Garage/carport
  Yard
  General: throughout house

Subenvironment: eating area

Activities
  Ingesting solid food
  Ingesting liquids
  Use of utensils
  Table manners
  Setting the table ⟶
  Clearing the table

Activity: setting the table

Skills
1. Takes plates and/or bowls to table.
2. Places plates in proper place on table.
3. Takes glasses and/or cups to table.
4. Places glasses and/or cups in proper place on table.
5. Takes napkins to table.
6. Places napkins in proper place on table.
7. Takes silverware to table.
8. Places silverware in proper place on table.
9. Takes serving bowls of food to table.
10. Places serving bowls of food in proper place on table.

SOURCE: Haas and Hanline (Note 1).

sliced, in turn, into many smaller steps that can be stated as objectives or as steps in a task analysis, as we shall see in the next chapter.

In general, the strategy to pursue in conducting environmental assessments, from Falvey et al. (1979), is the following:

1. Select an environment
2. Divide into relevant areas
3. Delineate activities germane to the area
4. Specify skill germane to an activity
5. Select the first skill
6. Combine with other standardized assessment data, if available
7. Write an instructional objective
8. Perform a task analysis to accomplish the objective

THE PRIORITY MATRIX

The system we have evolved for setting goals and objectives is based in part on the earlier work of the Madison group and in part on the work of Owen White and his colleagues at the University of Washington (White, 1980). Not long ago, instructional objectives for severely handicapped students were written on the basis of a logic that said, if the student fails on an item that is one of a sequence of items comprising a strand on a standardized check list, say the BCP (Behavioral Characteristics Progression, 1973), then the failed item would be specified as an objective. The item could be "points to circle, triangle, and square upon command"; or it could be "provides an indication of a basic need with a consistent action." One of these statements is representative of a critical function, expressive communication, the other is not.

Identifying Critical Functions. A *critical function* is a behavior that is defined or considered in terms of the purpose it serves for the student, rather than a behavior defined in terms of its specific motor characteristics (White, 1980). Furthermore, a critical function is behavior that is of immediate, critical importance to the individual's success in becoming more independent in multiple environments.

White (1980) and Bricker and Campbell (1980) have separately examined the educational needs of severely handicapped students in terms of critical functions. The concept provides a useful alternative to the logic of selecting goals and objectives from failed items on a check list. Pointing to a circle or naming it has behavioral form and possibly function (for example, recognizing shapes), whereas communicating an immediate need in a recognizable and consistent fashion is certainly a critical function. The former is a case of form without function, and the latter a critical function without form (for example, a manual sign for food or drink).

Figure 5.1 presents a *priority matrix* that examines eight critical functions for all severely handicapped students as a function of environmental domains. We now have a logic for the setting of instructional objectives that says, teach those skills first that provide forms to meet critical func-

	ENVIRONMENTAL DOMAINS			
	School areas	Vocational area*	Domestic area	Community areas
Eating				
Toileting				
Mobility				
Expressive communication				
Receptive communication				
Hygiene/appearance				
Recreation/leisure				
Horizontal social interactions				

CRITICAL FUNCTIONS

FIGURE 5.1
Priority matrix for the establishment of goals and objectives by relating critical skill functions to various environments

*Applicable to students in middle and secondary school programs.

tions in multiple environments, forms that increase the individual's independence in those environments.

Each of the critical functions specified – toileting, eating, receptive and expressive communication, mobility, and hygiene/appearance, recreation/leisure, and horizontal social interactions – is an aspect of a severely handicapped student's life that is in immediate need of further refinement. Each function is *critical* to successful participation in normal environments. Surprisingly, these functions have not until recently been the focus of initial educational efforts. Possibly this was so because in segregated environments, where little or no contact with nonhandicapped peers was possible, there was a higher degree of tolerance for a failure to exhibit increasing independence in these areas. With the current focus on increased independence in multiple environments as the basis for education of severely handicapped students, critical functions take on significantly more importance.

The toileting and eating critical functions are, of course, obvious skills with which to begin instruction with severely handicapped students. Communication is best approached as two separate functions, one having to do with *reception* of information provided by others (understanding speech, for example), and the other pertaining to *expression,* or how the student makes his or her needs and wants known to others. This distinction and its implications for curriculum are discussed in detail in Chapter 10. Mobility and personal hygiene, including appearance, are also considered critical first skills to be developed in a variety of environments. Recreational skills include, for example, the ability to amuse oneself in an appropriate manner when left alone, the ability to participate with others in an age-appropriate manner when left alone, and the ability to participate with others in age-appropriate recreational environments (cf., Brown, Ford, Nisbet, Sweet, Donellan, and Greunewald, Note 2).

Horizontal social interaction is included as a critical function in order to place further stress on the importance of teaching severely handicapped students to interact with age peers, including, certainly, nondisabled peers. The term *horizontal* refers to the age-peer dimension. Most interactions that involve severely handicapped students have been of the *vertical* variety, that is, orienting only to an adult upon whom the student is dependent in various ways. Often, it has proven difficult to establish meaningful social contacts between severely handicapped students and their age peers for the reason that these peers have held no particular social *value* for the student and, in fact, have more likely been in the position of competing with the student for the attention of a caregiving adult. Horizontal social interactions then represent as a critical function, the establishment, through teaching, of value in age-appropriate social contacts: side-to-side interactions as an alternative to one-way, up-to-down interactions.

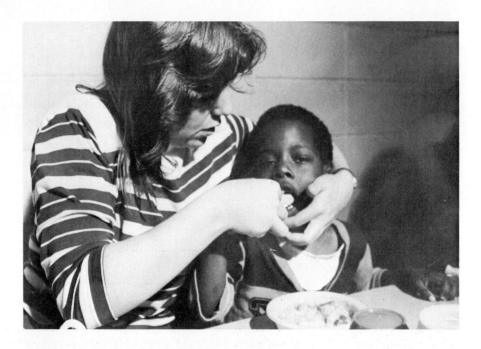

The process of establishing goals by use of the priority matrix is similar to the one described in Brown et al. (1979a). An initial series of questions is posed for any student for whom the setting of one or more educational goals is an immediate consideration.

1. What are the *present* environments that are available to the student for instruction (environmental domains on the matrix)?
2. What are potential future environments for this student (in one year)?
3. What are the requirements of these environments as a function of the student's *chronological age?*
4. What are the special needs of this student to assist *sensory* efficiency?
5. What are the special needs of this student to assist *motor movement* efficiency?
6. What are the special needs of this student to assist *communication?*

The answers to these six questions constitute *modifying characteristics* that may suggest the priority with which critical functions are matched with environmental domains in the setting of initial educational goals. The issue, then, is what functional life skills do we envision for our student as an outcome of instruction over one year? What special equipment will be necessary? What changes or modifications to various environments will be needed?

An Example of the Use of the Priority Matrix.   To illustrate the development of an educational goal with the priority matrix, let us consider a hypothetical student in a classroom for severely handicapped students in a segregated facility, say a special school or development center. Suppose the student, Joel, is a six-year-old male, has been institutionalized or kept at home much of his life, and is substantially health impaired. He is mobile with assistance in a specially adapted wheelchair, but is characterized by extreme spasticity, and must be repositioned frequently out of the wheelchair. He has no reliable expressive or receptive communication skills and is not toilet regulated. He is capable of tracking and scanning moving objects and has progressed in previous programs to increased range of hyperextremity motion and controlled assisted feeding. For purposes of our example, Joel is one of ten in a classroom of similar students with one teacher and a teaching assistant.

Joel's class is expected, under current planning, to be moved intact to a regular public school setting in one year under a district integration plan. The first step in the development of the first educational goal for Joel is to select a domain. Three of the four domains apply to Joel. The second, vocation, is reserved for students in or moving into middle-school, secondary-school-age or post-school-age programs. For the illustration, let's consider a critical function: recreation/leisure. The teacher should first forecast, as much as possible, the domains to which Joel will have access for leisure time in one year. The public school playground is, of course, one, but there are others that should be included. *Information from parents* is necessary to determine the student's total environmental context. A home visit at the early stage of program planning by the teaching staff is ideal.

The second stage in the process is to determine specific areas within each identified environmental domain that Joel will have available for recreation and that may be identified for skill development. Figure 5.2 presents a schematic expansion of the hypothetical areas within domains that are available to Joel for instruction in recreation and leisure. The principal of partial participation (Brown et al., 1979b) is very relevant in Joel's case and suggests that Joel should be taught whatever skills are realistically possible for him that will allow him to participate in an integrated activity partially and with assistance if necessary. The activity should also be appropriate to Joel's age group. A six-year-old severely handicapped child should not be taught skills appropriate to a younger age group (such as infants) just because these skills may more closely approximate his abilities.

For Joel, we have identified the playground at the public school to which he is being assigned in a year as the first of several environments to consider in formulating an educational goal for the critical function of recreation/leisure. We selected the playground for the first priority for goal setting because of the potential for success in this area to directly influence Joel's motivation to benefit from similar instruction in other areas. An age-appropriate skill in this area will bring Joel into direct and, it is hoped, pleasurable contact with nonhandicapped age peers. The selection of a specific skill to form a goal will now require the examination of *subareas* within each area (only the playground area is shown in Figure 5.2). The subarea that we have selected for Joel is the swing set at the school playground where Joel is to be placed in one year. The activities that will enable Joel to function more effectively in this environment include: (1) mobility to the area, (2) transfer from wheelchair to swing, (3) the act of swinging, (4) transfer from swing to chair, and (5) mobility to return to classroom or other area. We will select the activity of swinging as the place to begin. One of our goals for Joel, then, for the critical function of recreation and leisure is that in one year, he will be able to activate a swing for his own enjoyment. What remains is to specify the smaller skills needed which, when taught to Joel in sequence, will result in his ability to engage in the final action. This is the business of writing short-term instructional objectives and of designing instructional programs, which we will discuss in a later section.

"Joel will initiate and sustain the act of playground swinging." This is, most would agree, a very different kind of educational goal than, say, "Joel will improve in gross motor skill development." The goal we have specified for our hypothetical student has the following properties:

CRITICAL FUNCTION:
RECREATION AND LEISURE

ENVIRONMENTAL DOMAINS:
AREA AND SUBAREA FOR PLAYGROUND

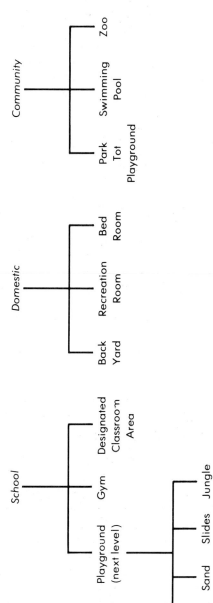

FIGURE 5.2
Expansion of environmental domains to reveal areas and subareas available for instruction in recreation and leisure skills for Joel

1. It is age appropriate.
2. It is anchored in a least-restrictive community setting.
3. It can be "visualized" as a specific, useful, "normalized" skill.
4. It is reasonable as an expectation of the student's abilities under intensive, carefully planned, and monitored instruction over a one-year time span.
5. It is capable of being broken down into subskills that can be taught in sequence as short-term instructional objectives.
6. It is a useful, functional skill that will increase the student's independence in a normal environment.
7. Together with other educational goals, it fits into a coherent, developmental pattern that lends unity and focus to the student's overall educational program.
8. It was derived from a systematic examination of the student's immediate critical function needs within multiple, normalized environments, taking into consideration modifying characteristics that might be needed, such as environmental modification or special equipment.

The process identified for Joel above applies to the establishment of each educational goal for a severely handicapped student. Should there be only one goal for each critical function? Not necessarily, but an attempt should be made to integrate instruction across as many of the relevant environmental domains as possible. Does this system require integration with nonhandicapped peers? Yes, at least some of the time each instructional day. How do we know that swinging is a realistic one-year goal for students as impaired as Joel? We don't. We begin our program and modify goals and objectives as we go along. *It is a place to begin* in a dynamic, changeable system. Similarly, how do we know that we haven't fallen far short in our expectations of Joel? What if he can learn this skill in only a few months? Fine. At that point we establish a new goal. Each day's effort to teach skills to Joel will result in new information for the teaching staff about what Joel is or is not capable of doing under optimal conditions. It is important to consider that the initial specification of educational goals is a "best guess" of where to begin on the basis of available information. The best system is one that can change in the face of new, incoming information. Educational goals for Joel may look very different at the end of six months of intensive instruction under this model than they looked at the outset of his program. Conversely, the more experience a teaching staff has with a particular student, and the more skills they have successfully taught to that student, the more accurate they become at identifying realistic goals, objectives, and their timelines. The student teaches the teacher in a dynamic system!

EDUCATIONAL GOAL SHEET	Date Set	Date Accomplished
1. Joel will initiate and sustain the act of playground swinging.		
2. Joel will communicate the request to be taken to the bathroom at appropriate times and in all environments.		
3. Joel will eat in the school cafeteria, with assistance, without drooling or spilling food.		
4. Joel will extend right arm, traverse an arc of 24 inches, crossing midline in the process, and touch any point within the arc, in all environments.		

FIGURE 5.3
Educational goals for Joel for year one

To summarize educational goals, they represent visualized skills to be exhibited by a student in one year's time under conditions of intensive instruction. They may span each of the relevant domains and critical functions identified above and, together, will form a coherent, focused educational program leading to greater independence in a normalized environment.

To return to the working program plan, Figure 5.3 presents a sample first page for the clipboard representing the program plan for our hypothetical student Joel. Five educational goals have been identified spanning three of the four environmental domains shown in Figure 5.1.

AN ASSESSMENT MODEL

The first step in the process of constructing a working program plan was the identification of one-year goals. The next step is the formulation of precise, specific, short-term objectives which determine the instructional operations necessary to initiate progress toward realization of the goals.

A BASIS FOR ASSESSMENT: TWO CONSTRUCTS

To approach the construction of short-term objectives, two *hypothetical constructs* are necessary. The first consists of a *sequence of objectives* that will move a student from a level of basal performance to the final level of performance indicated in the educational goal statement. The second construct is represented by data that provide a rough indication of the *student's present ability* vis à vis the long-term-goal outcome. These two hypothetical constructs represent a platform from which to begin instruction. The student's progress under instruction will determine the validity or the accuracy of the predictions derived from the constructs. In addition, they represent ways of thinking about a solution to the problem of what to teach. Both constructs may take various forms, depending on the particular styles of different teachers, prior to the writing of objectives. The sequence construct, for example, may be as detailed as a full stepwise lattice, with decision points specified along the way, as in a computer program. Alternatively, the construct may be represented by rough notes on a scratch pad or may even remain totally in the teacher's thoughts. We believe that at least a rough sketch on paper helps to keep a focus on the relationship of the goal to the time available to reach it.

The second construct, basal performance, usually consists of assessment data from various sources, some collected systematically using standardized instruments, some collected informally, and some unique to the particular student and teacher. It necessarily, however, involves data gathered from an analysis of both the environment and the individual as he or she functions within the various aspects of the total environment. The usual form of the basal-performance construct is a series of short statements that describe a student's current performance, under various conditions, relative to a long-term goal. Again, these specifications can take the form, at one extreme, of a series of fully specified, potential instructional objectives with which to begin or, simply, of sheets of completed assessment data with rough ideas for objectives within the teacher's thoughts. Again, we would opt for at least rough notes on each potential objective.

Why have these hypothetical constructs at all? Why not simply fill out a large check list assessment instrument like the AAMD Adaptive Behavior Scales and pick some objectives right off the instrument? Why not follow the logic, say, of the Stanford-Binet Intelligence Test scales and choose as an objective the first item the student "fails" in a sequence of items representing some skill or proficiency? This would certainly simplify the teaching task and save a great deal of time and strain on the staff.

The fact is, most teachers of severely handicapped students were doing similar things only a few years ago. The strategy makes sense, one, if (and only if) assessment instruments provide relevant items that are deserving of instruction, and two, if their sequences are valid, that is, if they represent an order from which a skill is likely to emerge under conditions of instruction. The answer to the question, "why not?" is that all the assessment systems available to teachers of severely handicapped students fail, and fail miserably, on both counts. They fail to contain relevant, functional, and therefore teachable items, and they fail to provide sequences of items that translate into meaningful long-term goals. The reasons for these failures are many, but the principal one is a lack of substantive knowledge on how patterns of learning under instruction with severely handicapped students differ from patterns of normal development upon which most standardized assessment systems are based. Secondarily, assessment systems have been constructed as if skills were able to develop in isolation rather than in relationship to each other and to the requirements of different environments.

We no longer teach to the dictates of checklists, in short, because we have failed in our efforts to achieve meaningful goals with that strategy. Many readers will have had the experience of visiting a classroom for severely handicapped students on two or more occasions, with large intervals of time in between, and noted that the students were working on the same tasks each time with no discernible differences in performance. These tasks often resembled the curriculum that characterizes preschools, regardless of the age of the students, with colors, body parts, and so on; coin-recognition tasks; puzzle and block constructions; and perhaps isolated dressing, washing, and eating skills. Instruction toward proficiency in those skills was attempted because those are the skills represented on the assessment check lists. That the student fails to progress under this instructional model is by now legendary.

The alternative, which admittedly requires a much greater outlay of intellectual energy on the part of the teacher, is to *generate* a curriculum for each student that is relevant, functional, and unique to the individual needs of that student. The role of assessment systems under this model is to provide a helpful structure for systematic observations of current performance levels in different situations. It is not to supply objectives to teach.

Hypothetical Construct One: A Sequence.   The process of generating an individualized curriculum requires the establishment of a microscopic logic of the type that characterizes the large assessment systems. The logic is microscopic in the sense that it provides a sequence, unique to one individual, that pertains to one set of skills only, namely, the set that constitutes a previously established educational goal. The logic has one further dimension that does not characterize standardized assessment systems, and that is a specific time frame. The time frame, which is almost entirely arbitrary, serves to place a constraint on the nature of the logical sequence. This constraint helps to ensure that the initial objectives are necessarily dynamic rather than static and immutable, and that they are *short-term* in reality rather than in theory only.

The process works like this. First, one of the educational goals is selected to set a curricular sequence in motion that will, *hypothetically,* result in its realization. We have selected the time frame of one year for realization of educational goals and *one month* for the realization of short-term objectives. Educational programs for severely handicapped students typically operate on a ten- to eleven-month basis. Thus, the number of instructional objectives that are required, when arranged in a sequence from basal performance level (the student's current performance level relative to the goals) to fulfillment of critical performance on the goal, is ten or eleven. Thus, to form the sequence construct, we need a specification of the final outcome, the goal, as short-term objective ten (assume a ten-month program), and a specification of basal level of performance (hypothetical construct two). We then need to sketch out a series of, say, nine steps that will form a sequence, beginning one step above basal performance, going one month at a time under optimal instructional conditions, culminating in the final performance objective (the goal) at the end of the one year. An impossible task? No, but initially, it is an arduous one because it requires an act of intellectual creativity. There is little to guide the teacher in the formulation of hypothetical goal sequences apart from knowledge of the student and his or her environment, previous experience with the student or with similar students, knowledge of the body of literature on education of severely handicapped students, and, perhaps most important, practice with the method. The first working program plans with this method will be difficult to construct. Later the task will seem much simpler. The rewards are in seeing one's predictions become more accurate over time and in seeing one's students move more rapidly toward higher levels of independent and adaptive living in normal environments.

So far, to return to our example student, Joel, we have established five educational goals that will enable him to function significantly more independently in one year's time in natural environments, present and future. We now consider each goal to be specifiable as an instructional objective (a process to be described later in this chapter) that will be the tenth in a string leading from current performance level to the final goal in each case. Fifty objectives! And if Joel is only one of ten students in a class where you are the new teacher, then five hundred objectives! Obviously, the meaning of the term *hypothetical,* as it applies to the construct, takes on new significance. Rough notes toward the development of a sequence in each case, at best, is all that time will allow. Nonetheless, the development of such a hypothetical sequence in each case is *essential* to the establishment of the first five objectives that will constitute the working program plan.

Hypothetical Construct Two: Basal Performance Level.   Before proceeding to an illustration, we must consider the case of the other hypothetical construct, the basal performance. One cannot construct a sequence of ten steps leading to a goal by proceeding backwards from the goal statement any more than one can proceed forward from basal performance ten steps to establish a goal. The end points must be determined first, and then the intervals can be fitted to the unit requirement, in this case, ten. The process is identical to the construction of an interval scale of measurement. We have predicted that Joel can accomplish some specified goal within one year of instruction. We now venture a somewhat more data-based prediction concerning his current performance relative to that goal. Our success in establishing a reasonable and realizable one-month, short-term objective, then, will depend largely upon the accuracy of our predictions regarding the limits of the sequence.

We stated earlier that this construct would be somewhat more data based than would the sequential construct. This is because we are predicting a present rather than a future state. The accuracy of our prediction is limited only by the means with which we study the phenomenon and the extent to which our student will reveal what he is capable of doing. The former problem can be alleviated somewhat by employing structured assessment instruments, although we must guard against the tendency represented by the fabled man who lost his house key on the dark street and who then proceeded to search for it only in those areas illuminated by street lights. Many assessment systems would have us look in the wrong places for a starting point to a functional, relevant goal. The latter problem is one of motivation and it is a difficult problem indeed. We may find that our first instructional objective represents a behavior not willingly *performed* rather than one not previously in the student's repertoire.

In any case, the task of the basal performance scheme is to determine as best we can what degree of performance our student is capable of in the present, relative to the performances required by the year-off goal.

To formulate this construct, we must gather assessment information on the student's current performances in relevant environments under optimally motivating conditions. One of the best approaches to assessment is to attempt to teach something, a pilot instructional program.

If one of our goals for a student calls, for example, for use of short conversational sentences in expressive speech to communicate wants and needs and we need to know in detail the student's current performance level for speech, then we may need to attempt to teach a word or two over a few days, in a few subareas, to establish that level. Obviously, the two constructs are dynamically interdependent. One does not precede the other, rather they are conceptualized together as a unit. Some information is needed about the current performance level to be able to specify a reasonable one-year goal. One must keep the goal in mind, however, to know where to look to specify current performance levels. Thus, the setting of both goals and objectives depends each upon the other, and the process is both simultaneous and lengthy. The days of writing a lesson plan for the school year the weekend before school starts are long gone for the teacher of the severely handicapped student.

STANDARDIZED ASSESSMENT

Sailor and Horner (1976) in the first volume of the series *Teaching the Severely Handicapped* reviewed a number of standardized assessment instruments available at that time and concluded that initial instructional objectives should be derived from one of the available comprehensive check lists (for example, Behavioral Characteristics Progression, Vort Corporation, 1973). Obviously, we have come at least "half circle" since 1975. We would now suggest that teachers treat these checklists as useful guides for approaches to gathering information about students in various situations on a wide range of variables. In this sense, the checklists are sources of assessment ideas rather than scorable items that translate into instructional objectives. The reviews by DuBose (1978), Haring (1979), and White (1980) should provide useful starting points for the selection of checklist systems with which to assist the assessment process. But if standardized assessment checklists are not the source of instructional objectives, then what is? Again there is no easy solution. The checklist strategy was not a good one, and the present solution is necessarily more complex and requires a greater expenditure of intellectual effort on the part of the teacher.

Four Standardized Assessment Systems.   Standardized assessment systems may best be grouped into four categories as they pertain to the education of the severely handicapped, as shown with some examples in Table 5.2. Group I systems, we will call screening instruments; Group II, intermediate-range assessment checklists; Group III, comprehensive or global assessment; and Group IV, specialized assessment techniques.

Screening instruments, such as TARC (Sailor and Mix, 1975) and Portage (Shearer, 1972), are mainly useful as aids to making early placement decisions. Group II instruments, such as the Pennsylvania Training Model (Somerton and Turner, 1975) and the UPAS (White, Haring, Edgar, and Bendersky, 1978), can provide useful guides for structuring activities to carry out with an individual to determine, *under optimally motivating conditions,* what that individual's basal performance may be in certain per-

TABLE 5.2

Standardized and Nonstandardized Assessment Instruments for Severely Handicapped Students

Group I Screening	Group II Intermediate	Group III Comprehensive	Group IV Specialized
Portage Guide to Early Education (Shearer, 1972)	Pennsylvania Training Model Individual Assessment Guide (Somerton and Turner, 1975)	Adaptive Performance Inventory (CAPE, 1980)	Callier-Azusa (Deaf-Blind) (Stillman, 1974)
TARC Assessment System (Sailor and Mix, 1975)	Learning Accomplishment Profile (Griffin, Sanford, and Wilson, 1975)	AAMD Adaptive Behavior Scale, Public School Version (Lambert, Windmiller, Cole, and Figueroa, 1975)	Camelot Behavior Checklist (adult/vocational/TMR) (Foster, 1974)
	Uniform Performance Assessment System (UPAS) (White, Haring, Edgar, and Berdersky, 1978)	Behavioral Characteristics Progression (BCP) (Santa Cruz County Public School District, 1975)	Ordinal Scales of Psychological Development (Piagetian) (Uzgiris and Hunt, 1975)
		Balthazar Scales of Adaptive Behavior (Balthazar, 1971, a, b)	Total Communication Checklist and Assessment (Communication) (Waldo, Barnes, and Berry, 1979)

formance areas (such as washing, toileting, and so on). Group III instruments are so global that relatively small portions of the behaviors they sample usually apply to severely handicapped students; thus, they are cumbersome to use. The most recent of these, however, the *Adaptive Performance Instrument (API)* (CAPE, 1980), provides a compendium of items, sequenced developmentally, that apply more generally to severely handicapped persons. According to CAPE (1980), the instrument offers the following advantages over traditional standardized checklists:

1. The API measures skills which are functional (skills which enable a child to perform in the environment) and which are potential programming targets. Small steps of child behavior are measured by the instrument, allowing for discrimination of the slow and gradual progress typically displayed by the target population.
2. Most of the instrument is designed to be administered through examiner observation of children as they behave in their environments. Direct testing is used primarily when a child does not display target behaviors during the observational sessions.
3. Most of the instrument's assessment targets provide adaptations in either the directions given to or the behavioral response required by children with sensory and motor impairments.
4. The API is program-oriented in that it assesses the child's ability to perform educationally relevant target behaviors. Examiners are requested to make a judgement regarding the rate, consistency, or age appropriateness of a child's performance. Thus, the direct service personnel obtain such programming information as what skills are appropriate and what aspects of performance to strengthen.
5. The API includes procedures for assessing the child's physical and sensory intactness. The Physical Intactness domain alerts the examiner to the necessity of referring children for specialized treatment, to the potential impact of sensory or motor difficulties on performance and performance assessment, and to the need to make necessary adaptations in administering the API.*

The Adaptive Performance Instrument is intended for use with severely handicapped children under the age of nine.

Table 5.3 presents the domains and strands sampled by the Adaptive Performance Instrument for purposes of illustration. Each of the strands within domains are further subdivided into specific behaviors called targets. Targets are intended to be approximately equivalent to steps in a task analysis (to be discussed in the next chapter). For example, a target

---

*Dale Gentry, *Consortium on Adaptive Performance Evaluation (CAPE)* (Washington, D.C.: U.S.D.O.E., Office of Special Education, 1980), pp. 1–2. Used by permission.

TABLE 5.3
Domains and Strands Sampled by the Adaptive Performance Instrument

PHYSICAL INTACTNESS (PI)
1. Extremities (EXT)
2. Head, Neck, and Trunk (HNT)
3. Oral, Facial Structures (OFS)
4. Breathing (BRE)
5. Sensory Organs (SOR)
6. Muscle Tone and Control (MTC)

REFLEXES AND REACTIONS (RR)
1. Oral Reflexes (ORE)
2. Grasping Reflexes (GRE)
3. Brain Stem Reflexes (BSR)
4. Righting Reactions (RRE)
5. Automatic Movement Reactions (AMR)
6. Equilibrium Reactions (ERE)

GROSS MOTOR (GM)
1. Balance on Stomach (BOS)
2. Voluntary Movements on Back (VMB)
3. Rolling (ROL)
4. Balance in Sitting (BIS)
5. Balance in Standing (BST)
6. Positional Changes (PCH)
7. Functional Utilization of Balance in Movement (FUB)

FINE MOTOR (FM)
1. Reach for Object (RFO)
2. Voluntary Grasp (VGR)
3. Bring Hands to Midline (BHM)
4. Hands to Mouth (HTM)
5. Voluntary Release (VRL)
6. Forearm Rotation (FRO)
7. Hands Cross Midline (HCM)

SELF-CARE (SC)
1. Ingestion of Foods and Liquids (IFL)
2. Self-Feeding (SFE)
3. Preparing and Serving Foods Using Utensils and Containers (PSF)
4. Washing/Drying Self (WDS)
5. Toileting (TOI)   (*Continued*)

SOURCE: Dale Gentry, *Consortium on Adaptive Performance Evaluation (CAPE)*
Washington, D.C.: U.S.D.O.E., Office of Special Education, 1980), pp. 4–5. Used by
permission.

TABLE 5.3
(Continued)

SELF-CARE (SC) *(Continued)*

   6. Personal Appearance/Hygiene (PAH)
   7. Functional Manipulation of Common Environmental Mechanisms (FMM)
   8. Avoidance of Environmental Danger (AED)
   9. Undressing (UND)
  10. Dressing (DRE)

SENSORIMOTOR (SM)

   1. Problem Solving (PSO)
   2. Vocal Imitation (VIM)
   3. Motor Imitation (MIM)
   4. Object Differentiation (OBD)
   5. Object Permanence (OBP)
   6. Grouping Objects (GOB)

SOCIAL (SO)

   1. Compliance (COM)
   2. Anticipation of Commonly Occuring Routines (ACR)
   3. Interaction with Adults (IWA)
   4. Responsiveness to Social Interactions (RSI)
   5. Maintenance of Interaction with Environment and Objects in Environment (MIE)
   6. Child-Peer Interaction in Free Play (CPI)

COMMUNICATION (CO)

   1. Response to Communication Context (RCC)
   2. Understanding of Phrases and Sentences (UPS)
   3. Understanding of Single Words (USW)
   4. Communicative Intent (CIN)
   5. Speech Production (SPR)
   6. Imitation of Lip and Tongue Movements (ILT)
   7. Production of Single Words and Phrases (PSW)

from the Gross Motor (GM) domain, Balance on Stomach (BOS) strand, is given as follows in the Inventory (Administrative Guide, pp. 6–7):

   GM   BOS 2.0 Child lifts head at midline and turns head;
                   2.1 to the right;
                   2.2 to the left.

According to the Administration Guide for the Adaptive Performance Instrument, certain targets are designated as critical targets. These are thought to be prerequisite to the development of complex skills, for example, the superior pincer grasp, as shown in Table 5.4.

TABLE 5.4

Critical Targets for the Development of Pincer Grasp from the
Adaptive Performance Inventory

TARGET

2. The child voluntarily grasps a thin, cylindrical object with the right
hand using:

  2.1 ulnar-palmar grasp
  2.2 radial-palmar grasp
  2.3 radial-digital grasp
  2.4 inferior-pincer grasp
  2.5 superior-pincer grasp

CRITERIA

  2.1 On at least 2 occasions, the child grasps and retains an object
  using primarily the middle, ring, and little finger to push the
  object against the palm of the hand and retains it without thumb
  opposition (i.e., ulnar-palmar grasp).

  2.2 On at least 2 occasions, the child grasps and retains an object
  using primarily the index and middle fingers to push the object
  against the palm and retains it without thumb opposition (i.e.,
  radial-palmar grasp).

  2.3 On at least 2 occasions, thee child grasps and retains an object
  using thumb, middle, and/or index finger. The object is not held
  against the palm and the side of the thumb is used in opposition
  (i.e., radial-digital grasp).

  2.4 On at least 2 occasions, the child grasps and retains an object
  using the tips of the thumb and index finger. The object is not
  held against the palm, the hand is supported on a surface, and the
  tip of the thumb is in opposition (i.e., inferior-pincer grasp).

  2.5 On at least 2 occasions, the child grasps an retains an object using
  the tips of the thumb and index finger. The object is not held
  against the palm, the hand is not supported, and the tip of the
  thumb is in opposition (i.e., superior-pincer grasp).

DIRECTIONS

Materials: Thin cylindrical objects (e.g., pen, rattle, ring)

Position: Any position which allows the child to grasp.

Procedure: Observation: Observe child's grasp of thin cylindrical objects,
on at least 2 occasions.

Direct test: Place object near the child and encourage the child
to pick it up. Test 3 times.

SOURCE: Dale Gentry, *Consortium on Adaptive Performance Evaluation (CAPE)*
Washington, D.C.: U.S.D.O.E., Office of Special Education, 1980), p. 19. Used by
permission.

Certainly the API instrument surpasses all of its forerunners as a check-list appropriate to the severely handicapped population, but again we caution against a procedure that would structure the specifics to be taught to a severely handicapped person on the basis of mismatches between current performance levels and expectations on the basis of normal childhood development. In our opinion, the API will have its greatest usefulness in suggesting short-term instructional objectives for young, handicapped infants in an early education program. For older chronological-age students, the instrument is best used as one more source of information about current functioning levels across multiple environments.

Finally, Group IV instruments are those that have been designed: (1) to provide performance data on specific subgroups within the severely handicapped population (for example, autism, deaf-blind), (2) to provide information on particular performance domains (for example, communication, physical-motor), and (3) to provide an assessment that is geared to a particular theoretical model (for example, the Callier-Azusa (Stillman, 1974), which represents a Piagetian approach to assessment).

Objective Banks.   In addition to assessment check lists, another useful source of guidelines with which to examine current performance levels in severely handicapped students can be found in what are called *objective banks*. These are large compendia of specific task analyses that have been gathered by school districts, special grant-funded projects, and others. Among these are, for example:

1. *APT,* A Resource Book, ed. J. F. Brody et al. (Spring City, Penn.: Pennhurst State School, 1975).
2. *STEP,* Sequential Tasks for Educational Planning, vol. 1 (San Diego, Calif.: Cajon Valley Union School District, Department of Special Education, 1978).
3. *Instructional Programming for the Handicapped Student,* ed. Anderson, Hodson, and Jones (Springfield, Ill.: Charles C Thomas, 1975).
4. *Observations,* Inventory of Developmental Tasks and Teachers Manual, ed. Gainer et al. (Santa Clara, Calif.: Santa Clara Unified School District, 1974).

USING THE ASSESSMENT DATA

Setting Instructional Objectives.   The priority matrix in Figure 5.1 combines the six critical functions with multiple environmental domains to provide an approach to answering the question, what do I teach first? Goals have been established as one-year targets that focus on adaptive functioning in the multiple environmental domains. Assessment data have been gathered on the student's current functioning in these domains and from the specific environments and subenvironments the student encounters. The two constructs of the assessment model, basal performance and one-month step sequences, now combine to set the initial instructional objectives from the priority matrix. An examination of the assessment data from the student and the environments will now enable the teacher to place numbers in the grid on the matrix that form a ranking of the *highest priority* short-term instructional targets.

To return to Joel, our example student, suppose we now re-examine his (hypothetical) priority matrix (Figure 5.4), considering the goals itemized earlier in Figure 5.1. Our assessment data have led us to consider toilet regulation at school to be the most immediate priority (1) because the odor associated with loss of control is offensive to Joel's nonhandicapped peers and therefore may act to isolate him and further retard his social development. The second priority was assigned to the box in recreation/leisure. The greatest opportunity for sustained interactions between Joel and his nonhandicapped peers will occur on the playground at recess, so teaching Joel to become mobile enough to participate partially (Brown et al., 1979b) in playground games and swinging, in particular, is important. Swinging was selected because assessment of this subenvironment turned up data suggesting that Joel's nonhandicapped, same-aged peers enjoy swinging him and seeing him laugh from the new experience. If Joel were your student, what would be your next three priorities in order to arrive at a working program plan of five objectives?

Figure 5.5 presents the second page of the working program plan as developed thus far, the *instructional objectives* page. This page lists in chronological order of establishment, each instructional objective set for the student, the date it was begun, the date it was modified or replaced, or the date it was completed. Some objectives don't work out and are modified; others are thrown out altogether. The strength of the model presented here lies in its flexibility and in its dynamic quality. A working program plan should be *changeable* to reflect decisions on the basis of progress or lack of progress, yet be precise and documented. This page of the plan is a *continuous, historical record* of the student's specific educational progress. It meets the need to demonstrate accountability and helps to show new teachers how far the student has come and in what directions.

For purposes of illustration, Figure 5.5 presents Joel's first (hypothetical) instructional objective. We had determined at the time of educational goal specification that Joel would be toilet regulated and would communicate the need to be taken to the bathroom in one year of educational effort. Our present assessment data tell us that Joel will usually defecate and urinate in the toilet when placed on it at opportune times during the day, but that Joel still has "accidents" at a rate of two or three per week for defecation, and in all environments. We therefore determine that

	ENVIRONMENTAL DOMAINS			
CRITICAL FUNCTIONS	School areas	Vocational area	Domestic area	Community areas
Eating	Goal: Eat in school cafeteria.			
Toileting	Goal: Communicate toilet request. (1)		Goal: Communicate toilet request.	Goal: Communicate toilet request.
Mobility	Goal: Extend arm.		Goal: Extend arm.	Goal: Extend arm.
Expressive communication	Goal: Communicate toilet request.		Goal: Communicate toilet request.	Goal: Communicate toilet request.
Receptive communication				
Hygiene/ appearance				
Recreation/ leisure	Goal: Playground— swinging. (2)			
Horizontal social interactions				

FIGURE 5.4
Priority matrix with first and second priority rankings for short-term instructional objectives shown for Joel

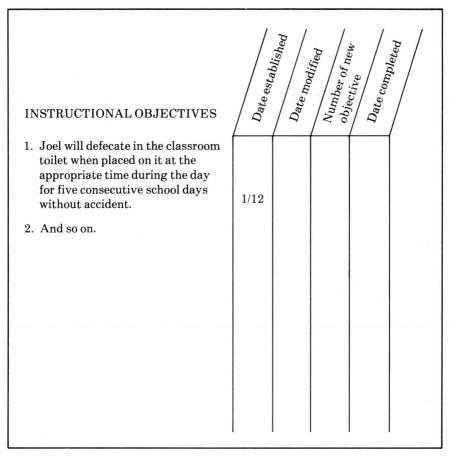

FIGURE 5.5
Illustration of instructional objectives page of working program plan with the first instructional objective for Joel shown as an example

the first of a string of eleven objectives (eleven months) leading to our toilet regulation goal should be to eliminate all defecatory accidents in one environment, the classroom. The next objective, if we are successful, will be to gain control in other environments, and so on.

The next instructional objective for Joel's working program plan will address the second priority and its goal, and so on. The working program plan should contain at least four specific objectives and at least one objective sequence (to be described in Chapter 8).

Writing Instructional Objectives. Some students reading this book in preparation for a career in the education of severely handicapped students will already have learned to write short-term objectives and will probably be familiar with the standard source, Robert Mager's *Preparing Instructional Objectives* (1975).

As a refresher, the basic components of the instructional objective are *performance specifications, conditions,* and the *criterion* for completion. The performance (by the student) specifications should be behavioral, that is, they should be capable of being observed reliably and being counted. "Joel will defecate in the classroom toilet . . ." is the performance component of the objective specified in our example in Figure 5.5. Conditions delimit the objective and reflect environmental considerations, equipment, or the actions of others that influence the performance. "When placed on it (the classroom toilet) at the appropriate time during the day . . ." specifies the conditions of this instructional objective.

Finally, the criterion provides a clear designation of when an objective has been met. For Joel, ". . . for five consecutive school days without accident" communicates a specific criterion for exit to the next objective in this particular sequence. The criterion also suggests the nature of the data that must be collected in order to determine progress toward exiting from the objective.

SUMMARY

In this chapter, we have presented the first part of a working program plan for severely handicapped students. This first part has been concerned with the establishment of educational goals, with assessment, and with the specification of short-term instructional objectives.

To review, the logic of this part leads the teacher to engage in the following sequence of activities when designing the initial instructional objectives that comprise each student's working program plan:

1. Specify from four to six educational goals in accordance with the student's IEP and the domains that comprise the student's current and likely subsequent environments.
2. Assess the student's current performance in the various environments comprising the educational program.
3. Assess the environments and specify the requirements of current subenvironments for the student's needs for increased independence.
4. Set priorities from the matrix of critical functions and domains, among five immediate targets for instructional objectives.
5. Determine the student's basal performance for each ranked area in terms of the educational goal that relates to that area.

6. Construct, at least mentally, a sequence of about ten objectives that would start with basal performance and culminate with realization of the goal.

7. Write the first five objectives, one of which will be a curriculum sequence (Chapter 8).

The second part of the working program plan pertains to the breaking down of the objectives into smaller, more easily obtainable units of behavior through the process of task analysis. This is discussed in the next chapter.

CHAPTER 6

Curriculum Development:
Task Analysis

TASK ANALYSIS DEFINED

In our model for curriculum development, we have already examined the necessary steps for constructing a working program plan for a severely handicapped student. These have included formulating educational goals, assessing the student in multiple environments, assessing the environments themselves and developing short-term instructional objectives. With task analysis, we continue to move from the general to the specific.

The term *task analysis* originated in business and industry. It refers to breaking the requirements of a job down into its specific components, leading to worker specialization. For example, a task analysis of auto assembly results in numerous specialized assignments. Mager (1975) adapted the term *task analysis* for education to refer to the sequence of steps that comprise an educational program. Thus, task analysis is a sequence of discrete behaviors or skills that are learned by the student. Gold (1975) used the term *content task analysis* to describe the steps that a teacher follows in an instructional program of the vocational type. The definitions are similar, but Mager stresses behaviors learned by the student, whereas Gold stresses the teacher's actions. Both are concerned with reducing a discrete task or skill into its component parts to facilitate instruction and learning.

In the education of severely handicapped students, task analysis has been described as the process by which curricular content is sliced into its smaller, more teachable components. Williams (1975) uses the term to mean only the discrete behavioral steps that form a chain leading to acquisition of a specific skill. Gold (1975) and Bellamy, Horner, and Inman (1979), on the other hand, use the term *task analysis* to include the process of instruction as well as curricular content. Bellamy et al., for example, define *task analysis* as the process of

1) breaking a task down into its component responses, 2) listing these responses and the stimuli that should ultimately come to control them, and 3) identifying a criterion for each response. (1979, p. 65)

Gold (1975) suggests that a task analysis should contain information about three functions: the method, process, and content of instruction. The *method* describes in general terms the way a target skill will be taught. For example, a student learning to wash up after a work task will need to be positioned at an accessible sink with soap and towels. Also necessary is a procedure that specifically combines the discrete actions required to complete the skill sequence. The *process* is the detailed specification of the teaching procedure to be used, such as prompting, fading, and so on. The *content* is the specification of the discrete behavioral steps (or actions) that the student must complete.

For purposes of this text, *task analysis* will refer to discrete behavioral steps in an instructional chain leading to acquisition of a skill. Our use of the term is thus consistent with the definition provided by Williams (1975). There is however, one important distinction that places our use of the term *task analysis* in a somewhat different perspective than its typical use by others. Task analysis usually refers to an analysis of a skill or task in a generic sense. That is, a given task analysis of sock removal, for example, would apply to all students for whom sock removal was specified as an instructional objective. Van Etten, Arkell, and Van Etten (1980) describe the task analysis operation as follows:

Although task analysis facilitates instruction, it is not part of the actual instructional process, per se. Task analysis provides a blueprint for instruction by furnishing the teacher with a layout of a skills sequence through which the student should proceed to achieve the terminal behavior. But task analysis does not specify *how* each component skill in the sequence should be taught. It simply specifies *what* component skills should be taught to facilitate mastery of the terminal skill. This distinction is very important! Task analysis is not a teaching methodology. A teaching methodology involves a series of descriptive statements, guidelines, and suggestions that explain *how* to instruct students on a particular task, along with what materials might be used. Teaching methodology also describes the behavior of the instructor in relation to the student and the task to be taught. Task analysis is not this specific; it only describes *what* skills should be taught. How they should be taught is a decision that must be made for each student. It is possible to use one task analysis for several students if all of the students need instruction on the same skill. However, each student would possibly have unique strengths and weaknesses, different needs, and various entry behaviors with regard to the task. It would therefore be inappropriate to teach the skills sequence in exactly the same fashion to all students. The individualization or modification of instruction would occur in the design of the lesson plan or in the teaching process. A task analysis should be general enough so that it is useful for a number of students needing instruction in the same skill areas. Providing for the special needs of individual students is done as part of the lesson plan, rather than as part of the task analysis. Task analysis, then, is not a teaching methodology – it is simply a blueprint for acquisition of a skill. Two teachers may use the same task analysis (blueprint) as the basis for teaching a task to children with very different needs, abilities, and disabilities. This process is much like the builder who takes a blueprint of a house and tailors the design of the house to meet the special needs of two clients.*

Our definition of *task analysis* is quite different. It places the process interactively, midway between the task and the individual who is to learn the task. In our definition, task analysis is conducted for a skill to be taught under certain conditions (which are also specified alongside the task analysis) to a specific individual. The task is analyzed in terms of the individual's characteristics, as best we can determine them, so that the individual may most rapidly acquire a skill under the instruction we provide.

Thus, a task analysis of blouse removal for Mary will not necessarily resemble the task analysis of blouse removal for Jean. The two may or may not share steps in common. Our task analysis for Mary may contain three large and quite general steps, whereas for Jean there may be ten very small steps. The obvious limitation of our definition of task analysis is also its primary strength: *specificity.* In our definition, each task analysis is unique to the individual for whom it was designed. This does not mean that the same task analysis cannot be used for more than one student, but it does mitigate against general utility.

If one is interested in building a standard curriculum for severely handicapped students, then our definition of task analysis will not prove helpful. It is our opinion that the field of education for severely handicapped students is far from any stage of development that would benefit from standard, general curricula. The individualization that accrues to a teacher-generated curriculum appropriate for each student in an educational program is currently worth ten published curricula, and this state of affairs is not likely to change for some years. The combination of task analysis and complete instructional procedure is provided in what we shall call the T-format, the next component of the working program plan.

---

*From Glen Van Etten, Claudia Arkell, and Carlene Van Etten, *The Severely and Profoundly Handicapped* (St. Louis, The C. V. Mosby Co., 1980), p. 163. Used by permission.

THE T-FORMAT

Suppose that in the development of your working program plan for a student an instructional objective was developed that aimed at improving appearance and hygiene in the domestic environment. The student is learning to perform independent self-help skills and, specifically, is ready to learn to remove a slipover shirt. To accomplish instruction in this discrete skill, an appropriate instructional objective was written, and a task analysis was performed and then combined with an instructional procedure. The entire instructional program was then specified in the T-Format shown in Table 6.1.

TABLE 6.1
T-Format for steps required to remove a slipover shirt

Long-Range Educational Goal(s): Robert will dress and undress independently when appropriate (except for shoe tying).

Short-Term Instructional Objective: When asked to remove his shirt, Robert will remove his slipover shirt. He will place it on a table in three consecutive sessions of instruction without physical assistance.

Task Analysis	Instructional Procedure
9. Grasp bottom of shirt with both hands.	*Setting:* Bathroom area. Use slipover shirt in locker if Robert is not wearing one; teaching staff as indicated on classroom schedule.
8. Raise shirt to underarms.	
7. Grasp shirt at back of neck over head with both hands.	*Materials:* Robert's shirt or slipover in locker.
6. Pull shirt over head.	*Procedure:* Backward chain; physical prompt and fade; use praise for effect and allow exit from bathroom after two trials; alternate with hair-combing objective as indicated on schedule.
5. Grasp shirt at left shoulder with right arm.	
4. Pull shirt off of left arm.	
3. Grasp shirt with left hand.	
2. Pull shirt off of right arm.	
1. Place shirt on table.	*Measurement:* Frequency of correct trials per day (odd sessions); graph by steps.
	Generalization strategies: Parent to instruct at home in A.M. daily.
	Next objective (if applicable): Pants removal.

The T-Format consists of two parts, the first of which is shown in the figure. The second part consists of graphed data reflecting progress on the objective or the skill sequence (to be discussed in Chapter 7). On the working program plan clipboard, the graph of *progress data* will usually be stapled to the T-Format. With one T-Format (and data record) for each instructional objective, the active, clipboard portion of the complete working program plan would include a set of four to six T-Formats including a curriculum sequence (Chapter 8). The remainder of the plan, the *file* portion, contains the running record of goals, the running record of instructional objectives, assessment data, and any *completed* T-Formats, that is, instructional programs that resulted in learned objectives.

Each T-Format is intended to convey a sufficient amount of information about the teaching of a discrete skill to enable various instructional personnel to carry out the program upon a single reading of the specifications from the T-Format.

As shown in Table 6.1, each T-Format contains a statement of the instructional objective. (Remember that this information also appears in the running record of instructional objectives in the file portion of the working program plan.)

Next, the T-Format is divided into two columns of information. The column on the left side of the T is headed "Task Analysis." The column on the right side is headed "Instructional Procedure." This T-Format is used both for instructional programs to meet a particular instructional objective, as shown in Table 6.1, or for programs to meet a functional curriculum sequence, which will be discussed in Chapter 8.

CHAINING: A METHOD OF TASK ANALYSIS

Robert Gaylord-Ross (1982) has recently provided a concise description of the process of developing task analyses for severely handicapped students. According to Gaylord-Ross, chaining procedures are the most commonly used methods of task analysis.

In the chaining procedure, the instructional objective is first sliced (broken down) into a discrete number of actions. The student is thought to be capable of learning to perform the actions in a program of systematic instruction. Using the shirt-removal objective in Table 6.1 as an example, the skill of shirt removal was sliced into nine discrete steps or actions. How did we determine the number of steps leading to a serial chain to teach shirt removal? Here we operate in the realm of speculation. As Gaylord-Ross points out, there are no research-based rules to rely upon. Deciding how to carry out a slicing operation is a critical teaching skill, which improves with practice. It requires a wide sample of students with different skill needs and repeated experience with each particular student. Familiarity with a student's demonstrated abilities on earlier acquired skills and with his or her learning rates under various conditions will facilitate the process of task analysis dramatically. The first task analyses with a new student, however, are difficult and often need redesigning after initial instructional efforts.

Slicing Errors.   Errors in slicing objectives into steps in a task analysis are usually of two types. First, and most commonly, it is assumed that the student will be capable of acquiring only the tiniest behavior actions. More steps are created in a chain than are typically needed in actual instructional practice. Fortunately, this error is the least costly to an instructional program because the student simply acquires the extra steps in a single training trial or session.

The more costly common error is to create a chain in which some steps are too difficult for the student to master. The result is wasted effort and often lowered motivation on the part of the student to perform the skill. It is obviously better to err on the side of too many easy steps than too few difficult ones.

Other types of slicing errors are made when teaching staff fail to adequately consider a student's motoric or sensory capabilities. If, for example, a step requires a greater degree of visual acuity than a student possesses, the result might suggest a failure of learning rather than a specific limitation of disability in the absence of prosthesis, as is the case.

DEFINITION OF CHAINING TERMS

Before discussing types of task-analyzed chains, it might be helpful to clarify some of the various terms used in this chapter. *Steps* in a task analysis are synonymous with *actions*. They always represent independent behaviors on the part of the student. They do not include, in part or in whole, any behavior of the teaching staff or others, unless specifically stated in the step specification. By *independent,* we mean without physical assistance by another person. Steps may, however, imply adaptive equipment, modified environments, or arranged cues from other persons. Steps are always discrete behaviors that may be counted in some way (see discussion of actions in Chapter 3).

The term *chain* refers to the fact that steps in a task analysis bear a relationship to each other in their common contribution to an objective. The chain can function as if it were analogous to a ladder, as in a *serial chain* where each link must be mastered before moving on to the next. It may also be analogous to a molecule, as in a *concurrent chain* where steps are taught simultaneously.

The basic unit in a task analysis is a *step*. The next higher unit is an *instructional objective,* and the next after that is an *educational goal.* An instructional objective is usually a *skill* but need not necessarily be one. Some instructional objectives may teach behaviors that are necessary prerequisites to the attainment of useful skills but have in themselves no functional skill value.

Finally, the number of steps in a task analysis can vary from one to many. Our experience has led us to believe that long chains are usually undesirable, and we seldom employ task analyses with more than twenty steps. On the other hand, some discrete motor objectives, for example, "raise head to midline," may require only one training step that is the same as the specification in the objective. In this case, the task analysis column in the T-Format is simply left blank, and the instructional operations are made clear on the procedure side.

SERIAL CHAINS

Serial chains, as mentioned, are analogous to steps on a ladder. Each step is taught independently, and each is prerequisite to the next in the chain. Serial chains come in three varieties: *forward* chains, *backward* chains, and *mixed* chains. These terms refer to the order in which steps in the task analysis are taught.

When an instructional objective is sliced into steps in a task analysis, the steps are always laid out in a forward order; that is, the first step in a logical chain appears at the top of the column in the T-Format, followed by the second in logical order, and so on down the column to the last in the serial order. Table 6.1 exemplifies this ordering for the steps in the shirt-removal task analysis. There is an important difference, however, between the *logical* ordering, which is always forward, and the *instructional* ordering, which may be forward, backward, or mixed. Logical ordering is always from top to bottom on the T-Format. Instructional ordering is always conveyed by the numbering system to the left of the steps in the chain. The shirt-removal chain in Table 6.1, for example, is numbered from bottom to top. The information conveyed is that the logical (forward) chain of steps is not to be followed in instruction, but rather instruction should occur from the bottom of the chain, in order, to the top. The process is called backward chaining.

Suppose we have task analyzed an eating objective. An example would be a student learning to eat from a bowl with a spoon at mealtimes. The logical order, or forward chain, might begin with grasping spoon, then

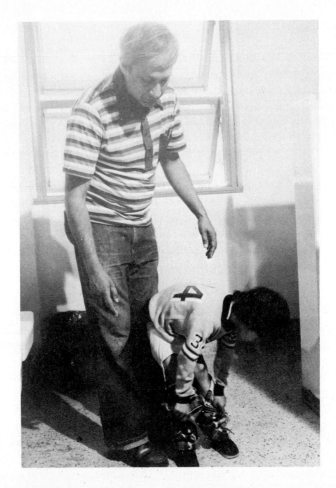

move to bowl, then scoop, then raise to mouth, then insert, then remove food and extract, and then return to bowl and so on. Would this objective be taught in a forward serial chain? Perhaps not. A better procedure might be to start instruction at the point of highest motivation in the system and back up from there. In the eating program, food extracting (assuming a preferred food) has the highest probability of maximal motivation. Accordingly, that would be the first step to be taught. This particular step, however, occurs in the middle of the logical chain as we have laid it out. By numbering the various steps in the order that we wish to proceed instructionally, we can convey mixed, backward, or forward chains on the T-Format while still retaining the conceptual ease of laying out our task analyses in a logical, forward order. A forward instructional chain means teaching each step in the logical order as laid out. A mixed chain means jumping around in an order determined by some logic other than forward

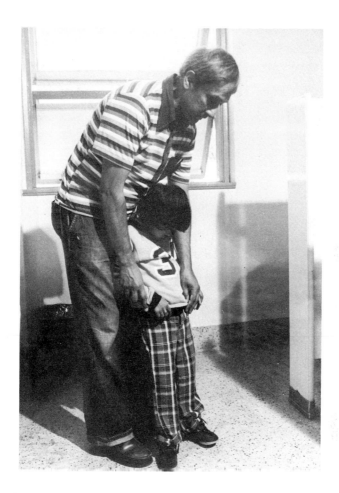

logic. Backward chaining means teaching the sequence in the reverse of the logical forward order.

Ideally, we should now be far enough along in our development as a field to specify rules for selecting an appropriate task-analysis system with which to teach any specified objective. But as in so many areas, we are not yet able to do so. Current and further research will provide more substantive guidelines. For now, we must use a few basic principles in constructing task analyses and be prepared to make changes in a spirit of flexibility if our initial decisions do not work out.

Ordering the Steps: Motivation.   If we have made an initial decision to construct a serial rather than a concurrent chain (more about that decision later), our next choice point is the order of instruction. How shall we order the steps in our chain? The first general principle to guide us is *motivation*.

The first step to be taught in a task-analyzed chain should be that step that is temporally closest to a natural contingency of reinforcement. In the eating example above, a mixed chain was constructed so that the ingestion of food, the positive effect, would fuel the effort that leads up to it.

Many self-care skills, such as the clothing-removal task analysis in Table 6.1, have little or no functional reinforcement value incorporated within them. They must be helped along initially with artificial reinforcers. In many cases, the most powerful contingency of reinforcement extant in the system is the exit from the demands of the instructional task, a positive subtracted effect ($E^{\pm}$), or negative reinforcement. Objectives of this type often readily lend themselves to backward chaining procedures, since the last step in the sequence completes the activity and motivates the steps leading up to it.

Ordering the Steps: Cues.   The second principle to guide the selection of a task-analysis procedure is *cue analysis.* Within a serial chain, where motivation is constant, steps should be taught in the order that maximizes the cue value of preceding steps in controlling the acquisition of subsequent steps. Suppose, for example, that a student is learning to communicate the desire for a drink of juice in a classroom environment. The student's expressive system is a ring-bound picture book with the drawing of a glass of liquid serving as the word for *drink.* The task analysis is laid out as follows: (1) grasp and scan booklet, (2) select word name, (3) turn booklet to display word name to other person, and (4) point to word name. The cue value of the earlier steps is relatively high in providing the student information concerning acquisition of the later steps in the chain. Motivation, although probably higher at the end of the chain, is still not as high as it would be, say, at the end of a drinking-instruction program where the effect of the last step is the consummatory response. So whereas the drinking program would be backward chained to make use of the motivation principle, the expressive-communication program would be forward chained to take advantage of the cue-analysis principle. Motivation generally takes precedence over cue value in this decision model.

Ordering the Steps: Another Method.   What about those cases in which neither motivation nor cue value seems to bear a direct relationship to the decision on selection of a serial chain? There are no further substantive guidelines on the issue. Smith and Snell (1978), however, provide a recommendation to aid the decision process. They suggest running a baseline session or two of each instructional program, once it is laid out in an initial order. The student may show that he or she has already mastered one or more of the steps or is far enough along toward acquisition that early success on one or several steps is likely. If these steps tended to fall at the end of a sequential chain, backward chaining the instruction of the series would lead to more rapid success and the experience of competence at the end of the activity. On the other hand, if the acquired or easier steps are at the front of the serial chain, forward chaining might lead to experienced competence early on and heighten motivation to perform well on subsequent, more difficult steps.

CONCURRENT CHAINS

Concurrent chains are set up exactly the same as serial chains – in a forward, logical order. In a concurrent chain, however, all steps are taught simultaneously rather than in a one-at-a-time, sequentially interdependent fashion.

Concurrent chains tend to be favored by persons working with cognitively higher functioning students, particularly teaching personnel associated with secondary severely handicapped programs. Gold and Pomerantz (1978) and Bellamy, Horner, and Inman (1979) specify types of concurrent chains as the preferred mode of task analysis in vocational preparation with severely handicapped adults. The reasons for this preference are twofold. First, the characteristics of the vocational preparation population have tended to self-select at the somewhat higher functioning end of the severely handicapped population spectrum. Students who are cognitively more complex can handle more complex stimulus configurations in acquiring a skill. Short-term memory is greater and can have a facilitating effect on acquisition of the whole in a task assembly. The second factor has to do with the greater complexity of typical vocational task analyses. Chains of greater than twenty steps are not uncommon in work assembly tasks, and there can be a wide variation in the capacity with which various steps throughout the sequence are mastered.

CHAINING IN OPERATION

In designing a task analysis using the T-Format, whether serial chaining (backward, forward, or mixed) or concurrent chaining is the desired system, the specification of steps should follow the same format. Each step should:

1. Consist only of *student* behavior (except in rare cases where the interactive behavior of others is written into the step)
2. Consist of a discrete quantifiable action
3. Be of equivalent generality and difficulty to all other steps to whatever degree possible
4. Be specified as a simple sentence (with no exit criteria provided)
5. Be an essential and indispensable part of the whole skill represented by the objective

In a serial chain, the step to which the number 1 has been assigned is taught systematically, whereas the other steps are simply cued and assisted whenever necessary. If prompting and fading comprise the instructional strategy for a given objective, systematic fading of the prompt occurs across repeated trials of step 1, and the student is put through all remaining steps not responded to on cue. When step 1 is mastered, fading of prompts begins on step 2, and the procedure continues. Thus, the cue is provided to the student to begin the sequence, and instruction begins at the level of step 2. After step 2 is mastered, the student completes 1 and 2 independently on the next trial, and instruction is concentrated on step 3. Training a serial chain continues until all steps are performed in a sequence independently without physical prompts or other intervening instructional procedures. The procedure is followed regardless of whether the serial chain is of the backward, forward, or mixed type.

In the shirt-removal procedure of Table 6.1, instruction begins by providing the initial cue, "Take off your shirt, please," and then by guiding the student physically through each step of the chain. The student is allowed as much leeway as possible to perform each component independently until step 1 is reached (at the bottom of the logical chain). At step 1, the student is reinforced systematically for increasing independence (less physical prompt required each trial) until the step is mastered across repeated trials. Should the entire sequence be repeated across several trials in a single session or just the final step in a backward chain? This is a matter of teaching preference and style, but usually the context of the whole skill is needed to aid the acquisition of one of its parts. We recommend putting the student through several trials of a whole sequence regardless of the type of chain. The number of training trials is another matter of style and is generally determined by the level of sustained motivation that can be expected from a given student in a given session. It is generally better to intersperse instructional trials across several different tasks with only one or two trials in succession with any given task. (This will be discussed more fully in Chapter 8.) It is better to vary situations and teaching personnel in order to promote skill generalization. In no case should long strings of training trials occur when there is little intrinsic motivation to perform the task being taught.

Two of the advantages to using serial chains are the relative ease of applying systematic reinforcement when needed and the relative ease of scoring the outcome of instruction. Concentration on one step at a time allows for a simple recording of correct or incorrect across each trial for presence or absence of independent responding on cue.

Use of a concurrent chaining strategy, on the other hand, presents problems for systematic, contingent reinforcement and for data recording as well. In this procedure, prompts are faded systematically on each step in a chain across all trials. The amount of instructional effort expended by the teacher is equal to the number of steps in the chain multiplied by the amount required in single-step instruction. Data become exceedingly important in concurrent chain instruction, because the teacher must be able to anticipate in advance those steps in which the student is apt to encounter difficulty and be able to intervene quickly with a prompt.

The advantage of the concurrent chain procedure is that it credits the student instantly with independent gains through the chain. A student who moves rapidly through most instructional programs, a fast learner, profits immensely from the concurrent chain procedure.

In many cases, a task-analyzed program can be begun as a serial chain but be converted rapidly to a concurrent chain strategy if the student displays a tendency to master various steps out of sequence. Since competence is the prime motivator, a strategy that capitalizes on the student's success en route becomes highly desirable.

INSTRUCTIONAL FORMAT

The T-Format exemplified in Table 6.1 specifies in the right-hand column information about how an instructional program is to be carried out. If task analysis can be conceptualized as the *content* variable according to the analysis by Gold (1975), then the instructional procedure embodies the *method* and *process* variables. Note that the information conveyed in the instructional procedure section is not intended to match or correspond in one-to-one fashion to each step in the task analysis in the left-hand column. Rather, information conveyed under instructional procedure is expressed in general terms that apply to the whole task-analyzed sequence, and it is expressed in a prose format rather than in a parallel format with short statements.

SETTING AND MATERIALS

Under this subheading, the information includes where the instruction is to take place, how often, by whom, and what materials or equipment are required.

PROCEDURE

The cue-control strategy selected for instruction is conveyed in this section. From the guidelines discussed in Chapter 4, a teaching method will be selected and specified in the briefest of terms. For example, if a physical prompt-and-fade procedure is to be used, as in the example shown in Figure 6.1, that is all the information required. If an imitation-cue paradigm is employed, as in many speech production programs, it would be so specified. Other instructional procedures might include auditory, visual, tactile, or verbal stimulus control, differential reinforcement or schedule (of reinforcement) management, and any behavior management procedure that might be called for. In each case, the minimum amount of information required to convey the nature of the procedure is specified.

This section can become somewhat more complex in cases where different steps in the task analysis require different instructional techniques, or when the teaching strategy calls for a shift at some point from a serial to a concurrent chain strategy. In the eating program discussed earlier, the initial step of grasping the spoon (the last step to be taught in the mixed serial chain) occurs only once in a session, whereas the other steps are recycled for a number of trials within each session. This information would be conveyed under the procedure section.

Finally, the issue of criteria for advancement from one step to the next in a serial chain may need to be addressed in this section. In general, task-analysis step criteria are left flexible and unspecified in order to maximize the teacher's flexibility in carrying out the instructional program. Some steps may be less crucial than others in contributing to acquisition of the next step in the chain. Where a given step need be mastered only to the extent necessary to launch proficiency in the next step, a lower criterion of acceptability may be warranted. Other steps may require a high standard of proficiency in order to go on to the next, and so on. Where this proficiency requirement is known in advance, as in some motor-movement programs, it may be important to specify a criterion for particular steps. For example, a program to develop proficiency on a communication board might call for an extension and forearm reach to a certain criterion of distance and time prior to starting a motor scan of the board. Since the reach proficiency is clearly prerequisite and requires a degree of motor relaxation and control in students with abnormal muscle tone, a particular criterion of proficiency may need to be required for this particular step. This information would be conveyed under procedure.

In general, all the information an experienced member of the teaching staff needs – necessary cues, schedules of reinforcement, criteria for exit from steps, and special reinforcement considerations – should be conveyed in the procedure section.

MEASUREMENT SYSTEM

Specifications in this subsection should convey to readers enough information so that they can read and understand the graph attached to the

T-Format page. The key components are the scales represented on the abscissa (vertical axis) and the ordinate (horizontal axis). If the data are presented graphically as percentage points across instructional sessions, and this scalar arrangement is constant for all the steps in a given serial task analysis, the specification would simply read "percentage of independent actions per session" or "percent correct per session." For a concurrent task analysis, the specification might read "percent correct steps per session." Measurement strategies can, of course, vary within task analyses, and, if so, the specifications for change should appear in this subsection. For example, in a serial task analysis, the first four of ten steps might be tracked by percentage correct per session and the last six by rate of correct responding. In this case, accuracy of independent responding was considered most important early in the learning sequence, and speed combined with accuracy (rate) in the latter stages of the sequence.

If the task-analyzed skill is time sampled (say, twice a week), but instruction occurs daily, then the definition of session on the ordinate will differ from the actual instructional sessions and should be so specified (by dates, for example). Measurement systems will be discussed in detail in Chapter 7.

GENERALIZATION STRATEGIES

The information conveyed here may overlap somewhat with that specified under setting and materials, but it should be reconstructed in this specific context. If the task-analyzed skill is of no functional value but is simply a prerequisite to some other more functional skill, then "not applicable" may be specified. For example, a student may be instructed to place clothespins on a card in order to strengthen the pincer grasp needed to operate a coat zipper. Generalization of the clothespin activity is deemed irrelevant for now, but the later objective of zipper manipulation will be generalized across clothing and situations.

On the other hand, if a student is learning to operate a head wand to indicate the symbol for *drink* on a communication board, then the specification might be: "The symbol for *drink* will appear in different positions across the communication board during ongoing instruction, and, as (the student) nears proficiency, the request for drink will occur in at least three different environments and be directed to the attention of at least three different persons."

The purpose of this subsection is to call to the attention of all teaching staff the importance of building functional, generalized skills that are useful and adaptive in a multiplicity of environments. Specification of procedures to accomplish generalization can help to ensure the generality of what is taught to a severely handicapped student.

NEXT PLANNED OBJECTIVE

The information conveyed in this subsection is intended to focus the attention of teaching staff on the sequential nature of instruction. Specification of the next objective helps to assist this process by putting instruction on any single skill in a larger perspective. Of course, any specifications of this type forecast the future and thus are necessarily hypothetical. Nevertheless, it provides a yardstick against which a teacher can measure his or her own accuracy in planning instructional sequences. Needless to say, the information coming back to teaching staff in the form of data during instruction on any one objective, or on any one individual curriculum sequence, can greatly influence or alter earlier judgments about what should be taught next. Again, students' performance under optimal instruction provides the most reliable assessment information for planning future instructional efforts.

In the example above, a student was learning to communicate drink on a communication board. The next objective may have been planned to be: "(Student) will learn to indicate the symbol for *eat*." However, the rate of progress of the earlier objective might have been such that a decision would now (during completion of the drink objective) be made to write a more complex (or less complex) objective as the next step. Teachers who use this system will find that as they become more accurate in their own forecasts of subsequent objectives, their students' instructional progress will increase. Getting to know a student's learning style automatically leads to more accurate and more functional program planning.

Finally, it should be noted that the specification "not applicable" would never appear in this subsection. There is always a next subsequent objective to be taught, even if the student is being moved on to another program or school or graduating altogether!

SUMMARY

Task analysis is the process by which a skill is broken down into component parts so that the skill becomes teachable to a particular student. Task analysis in this definition differs from its traditional meaning of subskills being generic to skills being individualized. Task analysis means subskills designed to fit an individual student.

Task analyses and instructional procedures come together in the T-Format, which together with the graphed data progress record, constitutes the fundamental unit of each student's working program plan.

Task analyses are typically either serial chains or concurrent chains. Serial chains can be taught in a forward, backward, or fixed format. Steps in a concurrent chain are taught simultaneously. Single-step task analyses are not uncommon and reflect the fact that some instructional objectives cannot or should not be sliced into component parts. Rather, they should be taught directly.

The instructional procedure part of the T-Format includes the setting; method of stimulus control to be employed, including cues; schedules of reinforcement and the nature of reinforcers, or motivational effects; strategies for generalization; and the next likely objective to be taught in the series. Additional examples of T-Formats in elementary programs are provided in Chapter 10.

CHAPTER 7

Curriculum Evaluation:
A Data-based Decision Model

MEASUREMENT

Of all the sophisticated instructional technology developed over the past decade for the education of the severely handicapped, no single component has simultaneously represented such a significant advance while facing more resistance on the part of those who apply it than data collection and management. Suppose an aircraft company builds a commercial airplane capable of flying twice the usual number of people in half the time and with half the fuel consumption. Yet airline pilots refuse to fly it because they claim the controls are too complicated. Would you fire the pilots and train new ones? Or would you acknowledge their arguments and try to simplify the controls? Many teacher training institutions seem to have adopted the "fire the pilot" approach. Teachers are provided with a sophisticated data management system and are then reprimanded for failing to use it after a year or two in the classroom. It is our belief that if a system is not used, it is the system, not the user, that is at fault.

The primary obstacle to utilizing a data management system is the extent to which it competes for time with the instructional process. Whether we like it or not, we are faced with a chronic, recurrent question: do we teach or test? Every college instructor faces the problem of sacrificing lecture hours in order to give examinations. Yet, are not exams part of the instructional process? They enhance the student's motivation to acquire new material. Measurement of instruction of severely handicapped students is also part of the instructional process – an indispensable part. It provides the information needed to adjust the instructional program, and it provides proof of learning, a function that in aggregate takes on increased importance in times of economic hardship for school programs.

By grounding our instructional model in a data management framework, we have devised a system with maximum utility for providing the information needed both for using a teaching program and for making changes in it. There is also a strong likelihood that the system will be used by teaching personnel on a long-term, continuous basis.

TARGET OF MEASUREMENT: INDEPENDENT ACTIONS

The first step in the design of a simplified, useful measurement system is to provide an easily accessible means for collecting raw data.

A task analysis and instructional procedure for a clothing objective for a hypothetical student are displayed in Table 7.1. Figure 7.1 shows a graph that illustrates the student's progress through each of the first 7 steps of the task analysis as measured on a particular scale (percent correct over sessions) on a particular kind of graph paper (2½-cycle logarithmic columnar-numerical).

For a working program plan, the information in the figure and the table, stapled together, are attached to a clipboard with the other T-Format components of the student's program. To begin to understand how the figure's lines came to represent the student's progress, we must first explain what was counted.

In all applications of the data management system represented, only *independent actions* are scored as correct, unless specifically stated otherwise in the task-analyzed sequence. For example, in step 1 of the backward (serial) chained task analysis for pulling pants up and down, if the teacher physically prompted the student, as called for under the procedure subsection of the T-Format, the completed *action* of pulling up pants, hips to waist, is actually a mix of teacher behavior and student behavior. It is scored incorrect.

Certainly, one could define what to count differently. One could devise a scoring system that differentially measures the proportion of teaching staff involvement in a student's action relative to the student's independent involvement. For example, on any one trial of step 1, the resulting action could be scored 0 for a full prompt, 1 for a reduced physical prompt, 2 for a partial prompt, or 3 for an independent action. This procedure is potentially a more sensitive measure of progress and, hence, is more complicated and cumbersome. Furthermore, judging the degree of a prompt is highly subjective. It might reduce the *reliability* of the system, or the degree to which the measurement system accurately samples the phenomenon. On the other hand, the simpler system we have opted for is not without its disadvantages. By counting only independent actions, we lose sensitivity to progress on the way to independent actions within each step. The choice is difficult, but our decision has been to leave subjective judgment to the

TABLE 7.1
Task Analysis and Instructional Procedure for Clothing Objective

Long-Range Education Goal(s): Betty will become independent in her dressing and undressing skills in all environments.

Short-Term Instructional Objective: While toileting and given unsnapped and unzippered pants, Betty will pull her pants up and down at the appropriate time without physical assistance for 80 percent of the trials on two out of three days.

Task Analysis (Pulling pants up and down)	*Instructional Procedure*
10. Thumbs hook waistband.	*Setting:* Bathroom 1–1.
9. Push down pants–waist to hips.	*Materials:* Betty's pants and panties.
8. Push down pants–hips to midthigh.	*Serial-backward Chain Procedure(s)* (inclusive of cues, actions, schedules and effects): T. gives cue, "Push *down* pants"
7. Push down pants–midthigh to knees.	and motors S. through #10–#7. After toileting, T. gives cue, "Pull up panties"
6. Grasp panties.	and motors S. through #6–#4. Then T. gives cue, "Pull up pants" and motors S.
5. Pull up panties–knees to midthigh.	through #1 and #2. S. does #1 without assistance. Next step, repeat same pro-
4. Pull up panties–midthigh to hips.	cedure of motoring through. S. must perform #2 and #1 on own and so forth.
3. Grasp pants	Score + or –. Mark + when S. does all steps from point where T. ceases to motor
2. Pull up pants–knees to hips.	S. through.
1. Pull up pants–hips to waist.	*Correction Procedure:* If incorrect or no response, return to missed position in steps. Repeat cue, allowing another chance. If still incorrect or no response, motor S. through. Score + only if S. responds correctly on first chance.
	Reinforcement: Praise for independent responses.
	Measurement: Graph progress of each step, 5× day. 80 percent mastery on two out of three days = criterion for moving to next step.
	Generalization Strategies: Betty will independently pull her pants up and down at the appropriate time in all toileting environments (home, restaurant, and so on).
	Next Objective (if applicable): While toileting, Betty will unzip and unsnap her pants at the appropriate time, without physical assistance for 80 percent of trials on two out of three days.

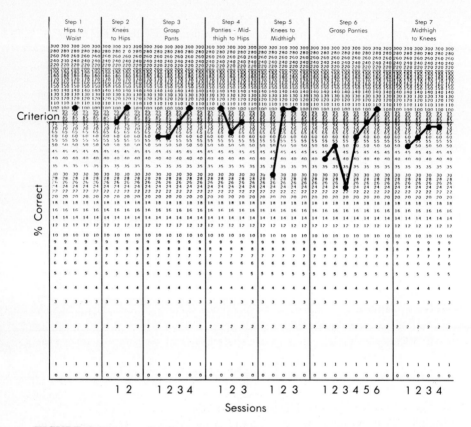

FIGURE 7.1
Betty dressing (pants up/down while toileting)

teacher and commit to paper only the most reliable index of progress—independent actions.

Wheeler and Fox (1972) suggested that a behavioral definition of what to count should include the following:

1. A description of the final outcome of the instruction in terms of observable behavior (the "action" described in Chapter 3, for example)
2. The conditions under which the performance may be observed (the instructional procedure, for example)
3. The criterion by which the performance may be judged (an *independent* action, for example)

Other highly relevant approaches to the question of what to count may be found in Haring (1977), White (1980), and Smith and Snell (1978).

Counting independent actions can occur in two ways: by counting the actions themselves or by tracking some aspect of the time or space over which independent actions occur.

COUNTING ACTIONS DIRECTLY

Counting independent actions most commonly occurs under one of two conditions: (1) when the length of a teaching session is fixed and the number of instructional trials is allowed to vary, or (2) when the number of trials is fixed and the length of instructional time varies. Which method of recording data is selected depends on the instructional objective and the teaching procedure. As a rule, if an objective is taught in a massed-trial format so that repeated opportunities to respond independently occur within a given session, then the fixed-trial, variable-time format may be used, and the measure is often *percent*.

In earlier days, most of what was taught to severely handicapped students could easily be charted in percentage formats. Settings were fixed, objectives were tied to specifications from standardized assessment systems, and the discrete-trial format of instruction was used. Typically, a child's educational day was divided into blocks during which she or he would receive from 10 to 25 trials (usually 10 for ease of recording) on tasks that were often irrelevant. Five correct block stacks out of 10 trials per session led to a dot at the 50 percent point on the scale for the day's block-stacking session.

Today, the instructional process is more complex, and using percent is less common because of its lack of utility for many objectives. As we move toward distributed rather than massed-trial instruction (see Chapter 8) occurring across a multiplicity of environments, we need systems for tracking progress that are not grounded in fixed-trial, variable-time formats. Clothing removal, for example, does not lend itself to massed-trial instruction. This is probably because the motivation to perform the desired activity is lost after the first effort or two. On the other hand, communication instruction (which can occur under highly motivating conditions), eating instruction, some recreation and leisure activities, and so on, may well lend themselves to this format. In general, where motivation to perform an action remains high across repeated instructional trials and where repeated actions would occur naturally, massed-trial instruction becomes feasible. Few instructional objectives, however, should be labored over repeated training trials under conditions of artificial cues and effects. If the number of instructional trials (opportunities to respond) is fixed, the number of those trials during which independent (unassisted) actions are performed, divided by the total number of instructional trials, times 100, yields the percent correct per session.

Suppose instruction time is fixed and the number of trials is allowed to vary across sessions. For the fixed-time, variable-trial format, the most common measurement methods are *frequency* and *rate*.

Frequency Measurement. Frequency is the simpler of the two to calculate and is usually used when accuracy of responding rather than speed is the critical factor. Rate, a more complex system, is used when both speed and accuracy are important (although see White, Note 1, for another perspective on rate data).

Both these measures are taking on greater utility in contemporary instruction relative to percent. Both are highly adaptable to functional content instruction in multiple environments. Frequency, however, suffers from a pronounced mathematical shortcoming – that is, the absence of a fixed common denominator representing the number of opportunities for independent actions to occur across sessions of instruction. *Frequency* is defined as the numbers of correct actions per session. Suppose, for example, that step 1 of a task-analyzed objective reveals the following pattern of acquisition:

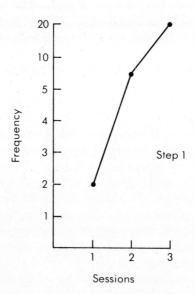

The number of correct responses, or independent actions, per instructional session is steadily increasing. Is the instructional program adequate to continue as is? Suppose we now learn that in session 1, the student had 4 trials (opportunities to respond); in session 2, 12 trials; and 60 trials occurred in session 3. If we had graphed our data in terms of percentage of correct trials, it would look like this:

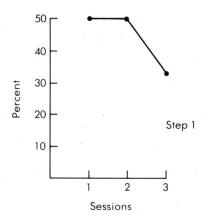

Which of these graphs *really* reflects the student's progress? The answer is neither. Percentage is meaningless without a fixed common denominator, the number of opportunities to respond. Two correct out of 4 is very different than 20 correct out of 40, yet both would result in 50 percent. Similarly, frequency means nothing if the number of opportunities fluctuates widely, even though the overall length of a session may be constant.

Rate Measurement.   Suppose we let the length of our instructional sessions serve as a common denominator. If sessions are 20 minutes in length, we can divide the number of correct actions by 20 for each session, and we get the number of correct actions *per minute*. By definition, this is *rate*, the number correct per minute. To return to our hypothetical data set for step 1, it would now look like this:

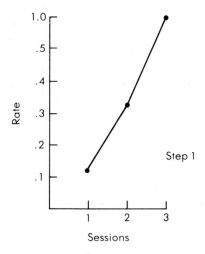

Do we now have an accurate measure of progress? The answer is possibly, *if* we are interested in the speed of correct responding and are satisfied with a very slow initial responsiveness. In this case, we consider the number of opportunities to respond (trials) to be relatively less important than instructional time; thus, the number is allowed to fluctuate. We then use time as the common denominator.

Because we are more likely to be able to fix time limits on instruction and let our teaching opportunities vary from session to session to capitalize on motivation, and so on, we tend to favor the variable-trial, fixed-time measurement option. But we must recognize the problem this option presents. Frequency loses its sensitivity, and hence its utility, if opportunities to respond vary more than a few trials from session to session. Rate, on the other hand, requires the extra step of computation and the use of a graph that is capable of wide ranges in scale representation. For example, suppose our step 1 data set represented a task-analysis step for which we feel that at least 1 correct response per minute should occur before moving on to step 2. Try to construct a graph that goes from .05 (1 correct in 20 minutes) to 1.00 (20 correct in 20 minutes) in linear, step-wise fashion. You get a very long scale.

To solve the scale problem, proponents of the rate measure recommend the use of semilogarithmic graph paper that covers 6 logarithmic cycles. Special rate-finders can be used with graph paper to reduce computation time. White and Haring (1976) and White, Note 1, have provided the most extensive discussion of the use of this system of charting.

In our opinion, although the use of rate as a standard measure for most instructional programs provides some useful solutions to the problems of equivalent scaling, it suffers from some deficiencies that rule it out for many situations. First, the technology of rate finding and plotting can be somewhat cumbersome and demanding. If its use is perceived as competing with instructional time, it will tend not to be used by teachers who have been trained in the procedures. Second, the measure can focus undue attention on the speed of performance. This attention can and does get translated into instructional emphasis, so that students become pressured to work quickly rather than more accurately. For most curricular content with severely handicapped students, accurate responding is paramount, and speed comes with extensive generalized practice.

Rate measurement is most often associated in contemporary educational practice with vocational instruction in application with the secondary population. Independent work production typically requires a student to become proficient in doing a reasonably accurate job in a reasonable amount of time. For this reason, charting progress as a function of rate can be a meaningful and reliable measure, particularly for vocational tasks.

TRACKING ACTIONS IN TIME OR SPACE

Duration and *distance* are examples of two common measurement tactics used in education of severely handicapped students. Suppose we are interested in how long an independent action occurs rather than simply whether or not it occurs. An example is head control. We may be more concerned with increasing the duration of head on midline during an instructional program than the number of times per session the student's head reached midline. In these cases, the numbers on the vertical axis might be seconds, minutes, or even days (as in no toileting accidents) rather than numbers of actions.

Similarly, the distance an independent action covers in space may be of primary interest. For example, a student with contractions learning to extend a forearm as part of a communication board actuation or of an eating program might better be measured by noting the increases in the distance traversed from forearm to bicep in response to each trial. A student learning to go from point A to point B in a wheelchair might have a training step measured in terms of increases in the distance traveled per training trial. In these cases, the numbers on the vertical axis represent millimeters, inches, feet, or even miles (jogged, for example, as in a recreation/leisure program) rather than numbers of actions. Which is the more appropriate measure: the *percentage* of 10 trials per session that the wheelchair traverses at least 4 feet; the *frequency* with which the wheelchair traverses at least 4 feet per trial with 8 to 12 trials occurring per session; the *rate* of wheelchair movement per session (the times per minute 4 feet is traversed); or simply the average number of feet traversed during trials per session? The latter measure gets at the training step with the most sensitivity and, at the same time, the most simplicity.

MEASUREMENT OF PERFORMANCE IN CONCURRENT CHAINS

Whereas percent, frequency, rate, duration, and length typify measurement schemes applicable to serial chains in task-analyzed objectives, a different procedure is usually applied to performance tracking in concurrent chains and curriculum sequences. The latter is described fully in Chapter 8, so we will skip measurement of curriculum sequences here and concentrate on tactics for the concurrent chain.

Instruction on a concurrent chain requires that all the steps in the chain be taught simultaneously on any one training trial. Whereas teaching on a serial chain task analysis limits systematic instruction and measurement to the particular step being taught and the student simply runs through the requirements of all other steps, measurement of performance in a concurrent chain format requires some indication of progress on all the steps in the task analysis for each training trial.

Table 7.2 presents the T-Format of an instructional objective for bed making. The skill for this student was task analyzed into 13 steps, the procedure calling for instruction on a concurrent chain. Sessions were conducted once a day in the morning at home with the student's mother as the instructor.

TABLE 7.2

T-Format of a Thirteen-step Instructional Objective for Bed Making

Goal: Catherine will straighten her bedroom by picking up and putting away clothing and making her bed.

Objective: Catherine will make her bed on three consecutive days with 100 percent accuracy within fifteen minutes.

Task Analysis	Instructional Procedure
1. Pulls top covers down to foot of bed.	*Setting:* Catherine's bedroom at home.
2. Puts pillow on floor.	*Materials:* Bed is mother-made, with 1 blanket, 1 pillow, contour bottom sheet, flat top sheet, and quilt spread. Catherine has slept in bed.
3. Pulls corners to smooth bottom sheet.	
4. Pulls up top sheet and puts evenly on bed.	*Procedure:* Concurrent chain. Teacher (mother) will demonstrate (imitative prompts) and verbally prompt student through the steps, fading prompts as possible.
5. Pulls up blanket and puts evenly on bed.	
6. Tucks top sheet and blanket in at bottom of bed.	*Schedule:* Once a day in the morning.
7. Tucks in corners at bottom.	*Reinforcement:* Social praise.
8. Folds top sheet back over blanket.	*Measurement:* Steps correct per session.
9. Puts quilt cover evenly over bed.	*Generalization:* Will help at home by making other beds.
10. Folds top of quilt back about one-half foot.	*Next Objective:* Sorting dirty clothes from clean clothes.
11. Puts pillow on fold line.	
12. Pulls quilt cover over pillow.	
13. Smoothes wrinkles.	

Figure 7.2 presents the data record of the student's progress under these conditions. Note that each column represents data for 1 trial per session. If the sessions had been defined in terms of several trials (several beds were made), each point in a column would have represented the average number of steps carried out correctly for each session (the total number of correct steps per trial, divided by the number of trials).

In concurrent chain instruction, stimulus-change procedures, such as prompting and fading techniques, are employed on all steps simultaneously. Therefore, measurement of progress can occur at any of a number of different degrees of precision. One, for example, could track the progress of each step within the chain independently of progress over the objective (all steps) as a whole. This information is readily available when sessions of instruction are carried out 1 trial at a time, as in the bed-making chain above. When several trials per session occur, the tracking of individual step progress becomes more cumbersome. We have opted to recommend a level of measurement for concurrent chains that sacrifices information on progress

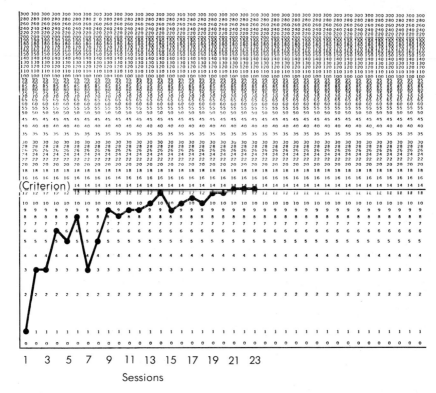

FIGURE 7.2
Data record of student performance in the bed-making task

within individual steps in the chain in favor of simplified tracking of progress on the whole chain.

Using the columnar-numerical graph paper illustrated in Figure 7.2, for example, measurement of the bed-making chain can be accomplished as follows. First, let each column from left to right represent a single session. Second, let each number in a column from bottom to top, represent the corresponding number of each step in the chain. Numbers 1 through 13 in each column equal steps 1 through 13 in the concurrent chain for bed making. As an instructional session is carried out, the teacher draws a slash through the number of each step the student accomplishes independently. This procedure can often be carried out by memory after a session, but for long chains, scoring may have to occur during instruction. At the end of a session, the numbers with slashes through them are added together, and the number in the column representing the sum of slashes is circled. This number stands for the number of correct steps per session. The graph of progress over time becomes the line that connects the circled numbers across columns from left to right. This procedure is illustrated (without slashes) for the bed-making chain in Figure 7.2. It required 23 sessions to achieve the criteria of 3 correct chains in a row with no errors for this student.

Criteria for completion of an objective taught in a concurrent chain are automatically established in the instructional objective. Criteria for individual steps within a serial chain, on the other hand, are set by the teaching staff and are *flexible* to allow for adjustments as a function of the student's progress under instruction. In either case, criteria can be represented by lines drawn from left to right on the graph paper at the number corresponding to the criterial performance requirement. The criterion for the concurrent chain in Figure 7.2 was drawn·at the number 13, since exit from instruction on this chain required 3 consecutive completely correct chains. For some objectives, a less stringent criterion might be specified, for example, an average of 80 percent of the steps correct for any one session. Eighty percent of 13 steps is about 10, so the criterion line for that specification of performance would have been drawn at the level of 10 steps. The issue is usually determined by whether or not the student is expected to master all steps but is permitted to forget a few from time to time, or if total mastery is needed at each occurrence.

In the case of serial chains, the criterion lines for each step may be different. They may also change during instruction, and for that reason they are usually penciled in lightly so they can be easily erased. We will have more to say about criterion specifications a little later in this chapter.

To return to the measurement of concurrent chains, progress on individual steps within the chain can be traced by examining the pattern of slashes that occur from left to right across the graph for each step. Having this step-by-step progress information available to the teaching staff can be valuable in suggesting possible modifications in stimulus-control procedures, reinforcement contingencies, and so on. In actual practice, however, instruction often leads to the same adjustments. In a concurrent chain, the tough spots come to be anticipated in advance over repeated sessions, and difficult steps become targets for concentrated effort on the part of the teaching staff. For this reason, in those task analyses in which more than 1 trial is provided per session and the data are averaged within sessions, we have elected to sacrifice step-by-step information in favor of a simplified tracking of the total chain.

Suppose, for example, that the circled numbers in each column represented the average number of correct steps in each session where instruction consisted of making 3 different beds each time. Scoring could occur on the graph paper during instruction as before, but now up to 3 slashes would have to appear for each step. The circled number would again be equal to the total number of slashes in a column, divided by 3 times the total number of steps in the chain. Obviously, the more trials that occur per session, the more cumbersome the dual function of the graph paper (scoring and charting) becomes. Probably anything over 3 trials per session would require separate collection of data during instruction, tabulation at the end of a session, and transposition of the average number of correct steps to the graph. In this case, no slashes would appear on the graph paper – only circled numbers connected by the continuous line of progress.

SELECTION OF GRAPH PAPER FOR SERIAL CHAINS

There are literally hundreds of different types of graph paper from which to choose for charting student performance over time. From this array, we have selected three types of chart paper that we feel fulfill our requirements for simplified functional recording. They are linear grid paper, logarithmic columnar-numerical paper, and 6-cycle logarithmic rate paper.

Our preference is for the columnar-numerical paper for two reasons. First, it frequently serves to eliminate one of the steps in data management – separate scoring forms. As in the concurrent chain–teaching example earlier, the scoring form and graph paper functions are combined. For serial chains, this dual function can usually be accomplished when the scale of measurement falls within the boundaries of 0 to 300. This is usually the case for frequency, percent, length, and duration. Since it is usually not the case for rate, this paper is not recommended for rate measurement.

Adjustment for Learning Curves.   The second advantage of the columnar-numerical graph paper is the 2½-cycle property just discussed. The "myopic" effect of the paper from bottom to top reflects the passage of the scale of 300 through 2½ logarithmic cycles. This mathematical property of the paper allows it to adjust automatically for a common property of all human behavior: the S-shaped learning curve. Figure 7.3 presents the initial portion of the theoretical curve of learning as illustrated with a hypothetical set of percentage data plotted on "regular" linear graph paper. It tends to be approximated each time an instructional program is carried out on a student, whether severely handicapped or not. The curve would be S-shaped if carried out for additional trials after asymptotic responding because it reflects the slowness of acquisition in the initial stages of learning, followed by steep and rapid progress in the next phase, followed by a leveling off where the highest level of performance of a learned response is achieved.

Because all actions taught to a student will tend to repeat this basic learning curve, the theoretical curve is always to be expected and should not be taken to represent errors on the part of the teaching staff in designing a task-analyzed curricular component or in carrying out instruction. Because this curvilinear phenomenon is always expected from the outset, it becomes desirable to eliminate it *graphically* so that the *actual* progress of the student can be readily examined over time free from the universal contamination of the learning curve. That is what the 2½-cycle paper, in part, accomplishes. The plotting of acquisition data on paper across these 2½ cycles as a deviation from linear scaling has the interesting effect of

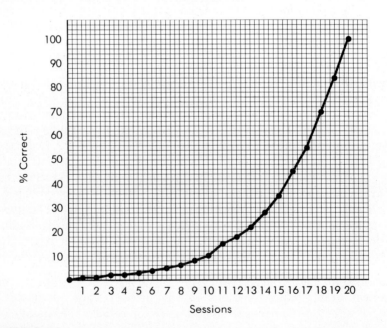

FIGURE 7.3
Hypothetical percent data plotted on linear graph paper to illustrate the lower portion of the learning curve

straightening the bottom portion of the theoretical curve. Figure 7.4 illustrates this effect by plotting the hypothetical data set, shown in Figure 7.3 on linear graph paper, on 2½-cycle percentage paper.

With the learning curve straightened mathematically by the graph paper, the data that we now plot on that paper (data that represent the *actual* performance of the student under instruction) represent the student's true progress more accurately (to the eye). The same effect is obtained for frequency data between 0 and 300 counts, when plotted on the 2½-cycle logarithmic columnar-numerical paper. It is easier to judge and predict performance over time when examining a straight line than when examining a curved line. Of course, severely handicapped students nearly always produce variable data under acquisition of learned behavior, so we almost never have straight lines of progress to look at in any case. Nonetheless, the removal of the theoretical learning curve has a flattening effect on the line of actual performance and therefore tends to render our predictions from visual inspection of those lines more accurate.

The columnar-numerical graph paper has the dual versatility of often eliminating the extra step of scoring and transposing to graph and of removing some of the curviness of the line of acquisition. It performs the latter function more efficiently to the extent that the entire range of the scale is utilized (0 to 300). Linear paper is recommended when the numbers 0 to 300 cannot fit the scale of meaningful measurement for a given task-analyzed skill.

Rate paper, on the other hand, progresses through 6 logarithmic cycles, so that it is theoretically possible to track acquisition of an action that would occur as few as 1 or 2 times per day to as many as 17 times per second. Of course, no single behavior of any severely handicapped (or, for that matter, nonhandicapped) student would traverse such a wide scale. Most human behavior under conditions of acquisition during instruction traverses no more than 2 logarithmic cycles. Nevertheless, convention has set rate paper at 6 cycles, and that is what we utilize when the number of correct actions as a function of the number of minutes of instruction is our common denominator in charting progress.

The effect of the 6 cycles traversed by the rate paper is to condense the line of progress into the middle of the paper. This tends to mitigate against its usefulness for prediction of progress on the basis of visual inspection. Nevertheless, it obviates the learning curve and makes a decision model based on the visual line of progress possible and desirable. White and Haring (1976) have presented a comprehensive data management system based on 6-cycle rate charting.

Chart Comparisons. To illustrate the three graphic options presented here, we have plotted the data from the two task analyses presented earlier, one serial and one concurrent, on each of three types of paper. We

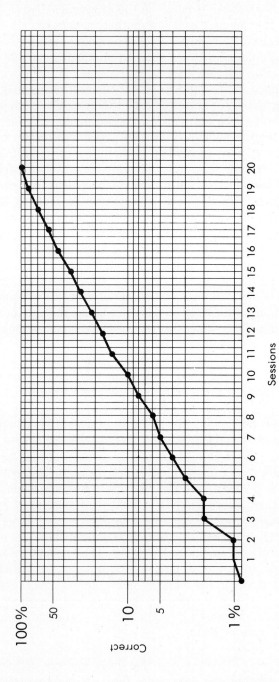

FIGURE 7.4
Percentage data plotted on 2½-cycle percentage graph paper

have assumed a common denominator of 20-minute sessions to calculate the rate specifications for Figure 7.10. Note the effects on the various lines of acquisition of the different scales represented by the four types of graph paper. Which do you find most helpful for predicting future progress on the basis of current data?

Figures 7.5, 7.6, and 7.7 present percentage data for clothing removal, serial chain progress, first on linear paper, then on 2½-cycle logarithmic columnar-numerical paper (as in Figure 7.1), and finally on 2½-cycle logarithmic percentage paper.

Figures 7.8, 7.9, and 7.10 present the concurrent chain bed-making data first on linear paper, then on columnar-numerical paper (same as Figure 7.2), and finally on 6-cycle rate paper. The calculation for rate was taken to be the number of correct steps per session divided by 20 to get the number of correct steps per minute (rate over an assumed 20-minute session). To simplify the visual display, the criterion line is not shown on these three figures.

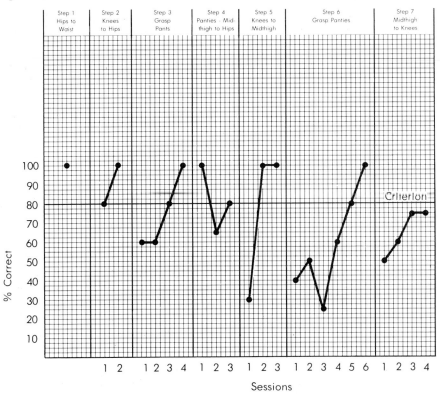

FIGURE 7.5
Clothing removal, serial chain progress data plotted on linear paper

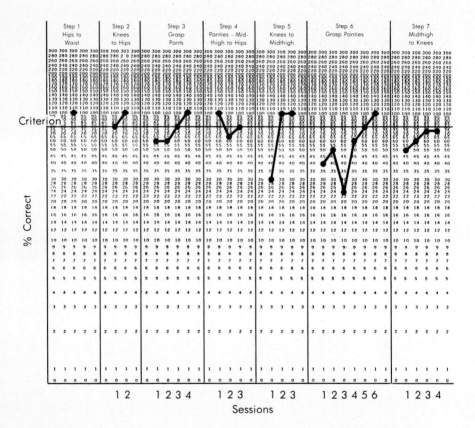

FIGURE 7.6
Clothing removal, serial chain progress data plotted on columnar-numerical paper

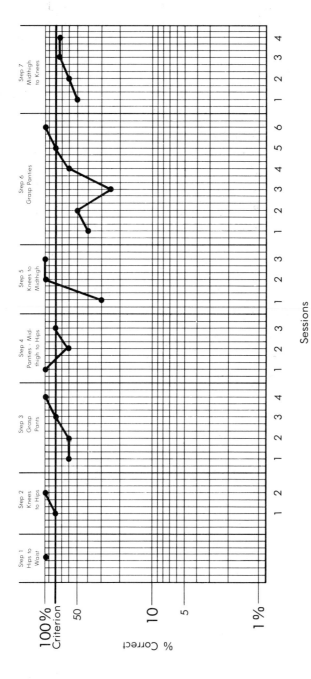

FIGURE 7.7
Clothing removal, serial chain progress data plotted on 2½-cycle logarithmic percentage paper

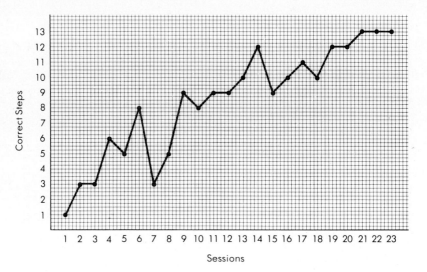

FIGURE 7.8
Bed-making concurrent chain progress data plotted on linear paper

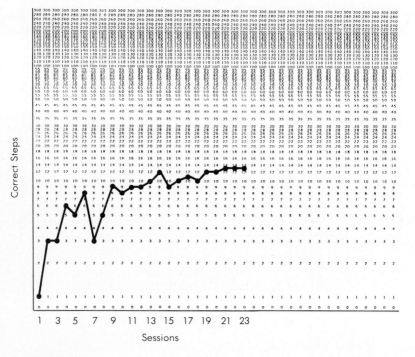

FIGURE 7.9
Bed-making, concurrent chain progress data plotted on columnar-numerical paper

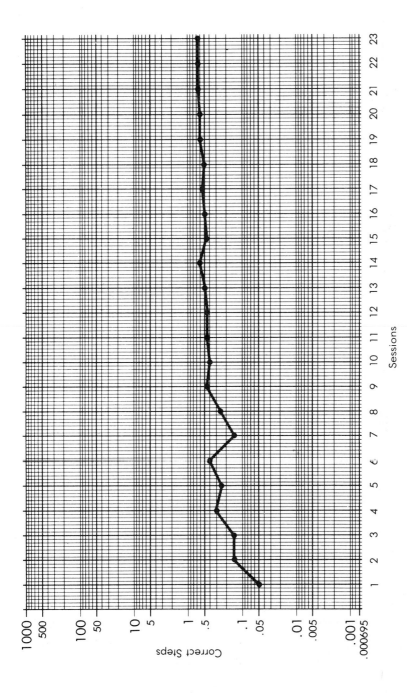

FIGURE 7.10
Bed-making, concurrent chain progress data plotted on rate paper

FREQUENCY OF DATA COLLECTION

TEACHER DIFFERENCES IN DATA COLLECTION

Both our teacher training programs, one at the University of Kansas and one at San Francisco State University, since 1976 have placed a strong emphasis upon measured instruction. Fredericks, Anderson, and Baldwin (1979) at Teaching Research in Oregon discovered in a large-scale research project on the parameters of teacher-training effectiveness that *measured instruction* was one of the few variables of many they studied that reliably predicted child change as a function of teaching effectiveness. The more teachers collect and utilize their data, the faster the student's progress.

This finding corresponds to our own anecdotal observations of teachers who graduated from our respective programs. The most successful and also the most satisfied (least likely to burn out) teachers are avid data collectors. We did, however, further note that these teachers tended to fall into two groups. First, those who measured session by session all specified instructional objectives were continuing to display two and three years after graduation the competencies in measurement they had been taught in the university programs. Their data-collection schemes were close to identical, as a group, to the schemes taught to them. The second group, nearly as large, had evolved more idiosyncratic data-collection schemes, which resembled, but were different from, those that had been taught to them. The primary distinguishing characteristic of the schemes devised by the second group was a tendency toward intermittency in organizing data collection. The first group would track, on the average, five instructional objectives per student on a session-by-session basis. The second group would track one or two objectives session by session and time sample others. Some would initiate session-by-session data collection on some objectives and then move to time sampling as the speed of acquisition increased.

The first group of teachers were highly data-dependent as a group. They would typically resist suggestions that they could collect fewer data points per child and thus save some work without sacrificing utility. Some would say that they actually felt insecure without the process of data collection. The second group seemed to feel data-bound. For them, the process of measurement was somewhat bothersome. They would rather not bother with it at all, but they, too, felt that its utility justified the effort and expenditure of time and energy. Both groups were effective teachers.

It would seem, then, that the answer to the question, "How often should I measure?" requires an answer that is tailored to the needs and preferences of the individual teacher, as long as enough data are collected to allow for day-to-day decisions regarding the adequacy of ongoing instructional programs tied to objectives.

TECHNIQUES TO REDUCE DATA-COLLECTION FREQUENCY

As mentioned earlier, measurement of any kind is a form of testing. Where teaching time is a scarce commodity, testing can compete for instructional time. We have seen teachers who were so test oriented that their use of data actually mitigated against their overall teaching effectiveness, and ironically, the data reflected the deterioration of child performance over time.

An optimal instructional program needs a balance of teaching and testing to enhance student progress. Two techniques for reducing the amount of testing relative to teaching time but retaining the important collection of measurement data are probes and time sampling.

Probes.   In a serial chain, instruction is concentrated on one step at a time, and the student is prompted or physically put through all the remaining steps. When a step is nearing criterion for advancement to the next step in the chain, a probe can be administered to determine the current level of performance on all remaining steps. A probe is accomplished by switching occasionally for one training trial to a concurrent chain. Each step is instructed during this trial so that the student has the opportunity to display independence on all steps in the chain. Across repeated probes, a pattern of performance emerges that can be helpful in determining whether the existing chains will need to be taught as originally designed or whether some time-saving procedures can be instituted instead. Some steps in a chain will be found to emerge without much direct training. The probe procedure can lead to decisions like these: (1) concentrate a few teaching trials on other steps in addition to the step being taught in order to reach independent performance ahead of schedule, (2) switch to a concurrent chain from a serial chain, or (3) modify the existing chain by creating fewer steps and combining existing steps.

Results of probe trials are usually not plotted alongside existing data since the number of probe trials are discontinuous with acquisition trials, but the results may be noted and used to determine whether to advance to later steps ahead of criterion, to switch to a concurrent teaching strategy, or to continue instruction as is. In this procedure, probing becomes a way of sampling ahead of schedule to forecast the overall outcome of instruction. It can save testing time later by conserving teaching time in the present.

The probe method does not apply to measurement of concurrent chains, since each datum point collected represents an ongoing probe of the attainment of all steps in the chain.

Time Sampling.   The teach-test time ratio can be further increased by systematically thinning the schedule of measurement of an instructional activity in much the same way that you would thin a schedule of reinforcement. Many objectives will not require session-by-session scoring, and the relative freedom from the need to score each action can allow a teacher to concentrate attention more effectively on instructional procedures. Time sampling, however, is not for everyone. Some teachers report that their own evaluations of their teaching effectiveness decrease upon shifting to a thinner measurement schedule. These teachers seem to need the security of session-by-session feedback on child performance. Others feel their effectiveness increases when they can concentrate completely on the teaching task, knowing that measurement will occur at a later time.

Time sampling is the process of taking measurements of performance only at selected times, rather than trial by trial and session by session. Where instruction on a particular objective is occurring over repeated trials during a single session, as in, for example, an eating program, certain trials can be selected for scoring rather than performance on each trial. Selected-trial scoring requires that the trial or trials to be scored during any one session be *determined in advance* to avoid introducing a bias in the selection of trials to be scored. The procedure also requires that an *equal number* of trials within sessions be scored in order to render the data across sessions equivalent. In general, selection of trials to be scored within sessions should usually aim for sampling the approximate middle and end of the series. The first and last trials are usually not selected for scoring. For example, in a series of 12 trials per session, numbers 4, 7, and 10 could be selected. The graphed datum point for that session would then be the average of the 3 sampled trials.

Time-sampling sessions, the more common procedure, similarly requires caution in the selection of test sessions. The following are some general rules for time sampling:

1. Score the first 3 sessions of any instructional program in order to gauge the student's responsiveness to the program as structured.
2. If performance is such that there are no correct (independent) actions during initial sessions but you feel progress in fading prompts, and so on, warrants continuing the program as is, discontinue scoring for several sessions or until you get the first scorable response.
3. If progress on a step (serial) or on a chain (concurrent) is steady but slow and no changes seem to be indicated, score only every third or fourth session. Return to session-by-session scoring only if criterion performance is at hand or if problems are sensed or encountered during ongoing instruction.
4. Where instruction on similar objectives is occurring in a group format, time sample by scoring performance on only one member of the group on any given session. By rotating group members who are tested, the

higher demands of scoring during group instructions are reduced, and time sampling is spread across several individuals simultaneously.

The use of time sampling causes minor problems for the construction of graphic records. Where data are equivalent and continuous across sessions, the line connecting the data points should be unbroken. Where a session or several sessions in a row are not scored, either because of time sampling, absence, or whatever, the points prior to and following the missed sessions should not be connected. The space where a datum point would have been entered should be skipped. In other words, the sessions specified on the ordinate should be fixed and immutable for record purposes.

The fundamental rule of time sampling is to reduce the burden of measurement to whatever degree you can without sacrificing its key function – the provision of information on performance needed to make decisions concerning the ongoing effectiveness of an instructional program. The process can often lead to difficult decisions.

MEASUREMENT-BASED TEACHING DECISIONS

A DECISION MODEL

Much if not most of the important work done on the science of measurement and curriculum evaluation as it directly applies to educational programs for severely handicapped children has been carried out over the past six years at the University of Washington by Norris Haring, Kathleen Liberty, and Owen White (1980). This impressive group not only has designed a sophisticated technology for measurement based on earlier pioneering work by Lindsley (1964) but also has conducted valuable and systematic research on key variables that affect teaching decisions growing out of measured child performance. The decision model presented here is based loosely on the work of this group.

The Washington group devised a strategy whereby a teacher would run a few sessions, plot a few data points, and then select a *desired* date for completion of the skill being taught (or step in a serial chain). A minimum celeration line would then be drawn from the cluster of initial data points to a point of intersection with the criterion line (Liberty, 1972). The criterion line, it will be recalled, is the line parallel to the ordinate at the point on the scale where criterion is met to advance to the next step of the next objective. Typically, a student is advanced as soon as the line of progress (the graph) intersects the criterion line, unless the criterion calls for some repetition of critical performance, such as 3 sessions in a row. The criterion line is drawn to correspond to a predicted, acceptable date for completion. When the line was drawn, additional data points would be collected during instruction and a decision made to change something, if 3 consecutive data points on the performance line fell below the minimum celeration line (White and Haring, 1976).

Haring, Liberty, and White suggested on the basis of their research that a student's performance under instruction could be examined for decision purposes in terms of three phases that correspond to the phases of the theoretical learning curve (Figure 7.4). They called these phases acquisition (initial progress), fluency building (accelerated progress), and compliance (motivated performance of already learned behavior). The authors suggested that the decision to change teaching tactics should depend on the particular phase in which errors are detected during ongoing instruction. For breakdowns in the instructional pattern, as reflected in 3 or more successive data points falling below the minimum celeration line, that occur in the *acquisition* phase of instruction, the remedy should be adjustment of the stimulus-control procedure. The problem here, according to the Washington group, is likely to be one of directions, demonstrating physical guidance, prompts, modeling, materials, or feedback to the student on accuracy of performance.

Problems that occur during the *fluency-building* phase, according to these authors, are likely to be problems of motivation and efficiency. Typical strategies to remedy problems in the fluency-building stage would include repeated practice, modification of instructions, and manipulation of effects (reinforcers). Finally, problems occurring in the final maintenance, or *compliance,* phase would suggest remediation by consequence (effect) manipulation and application of behavior management procedures.

It is our opinion that the work of the Washington group represents an impressive and important beginning to the process of formulating a set of general data-based decision rules. We feel, however, that much more research is needed before such a set of rules can be put forward with confidence. Our own experience with a decision model suggests, for example, that problems occurring in the early stages of acquisition of a skill or step are about equally as likely to accrue to faulty stimulus-control tactics as to faulty task analysis. It is difficult to know what to change when things go wrong early in the teaching program. Since instructional procedures tend to be fixed and general, whereas task analyses tend to be highly individualized, we would be more inclined at this stage to slice a difficult step in the chain differently than to shift the instructional procedure. White (Note 2), however, reports that recent research he and his colleagues have conducted tends to suggest that further slicing of steps in a task analysis, where errors are occurring, often leads only to more errors. He reports that errors are more likely to decrease when more *difficult* steps are arranged following an error analysis than when steps are made easier. It is as if the student becomes bored and needs the challenge of a new problem during ongoing instruction. We would agree that problems occurring after initial acquisition tend usually to be motivational (boredom, for example).

If a skill is practiced repeatedly without efforts to generalize it across settings, persons, and materials, and if the skill is not reinforcing in and of itself, the student's motivation to perform will naturally wane. For this reason, flexibility in setting criterion lines for step acquisition in serial chains is preferable to fixed, high criteria for advancement. Most teachers are familiar with a type of boredom effect, in which a student will approach or initially cross a line of critical performance for advancement, only to deteriorate in performance short of final criterion. In no case would we suggest a forced compliance approach to problems in performance of an initially learned action. Severely handicapped students must be pulled on the pleasure principle rather than pushed on the pain principle in order to attain self-motivation for learning new skills.

DECISION-ANALYSIS RULES

Again, borrowing heavily from Haring, Liberty, and White, we would propose the following data rules preparatory to a decision analysis:

1. Begin initial instruction and record data until a total of 6 *nonzero data points* have been collected. Because only independent actions are scored as correct, many initial data points will be 0. Time sampling can be employed until non–0 points begin to appear. We would suggest continuous session-by-session scoring then be instituted until the 6-point specification is met.
2. Find the midpoint of the first 3 (nonzero) data points by making a plus sign at the intersection of the second highest point of the 3 with the second day of the 3 (as in Figure 7.11).
3. Repeat the second procedure for the second 3 data points.
4. With a clear plastic ruler, draw a line (which we will call the *prediction* line) that intersects the two plus signs and extends to the point where it crosses the *criterion* line (all intersect lines should be drawn in light pencil). Do not draw the line if it is not ascending and if it does not cross the criterion line in an amount of time that seems reasonable and acceptable.
5. If a line is drawn, drop another straight line from the point of intersection of the prediction line with the criterion line down to the ordinate (as in Figure 7.11). The intersection of this line at the ordinate is the predicted session at which criterion will be reached on this step or skill. The prediction is actually made by the *student* based on early performance returns. The prediction represented by the prediction line will tend to be more accurate when applied to the columnar-numerical graph paper or rate paper for the mathematical reasons described earlier.

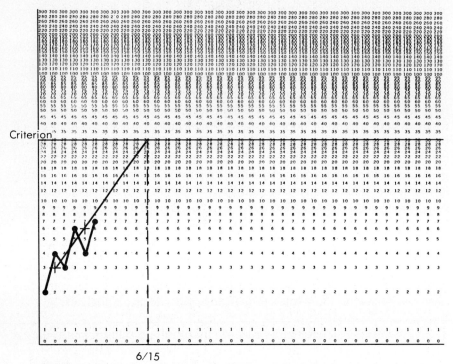

6/15

FIGURE 7.11
A hypothetical data set illustrating a prediction line, a criterion line, and resultant intersect with ordinate to show projected date of criterial performance

Teaching staff will find that, with repeated practice at drawing prediction lines, the procedure detailed above can gradually be replaced by simply "eye-balling" the 6-point data set with the clear plastic ruler and estimating the trend. Occasional checks on lines drawn by estimate will help to improve accuracy. The estimated line should aim for half the data points to fall below the line and half to fall above. Often, the line will have to be drawn through one or more points to accomplish that.

New prediction lines should be drawn following a decision to change the instructional program according to rules we will specify a little further along.

The First Decision.   If a decision was made *not* to draw the prediction line, a problem has been identified early in the instructional process. If the prediction line would have sloped downward or paralleled the ordinate and criterion lines, the student is indicating with his or her performance that there is no progress. If the line would have intersected the criterion line at a point too distant for acceptability, progress is occurring but is insufficient.

Either way, something is wrong, and something must be changed. The following is a check list of potential trouble spots. The first yes answer to the series of questions stands a reasonable chance of indicating the fault, and an appropriate adjustment at that level would merit the collection of 3 additional data points:

1. Is the step or chain too difficult for the student as presently constructed?
2. Is the stimulus-control procedure ineffective as presently specified?
3. Is the effect of the required action sufficiently motivating?
4. Does the action require prosthesis?
5. Does the environment require adaptation in order for the required action to be performed?

If the answer to each of the above questions is no, then a decision to collect an additional 3 data points and redraw the line would be warranted.

The new prediction line in the case above would be drawn on the 6 data points that consist of the last 3 points in the old set plus the 3 new points following the decision to alter something or to continue.

In a case where the initial prediction line indicated satisfactory progress and a reasonable predicted date of completion of the step or skill, the decision would be to continue instruction until criterion is reached or until 3 consecutive data points fall below the prediction line.

The Second and Subsequent Decision.   The second decision point and all subsequent decisions for changes are made on the basis of the 3 consecutive points below the line of prediction rule. Figure 7.12 presents an example of a case where a change was made following 3 points below the first prediction line. A second line was drawn on the basis of the last 3 points of the first set combined with the first 3 points of the second set (post change), and finally, criterion was attained as predicted on the basis of the second line.

The second and subsequent decision usually must be made when initial progress has taken a disappointing turn. The check list of potential remedies above applies to this situation as well, but the likelihood of the problem being in the realm of insufficient motivation increases the further along the line of acquisition a problem occurs.

Each time a new prediction line is drawn, a new intersect line can be dropped to the ordinate to ascertain the new suspected date of completion of instruction on this skill or step. A determination is made each time as to whether the anticipated progress is satisfactory. If not, another change should be made, a new line drawn, and so on.

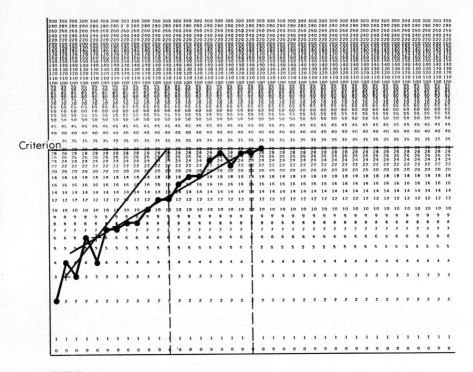

FIGURE 7.12
Example graph showing a new prediction line based upon the second 3 points of the first set of data points and the first 3 points of the second set of data points

Can time sampling occur and the decision model still be activated? The answer is yes. Spaces between the consecutive data points do not alter the expectations and can, in fact, lend additional strength and confidence to the resulting decision by extending the length (data base) of the prediction line.

Once the decision model process has been tried a few times, the lines can be drawn reasonably accurately by eye. Some decisions for change have resulted in dramatic progress on the part of one or two students, and, believe it or not, the process can become *fun* as well as scientific. Only when you have become an experienced user of a data-based decision model do you begin to realize fully the power of the technology that has evolved over the past decade in the field of education of severely handicapped students. No other aspect of the teaching process is as impressive (if not astounding) to educators from other fields than the process of adjusting teaching procedures on the basis of a severely handicapped child's own prediction of his or her future performance under instruction.

SUMMARY

Curriculum is most efficiently evaluated by systematic measurement of student performance under specified conditions of instruction. Measurement always occurs at the level of *independent* (nonprompted) actions. Actions may be measured by use of various scales. Scales are fitted to the particular action to be counted and, for serial chains, may include: percent, frequency, rate, duration, and length, among others. Frequency, when length of session and number of opportunities (trials) are equivalent, is becoming the preferred scale for many kinds of objectives. Rate is a useful measure when numbers of trials and session times vary during an instructional program and when speed as well as accuracy of performance is important.

Actions measured under conditions of concurrent chain instruction are tracked by steps to criterion or the number of steps in the chain correctly accomplished each session. Criteria for advancement are flexible within steps of a serial chain and equal to the criterion for exit from the instructional objective for the concurrent chain. In serial chain measurement, criterion is usually reached when one datum point falls above the specified criterion line. Flexibility in setting criteria within steps is critical.

Measures of performance can be plotted on various kinds of graph paper. Rate paper (6-cycle logarithmic) is preferable when rate is the scale of measurement. Linear paper is an option whenever data cannot be fitted to the scale of 2½-cycle columnar-numerical paper, which is preferable for most measurement needs.

Data can be collected trial by trial and session by session, or time sampling can be instituted to reduce the time spent in measurement. Time sampling should not sacrifice the amount of data necessary to make ongoing decisions for change in instructional procedure.

Probes can be added to the measurement process to determine if later steps in a serial chain are emerging prior to instruction. Probes can save instructional time by providing data on later skill targets easily.

The first 6 nonzero data points gathered in an instructional program can form the basis for a decision model. A prediction line drawn through the 6 points that approximates a trend line, or line of best fit, provides the student's own revealed prediction as to the date of completion of the current step or skill. This date is determined by the session number that corresponds to the intersection of the prediction line and the criterion line.

When 3 data points in a row fall below the prediction line during ongoing instruction, the indication is for a change in the specified instructional format. The change may occur in the task analysis; the instructional procedure, including stimulus control and reinforcement effects; and the relationship of the student to the instructional environment, including prosthetic and/or adaptive equipment needs.

CHAPTER 8

Curriculum Sequencing

The previous three chapters discussed the working program plan as the basis for developing a curriculum for severely handicapped students. The plan included procedures for identifying goals and objectives for the education of individual students (Chapter 5), approaches for arranging objectives into smaller and more obtainable instructional units (Chapter 6), and a database decision model for evaluating student progress in meeting instructional objectives (Chapter 7). Each chapter emphasized the importance of directing effort toward the educational needs of individual students, as opposed to adopting a standard curriculum for an entire class.

This chapter extends this orientation by presenting a model for arranging curriculum content according to the educational goals and objectives for individual students in the classroom. Emphasis here is placed on organizing the curriculum in a manner that cuts across traditional content areas and that effectively provides for the teaching of skills in a natural and functional manner. Whereas the previous three chapters were concerned primarily with the initial steps required to provide and evaluate instruction in specific skill areas, the present chapter presents a rationale and strategy for integrating some identified instructional objectives into a cohesive training sequence for individual students.

BASES FOR A CURRICULUM-SEQUENCING APPROACH

The severely handicapped student presents a number of demands not usually encountered in curriculum development for less handicapped populations. For example, curriculum development for mildly mentally retarded students is based on the already existing framework for the academic curriculum of nonhandicapped students. Content must still be decided upon, but a basis exists for selecting, sequencing, and organizing the courses. For other disability groups such as persons who are visually and hearing impaired, the same considerations apply, but in this case, an additional dimension of instructional technology is needed.

For the mildly handicapped student, the nature of the curriculum permits wide variation in the selection of teaching strategies. The curriculum sets forth what is to be taught (the content), but teachers are usually free to employ the instructional method that works best for them. Because of the cognitive abilities of mildly handicapped students, different approaches to teaching the same content are likely to be equally successful.

For severely handicapped students, however, the present range of effective teaching strategies is greatly restricted. There are no validated curriculum specifications, nor are existing assessment strategies precise enough to determine needed behaviors and to assess progress during attainment. It may be argued that for severely handicapped students, curriculum content, teaching procedures, and assessment strategies constitute an interrelated problem (cf., Filler, Robinson, Smith, Vincent-Smith, Bricker, and Bricker, 1975). This argument is supported by noting that the current primary curriculum approach for severely handicapped students emphasizes instructional procedures whereby teachers help students acquire behaviors specific to their needs. This approach can be contrasted, for example, with that for other populations wherein most curriculum decisions involve choice of subject matter and not necessarily choice of teaching strategies. For the severely handicapped population, teaching strategies become a major focus of the curriculum–a point that is missed by many teacher-training institutions, which still separate courses for assessment (like "Psycho-Educational Diagnosis") from courses on methods of instruction.

There are two requirements that are especially important to curriculum design for severely handicapped students. These are:

1. The teaching of skills in clusters that maximize the functional interdependence of content areas
2. A teaching strategy that capitalizes on the sequencing of skills in a manner that is natural to the various environments in which the student is expected to perform

TEACHING SKILLS IN CLUSTERS

Many would now agree that we should not teach isolated skills to severely handicapped students, but rather, that we should teach a number of skills concurrently. The best way to achieve this is to group skills into clusters. A skill cluster might include, for example, teaching a multiply handicapped infant to (1) raise her head (gross motor), (2) visually fixate on a favorite toy (sensory), (3) produce a sound that approximates the name of the toy (communication), (4) reach for and grasp the toy (fine motor), and (5) engage the toy in an appropriate manner (motor and cognitive).

The logic underlying the recommendation to *teach skill clusters* is that naturally occurring behaviors are rarely present in isolation. We are required to emit many behaviors at the same time when faced with the complexities of the environment. Ecologists refer to the "stream of behavior" as the organism interacts with the environment, developmental psychologists and others often refer to treating the "whole child", and behavioral psychologists refer to "stimulus arrays." Regardless of one's particular specialty, the message is the same: the person must learn to emit many different types of actions either concurrently or in rapid succession if adaptive behavior is to occur.

For severely handicapped students, we emphasize the teaching of behaviors that occur naturally in normal environments. This strategy, in effect, requires a curriculum that teaches skills in logically arranged clusters directly reflecting, or occurring within, the student's environments. Once the skills that comprise a cluster are identified, the obvious problem is to decide exactly how the clusters should be arranged. Which behaviors should be taught together, and in what sequence should they be logically ordered? Our premise is that the phenomenon referred to as *response classes* may provide a method for identifying, arranging, and subsequently teaching skill clusters to severely handicapped students. To better understand how and why this can be done, let us first review two logical systems that are prevalent in the design of programs used with severely handicapped students. We can then see how the two systems can work together to provide a basis for the identification of skill clusters.

Developmental and Remedial Logic.   *Developmental logic* draws heavily on cognitive theories of learning. This logic assumes that the best way to teach handicapped children is to follow the same learning sequence of nonhandicapped children (cf., Cohen, 1979a, b). The basic premise is that since human behavior is complex, the acquisition of individual skills depends on already mastered skills. This assumes, for example, that before teaching children self-feeding skills, they should already be able to reach for and grasp objects and hold their heads in an upright position. Or before teaching children to talk, they must realize that objects exist even when the objects are out of sight. Other readiness skills for speaking might include the ability to imitate actions previously observed by the child and to demonstrate knowledge of how common objects are used.

According to developmental logic, skills are acquired within limited alternative sequences, at least in the case of children who are learning such skills in the process of their normal development. This hypothesis is bolstered by the reported uniformity with which children acquire a large number of sensory, motor, and cognitive skills.

Remedial logic, in contrast, notes that severely handicapped children must be taught many basic skills of development much later in life than usual (Guess, Sailor, and Baer, 1978b). These children usually do not possess the same collection of abilities and deficits as do nonhandicapped children. On the contrary, the severely handicapped child might possess certain *deviant* means of interacting with the environment, none of which is representative of the knowledge or ignorance, ability or inability of the normally developing young child.

Remedial logic does not assume the order in which the handicapped child needs to learn motor, sensory, cognitive, and social skills. It asks rather which skills in what order, when acquired most quickly, will accomplish some improvement in the severely handicapped child's ability to interact successfully with the environment. Remedial logic has a history of experimental efforts to teach quite arbitrary skills with virtually no regard for the child's readiness to learn each particular element. In these cases, at least, no attempts were made to base the training effort on the presence of other existing skills that some persons might perceive as critical developmental prerequisites for successful learning. Instead, the selection of skills for training was more influenced by the need to teach behaviors that would improve the child's ability to better interact with the environment (cf., Guess, Sailor, and Baer, 1974).

In all likelihood, the distinction between the two logics is artificial in practical application. A more important matter is the age of the students with whom one is working. A developmental approach is more readily adopted with young severely handicapped children, and a lesser concern for developmental prerequisites occurs when one is working with a severely handicapped adolescent or young adult.

The teaching of skill clusters draws heavily from developmental logic in helping to identify behaviors that should be taught together, based upon the expected age of emergence. Remedial logic serves as a reminder that skill clusters should be arranged in a manner that allows for the acquisition of learning in small, obtainable steps, and that environmental adaptations (like prosthetic devices) may be needed when the student exhibits grossly uneven or abnormal patterns of development.

Identifying Functional Responses.   The organization of instructional units into clusters of related skills fits very nicely into an educational service system that occurs in multiple, normal environments. Skills that can easily be sequenced together in a cluster are often those skills that are the most useful and meaningful to the student. This aspect of the shift in curriculum has most frequently been discussed in terms of functionality.

How do we make education for severely handicapped students more functional? This may well be the most critical issue facing providers of educational services to severely handicapped students. More basically, how do we define *functionality?*

Guess, Horner, Utley, Holvoet, Maxon, Tucker, and Warren (1978) have made an initial effort to define *functional responses,* with the assumption that training programs and curricula are based on teaching a multitude of individual responses. According to their definition, *functional responses* have the following characteristics:

1. They produce an immediate effect.
2. The effect is motivating.
3. The combination of actions and effect should be natural to the students' interaction with the environments in which they now live or will live in the future.

Brown, Branston, Hamre-Nietupski, Pumpian, Certo, and Gruenewald (1978) have recently provided a broader definition of *functionality* as it relates to the teaching of skills.

> Functional skills, as the phrase is used here, refers to the variety of skills which are frequently demanded in natural domestic, vocational, and community environments. Functional skills are not limited to performances which affect the actual survival or physical well being of an individual; they also include the variety of skills which influence a student's ability to perform as independently and productively as possible in home, school and community settings. Nonfunctional skills, by contrast, are those which have an extremely low probability of being required by daily activities. (p. 3)

It is interesting to note that the attempts by Guess et al. (1978) to deal with the issue of functionality evolved from work with young and early-school-aged severely handicapped students, whereas the writings of Brown et al. (1978) reflect, to a great extent, their efforts to serve school-aged severely handicapped students who are being prepared for community living. In both cases, however, the message is the same, the teaching of functional responses and skills must assume a more prominent role in curriculum and programming efforts for severely handicapped students.

A FUNCTIONAL CURRICULUM-SEQUENCING MODEL

In an earlier paper, Guess et al. (1978) described a model for constructing and developing a curriculum that would combine the positive features of both developmental and remedial logics in a manner that provides a basis for teaching functional skills to severely handicapped students. The model assumes that any curriculum for teaching this most difficult-to-teach population must have a strong and validated empirical base. It further assumes that this empirical base cannot be developed in a short time and that it cannot be derived from "armchair analysis." Indeed, the foundation of the curriculum must come from intensive research that feeds into a flexible model that allows data from performance of severely handicapped students to answer the questions, "What should I teach?" and "In what order should skills be taught?"

Response Generalization: A Basis for the Model.   The functional curriculum-sequencing model is predicated conceptually and operationally on the phenomenon of response generalization, discussed briefly in Chapter 4. This term is used to describe the fact that actions or skills of similar topographical and/or functional components can best be taught within behavioral classes, and importantly, the transfer, or generalization, of one action or skill to the other is most likely to occur *within* that class.

Topographical similarity refers to the actual physical commonality between two or more actions, regardless of their function. As an example, teaching a student to pull down a shirt as the terminal step in a backward chaining procedure for a dressing program is topographically similar to teaching the same student to pull paper towels from a dispenser (which may be a part of a washing program). In both cases, the actions needed to complete the task are physically similar. As such, they might well be members of the same response class.

Functional similarity refers to the fact that two or more actions may have the same meaning for the student, yet there may be a considerable variation in the actual physical characteristics of the actions. In language training, for example, a student may be taught to discriminate a ball from other objects and also to produce orally the word *ball.* The physical act of pointing to a ball is, of course, quite different from saying the word *ball.* Yet, both actions are emitted for the same purpose and, hence, are considered to be functionally similar.

Response Classes.   The research literature includes many examples showing that acquisition of new behavior is more likely to occur within *response classes,* that is, groupings of actions that have similar physical or functional similarities (Garcia, Baer, and Firestone, 1971; Guess and Baer, 1973). This phenomenon of response generalization has not, however, been systematically applied to the development of curricula for severely handicapped children.

The model proposed by Guess et al. (1978) argues for a curriculum approach that recognizes the need to teach skill clusters, which are close approximations to response classes (as generally referred to in the experimental literature). The distinction is actually one that requires empirical verification. A skill cluster is arranged as a potential response class, which can only be demonstrated as such if systematic changes can be observed among responses in the class as a result of some type of manipulation. (These changes typically mirror response generalization as discussed earlier in Chapter 5.)

Included in the model presented by Guess et al. was a discussion of how skill clusters might be arranged across typical content domains, including communication, socialization, sensory/motor, self-help, preacademic, and vocational areas. The authors suggested that training programs might best be developed in a manner that teaches skills from various content areas in an interdependent way. This implies, for example, that motor, communication, and self-help training might be taught together as a skill cluster. It was further suggested that skills included in the clusters should be arranged in a sequence that is functional for the child in interaction with the immediate demands of an environment.

Subsequent to the original presentation of the functional curriculum-sequencing model by Guess et al., an effort was made to specify and identify more clearly the underlying premises of the model, and to develop from it a practical teaching strategy that could be used with severely handicapped students. The teaching strategy that evolved from the model has been referred to as the individualized curriculum sequence (ICS) (cf., Mulligan and Guess, Note 1). The ICS strategy provides for each student a learning sequence containing a meaningful series of training trials in which one response logically sets the occasion for the next response. The ICS is a deliberate attempt to teach functional skills in a manner that facilitates optimum generalization across materials, persons, settings, tasks, and contexts.

MAJOR COMPONENTS OF THE ICS

FUNCTIONAL SKILLS

The issue of identifying and teaching functional skills was discussed above as part of the functional curriculum-sequencing model. To elaborate on this point, Brown, Nietupski, and Hamre-Nietupski (1976) have referred to the "criterion of ultimate functioning" as a standard by which classroom curriculum content should be measured.

> *The criterion of ultimate functioning* refers to the ever changing, expanding, localized, and personalized cluster of factors that each person must possess in order to function as productively and independently as possible in socially, vocationally, and domestically integrated adult community environments. (p. 8)

These authors pose six questions that should be considered by the classroom teacher and other service delivery personnel before initiating training activities. These questions are as follows:

1. Why should we engage in this activity?
2. Is this activity necessary to prepare students to ultimately function in complex heterogeneous community settings?
3. Could students function as adults if they did not acquire the skill?
4. Is there a different activity that will allow students to approximate realization of the criterion of ultimate functioning more quickly and more efficiently?
5. Will this activity impede, restrict, or reduce the probability that students will ultimately function in community settings?
6. Are the skills, materials, tasks, and criteria of concern similar to those encountered in adult life? (p. 9)

Whether these questions would also apply to young severely handicapped children is debatable, since predictions of their future adult environment might change considerably during their school years. Nevertheless, the principle remains the same. Classroom activities and tasks should reflect those behaviors and skills that would enhance the students' successful interaction with the natural environment, presently and in the future. The ICS is an attempt to teach functional skills in terms of both *content* and *sequence* of presentation.

DISTRIBUTED-TRIAL PRESENTATIONS IN THE ICS

A second major issue centers around the presentation of massed, spaced, or distributed trials during training. Trials from a program are *massed* if two repeated trials occur so closely together that no other behavior can be expected to be emitted between the two. In spaced- and distributed-trial sequencing, periods of time occur between trials of the same program. Trials are considered to be *spaced* if a rest period or pause occurs between two repeated trials from the same program. Trials are *distributed* if trials from another program occur between two repeated trials from the same program. Figure 8.1 shows, schematically, the differences between these three types of trial schedules.

In the past, most training programs for severely handicapped students have deliberately used massed-trial procedures. Trials are presented in rapid succession in blocks that typically range from ten to fifty presentations per session. For example, a student might be required to label (or point to) the same object for a large number of successive trials. A common observation of this procedure is that performance decelerates over the training session. Explanations for this deceleration include fatigue,

TRIAL DISTRIBUTION	THREE TYPES OF SCHEDULES
1111111111 → 2222222222	Massed-trial sequence for skills 1 and 2
1→1→1→1→1→1→1→1→1→1	Spaced-trial sequence for skill 1
12121212121212121212	Distributed-trial sequence for skills 1 and 2

FIGURE 8.1

Different trial arrangements over time for massed, spaced, and distributed trial training

The 1 represents one action being trained; the 2 indicates a second type of action. Time is indicated by the arrows.

boredom, and reinforcer satiation. A frequent outcome is to break up the training sessions into smaller blocks of trials with more sessions scheduled during the child's day, a procedure that more closely approximates spaced- or distributed-trial presentations.

Mulligan, Guess, Holvoet, and Brown (1980) reviewed the literature pertaining to massed-, spaced-, and distributed-trial training among both nonhandicapped and mentally retarded learners. This review indicated consistent findings favoring distributed-trial over massed-trial procedures in the acquisition of motor and, especially, cognitive skills. The literature thus supports the conceptual basis of the ICS strategy, which in part is based on distributed-trial sequencing. This support is, however, offered with the caution that most of the studies reviewed by Mulligan et al. were conducted with nonhandicapped-subject populations, and the studies often included learning content not appropriate to the skill level of severely handicapped students.

CONCURRENT-TASK SEQUENCING IN THE ICS

The third component of the ICS involves the issue of concurrent- versus serial-task sequences of the content included in training programs. In a *serial-training sequence,* one action is usually taught to criterion, then a second action is taught to criterion, a third action is taught, and so on. For example, a student might be trained on one imitative action (such as clapping hands), then a second action (such as touching the table), and so on. In this type of training, the first action is taught to a specified criterion level before the second action is taught. A serial task-sequencing procedure is frequently used with massed-trial training. *Concurrent-task sequences,* on the other hand, require that two or more skills be taught at the same time during a training session. An important difference between concurrent- and serial-task-sequencing approaches is presented schematically in Figure 8.2.

SERIAL-TRAINING SEQUENCE

Sessions

(1)	1	1	1	1	1	1	1	1	1	1	1	1	1	1	1	etc.
(2)	1	1	1	1	1	1	1	1	1	1	1	1	1	1	1	etc.
(3)	1	1	1	1	1	1	1	1	1	1	1	1	1	1	1	etc.
(4)	1	1	1	1	1	1	1	1	1	1	1	1	1	1	1	etc.
(5)	1	1	1	2	2	2	2	2	2	2	2	2	2	2	2	etc.
(6)	2	2	2	2	2	2	2	2	2	2	2	2	2	2	2	etc.

etc.

CONCURRENT-TRAINING SEQUENCE

Sessions

(1)	111	222	111	222	111	222	111	etc.
(2)	222	111	222	111	222	111	222	etc.
(3)	111	222	111	222	111	222	111	etc.
(4)	222	111	222	111	222	111	222	etc.
(5)	222	333	222	333	222	333	222	etc.
(6)	333	222	333	222	333	222	333	etc.

etc.

FIGURE 8.2
Schematic presentation of serial versus concurrent training sequences

In this example, the numbers 1, 2, or 3 are used to indicate different actions being trained. In the serial-training procedure action 1 is trained to criterion across sessions before training begins on action 2. In the example provided for concurrent training, actions 1 and 2 are presented together (in blocks of three trials) across sessions. When criterion performance for action 1 is obtained, action 3 is introduced into the sequence, and so on. *Note that concurrent-training sequences are not the same thing as concurrent task-analysis teaching strategies, where all actions comprising the skill are taught simultaneously.*

Studies using concurrent-task sequencing have shown greater generalization of correct performance to skills within targeted areas that were not directly trained. One of the first investigations to demonstrate this finding was conducted by Schroeder and Baer (1972) in a study that compared serial-versus concurrent-task sequencing in teaching verbal imitation skills to two retarded females. No differences were found between the two procedures in terms of acquisition rate; that is, verbal imitation skills were acquired equally well under both the concurrent- and serial-training conditions. Importantly, however, consistent differences were found in favor of the concurrent-training procedure on measures of generalization to nontrained imitations.

The study by Schroeder and Baer thus demonstrated the advantages of concurrent training in an *intra* task sequencing situation; that is, the content taught was within the same general response class.

A second important study by Panyan and Hall (1978) compared serial-versus concurrent-task sequencing in an *inter*task-training situation. In this study, two nonrelated tasks, tracing letters and verbal imitation, were trained, using either concurrent- or serial-task sequencing procedures with two severely retarded females. Again it was found that there were no differences between procedures in acquisition rates of the two tasks. Again, however, significant differences in generalization to nontrained skills within each task were found in favor of the concurrent-task-sequencing procedure.

COMBINING DISTRIBUTED-TRIAL PRESENTATIONS AND CONCURRENT-TASK SEQUENCING

Discussion thus far has indicated that distributed-trial presentations produce faster acquisition in learning tasks and that concurrent-task sequencing produces greater generalization to nontrained skills within those task areas. The ICS is a strategy that capitalizes on both these strengths by combining distributed-trial presentations with concurrent-task-sequencing procedures. This is accomplished by designing for each student a sequence, or chain, of behaviors that are functionally related in such a way that completion of the first task in the chain logically sets the occasion for the occurrence of the second task, the completion of the second task sets the occasion for the occurrence of the third task, and so on. This, in itself, constitutes a concurrent-task-sequencing procedure, since two or more behaviors are being trained during each session. The entire sequence is then repeated in a second session, a third session, and so on. This aspect of the strategy results in a distributed-trial presentation; that is, trials are repeated across time as they occur within the total sequence of interrelated tasks. This arrangement of combining concurrent-task sequencing and distributed-trial presentations is presented schematically in Figure 8.3.

STIMULUS VARIATION IN THE ICS

Numerous writers have pointed out the importance of systematically varying stimulus presentations when teaching severely handicapped students. Brown, Nietupski, and Hamre-Nietupski (1976) have stated, for example, that "when a student is taught to perform specific skills in response to a particular verbal language cue, the task should not be considered mastered until the student performs the task in response to the

INDIVIDUALIZED CURRICULUM SEQUENCING (ICS) STRATEGY

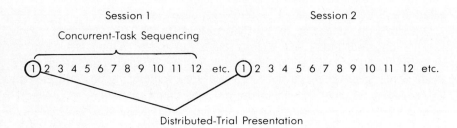

FIGURE 8.3
Schematic of the ICS showing how concurrent-task sequencing is
combined with distributed-trial presentations.

The numbers (1, 2, 3, etc.) represent different actions being trained concurrently in
the sequence. The representation of the same actions (e.g., 1) across sessions
exemplifies a distributed-trial presentation.

other verbal language cues in his natural environment that require the
same response" (p. 13).

Bijou (1980) also stressed the need to avoid using the same verbal cues
when providing instruction to severely handicapped students. He pointed
out that fixed-format instruction may become boring to the student, thus
resulting in an aversive situation that produces behaviors that compete
with the learning objectives. Bijou further noted that fixed instruction promotes rigidity and leaves little room for generalization. Within this context,
it should be noted that one of the strategies identified by Stokes and Baer
(1977) for producing generalization is referred to as *loose training*. This
strategy is a reversal of the usual tactic for producing discrimination
learning. In a loose-training procedure, the teaching process exerts as little
control as possible over the range of cues presented and the actions allowed
in an effort to maximize the potential sampling of relevant dimensions for
transfer to other situations and forms bearing on the class or behavior
being trained (cf., procedures for promoting generalization in Chapter 4).
This implies that during training, systematic variation should occur in
the materials used, the settings or positions where the student is taught,
the number of persons who serve as teachers, and the types of verbal
instruction used.

Thus, in application, the ICS is a teaching strategy that advocates pur-
poseful variation in cue and action conditions while new behaviors are being
acquired by the student. This premise is consistent with the conceptual
basis of the ICS as a strategy that produces both optimal generalization
and new skill acquisition.

PRACTICAL APPLICATION OF THE ICS

FUNCTIONAL-TASK SEQUENCING

Functional-task sequencing involves arranging certain instructional objectives and other behaviors into a chain so that movement through the chain is logical and meaningful to the student. Additionally, skills in the chain should be arranged in a manner that would most closely approximate these same events as they occur naturally in the environment. The chain, as used in this context, is basically the same as a behavioral cluster. Both terms are used to imply the grouping of skills from various content areas in a natural and functional manner.

Characteristics of Sequences. Sequences can be long or short. They can include one or many content areas, depending on instructional objectives and the creative abilities of the instructional personnel to arrange the objectives in a functional and natural order. A short sequence might include, for example, having the student use a walker to go to a certain area in the classroom to select a drink for snacktime. If use of the walker is a priority objective for the student, the sequence could be varied to have her go to other areas in and out of the classroom at appropriate times during the day.

A longer and more complicated sequence might include all of the necessary responses for a student to go to the toilet, make appropriate clothing adjustments during the process, and wash his hands afterwards, as will be illustrated shortly in an example ICS program.

Single-skill Presentation.   Within a sequence, it is often necessary to include training in specific skills that are somewhat unrelated to the other tasks. These isolated behaviors may include the deceleration of inappropriate behavior, or they might include increasing an appropriate behavior that is not functionally related to other tasks in the sequence (like periodically praising a student for keeping his or her glasses on during the session). These single-skill instructions may be incorporated into the sequence at opportune times, thus further serving to remind the teacher to attend appropriately to these behaviors throughout the day.

SELECTING FUNCTIONAL MATERIALS

The next major step in the implementation of the ICS is to identify and locate instructional materials that are both functional and age appropriate for the student. Obviously, there is a preference for objects and materials found in the student's natural environment. It is important also to remember that variations in objects and materials are desirable. For example, in teaching washing skills, the student should be exposed to bars of soap of different colors, shapes, sizes, and fragrances.

IDENTIFYING APPROPRIATE TIME OCCURRENCES

The final major step in implementing the ICS is to identify times during the day in which a particular sequence would be most appropriate. Sequences that involve eating skills should occur around snack times and meals, sequences involving toileting skills should be scheduled at those times when the student is most likely to urinate or have a bowel movement, and so on.

A further elaboration on the procedures for developing an ICS can be found in a publication by Holvoet, Guess, Mulligan, and Brown (1980).

EXAMPLE OF ICS SEQUENCE WITH A DEAF/BLIND STUDENT

Figure 8.4 shows an ICS that was used with a ten-year-old severely retarded student who was totally blind and had a severe hearing loss. The particular sequence presented in the figure is represented by a sample data

STUDENT: Greg				

	Date 12-1-83		12-2-83	
Content Area		AVR		AVR
(Orientation) Go to toilet area (teacher 1).	−	111	−	1
Check Phonic Ear.	+		+	
(Self-help; undressing) Check stereotyped posturing.	+		+	1
Unsnap pants.	−		−	
Unzip pants.	−	1	−	
Take pants down.	+		−	1
Take underpants down.	+		+	
Check Phonic Ear.	+		+	
Check stereotyped posturing.	+		+	
Self-help; toileting) Use of toilet.	−	1	−	
Pull underpants up.	−		−	
(Self-help; dressing) Pull pants up.	+		+	
Zip pants.	−		−	
Snap pants.	−		−	
Check Phonic Ear.	+	1	+	
Check stereotyped posturing.	−		+	
(Orientation) Go to sink.	+		+	1
Turn on water.	+		+	

(Continued)

(Self-help;	Place hands in water.	+		+	
washing)	Wash hands.	−		−	
	Find towel.	−		+	1
	Use towel.	+		+	
	Throw away towel.	−		−	
	Check Phonic Ear.	+		+	
	Check stereotyped posturing.	+		+	
(Orientation)	Go to teacher 2.	−	1	−	
	(Another sequence)				1

FIGURE 8.4

Example data sheet showing total cycle sequencing involving room orientation, undressing, toileting, dressing and hand washing

"Check Phonic Ear" indicates teacher reinforces student if apparatus is in place at that time; "check stereotyped posturing" indicates teacher reinforces student if the posturing position is not occurring at that time. The marks under AVR (any vocal response) indicate the number of times the student vocalized during that particular segment of the sequence. The pluses (+) and minuses (−) indicate the student's performance on each of the identified responses in the sequence. It should also be noted that scoring systems other than + or − are frequently used. A 1, 2, 3 numbering system, for example, might be used to indicate the extent to which the student required physical (and verbal) assistance from the teacher.

sheet. For purposes of illustration, particular content areas are identified for the various skills included in the sequence. The objective, "check Phonic Ear," that appears several times throughout the sequence was necessary because the student frequently took off this apparatus. At the times indicated in the sequence, the teacher would mark a + if the Phonic Ear was in place and a − if the apparatus was taken off. The student was then reinforced and a + was marked. Similarly, this particular student frequently engaged in an unusual stereotyped posture. Again, a + or − mark on the data sheet was used to indicate whether or not the behavior was occurring at specified places in the sequence. If the behavior was not present (+), the student was reinforced. It should be noted that this DRO (cf., Chapter 4) procedure was scheduled at times in the sequence when the student would likely not be engaged in the behavior (while snapping his pants, for example).

This nonverbal student had a low vocal rate. A mutual, or reciprocal imitation procedure was used wherein the teacher would imitate any speech sound spontaneously produced by the student during a session. These sounds and the time they were produced in the sequence were indicated by marking the occurrence of each one under the AVR (any vocal response) column. This procedure allowed the teacher, over time, to determine if there were certain activities that were more likely to produce vocal behavior in the student and, of course, if the behavior was increasing over time.

It should be remembered that each skill area in the sequence represents a training phase within that particular educational objective. Accordingly, a + does not necessarily mean that the objective was independently completed. It does mean that the student successfully engaged in the particular phase of that objective where training was directed. A − indicates that the particular skill (or phase within a skill) was not produced. The teacher would then execute the appropriately designated correction procedure, usually verbal instruction, followed by a physical prompt.

USE OF THE ICS WITH GROUP ACTIVITIES

It is important that severely handicapped students be provided with group activities for developing appropriate social interaction skills, and as a method of promoting better utilization of staff time. A study by Favell, Favell, and McGimsey (1978), for example, demonstrated that group teaching of word recognition with severely retarded individuals produced acquisition rates comparable to individual instruction. Significantly, however, group training proved to be far more efficient in terms of teacher time. The students who were trained in a group acquired considerably more skills in less teacher time than did those students who received individual instruction. Similar results have been found by Storm and Willis (1978), using gross and fine motor tasks. Even more encouraging are the findings by Frankel and Graham (1976) and Goldstein and Alberto (Note 2) who found that group instruction of severely handicapped students in many cases resulted in faster learning than individual instruction.

Brown, Holvoet, Guess, and Mulligan (1980) have presented a detailed description of procedures for extending the ICS strategy to small-group instruction for severely handicapped students. A distinction is made by Brown et al. between two types of group instruction, intrasequential and intersequential. In the simpler *intra*sequential structure, each student's individual programs are sequenced, using the behavior clusters following the ICS format. However, in this type of group, there is no systematic structuring of peer interactions. Each sequence (or cluster) of programs is presented by the teacher, and this involves only the student to whom it is being presented. This structure still allows both for observational learning among other students in the group and for spontaneous interactions that might occur as a result of having two or more students together in close proximity.

An *inter*sequential group structure, as described by Brown et al. (1980), provides for systematic and planned interactions among members of the group. In this type of interaction, a response made by one student serves to cue (or set the occasion) for another student to perform an action. An example of intersequential group interaction is shown in Figure 8.5.

ICS DATA COLLECTION AND ANALYSIS

Data collection procedures using the ICS are quite straight-forward. Scores for each of the content areas in the sequence are taken for each session (cf., Figure 8.4) and then plotted in a manner identical to that described for concurrent chain instruction in Chapter 7. Holvoet et al. (1980) have also presented a data sheet for use with the ICS, which allows the teacher to record progress for each total sequence and also to record (in blocks of 10 trials) the percentage of correct responses for each individual trial behavior in the sequence.

As usual, changes in the students' performance (or the lack thereof) require adjustments in the training programs. Since behaviors are to be sequenced functionally in the ICS, the teacher should also be especially sen-

STUDENT A   STUDENT B

1. "I want (_____)*

                                                      2. Point to named object
                                                      3. Pass object to student A*

4. Receive passed object*

FIGURE 8.5

Example of an intersequential interaction

The asterisks indicate those skills that make up the systematic interaction between students. The numbers represent the order of the intersequential cluster; that is student A has one trial ("I want_____"), student B then has two trials ("Point to named object" and "Pass object to student A", and student A completes the interaction with one trial "Receive passed object").

sitive to how one skill in the sequence effects (either positively or negatively) other behaviors that are chained to that particular skill. This reflects, conceptually, the dynamic intent of the ICS where behaviors should be clustered or sequenced in a manner that accelerates acquisition of skills that are topographically and/or functionally similar.

ADVANTAGES OF THE ICS

The primary purpose for designing the ICS was to make available a teaching strategy that promotes faster learning and better generalization among severely handicapped students. Available literature and research findings tentatively support the type of distributed-trial presentations included in the ICS. More solid research findings (reported earlier) support the concurrent training of skills to increase generalization. Combining distributed-trial presentations and concurrent-task sequencing with deliberate cue variations and functional-task content would seem to represent a logical teaching strategy, according to our present knowledge of the characteristics of the severely handicapped student. There are, however, additional advantages that support use of the ICS. These are described briefly below.

Student Doesn't Miss Program.   The ICS combines in each sequence a number of content areas. Accordingly, the student receives daily training on those skills that might otherwise be missed when individual therapy sessions are canceled because of daytime medical appointments, absences of therapists, and a variety of other classroom interruptions.

Consistency and Communication.   The fact that the ICS incorporates a variety of skill areas from numerous disciplines and professions makes everyone more aware of what skills students have and what skills are being trained. Ideally, any person coming into contact with the student in the classroom and home settings should be taught the skills necessary to implement the program.

Management of Behavior Problems.   As was pointed out in the discussion of the ICS for the deaf/blind student (Figure 8.4), procedures for managing inappropriate behavior can be inserted in the sequence, thus reminding teachers (and others) to systematically use those procedures during the class period.

Reduction of Extrinsic Reinforcers.   Teachers using the ICS have reported a sharp reduction in the need to provide extrinsic reinforcers. This is possible because a functional sequence includes many behaviors that produce inherent motivating effects. Secondly, the chain of different behaviors in the ICS reduces the fatigue and boredom (for both student and teacher) common to massed-training-trial procedures. This results in a lesser need to motivate each behavior with extrinsic reinforcers. The combination of inherently reinforcing actions and fewer extrinsic effects is, of course, more similar to conditions that are present in the natural environment.

Instructional Format Options throughout the Working Program Plan. The ICS strategy provides a vehicle for combining instructional objectives in the working program plan with other behaviors that are not T-Formatted (cf., Chapter 4) as objectives, in a natural sequence that allows for instruction on each objective, whether arranged to occur in either ICS or non-ICS format or both. A teacher may find for example that a dressing skill that was originally T-Formatted for individual instruction actually is showing more rapid acquisition when combined with other objectives and behaviors in an ICS. The teacher may elect, in this case, to teach the dressing skill only in ICS format. Where problems in acquisition occur in the ICS procedure on a specified objective, the teacher may elect to teach the skill as individually T-Formatted or to use a combination of both strategies.

Not all instructional objectives will lend themselves to an ICS procedure, nor will some ICS objectives be better taught with the independent T-Format instructional procedure. The primary advantage to the teacher is the combination of either or both strategies to meet any educational need. Future research will help to shed light on the preselection of some objectives for ICS format and others for individual T-Format. For now, each working program plan should contain a mixture of both for optimal instruction.

SUMMARY

In this chapter, we have discussed two major and interrelated components for developing a functional curriculum for severely multiply handicapped students. In the first section, a model was presented for grouping and sequencing skills for essential content domains (for example, self-help, sensory/motor, communication). Response classes, both functional and topographical, were discussed as a potential method for identifying skill clusters and a training sequence. In the second section of the chapter, we presented a curriculum-sequencing strategy that relates to the teaching of functional skills described in the earlier section. This strategy is offered as a method to incorporate the concurrent training of skills in a more functional manner. Organizing some parts of a total curriculum into skill clusters that combine content domains and individualized sequencing of these clusters is considered critical to the development of a truly functional and effective instructional methodology for this difficult-to-teach population.

CHAPTER 9

The Infant and Preschool Program

Early intervention for severely handicapped infants and young children is the cornerstone of a lifelong education and training process. This process will involve a multitude of professional services interwoven with active parent participation and support. As educators and therapists, we cannot afford to waste any time between the point at which an infant is identified as handicapped and the beginning of the process. As Haring (1976) has stated, "Education must recognize that for the severely handicapped child, programs that begin in infancy are very nearly the main hope: They should be our first priority from today onward" (p. 19).

Using consensus figures for 1977, Hayden (1979) estimated there were 1,636,420 handicapped children ranging in age from birth to three years old. Although a relatively small percentage of these children would be considered severely handicapped, there is little reason to assume that appropriate early intervention services are being provided to them and their families. The Council for Exceptional Children in 1977 (*Exceptional Child Education at the Bicentennial: A Parade of Progress*) estimated that only about 25 percent of preschool handicapped children were receiving appropriate educational services. This estimate is supported by a recent survey reported in Cohen, Semmes, and Guralnick (1979) that shows only four states have mandated programs for handicapped children ages zero to five; an additional seven states have mandated programs for handicapped children ages three to five. In some cases, however, the mandates have not been translated into direct services. A more recent report by Smith (1980) of the Policy Options Project, Council for Exceptional Children, found that twenty-one states had at least one policy document requiring services for some portion of handicapped children, from birth through five years. This report also concluded, however, that there has been a significant reduction of services since the passage of PL 94–142 in 1975. Thus, infant and preschool services for severely handicapped children need to be extended far beyond our present level of commitment.

   The purpose of this chapter is to provide guidelines and directions for
establishing and implementing services to severely handicapped infants
and preschool children. We will discuss the process of interrelating the
educational and treatment objectives of services to fully utilize the input
from the many disciplines that must work together, with parents, to maximize the growth and development of the severely handicapped child.
Parent involvement in early intervention programs is vital to the education
and treatment process. This involvement includes parents as a source of
information, as intervention agents, and always as active members of the
education and treatment team. Two important considerations in early
intervention efforts are the type of education/treatment model used and
the type of delivery model adopted to provide services to both children and
their parents.

A TRANSDISCIPLINARY EDUCATION AND TREATMENT MODEL

The large number of behavioral deficiencies, sensory and motor delays, abnormalities, and delicate health conditions often found in severely handicapped children requires an education/treatment model that enhances the coordination between service providers and parents in early intervention programs. In essence, the education/treatment model must provide cross-pollination of professional expertise and parental knowledge in a manner that bears directly on the particular needs of a specific severely handicapped infant or child. These considerations have prompted many persons (the authors included) to advocate the use of a transdisciplinary model for early intervention with infants and young children who have severe and multihandicapping conditions.

The *transdisciplinary (TD) approach* is an education/treatment team model that effectively integrates program goals and objectives from various disciplines and professions. The integration begins in the assessment process and extends through direct programming efforts. In this approach, each team member is responsible for sharing information and skills so that multiple interventions with the child can occur simultaneously.

A publication by the United Cerebral Palsy Association (Haynes, Patterson, D'Wolf, Hutchison, Lowry, Schilling, and Siepp, 1976) was one of the first to identify the importance of the transdisciplinary approach. This publication also provided staff development procedures for training personnel in the TD process. More recently, McCormick and Goldman (1979), Lyon and Lyon (1980), and Filler (1982) have discussed use of the TD approach with severely handicapped children.

The TD approach evolved from the need to provide a coordinated effort in the treatment and education of severely handicapped children. As Conner, Williamson, and Siepp (1978) stated,

> Just as human development is the coordination and integration of a variety of physical, mental, emotional, and social processes, so must intervention to aid that development be a coordinated and integrated effort. (p. 273)

Thus, the TD approach, originally conceptualized by Dorothy Hutchison, is "a deliberate pooling and exchange of information, knowledge and skills, crossing and recrossing traditional boundaries, by various team members" (p. 2, Haynes et al., 1976).

As a process, the TD approach involves a willingness and motivation among all team members to share information and skills appropriate to the needs of the infant or young child. This willingness implies that all professions and disciplines can best provide services to the child only if each is committed to working as an equal team member in supplying the educational and medical needs of the child.

THREE CHARACTERISTICS OF THE TD APPROACH

Lyon and Lyon (1980) have pointed to three important characteristics of a TD approach. The first assumes a *joint team* effort, implying that a team or group of professionals must perform the various aspects of program delivery together. Second, the TD orientation requires a *staff development* approach. This characteristic points to the need for the team members and parents to train one another, drawing from their particular areas of expertise or information. "To function in a transdisciplinary manner, the members of an educational team need to realize and accept that other individual professionals bring uniquely different experience, information, and skills with them into the group" (Lyon and Lyon, 1980, p. 253).

The third, and perhaps most important characteristic of the TD approach discussed by Lyon and Lyon involves *role release*. Role release provides the mechanism wherein various professions and disciplines teach others (including parents) to implement training procedures and skills that, by tradition, have been considered to be the responsibility of a particular profession or discipline.

As identified by Hutchison (Note 1), "role release is the authorization by a particular discipline:

- for a team member to carry out the learned interventions as program facilitator for a particular individual or individuals as assigned by the team;
- to parents as primary programmers to carry out interventions specific to the needs of their own child following systematic instructions and supervised practice by the program facilitator or selected member of the team" (p. 17)

The term *program facilitator,* as used above, generally refers to any member of the TD team who has the responsibility to coordinate and integrate the delivery of services from several professionals. In many cases, the program facilitator role is assumed by the classroom teacher who typically has the most contact with the severely handicapped child. This role is close to that of the *educational synthesizer* described by Bricker (1976)—a teacher who gathers information from a variety of disciplines and incorporates this information into effective intervention strategies.

Regardless of who assumes the role of program facilitator, the concept of role release among all professional disciplines is central to the TD approach. The program facilitator would have little to facilitate without agreement from other professions and disciplines that, indeed, they do have skills and knowledge that can and should be shared.

As a point of clarification, role release does not imply that professional responsibilities be abdicated. Hutchison made this clear when she noted that professional accountability is not relinquished in the transdisciplinary approach. Team members must remain accountable for what they teach to others and for how well the skills are acquired.

The releasing of roles from one professional to another person can take several forms or levels, each involving a contribution of varying degrees of technical knowledge and expertise. A transdisciplinary model implies differing levels of role release among the participating team members. These levels may, in fact, vary somewhat across teams depending on the skills and composition of the team members.

LEVELS OF ROLE RELEASE

Lyon and Lyon (1980) discuss three levels of role release on an applied basis. Level one involves the sharing of *general information* between members of the TD team (including parents). A speech/language therapist might, for example, share general information on normal language acquisition, a nutritionist might provide information on special diets for children with metabolic dysfunctions, a classroom teacher might provide information regarding classroom schedules, and so on. This general information is shared to increase the understanding and knowledge among team members about basic content within particular discipline areas of expertise.

Level two involves teaching other team members to correctly make specific judgments or decisions. This is referred to as sharing *information skills*. A physical therapist might, for example, teach other team members to recognize when a child is not positioned correctly, a psychologist might help others identify reinforcing items or events for a child, and a nurse might help others recognize when a child is having seizures.

Level three involves sharing *performance competencies* wherein team members teach others to correctly perform overt physical actions. Examples include an occupational therapist training a parent to correctly use the jaw control feeding method to develop independent eating skills, a speech/language therapist instructing other team members how to elicit and reinforce vocal utterances in infants, a teacher training the use of a correction procedure when working with severely handicapped children, or a parent showing other team members how to best stop a child from crying during test periods.

All three levels – general information, information skills, and performance competencies – are central to the TD team approach and the application of the education/treatment model to early intervention programs with severely handicapped infants and young children. Haynes et al. (1976) have described procedures for staff training, using a transdisciplinary approach. They have included in their manual suggestions and processes for achieving various levels of role release among the team members.

SERVICE DELIVERY MODELS USING THE TD APPROACH

The TD approach can be utilized in early intervention efforts in a variety of ways. Importantly, this may vary with the type of service delivery model adopted by a specific agency and with the age of the child.

HOME-BASED INTERVENTION PROGRAMS

The first model to be discussed, the home-based intervention program, is primarily intended for severely handicapped infants being served in the home with the parents as the primary interventionists. This is compared to a school-based model (to be described later) in which the intervention program is primarily conducted in a setting outside the home. It should be pointed out that the distinction between home- and school-based programs is usually not clear-cut since each usually contains components of the other. The distinction here refers to where the *majority* of intervention efforts take place – in the home or in a centralized location. Indeed, a typical program would likely include infants and children receiving services from both models and would include a transition between the two (as discussed later).

This TD model is intended to be highly *individualized*. Campbell (1982), for example, faults earlier transdisciplinary approaches for having fixed treatment teams that engaged each family case whether or not individual members of the team had something to contribute to the case. Campbell calls instead for an individualized team model that brings specific expertise to bear on each individual case as needed. We endorse that approach and suggest that the TD model outlined here will best accomplish that effort. As depicted in Figure 9.1, a facilitator is identified as the person who has primary responsibility for assisting the parents to implement the home-based intervention program. The facilitator could, of course, be any member of the TD team. The heavy lines in Figure 9.1 emphasize the flow of information from the various disciplines to the facilitator pertaining to the treatment and educational needs of the infant. The facilitator, in turn, organizes this information into a comprehensive intervention program for the infant, which is primarily implemented through the parents (or primary caregivers).

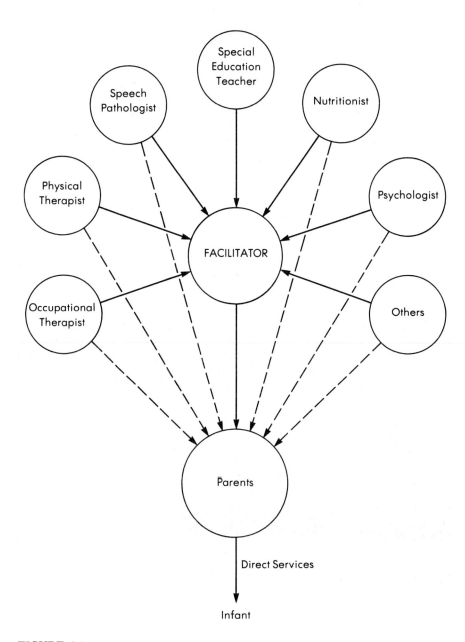

FIGURE 9.1

Transdisciplinary model for providing direct services to severely handicapped infants in the home, using parents as the primary interventionists

It should be noted that a TD approach applied to a particular child does not have to have either the specific disciplines presented in this figure or as many.

Team members may have additional contact with the parents and the infant, as indicated by the broken lines in the figure. Contact would include the initial assessment of the infant by the team member, the monitoring of the progress being made in the intervention program, and the discussion of specific problems requiring more in-depth assistance from a member of a specific discipline or profession. Additionally, the various members of the TD team would monitor the accuracy of the education/treatment information transmitted by the facilitator to the parents.

The TD approach simplifies lines of communication between parents (as the primary intervention providers) and the numerous professions and disciplines ideally involved in an early intervention program. Specific problems or areas of concern are directly communicated to the facilitator who, in turn, has rapid access to the other team members appropriate to the type of problem that is occurring. If, for example, a feeding problem was encountered, the facilitator might contact both the occupational therapist and the nutritionist on the TD team. These team members would then meet with the facilitator, parents, and infant to revise the existing feeding program or develop a new one, if necessary.

An effective TD team for home-based early intervention programs should include a number of disciplines and professions, or at least ready access to their services should be available on a continuing basis. Each of these disciplines would be involved in assessing the infant (discussed later), establishing specific education/treatment objectives, and monitoring programs to maintain effective implementation. Additionally, each member of the team should be willing to release roles to the parents who will implement the intervention. Some of the major disciplines and professions who might be members of the TD team for home-based early intervention efforts with severely handicapped infants and young children are listed below.

Occupational Therapist.   The occupational therapist (OT) is an important team member because many severely handicapped infants will have a varying degree of motor impairments requiring specific exercises and body positioning. The OT is especially important in helping develop appropriate feeding programs for the severely handicapped infant.

Physical Therapist.   The physical therapist (PT) assists in programs to develop gross motor skills, to train in the use and care of special prosthetic and adaptive equipment, and to teach appropriate body positioning and alignment. The PT (and/or OT) can be especially useful in teaching parents how to physically handle and move infants with severe motor impairments and in making suggestions for how the infant should be positioned when speech and other cognitive activities are being trained.

Nutritionist.   A nutrition expert is valuable to the TD team for helping devise special feeding programs and diets for the severely handicapped infant. The nutritionist is especially needed when working with infants who have metabolic disorders (for example, proprionic acidemia) that require special diets.

Special Education Teacher.   A special education teacher who is trained to work with young children who have handicapping conditions is another important member of the team. The teacher can provide assistance in programming for cognitive and sensory motor skills. Involvement of the special education teacher in early intervention efforts for severely handicapped infants is also important for maintaining continuity as the child later advances to preschool programs.

Speech Pathologist.   This member of the team should provide input to parents in procedures and techniques for communication and for facilitating speech and language development.

Psychologist.   The psychologist plays a major role in the early assessment and evaluation of the infant's cognitive skills and development. This team member also should help devise programs and procedures for working with specific behavioral problems (like excessive crying) and for preventing deviant behavior (like self-injurious stereotyped movements).

Nurse.   A pediatric nurse helps parents to deal with continuing medical and health problems often associated with severly handicapping conditions. This would include the daily maintenance and care of special prosthetic devices (like braces), and procedures for the prevention of secondary health problems, such as diaper rash and bed sores.

Other Members of the TD Team.   There are several other professions and disciplines that might be included, depending on the need. A *neurologist* would be involved with infants and preschool children who have seizures, an *ophthalmologist* would be needed for assessing infants suspected of having visual problems, an *audiologist* would be needed for assessing infants with suspected hearing problems, and an *orthopedic specialist* would be important for some infants and children who need braces or corrective surgery. Additional personnel could include a *dentist* or *orthodontist* for teeth and gum problems and a *social worker, family counselor,* or *clergy member* for situations where parents are having difficulties in coping with the problems associated with raising a severely handicapped infant or young child.

Of course team membership will depend on the availability of services in a given area. The important thing is that services to handicapped infants *be provided* and in no case should an infant program fail to be established for want of the comprehensive group of professionals listed here. The ideal of a metropolitan program based at a medical center, however, provides a useful comprehensive framework within which to view a service structure to meet the needs of smaller communities.

SCHOOL-BASED INTERVENTION PROGRAMS

School-based intervention programs are primarily oriented toward providing educational and treatment services for the severely, multiply handicapped child in one particular location. This setting is ideally a community school, but could also be a clinic, a medical facility, or any other physical arrangement that provides classroom space. Infants and young children are brought to the classroom setting on a scheduled basis. There are several advantages to school-based programs that are not available to home-based programs. One of the more prominent advantages is the typically greater accessibility of a variety of professions and disciplines to deliver services. Certainly, the positive features of a transdisciplinary education/treatment model can be more readily implemented in a school-based program.

A second advantage of a school-based program is the opportunity for the parents to receive respite from the day-to-day care of a severely handicapped child. The fact that the child is out of the home for varying periods during the day allows parents to engage in other employment, family and household related activities.

A third advantage of school-based intervention programs is the opportunity for parents to interact regularly with other parents of handicapped children and, thus, share information, concerns, and feelings about the responsibilities associated with their roles. It should also be noted that most school-based programs usually include assisting parents in home care, child management, and skill-development procedures.

Exemplary school-based programs that include infant and preschool severely handicapped children have been implemented at the University of Miami (Bricker, Bricker, Iacino, and Dennison, 1976; Bricker and Iacino, 1977), in Madison, Wisconsin (Vincent and Broome, 1977), in Chicago (Brackman, Fundakowski, Filler, and Peterson, 1977), in New York (Appell, 1982), and in San Francisco (Hanson, 1981). One school-based program using a transdisciplinary model to serve severely, multiply handicapped children up to five years of age has been described by Guess, Jones, and Lyon (Note 2). The model used in this program is similar to the one presented in Figure 9.2.

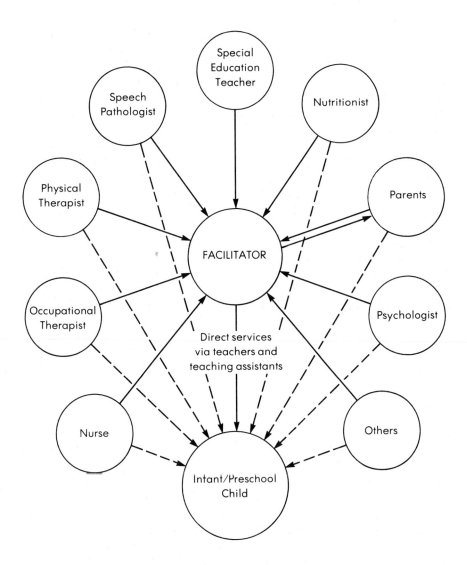

FIGURE 9.2
Transdisciplinary model for providing direct services to severely
handicapped infants/preschool children in a school-based program

This school-based program, which uses an individualized transdisciplinary model, differs in several ways from the one previously presented for infant intervention programs. First, the classroom teacher and teaching assistants assume major responsibility for the direct delivery of services while the child is at the school. This model, of course, is extended when appropriate (and feasible) to the home where parents provide additional training for the child, a process that is conceptualized in the figure by the extra arrow going from the facilitator to the parent. Second, the parents become more formalized members of the transdisciplinary team as increased direct child services are provided by staff members in the school.

TRANSITION FROM HOME- TO SCHOOL-BASED PROGRAMS

The transition from a home- to a school-based intervention model must, first, provide continuity for severely handicapped children and their parents. The continuity is enhanced if members of the school-based team also provide service delivery to the home consistent with the transdisciplinary model presented in Figure 9.1. A member of the school-based team, not necessarily the classroom teacher, should serve as the facilitator to work with parents to provide early intervention in the home. The services for the child are then gradually shifted to the school-based program as early as circumstances permit. It should be pointed out that this transition model makes a rather arbitrary distinction, since, as pointed out earlier, many home-based programs extend from existing school-based locations. The important point is the interfacing of home- and school-based intervention efforts to correspond to the needs of children as they grow older.

The model as proposed (1) provides support to parents who serve as primary early interventionists, (2) extends services of school-based programs into the home at the earliest possible time, (3) moves the infant or young child from the home to the school-based program as soon as possible, and (4) continues to assist parents with home-care problems and home-training programs. The model provides stability and continuity to both parents and children because the same treatment team is working with the child from infancy through the preschool years.

ROLE OF THE TEACHER

School-based programs that use a transdisciplinary model place many responsibilities on the classroom teacher, in addition to those required in more traditional service delivery approaches. It is our contention that the classroom teacher should serve as the facilitator in this model because it is the teacher who has the most extensive and continued contact with the children and their parents.

As the facilitator, the classroom teacher needs to arrange for and organize input from the various disciplines in the screening, assessment, program planning, education/treatment, and evaluation of progress for each child. This requires that the teacher be familiar with what services each discipline has to offer and with how best these services can be utilized in the school-based program. In many respects, the teacher-as-facilitator is analogous to the conductor of an orchestra who sees to it that each section (or team member) is cued at the right time so that each can make a maximum contribution to the total effort. As in the orchestra, all members of the transdisciplinary team must be prepared to make a significant contribution when their skills are required.

WORKING WITH PARENTS

Another major role of the teacher working in a transdisciplinary early intervention setting is to actively coordinate program efforts with parents who are members of the TD team. We discussed earlier the transition from home- to school-based programs in relation to parent involvement. The teacher in the school-based program has the additional responsibility of assisting parents to place their child in a public school classroom when they reach mandated school age. Careful planning is needed in this transition process. The teacher should visit potential classrooms in public school settings with the child's parents. This is necessary to inform the receiving teacher of the child's skills and deficits, and to help identify and secure any additional services that may be needed, such as OT and speech therapy.

In brief, the preschool teacher must remain a strong advocate for the severely handicapped child throughout the infant and preschool years by working with parents in securing needed services in the community at whatever level is required.

CURRICULUM DEVELOPER

Later in this chapter, we will review curriculum approaches with infant and preschool severely handicapped children. At this point, however, it is necessary to mention that a major role of the teacher in school-based programs is to pull together a comprehensive education/treatment program that actively involves the various members of the transdisciplinary team. As a facilitator, the teacher must make sure that the education/treatment program for each child includes those areas where identified behavioral deficits exist, and that the program schedule accurately reflects adequate attention to each deficit area.

INSTRUCTOR

Providing direct instruction to children in the program is, of course, the most important role of the teacher. The skill and expertise demonstrated by the teacher provides a model necessary for a successful intervention effort. Within this context, the teacher must also provide training to teaching assistants who will share a major part of the instructional program. This training should be combined with the areas of role release provided by the other professional members of the transdisciplinary team.

CLASSROOM DESIGN

The classroom design is critical to a successful intervention effort. The design, including needed equipment and supplies, should reflect a physical environment that provides optimal educational opportunities for the children, an efficient organization for staff members working in the setting, and careful attention to the health and safety needs of both children and service delivery personnel.

Probably no two classrooms will be arranged physically in exactly the same way. The design will vary with the size and shape of the room, location of the room within a particular building, the needs of the children being served, and importantly, the funds available for purchase of materials and equipment. There are, however, certain features that should be common to any classroom serving severely handicapped infants and preschool children.

MATERIALS AND EQUIPMENT

A properly designed preschool environment for severely handicapped children needs to include specialized equipment for proper positioning and handling, as well as materials and supplies necessary for any early education environment (toys or mats, for example). Of particular importance is equipment for proper positioning and body alignment, including such items as mats, bolster pillows, wedges, standing tables, support chairs, and adapted wheelchairs. Maloney and Murphy (Note 3) have described a number of standard equipment items important for positioning severely handicapped children, many of which can be economically made by the classroom teacher. They also suggest equipment suitable for playgrounds, mobility training, and transportation needs.

Other types of equipment necessary for specialized training in feeding and toileting may also be needed. Adapted spoons, bowls, plates, and cups for teaching feeding and drinking skills are essential items, as well as adapted potty chairs for toilet training. The manual by Maloney and Murphy describes many of these items and where they can be purchased. Other sources for descriptions of specialized training equipment include Finnie (1975) and Bigge (1982). The book by Finnie is especially useful for suggestions pertaining to specialized equipment for children with cerebral palsy.

When procuring specialized equipment items for the classroom, it is helpful to involve occupational and physical therapists if they are members of the transdisciplinary team. They are needed to match the physical needs of the child with the types of equipment and devices that best promote treatment and education objectives.

Other useful equipment items for a preschool classroom include a refrigerator and stove for food preparation, several child-height tables and chairs for feeding and group instruction, and a number of storage bins so that training and instructional materials for each child can be kept separate from other classmates (a necessary health precaution).

ARRANGING THE CLASSROOM ENVIRONMENT

Jones and Taylor (Note 4) have described, in detail, considerations for arranging the physical environment of classrooms serving severely, multiply handicapped preschool children. Figure 9.3 presents a diagrammatic example of a preschool classroom that includes the major space areas necessary for various components of the instructional program. The design presented is intended to accommodate eight children, one teacher, and two teaching assistants. The reader is referred to Jones and Taylor for a more explicit discussion of the types of activities conducted in each area, as well as more detailed descriptions of materials and equipment included in the classroom environment. It should be cautioned that this example of classroom design depicts a physical arrangement to expedite program implementation in relation to the space available, storage areas, the plumbing arrangement in the room, and the location of doors. The design does not imply that specific types of training should be limited to a certain area of the room. To the contrary, it is important to combine instructional objectives across content areas. This issue will be addressed later, when we discuss approaches.

In the receiving/departing area (Figure 9.3), parents bring and pick up their child each day. The area is equipped and arranged for optimal interaction between parents and staff members. It includes a daily sign-in sheet, a health-check form (to be described later), and a bulletin board to display important information for parents. The area includes shelves for each child to store extra clothes, diapers, and other personal items. As noted in the diagram, there is a storage area located next to the receiving and departing area that may be used for wheelchair/stroller storage. Coat hooks are also located on the wall in the wheelchair storage area.

The individual training area is equipped with appropriate mats, standing tables, bolsters, and wedges. Storage bins for each child are also located in this area as well as cabinets for storing a variety of instructional materials and equipment.

The gross-motor/large-group area, located in the center of the room, contains parallel bars, walkers, therapy balls, bands, and rolls for individual work in large-motor skills. A small-sized (4 feet by 6 feet) water bed, especially made for the classroom, is located there. This area of the room serves for group training when all children are involved in music, art, water play, and other messy activities. The nap and rest area, which includes mats, mobiles, and musical toys, is in a relatively quiet area of the classroom where the traffic flow is kept to a minimum. A toileting and diapering area is enclosed by room dividers and a large clothing bin. It includes potty chairs for toilet training, a diapering table, diaper pails, and other toileting and diapering supplies.

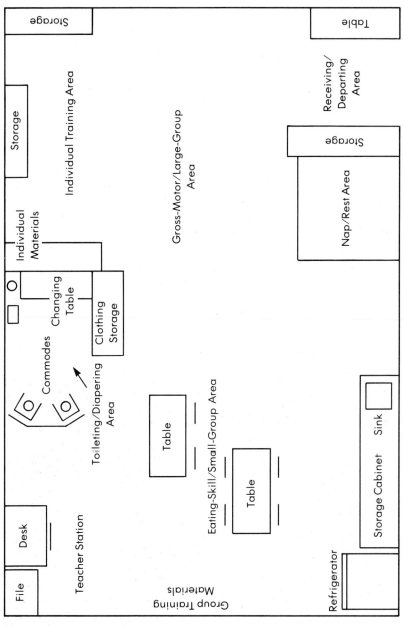

FIGURE 9.3
Physical arrangement of classroom for preschool handicapped children

SOURCE: From Jones and Taylor (Note 4). Used by permission.

A small-group training area is located at the far end of the room and includes tables, chairs, and storage space for instructional materials. It also serves as a feeding area for children in the classroom and is equipped with sink, food storage cabinet, and refrigerator. The far corner of the room includes a filing cabinet and desk for the classroom teacher and teaching assistants.

This diagram of one classroom arrangement for preschool severely handicapped children illustrates the types of instructional areas that should be considered. Obviously, other classrooms will differ, depending on the size and shape of the room. Considerable planning should be undertaken to provide a physical environment that is optimally efficient for both staff members and children. Planning might include a work-up of the classroom design on paper, with cutouts (to scale) of large furniture and equipment items, which can be moved around on the drawing. Team members can then provide suggestions and recommendations for the classroom arrangement. The diagram can also be Xeroxed which will make it possible to design and compare several tentative layouts. These procedures can often save unnecessary moving of large pieces of equipment and furniture.

HEALTH PRECAUTIONS AND EMERGENCY PROCEDURES

Severely handicapped children are especially susceptible to sickness; many of these children have chronic health problems that require continual monitoring. In past years, these delicate health conditions might have discouraged efforts to provide educational opportunities for these children. In fact, a preoccupation with the children's health problems might have overridden needed educational programs. We are not advocating here that the education and treatment of preschool handicapped children should take place in sterile, hospital-type environments. What we are proposing is that some common sense health precautions and emergency procedures will reduce certain health hazards, thereby providing an environment in which the task of education can be more fully realized. It is our experience that some simple and easily administered health precautions undertaken in the classroom setting reduces absenteeism resulting from illness among children and staff members.

Jones and Taylor (Note 4) have discussed a number of medical and health related procedures pertinent to preschool classrooms for severely handicapped children. Their suggestions include procedures for disinfecting classroom materials and equipment and for maintaining a sanitary classroom environment. Most of these recommendations can be implemented easily in the classroom, provided that all staff members participate in the procedures.

Recommendations include removal of shoes by an person entering the classroom beyond the receiving/departing area (see Figure 9.3), the convenient placing of disinfectant supplies in the various areas of the classroom (and out of reach of the children), individual bins for separately storing each child's instructional materials, and designating times and situations when staff members are required to wash their hands. A health check is also given to all children when they arrive in the morning for class. Staff members have been trained by the classroom nurse to check each child on arrival, using the guidelines found in Table 9.1. When conditions are suspect, the nurse is called in for consultation, and if warranted, the parents are requested to take their child home.

Emergency procedures should be included as another important component of the classroom design for preschool severely handicapped children.

TABLE 9.1
Health Check Guidelines

	Normal Findings	*Suspect Findings*
Hair	Smooth, resilient texture	Dry, coarse, brittle texture, bald spots, white flakes.
Scalp	Smooth, pale or pink	Crusty; flaky, bright pink or red patches.
Eyes/eyelids	White sclera; pink conjunctivae	Yellow or pink sclera, drooping eyelids; red conjunctivae; discharge, crusting.
Nose	Pink mucous membrane	White or yellow discharge.
Lips	Pink and moist	Dry, red; swelling, cracking, especially at corners.
Mouth/throat	Pink, smooth mucous membranes	White patches, red and inflamed membranes.
Neck	Musculature and bony structures palpable	Nodules or bumps behind or in front of ears, under chin, sides of neck.
Skin		
Color	Individual variations	Pallor, flushing, yellow tinge or blush.
Texture	Springy	Dry, flaking, does not spring back.
Temperature	Individual variations	Warm over face, abdomen, back.
Lesions	None	Rashes over face, abdomen, back (particularly suspect).

SOURCE: From Jones and Taylor (Note 4). Used by permission.

In this case, preplanning is essential. It is recommended that all classroom personnel have first-aid training, with special emphasis on emergency procedures for handicapping conditions (for example, using a suction machine or handling seizures). Each staff member also should be familiar with the special health problems of each child (heart disorders, food allergies, respiratory problems, shunts, and so on). Much of this information can be included in a health information alert that is made available to all staff members. Figure 9.4 shows one type of health information form presented by Jones and Taylor for use in preschool settings.

A medical treatment authorization form (Figure 9.5) is also important. This form authorizes classroom personnel to contact appropriate medical persons in case of an emergency. The form, signed by the child's parents or legal guardians, also helps protect classroom personnel from possible liability in emergency situations.

The classroom emergency procedures should be planned in consultation with the school nurse and parents of the children. All staff members, including nonteaching personnel, need to be well acquainted with the emergency procedures.

SCREENING AND ASSESSMENT

The screening and assessment process described here is applicable to severely handicapped infants being served in the home or in school by a transdisciplinary team. In either case, the process involves active participation by all members of the team. For infants being served in the home, the purpose is to identify the severity of the handicapping condition through an initial screening process, and then to conduct a more intensive evaluation to determine areas where remedial education/treatment are most needed. The screening process for a school-based program is designed to identify potential students for the classroom. In many cases, it may be necessary to screen out more capable candidates who should be referred to other preschool programs.

SCREENING

A screening session for an infant or young child can be completed in a relatively short time by a few members of the transdisciplinary team. Ideally, any member of the team should be able to conduct the screening, provided that role-release among professionals has taken place in accordance with the transdisciplinary model. Parents participate whenever possible in the screening session.

The primary purpose of the screening is to appraise the child's sensory, motor, and cognitive skills. This initial evaluation provides the framework

```
+------------------------------------------------------------------+
|                     HEALTH INFORMATION                           |
+------------------------------------------------------------------+
| Child's Name: _____   Birth Date: _____ |
|                                                                  |
| Physician's Name:_____|
|                                                                  |
| Physician's Address:  _____   Telephone: _____ |
|                                                                  |
| Specialty Clinics                                                |
|                                                                  |
|   Neurology:  _____   Ophthalmology:_____|
|                                                                  |
|   Orthopedic: _____   Other: _____ |
|                                                                  |
|   Cardiology: _____                                  |
|                                                                  |
| Medical History                                                  |
|                                                                  |
|   Diagnosis: _____|
|                                                                  |
|   Major Illnesses/Hospitalizations: _____|
|                                                                  |
| Chronic Illnesses and Health Problems                            |
|                                                                  |
|   Seizures (type and frequency): _____|
|                                                                  |
|   _____ |
|                                                                  |
|   Orthopedic Abnormalities: _____|
|                                                                  |
|   Heart Disease: _____|
|                                                                  |
|   Respiratory Disease: _____|
|                                                                  |
|   Sensory Deficits: _____|
|                                                                  |
|   Nutritional Problems:_____|
|                                                                  |
|   Allergies: _____|
|                                                                  |
|   Bladder/Bowel Habits: _____|
|                                                                  |
|   Other:_____ |
|                                                                  |
| Current Medications                                              |
|            Name            Dosage            Time                |
|   _____ |
|                                                                  |
|   _____ |
+------------------------------------------------------------------+
```

FIGURE 9.4

Health information form for preschool classroom serving severely handicapped children

SOURCE: From Jones and Taylor (Note 4). Used by permission.

MEDICAL TREATMENT AUTHORIZATION

Child's Name: _____   Physician: _____

Birth Date: _____   Physician's Phone: _____

Parent's Name: _____

Address: _____   Home Phone: _____

Business Phone: _____

Person to contact if parent cannot be reached: _____

1. _____   Phone: _____

2. _____   Phone: _____

   I authorize the preschool staff to take whatever emergency medical measures deemed necessary for the protection of my child while s/he is at school. I understand that this authorization includes contacting the pediatrician, implementing his/her instructions, and transporting my child to the emergency room if necessary, without first obtaining my consent.

Parent Signature: _____

Date: _____

FIGURE 9.5
Emergency medical treatment authorization form used in a preschool classroom for severely handicapped children

SOURCE: From Jones and Taylor (Note 4) Used by permission.

for more intensive follow-up assessments, as well as a strategy for coordinating members of the team so that priority areas for assessment can be identified and scheduled.

A number of developmental screening instruments are available for infants and preschool age children. Table 9.2 presents several examples, along with the age ranges for which they were intended and the time required to administer the instruments. Figure 9.6 presents an initial screening form for preschool severely, multiply handicapped children that is used at the University of Kansas (Jones and Rues, Note 5). This screening test is easily administered in about thirty minutes, and it provides information concerning gross-motor development, environmental interactions with objects, and communication skills. It should be cautioned that these

TABLE 9.2
Developmental Screening Tools

Instrument	Age Range	Time Required
The Boyd Developmental Progress Scale Robert D. Boyd, Ph.D. Inland Counties Regional Center, Inc. 808 North Arrowhead Avenue San Bernadino, California 92401	Birth to 8 years	10 minutes
The Denver Developmental Screening Test W.K. Frankenberg and J.B. Dodds LADOCA Project and Publishing Foundation East 51st Avenue and Lincoln Denver, Colorado 80216	Birth to 6 years	30 minutes
Developmental Screening Inventory Developmental Screening Supplement H. Knoblock and B. Pasamanick Developmental Diagnosis Harper and Row, New York	Birth to 6 years	20 minutes
Guide to Normal Milestones of Development Una Haynes U.S. Government Printing Office	Birth to 3 years	15 minutes
Minnesota Child Development Inventory Behavior Science Systems, Inc. P.O. Box 1108 Minneapolis, Minnesota 55440	Birth to 6 years	15 to 30 minutes

SOURCE: From Jones and Rues (Note 5). Used by permission.

RESPONSE	COMMENTS

Child's Name: Participants:

Birth Date:

Date of Screening:

MOTOR	

Place the child in prone:

_____ 1. Does child raise head from floor?

_____ 2. Does child maintain head control?

_____ 3. Does child prop on forearms?

_____ 4. Does child use arms in prone?

_____ 5. Does child roll to supine? Describe assistance needed:

Place the child in supine:

_____ 1. Does child maintain head control?

_____ 2. Does child have free use of arms?

_____ 3. Does child roll to sidelying? Describe assistance needed:

_____ 4. Does child maintain sidelying?

_____ 5. Does child push from sidelying to sitting? Describe assitance needed:

Place the child in a sitting position:

_____ 1. Does child require support? Describe:

_____ 2. Does child maintain head control?

_____ 3. Does child maintain trunk control?

_____ 4. Does child stand up from sitting? Describe assistance needed:

FIGURE 9.6
Initial Screening Form for a Preschool Serving Severely, Multiply Handicapped Children

Place the child in a standing position (if possible):

_____ 1. Does child require support? Describe:

_____ 2. Does child bear weight correctly?

_____ 3. Does child take steps or cruise?

RESPONSE TO ENVIRONMENT

Place several toys on the floor near the child:

_____ 1. Does child look at the toys?

_____ 2. Does child reach and touch the toys?

_____ 3. Does child track objects? How many degrees?

_____ 4. Does child imitate movement with a toy?

_____ 5. Does child imitate motor movement? Describe:

_____ 6. Does child respond to sounds?

_____ 7. Does child make vocalizations? Describe:

_____ 8. Does child respond to his/her name?

_____ 9. Does child respond to directives? Describe:

SUMMARY

1. Behaviors that may facilitate instruction:

2. Behaviors that may interfere with instruction:

3. Possible positive consequences:

4. Means of locomotion:

Team Recommendation: _____ Placement for Evaluation

_____ Referral to Other Agency

FIGURE 9.6
(Continued)

screening devices are not assessment and evaluation tools; they provide only gross indicators of skill development.

ASSESSMENT

The assessment process that follows the initial screening is again accomplished best through a transdisciplinary model, actively involving all members of the treatment/education team. Assessment sessions provide an ideal opportunity for team members to jointly evaluate the child and share information during the process – information that will ultimately be used in determining education/treatment objectives (the child's IEP and working program plan, as discussed in Chapters 5 and 6).

Jones and Rues (Note 5) have presented a diagram showing the relationship between screening, assessment, and the IEP program for severely multiply handicapped children. This process, shown in Figure 9.7, involves several major components.

The Assessment Procedure.   First, the initial screening is used to identify skills and performance deficits. From the screening, areas of further assessment are placed in priority, and the discipline-specific evaluations are scheduled. If, for example, the screening session indicated severe problems in the area of gross-motor development, then this would emerge as a high-priority area in the assessment process. Attempts would be made to schedule this evaluation at an early date by members of the team who have expertise in gross-motor development. If feeding problems were indicated to be severe during the initial screening, then more extensive evaluations might be scheduled for the team's nutritional expert and occupational therapist. Results from the discipline-specific evaluations are then summarized and combined with findings from the original screening session to plan and conduct a future, more global assessment of the child.

The next step of the assessment process is to administer tests that are designed to provide a wider appraisal of the child's abilities and deficits and to form instructional objectives. In many situations, even more specialty assessments (such as audiology, neurology) are recommended, following the general assessment process. These further assessments may involve professions and disciplines not actively represented on the transdisciplinary team.

General Assessment Instruments.   Professionals serving severely handicapped infants and young children are acutely aware by now of the fact that current assessment instruments are not very suitable for this population. In most cases, traditional developmental scales and check lists are not sensitive to the behaviors exhibited by the young severely handicapped child. The behavioral descriptions found in these scales are too gross to

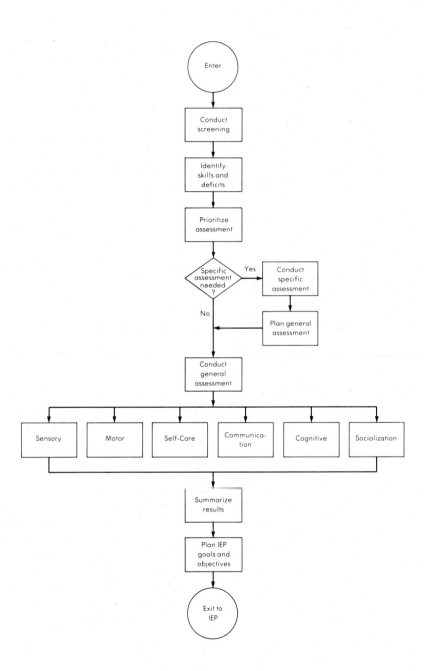

FIGURE 9.7
Relationship of assessment to screening and IEP development

SOURCE: From Jones and Rues (Note 5). Used by permission.

detect the relatively small changes in behavior typical of a severely handicapped child. Additionally, most developmental scales and check lists are based on the developmental milestones of nonhandicapped children. As mentioned earlier, it cannot be assumed that severely handicapped children follow a normal developmental sequence.

A distinction also needs to be made between criterion-referenced curricula and formal assessment instruments. The former include assessment instruments that are directly related to the identification and selection of program objectives. These assessment-linked curricula will be discussed in the next section. Formal assessment instruments provide an overall evaluation of the child, but do not directly specify instructional objectives that are based on the outcome of the evaluation. These assessment scales provide important information about the child that can be used with discipline-specific evaluations to determine intervention needs. Following are short descriptions of two of these assessment instruments.

The *Bayley Scales of Infant Development* (Bayley, 1969) is a standardized scale of assessing cognitive and motor development up to thirty months of age. The scale includes 82 motor and 163 cognitive items that are arranged in a normal developmental sequence. The assessment requires direct observation of the child combined with parental report. Some training is required for a valid administration of the instrument. As reported in a survey of preschool programs by Lowry (Note 6), the Bayley remains one of the most frequently used instruments for assessing handicapped infants and young children. This occurs in spite of the fact that many of the items are too high for the typical severely, multiply handicapped infant or young child.

The *Callier-Azusa Scale* (Stillman, 1975) is a nonstandardized assessment instrument that is specifically intended for deaf-blind and multiply handicapped children. It includes major sections for assessing direction following, motor development, perceptual abilities, daily living skills, language development, and socialization. The items in the scale follow a normal developmental sequence and are assessed through direct observation of the child by a person who is very familiar with the child's behavior.

A third assessment system, the *Consortium of Adaptive Performance Evaluation* (CAPE) System, was discussed in some detail in Chapter 5.

CURRICULUM APPROACHES FOR INFANTS AND PRESCHOOL CHILDREN

TRADITIONAL DEVELOPMENTAL MODELS

Curricula for infant and preschool programs for severely handicapped students typically follow a developmental model. The basic assumption of such a model is that the normal sequence of development provides the most logical ordering of instructional objectives and suggests behaviors appropriate for educational goals. As stated by several authors, a developmental curriculum is central to the overall goal of early intervention by providing intervention to allow handicapped children to follow normal development as closely as possible (Allen, 1976, 1978; Gentry and Adams, 1978; Haring and Bricker, 1976; and Hayden, McGinnes, and Dmitriev, 1976). Haring and Bricker contend that the developmental model is reasonable because information currently available (Bricker and Bricker, 1974; Bricker, Vincent-Smith, and Bricker, 1973; Hayden and Dmitriev, 1975; Hayden and Haring, 1976; and Miller and Yoder, 1974) suggests quantitative, not qualitative, differences in development among handicapped and nonhandicapped young children.

Proponents of the developmental model acknowledge that the model may not constitute the complete infant and preschool curriculum. For example, Bricker, Bricker, Iacino, and Dennison (1976) note that a "corrective strategy," decelerating maladaptive or undesirable behaviors, may need to be employed to support efforts in a developmental curriculum. Allen (1978) mentions that a developmental sequence should be used cautiously since severely handicapped children may arrive at normal milestones via atypical routes; and Hayden, McGinnes, and Dmitriev (1976) suggest that in addition to the developmental sequence, behavior described as *tool skills* (skills critical for learning more advanced skills, such as imitation) should be included in the infant/preschool curriculum. The importance of including objectives that are of immediate and functional use, meeting the "criterion of ultimate functioning" (Brown, Nietupski, and Hamre-Nietupski, 1976), was mentioned as a curricular consideration supplementary to the developmental model by Gentry and Adams (1978) but was deemphasized since it was felt that the "normal" developmental sequence *is* functional for the young, severely handicapped population.

The emphasis of the developmental model is on the specification of content and the selection of instructional objectives, rather than on intervention strategies for achieving those instructional objectives. Within the developmental model, content is specified according to categories of behaviors, generally referred to as *content domains*. Gross motor, fine motor, language/communication, social, self-help, and cognition are the common content domains. A detailed listing of behaviors for each content domain sequenced in the order of "normal" acquisition serves as the assessment for a developmental curriculum, and the first few assessment items failed by a child in each content domain are targeted as instructional objectives. In this way, the developmental sequence serves as both an assessment sequence and a guide for selecting appropriate instructional objectives. Since assessments and curricula are closely related and are frequently the *same* listing of behaviors, the developmental model is often characterized as an "assessment-linked" curriculum (Bricker, Bricker, Iacino, and Dennison, 1976; Gentry and Adams, 1978).

Instructional programming within the developmental model may utilize systematic behavioral procedures. Targeted objectives for each content domain are task analyzed. Each step of the task analysis is then operationalized in precise, measurable terms and specified to criterion; antecedent arrangements, cues, consequences and contingency ratios, and number of trials per session are defined; and data are collected on a continuous basis for the purpose of monitoring behavioral change and indicating the need for programmatic changes (Bricker, Siebert, and Casuso, 1980; Gentry and Adams, 1978).

A large number of developmental curricula are available in the literature and for purchase. A few examples that are commonly used include: (1) the *Learning Accomplishment Profile for Infants* (Griffin, Sanfad, and Wilson, 1975); (2) the *Behavior Repertoire for Handicapped Infants* (Gentry, Adams, Andrew, Chandler, Freedman, Kelley, Livingston, Robinson, Rusch, Stade, and VanderVeer, 1977); (3) *Teaching Your Down's Syndrome Infant: A Guide for Parents* (Hanson, 1977); and (4) *Developmental Programming for Infants and Young Children* (Schaefer and Moersch, 1977). Such curricula generally include a listing of developmental sequences divided by content domains, specific instructions for use of the sequences as assessments, and activity and/or programming suggestions corresponding to each behavior listed in the developmental sequence. Often it is left up to the teacher to develop the systematic programs for individual children. The activities and/or programs included in the curriculum are only provided to serve as suggestions or examples.

Variations of the Developmental Model. In addition to the traditional developmental curricula, such as those listed above, some variations of the developmental model are available. Connor, Williamson, and Siepp (1978) in the *Program Guide for Infants and Toddlers with Neuromotor and Other Developmental Disabilities* suggest four approaches to programming within the developmental curriculum. These are the use of "(a) sequential task analysis, (b) a major activity and its possible consequences across developmental areas, (c) integrated activities meeting multiple objectives, and (d) multiple interventions to meet a general behavioral objective" (p. 275). The use of "integrated activities" acknowledges that skills do not develop in isolation from one another, even though they may be categorized by content domains for programmatic purposes. The authors provide several examples of integrated activities. One example given is as follows:

motor: Place Kathy in an upright, symmetrical sitting position in an infant seat, pillow at nape of neck to provide flexion.

pre-speech: Use jaw control . . . to encourage lip closure over spoon presented in midline. (Caution: Initially, jaw control should be used only once during the day to avoid frustration for mother and child. Later it may be gradually increased until it is used for each meal.)

language: Introduce the concept of "more" by saying the word just prior to moving the food toward her mouth; talk to Kathy about the food and her eating during the meal

social-emotional: Encourage the mother to use mealtime to establish interaction with Kathy and to note Kathy's evidences of pleasure (e.g., smiling, eye contact) upon eating food of various textures, consistencies, and flavors. (p. 294)*

This guide, however, does not include developmental sequences, but refers the reader to other sources to obtain them. Systematic programming is not stressed, but sample program forms included in the appendix of the guide suggest the use of behavioral procedures.

A second variation of the traditional developmental curriculum, which was influenced by the Piagetian model, is the developmental interaction model (Bricker, Seibert, and Casuso, 1980), referred to elsewhere as the constructive interaction adaptation model (Bricker and Bricker, 1974; Bricker, Bricker, Iacino, and Dennison, 1976; Bricker, Dennison, and Bricker, Note 7). This model is based on three tenets: (1) development proceeds from simple to complex, (2) development follows a sequential hierarchy, and (3) development requires the production of disequilibrium in order to proceed.

In this model, developmental assessments, such as those previously listed, are recommended for evaluating the children and for targeting objectives. However, an additional assessment suggested is the Uzgiris-Hunt Scales of Psychological Development (Uzgiris and Hunt, 1975), or a comparable assessment that outlines cognitive development as conceptualized by Jean Piaget (1952, 1954, and 1962, in Bricker, Seibert, and Casuso, 1980). Instructional objectives in the cognitive domain based on the Piagetian sequence are central to this developmental curriculum and are absent from most other developmental curricula.

Instructional programming is also modified to accommodate the Piagetian influence. Major emphasis is placed on the arrangement of antecedent events and the structuring of the environment, rather than on reinforce-

---

*Reprinted from Frances P. Connor, G. Gordon Williamson and John M. Siepp, *Program Guide for Infants and Toddlers with Neuromotor and Other Developmental Disabilities.* (New York: Teachers College Press, ©1978 by Frances P. Connor, John M. Siepp and G. Gordon Williamson), pp. 275 and 294.

ment and other consequent events (although reinforcement is not completely eliminated). The goal in arranging antecedent events is to produce conflict in the child and, thereby, create what Piaget has termed *disequilibrium.* The discomfort of being in the psychological state of disequilibrium "motivates" the child to respond in an effort to restore equilibrium, a basic psychological process in Piaget's developmental theory. Bricker et al. (1980) emphasize that environmental interaction is a critical dimension of the developmental interactive model, for it is the environment that is the source of disequilibrium, and it is only through interaction with the environment that equilibrium can be restored. An example of this principle may be observed in the teaching of *object permanency,* that is, the concept that objects still exist even though they may be out of sight. In teaching this concept, a child's favorite toy might be covered up by a cup or cloth material. This provides a source of discomfort, or disequilibrium, that motivates the child to seek out the toy through interaction with the environment and, thus, re-establish psychological equilibrium.

Lastly, this Piagetian model emphasizes that assessment, selection of objectives, and the formulation of programs should take into consideration the interrelationships among behaviors within and across content domains. It is suggested that lattices (Bricker, Bricker, Iacino, and Dennison, 1976; Bricker and Iacino, 1977; and Woolman, Note 8) be constructed, based on existing knowledge of child development, to be used as maps to illustrate the interrelationships. The lattice also serves as a curriculum tool that assists the teacher in following the order of the developmental sequence in training and in program planning (Bricker and Iacino, 1977). An example of a language training lattice is presented in Figure 9.8.

The major difference between the developmental interactive curriculum approach and other developmental curricula lies in the area of targeting objectives and formulating programs. In the developmental interactive curriculum, actual program implementation follows a systematic behavioral approach.

REMEDIAL CURRICULUM MODELS

The remedial cuurriculum model assumes that severely handicapped children are different from normally developing children and the normal sequence of development does not necessarily describe the most logical ordering of instructional objectives for intervention (Guess, Sailor, and Baer, 1977b). Additionally, instructional objectives that might be chosen as "appropriate," based on a developmental curriculum, may have little relevance and may not be functionally useful to the child. A case in point: in describing the *Developmental Programming for Infants and Young*

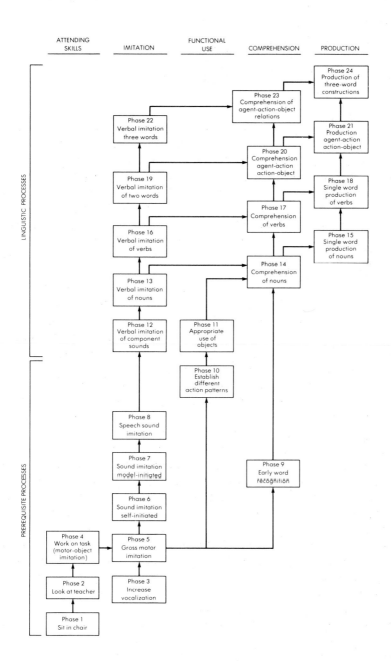

FIGURE 9.8
Language training lattice

SOURCE: From Bricker, Dennison, and Bricker (Note 7). Used by permission.

Children, the developmental curriculum by Schafer and Moersch, eds. (1977), an example of an item that might be selected as an instructional objective was "uses ulnar-palmar prehension." This is an acceptable goal within the developmental curriculum model, but it is probably unacceptable in a remedial curriculum. A remedial curriculum requires that the objective be functional, that is, of practical use to the child; the ulnar-palmar grasp is a very awkward grasp that, in spite of its occurrence in normal development, is rarely useful in tasks requiring grasping. The radial-palmar grasp (fingers extended with partial thumb opposition) would be selected as the objective in the remedial curriculum since it would have relevant application to other skills, such as holding a spoon for self-feeding. A remedial curriclum may draw from developmental data, but the ultimate selection of curricular objectives is based on relevance and usefulness to the child in relation to the environment.

Two remedial curriculum models that are compatible with one another are currently under development: (1) an approach emphasizing the criteria of the next educational environment (Vincent, Salisbury, Walter, Brown, Gruenewald, and Powers, 1980), and (2) the individualized curriculum-sequencing model (based upon the curriculum considerations described in Chapter 8).

Criteria of the Next Educational Environment.   This curricular approach is an outgrowth of the philosophy of the criterion of ultimate functioning (Brown, Nietupski, and Hamre-Nietupski, 1976), which focuses on skills needed by severely handicapped adults to perform productively and independently in the community. The criterion of ultimate functioning is difficult to apply to infants and preschoolers because objectives formulated from this principle would be so distant (temporally) that they would be irrelevant and essentially nonfunctional. Therefore, the principle was extended downward as the *criteria of the next educational environment,* that is, the public school kindergarten. LeBlanc, Etzel, and Domash (1978, in Vincent et al., 1980) recommended that future environmental settings be taken into consideration when setting goals for handicapped preschoolers.

The criteria of the next environment principle has implications for both the content and the instructional methodology components of curriculum. Vincent et al. (1980) provide evidence that developmental assessments and standardized intelligence tests cannot predict success or failure in a regular kindergarten placement. Research suggests that preacademic skills are only a small portion of the requirements for a handicapped child's success in regular kindergarten; "survival skills" (social/behavioral) are the more critical skills that determine success or failure in the next environment. Survival skills consist of such behavior as compliance, attending, social interaction, and following directions.

Vincent and her colleagues (Vincent et al., 1980) are presently engaged in four strategies for the purpose of identifying the skills required for kindergarten. These strategies are (1) kindergarten try-outs, (2) follow-up, (3) kindergarten teachers generating skills, and (4) objective measurement (cf., Vincent et al., 1980, for a complete description of these strategies). The first two strategies, try-outs and follow-up, resulted in pinpointing the critical importance of the survival skills. Try-outs include temporarily placing the child in a kindergarten classroom; follow-up consists of providing feedback to preschool teachers pertaining to academic and social skills areas where additional training is needed for successful placement of children in a kindergarten setting. The third strategy, teachers generating skills, helped broadly define the survival skills for kindergarten. This strategy has kindergarten teachers identify critical skills necessary for successful kindergarten placement. The final strategy of objective measurement is being used to more precisely specify and quantify the survival skills. This strategy requires direct observation of kindergarten classes to identify behaviors that frequently occur and that are essential to performing well in these settings. The objective measurement has resulted in a survival skill check list that is currently being field tested.

In addition to identifying survival skills as a critical content domain in infant and preschool programs, the criteria of the next educational environment principle has implications for instructional methodology. The precision teaching that characterizes instructional methodology for the severely handicapped does not occur in regular kindergartens. Vincent et al. (1980) suggest two ways to modify the instructional environment of special education in consideration of the next environment: (1) gradual modification of the special education environment to approximate the kindergarten, and (2) modification of the special education teacher's behavior to approximate the regular kindergarten teacher's behavior.

The authors note that this is only the beginning of the strategy of the criteria of the next environment. Much research and more data are still needed to further specify and validate the model. Included in this research should be procedures that also help nonhandicapped children to better interact with their handicapped peers. It might be argued, for example, that regular kindergarten classes have more freedom and opportunity for change. Thus, successfully preparing handicapped children for this type of setting is best accomplished when kindergarten classes are changed to better accommodate handicapped children coming into them.

Individualized Curriculum-Sequencing Model. Another remedial approach to curriculum has been developed and implemented at the University of Kansas. This model follows the functional curriculum considerations described earlier in Chapter 8. The implementation of the model with severely multiply handicapped preschool children has been described in detail by Bronicki, Holvoet, and Guess (Note 9). The model presents a strategy for developing individual curricula for each child in a manner that systematically plans for response generalization and emphasizes environmentally functional skills. The model also uses a distributed- rather than massed-trial format as also discussed in Chapter 8.

The *individualized curriculum-sequencing (ICS) model* for the preschool setting described by Bronicki et al. (Note 9) is interfaced with a transdisciplinary education/treatment approach. Assessments from the various team members are translated into specific teaching objectives. These objectives are then placed in priority to meet the needs of each child. A training program for each objective is designed, following typical task-analysis procedures. Following this, the objectives are located along an activities matrix sheet. The matrix identifies activities and events that offer appropriate opportunities for the behavior to be trained in a functional manner.

From the activities matrix, individual curriculum sequences are developed. These sequences combine skill training across content areas in a logical manner so that one behavior (or response) leads to the next behavior in the training sequence. Some examples of sequences are presented in Table 9.3. These sequences show training programs conducted in both 1:1 and small group settings.

It is important to note that the training sequences can be repeated at various times throughout the day, and that high-priority objectives can be included in two or more training sequences. Additionally, the sequences can be conducted by two or more persons (including parents) to further enhance generalization. The fact that a transdisciplinary approach allows for role release among professions and disciplines makes it possible for numerous persons to conduct training that combines content skills from the various team members.

The compatibility of the individualized curriculum-sequencing model with the remedial model based on the criteria of the next educational environment (Vincent et al., 1980) is worthy of comment. Two of the defining characteristics of the individualized curriculum-sequencing model, functionality and emphasis on the use of naturally occurring discriminative stimuli, also typify the model of the next educational environment. The definition of functionality, including age appropriateness and a consideration for present and future environments, is of optimal concern in planning for entry into a regular kindergarten; and the use of natural discriminative stimuli is supportive of the recommendation of Vincent et al. (1980) to approximate the kindergarten environment within the special education program.

TABLE 9.3

Sample Sequences in a Child's Daily Schedule.

Period: 9:30–10:00
Trainer: Nurse or teacher aide
Activity: Arrival: Health check
Setting: 1:1; Classroom entrance

Program	Cue	Action
Vocal Imitation	"Say 'up.'"	Imitates "up" within 5 seconds
Standing	"Stand up"; prompt hips.	Pulls to stand within 10 seconds
Standing	"You're standing"; prompt hips.	Maintains supported standing 1 minute.
Obj. Discrimination	2-choice obj.; "Find baby."	Touches doll within 5 seconds.
Vocal Imitation	"Say 'baby.'"	Imitates "ba-ba" within 5 seconds.
Obj. Discrimination	2-choice obj.; "Finds comb."	Touches comb w/in 5 seconds
Vocal Imitation	"Say 'comb.'"	Imitates "om" within 5 seconds.

Period: 10:00–10:20
Trainer: Teacher aide
Activity: Making snack
Setting: Small group; seated at table

Program	Cue	Action
Obj. Discrimination	Holding 2 objects; "Give me baby."	Hands trainer doll within 10 seconds.
Obj. Discrimination	Holding 2 objects; "Give me comb."	Hand trainer comb within 10 seconds.
Accelerate Activity Participation	"Do this."	Participates in activity.
Decelerate Tantrums	Behavior tantrum	No crying, whining, or tantrums for 5 minutes.
Accept Liquid	"Take drink"; tip fluid into mouth	Maintains head in midline & hands down without crying.
Vocal Imitation	"Want comb? Say 'om.'"	Imitates "om" within 5 seconds.
Vocal Imitation	"Say 'baby.' Say 'ba-ba.'"	Imitates "baba" within 5 seconds.

The sequences were derived from the activities matrix that identified training objectives in relation to classroom opportunities for the behaviors to occur. The "cue" indicates stimuli (verbal or nonverbal) provided by the trainer. The "action" indicates student behavior.

Additionally, the individualized curriculum-sequencing model reported by Bronicki et al. also teaches skill clusters discussed earlier in variations of the developmental model described by Connor, Williamson, and Siepp (1978) and the Piagetian model of Bricker, Siebert, and Casuso, 1980.

SUMMARY

In this chapter, we have presented some major components for developing and implementing intervention programs and services for severely handicapped infants and children. It has been stressed that the education/treatment team model and service delivery approach are closely related to the total intervention effort that starts in early infancy and continues through the preschool years. We have advocated the use of a transdisciplinary education/treatment team model in combination with a service delivery system that provides continuity for both the handicapped children and their parents.

This chapter does not present a detailed discussion of every component necessary for early intervention. It does offer a coherent path to follow, with sufficient references to enable the reader to obtain supplemental information pertaining to the overall model presented.

There are, of course, many areas of inadequate knowledge that await further research and evaluation. These include the inadequacies that exist in our current assessment instruments and the efficacy of various, and often quite different, approaches that can be taken in selecting curricula for this population of infants and young children.

The next chapter will discuss considerations for implementing educational programs for severely handicapped students in elementary-level classrooms in public school settings.

CHAPTER 10

The Elementary Program

DETERMINING THE PROGRAM'S STRUCTURE

Since most severely handicapped children who are served under PL 94–142 are of elementary school age, the elementary program is the most common educational group. Programs vary widely from state to state and across localities within states. The most significant factors determining the structure of these programs include (1) disability characteristics, (2) chronological age, (3) area population density, and (4) service delivery policy. Each factor is an important parameter in determining the structure of a relevant and functional elementary program. Nevertheless, few systematic studies have been made on the contribution of each to the structure of a program.

DISABILITY CHARACTERISTICS

During the first half of the 1970s, programs for severely handicapped students were frequently structured around disability characteristics, with extent of disability the most heavily utilized characteristic and type of disability a close second. In many cases, the terms *prekindergarten, elementary,* and *secondary* had no particular relevance, since chronological age was often disregarded when establishing educational programs. It was not unusual to see students grouped according to whether they were low functioning, low functioning/nonambulatory, medically fragile, or behaviorally disordered. Often, the primary determinant would be such factors as whether they could use wheelchairs or which sex was necessary for the teaching staff (large or aggressive students, for example, required male teachers). It was not unusual to see young adults of sixteen to eighteen years in the same room with seven to nine year olds when disability characteristics determined groupings.

During this period, many states created categorical programs for seriously emotionally disturbed (SED) students, and the programs constituted a type of severely handicapped class grouping. Referrals to this class were usually based on exclusion or termination from other less restrictive programs. Often, the staff for an SED class consisted of specialists in behavior modification, and a substantial part of the curriculum was comprised of a wide variety of punitive efforts to control aberrant behavior. In urban areas, SED programs were often found in private schools. Local school districts were only too happy to contract out responsibility for severe behavior problems and to take advantage of private facilities where specialized funding was available.

Frequently, severely handicapped students were grouped according to the diagnostic category to which the student was assigned on the basis of screening and referral. When specialized funding sources were available for certain diagnostic groups, such as autism and deaf/blind, the programs would frequently operate on this basis. Again, however, this occurred more often in urban settings, where a sufficient population base made the maintenance of such a class more likely.

Problems were encountered early with both types of disability characteristic groupings. In the late seventies and early eighties, it became apparent that factors accruing to chronological age far outweighed the homogeneity-of-disability factor in importance of program structure (cf., Sailor, Wilcox, and Brown, 1980). It was discovered that small female teachers could indeed manage large aggressive students and that putting all the behavior problems in one room simply exacerbated each student's problem.

The state of California, with its large population base (23 million in 1982), recently passed new special education legislation designed to free its service structure from the increasing burden of using categorical disability as the determinant of classroom placement. Now, instead of classrooms for TMR (trainable mentally retarded), severely handicapped, SED, and so on, there are only students with disabilities, some of whom will be appropriate for "special classes." Clearly, not all placement problems are solved with this noncategorical approach, but at least the stage has been set for focusing on placement factors more relevant than diagnostic labels.

CHRONOLOGICAL AGE

When mental age was considered to be a primary factor in curriculum determination, biological age was deemed relatively unimportant. The recent shift in focus away from cognitive development and the remediation of missed developmental milestones has reinstated the importance of chronological age as a placement factor. Elementary programs for severely handicapped students are now age-appropriate within somewhat flexible

ranges. For the most part, we no longer see fifteen-year-old students in a preschool environment.

It is our feeling that the primary factor in determining placement in a special class should be similarity of instructional objectives with other students in the class *within reasonable boundaries* of chronological age conditions. We would not favor the placement of high school (or secondary) age severely handicapped students on an elementary school campus, or vice versa, in any case. Within the elementary school age range, placement in special classes should be on the basis of curricular homogeneity. Partial mainstreaming in regular programs and all other contacts with nondisabled or mildly disabled peers should be concentrated on chronological age-appropriateness. We are opposed to the policy of placing all severely behavior-disordered students in a single behavior modification class. The presence or absence of behavior problems as a key factor in program selection should be de-emphasized whenever possible; instead, a strong focus should be placed on similarity among instructional objectives.

AREA POPULATION DENSITY

Considerations for serving severely handicapped students in rural, sparsely populated areas often contrast with urban considerations. The placement of severely handicapped children on regular public school campuses and partial mainstreaming are often more easily and naturally accomplished in the rural service model. Segregated service structures have been primarily an administrative luxury of large urban school districts.

In small, isolated communities, service for a severely handicapped student can be expensive and difficult to obtain. Often, the solution to rural service problems has been a long bus ride to a designated rural, cooperative school for special education services. We feel that long bus rides are detrimental to severely handicapped students and should be discouraged in most cases. Students who are subject to seizures are in clear and present danger if a strong seizure occurs during bus transportation. In cases where the bus ride entails a long, winding route, hypertonic students will often show an increase in tonicity during the ride. Stereotyped behaviors, like self-stimulation and self-destructive acts, frequently occur during long transportation runs.

Severely handicapped students should not have to endure bus rides over one hour in length. It is better, even if more expensive, to transport support services to a remote school site serving only a few students than to transport the students a long distance to the school where county or regional special education classes are clustered. It has been our experience that small community school programs often have the potential for a more realistic, functional life skills program for a few severely handicapped students than do large urban programs concentrated in more isolated or segregated environments. Students from small rural communities, under this plan, have the added advantage of maximized contact with their local physical environment and with accepting and caring people in their own communities. This increases their opportunity for independence and successful later adaptation to home communities.

In the rural model, placement by chronological age and proximity to home are key determinants in all cases except those for which necessary specialized professional services cannot be procured. A failure to *procure* needed services, however, is a different matter than failure to *provide* needed services because of administrative or budgetary convenience.

SERVICE DELIVERY POLICY

The final determinant in placement of severely handicapped students is often historical in nature. A particular school district or cooperative (consortium), for example, has been serving disabled students according to a particular model for years, and that model still dictates all new placement decisions. Problems are encountered when changes in educational knowledge, expertise, and technology require changes in educational techniques.

In a city or rural school district where all services to handicapped children have been traditionally provided at the handicapped school or at the state institution for "the retarded," there is a marked contrast between standard educational practice requirements for a severely handicapped pupil and the service delivery system offering that education. In these cases, efforts must be made to help the delivery system conform to standard practice. The alternative is a greatly substandard educational effort.

AN ELEMENTARY PROGRAM MODEL

To illustrate the kind of elementary service delivery system that we favor, we will provide a hypothetical model, which is relevant to almost all service systems, whether urban or rural. The model is intended to serve as a realistic basis for *standard practice* rather than representing the state of the art or the ideal. It will illustrate a program that can operate at a realistic funding level and in some form in most American communities.

Our hypothetical school is operated by a multicounty, cooperative district consortium in a rural area in the Midwest. It is located in a small town of 2,500 in population about twenty-five miles from a medium-sized city of 150,000. Elementary school-age children are bused to the school from a number of towns and rural residences within a twenty-mile radius. No bus ride is longer than fifty minutes for nondisabled or special education students.

PHYSICAL CHARACTERISTICS

The School. The school serves grades 1 to 6 and has twelve classrooms plus a gymnasium, a large outdoor playground, and a cafeteria that provides a hot lunch program.

Three of the twelve classes are special classes for special education students. Of the three, two classes consist of student populations that fit the definition of the severely handicapped presented in Chapter 1. The third class is for higher functioning students enrolled in a remedial academic curricular program.

Of the two classes serving severely handicapped students, classroom 1 contains nine students, ranging in age from six to ten, and all functionally severely retarded. All but two of the students are physically impaired and require adaptive wheelchairs for mobility. The other two students are ambulatory and possess a wide range of behavior disorders. They have been diagnosed as autistic in previous assessments.

Classroom 2 has nine children, ranging in age from nine to eleven. These students are generally more functionally competent than the students in classroom 1. All but two of the students are ambulatory without assistance. Only four of the students have a specific motor disability.

The three special education classes are dispersed throughout the school in order to maximize the degree of integration at the school. Recess and lunch occur at the same time for all classes for the same reason. The two classes for severely handicapped students eat in the cafeteria with non-disabled students, and classroom 2 students are often dispersed across the cafeteria with nondisabled or more mildly disabled students. Classroom 1 students tend to be more clustered within the cafeteria. Most eat lunch in their wheelchairs with top trays. They are assisted during mealtimes, however, by sixth graders in some cases.

The school has an adaptive physical education (PE) program, and both severely handicapped classes are partially mainstreamed into this program and receive instruction alongside nondisabled peers. Classroom 2 is partially mainstreamed into an art and music program for fourth- and fifth-grade students.

Transportation to the school is conducted on regular school buses. The physically handicapped students are transferred from chair to bus seat by the children's parents when they are picked up. Wheelchairs are folded and stowed at the back of the bus. For several children, foam cut-out bolsters are used on the bus seats to maintain position. Each severely handicapped student has a seatmate (usually a sixth grader) who assists in the transportation process. The nonambulatory severely handicapped students are transferred from bus to wheelchair by the teacher upon arrival at the school.

Classrooms.   Both classrooms for severely handicapped students are large (1,000 square feet) and well lit, with a row of windows along one wall. Each has two sinks with hot and cold water. Classroom 1 is fully carpeted, and about a quarter is covered with large vinyl mats with an assortment of wedges and bolsters. Classroom 2 is half-carpeted and is equipped with small circular and semicircular tables and chairs. Each classroom has a desk with file drawers for the teaching staff, and each is equipped with an intercom to the central school office.

Figure 10.1 shows a schematic design for classroom 1. The use of mobile partitions to create specialized areas within the classroom is illustrated as well as the strategic placement of equipment and furniture to allow wheelchair mobility and mat space for transfer and position change. The classroom is decorated in bright colors.

Table 10.1 presents a sample list of equipment used in classroom 1. This list is representative of the minimal (low-budget) equipment for a classroom of this type.

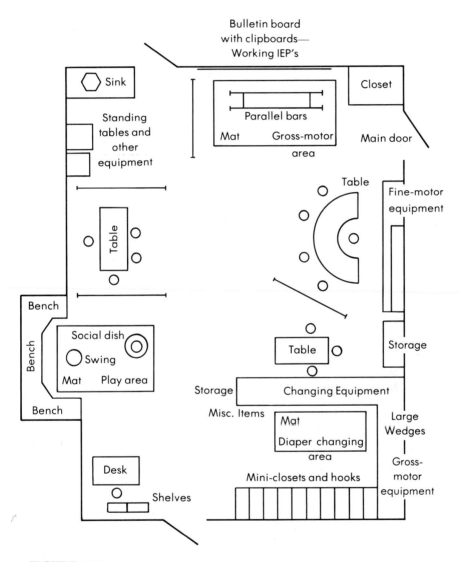

FIGURE 10.1
Design for classroom 1, showing location of equipment, storage facilities, and activity areas

TABLE 10.1
Equipment List for Classroom 1

Two twin-handled drinking cups with lid
One single-handled drinking cup with lid
Four sandbags (3.3 lbs. each)
One saucer twirl
One incline mat (small: 36 × 72 × 16″)
One foam cylinder (15 × 18″)

Foam wedges:
One 8 × 20 × 22″
One 8 × 20 × 24″

Two small foot-placement holders
One 90° support chair and base
Two 4 × 6′ floor mats (2″ thick)
One prone stander (child-size) with tray

EQUIPMENT, SELF-MADE OR FROM LOCAL STORES:
Foam cylinders for spoons
Vibrator
Headphones (for a cassette deck)
Flyer wagon
Door mirrors or mirror tile squares
Pegboard screen dividers (2), 49 × 60″ each
Balance beam, 2 × 4 × 8″, with portable supports on the ground made
    of 2 ×4″s
Corner floor chair
Adjustable parallel bars, sitting and standing equipment
Circular "dish" bean chair

Classroom 2 is arranged according to an instructional ratio format for different objectives. As illustrated in Figure 10.2, classroom 2 is set up in a manner conducive to one-on-one activity at the same time that small-group instruction and free time are occurring. This zoning by instructional format provides a useful alternative to the content zone approach, in which a classroom is divided according to the nature of the particular activity to be taught. Our own preference is for a classroom that allows instructional content to vary as a function of space rather than one having a language area, a motor area, and so on.

The use of mobile partitions allows the rapid creation of a limited space for a particular instructional activity. The best classroom design is the one that is the most *dynamic,* that is, the one that is most readily adaptable to new combinations of students and staff as instructional objectives are met and activity requirements change. Conversely, a fixed classroom

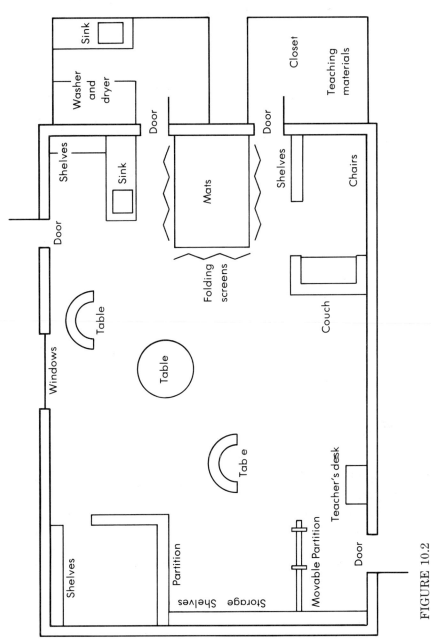

FIGURE 10.2
Design for classroom 2, showing location of equipment and training areas

model, with permanent curriculum areas and materials, tends to create a *static* program, in which students may be retrained in particular areas, even though they have exhausted the learning potential of the combinations of materials and staff patterns associated with the area.

Table 10.2 presents a sample list of the minimal equipment required to supply a classroom like number 2.

It is important to consider in the context of equipment, supplies, and instructional materials that, for both classes illustrated here, only a portion of each student's instructional day will occur in the classroom. Other instructional environments will include the cafeteria, the playground, the residential environment (and/or training area for home living skills), other areas of the school, and areas within the community at large, including recreation and leisure environments. Finally, the classroom designs we have presented here are only examples. Instructional environments will vary greatly from program to program, and there is no reason, at this stage in our evolution, to assume that fixed standards are needed for the physical layout of classrooms for severely handicapped students.

INSTRUCTIONAL STAFF

Both classrooms have full-time teachers with appropriate certificates reflecting specialized training for teaching severely handicapped children. Additionally, each class in our example has two teaching assistants, one full time and one half time (mornings only). The staffing pattern falls within a staff-student ratio that is generally acceptable for an educational program for severely handicapped students (Filler, Note 1). In addition to the core teaching staff, the district provides a motor-movement-disorder therapist and a language therapist, each of whom is assigned to classroom 1 on a 20 percent FTE (full-time equivalent) basis, resulting in about eight hours per week per therapist. Additional personnel available to this class on an unscheduled basis include a student's mother who volunteers time in the afternoons, and a student from a nearby college, who is placed in the classroom for supervised practicum experience.

Both of the teaching assistants have received specialized training relevant to their student populations, one within the class conducted by the teacher, the other as part of a specialized program at an area community college.

Both the therapists have received specialized in-service training appropriate to the severely handicapped population, and both use a version of the integrated/consultative-therapy model (cf., Sternat, Messina, Nietupski, Lyon, and Brown, 1977). Under this model, the therapist spends a portion of the time allotted to each child in hands-on therapy in the classroom and/or within the context of instruction in other environments. Additional

TABLE 10.2
Equipment List for Classroom 2

General Equipment	*Special Equipment*
Teacher desk and chair	Two wheelchairs
Cabinet for paper supplies	Two wheelchair trays with
Paper supplies, pens, pencils, stationery	plastic insert for
supplies, masking tape	communication board
Shelves and cupboards for recreational	Standing table
equipment and age-appropriate	Table with circular cutout for
toys, dishes, sanitary supplies	wheelchair use
Dishes, silverware, cups, bowls, paring	Velcro straps, seat belts
knife, bottle opener	Pillows, beanbag chair,
Two dishpans, dish drainer	sandbags
Two cup holders, two adaptive dish	Instructional materials
holders, four scoopy dishes, four	
adaptive spoons	
Dicem and octupuses	
Sink, hot and cold water	
Accessible refrigerator, washer,	
and dryer	
Toileting facilities	
Disposable diapers, toilet paper,	
paper towels	
Towels, washcloths, plastic gloves,	
sponges, safety pins	
Cleaning supplies, disinfectant	
Plastic straws, flexible and straight	
Mats for positioning and changing	
Changing table	
Combs, brushes, toothbrushes for	
each child	
Blender or food grinder	
Student clipboards	
Large wall charts for objectives and	
schedules	
Record player and records	
Radio or cassette player	
Four adult-size chairs, four smaller	
chairs	
Three-wheeled stools	
Three adjustable rectangular tables	
Two tables, semicircular, kidney-shaped,	
or trapezoid-shaped with adjustable	
legs	
Divided cubicles for students' coats	
and personal supplies	
Plastic tubs for individual student	
materials	
Movable dividers	
Large three-section standing mirror	
or table speech mirror	

time is allotted by the therapist for consultation with the teacher concerning therapeutic recommendations for the total instructional program. This model contrasts, for example, with isolated-therapy models that remove students from the overall instructional context and work with them in an isolated room or specialized area. The integrated model means that language and motor movement therapies are integrated with, and thus cut across, all aspects of the complete instructional program.

The language therapist has a similar time commitment to classroom 2, but the motor movement therapist has only a 5 percent FTE assignment to classroom 2. The second classroom has the services of two students in supervised practicum on an unscheduled basis.

CLASSROOM ORGANIZATION AND SCHEDULE

The single most difficult problem a teacher of severely handicapped students usually has to face is the design and implementation of the class schedule. Many variables enter into the process. To complicate things further, the schedule must be dynamic and capable of responding to changes in students, resulting from ongoing instruction.

The key components of an organizational schedule are (1) *staff members,* (2) *units of time,* (3) *instructional programs,* (4) *student groupings,* and (5) *instructional environments,* including transportation to and from school, adaptive equipment, materials and supplies, and so on.

Consider classroom 1. We suggest adherence to the principle that only regular and permanent staff be scheduled. The classroom program is thus organized as if the teacher and two teaching assistants were the only instructional personnel available. Others are utilized within this framework but on a more flexible (unscheduled) basis. We also recommend posting an organizational schedule somewhere in the classroom in a conspicuous place, one that is large enough to be readily visible to anyone in the classroom. Finally, we recommend that the posted organizational schedule be mounted on clear plastic with schedule information entered with multicolored large felt-tipped pens so that entries can be easily wiped off and new entries made with a minimum of effort. Blackboard schedules suffice for this purpose, but blackboards have virtually no other use in an SH classroom. They consume needed wall space, and blackboard schedules tend to be messy and unattractive. The organizational schedule is the hub of the instructional program and should be maintained in a systematic and professional way.

There are a number of ways to design a schedule. Most organizational schedules tend to reflect the emphasis of the program philosophy. Programs that, for example, stress curriculum blocks might show such entries as art, language, gross motor, self-help, snack, recess, nap, and toileting down the left-hand side of the chart, with staff names listed across the top.

The resulting grid is then used to enter students' names and times for each block and staff member.

Of all the organizational schemes that we have used or encountered, the system that seems most suited to the model we have presented in this book is the time-×-staff grid. This system divides the instructional day into thirty-minute time units and lists these units from top to bottom on the left side of the grid, as shown in Figure 10.3. Scheduled staff members are listed from left to right at the top. Time-×-staff schedules are usually single-day schedules but can be in two-day formats, when significant program changes occur every other day. In general, it is better not to have fixed weekly activities, such as swimming on Friday afternoon, art on Tuesday morning, field trips on certain days, and so on. One- or two-day schedules provide the most flexibility when possible.

With every organizational schedule, a certain amount of useful information can be posted, and a certain amount is sacrificed. There is virtually no visual system to our knowledge that can adequately communicate information on all five variables listed earlier. We favor a system that communicates time, staff, student, and environment but leaves the content of the instructional task unspecified. Quick reference to the working program plan clipboard readily supplies the missing information on content. This system seems to have the advantage of focusing scheduling efforts on *individualized* curriculum needs and away from fixed curricular blocks, such

		TEACHER	ASST. 1	ASST. 2	
DAY ONE	9–9:30	3B	3B	3B	
	9:30–10	4B	1B	4B	
	10–10:30	3B	3B	3B	
	10:30–11	Break/desk	5G	4G	
	11–11:30	4R	Break/2B	3B	2B/Asst. 1
	11:30–12	4R	3B	Break/2B	2B/Asst. 2
	12–12:30	3Y	3Y	3Y	
	12:30–1	1Y	4B		4B
	1–1:30	3B	4R		2B
	1:30–2	1B	4R		4B
	2–2:30	9G	Break/G		
	2:30–3	4B	5B		
DAY TWO	9–9:30	3B	3B	3B	
	9:30–10	1B	4B	2B	2B
	10–10:30	3B	4B	Break/3B	2B/Asst. 2
	10:30–11	Break/desk	5G	5G	
	11–11:30	3B	Break/2B	4R	2B/Asst. 1
	11:30–12	3B	2B	4R	
	12–12:30	3Y	3Y	3Y	
	12:30–1	3B	1Y		5B
	1–1:30	3R	3B		2B
	1:30–2	3R	1B		5B
	2–2:30	4G	5G		
	2:30–3	5B	4B		

FIGURE 10.3
Two-day time-×-staff organizational schedule for classroom 1

The number-letter combinations (e.g., 3B) in the grid refer to the number of students (3) and the color code for environment (blue). 5G means 5 students, green environment. Students' names would appear in colored ink rather than a number, as shown.

as gross motor, language, and so on. Since each student will have least five instructional objectives and classroom 1 has nine students, the three staff members must somehow organize their time to manage at least forty-five curricular components. With a large class such as this, we have found two-day schedules to be the most flexible. Each consecutive two-day block functions as a single instructional period divided into half-hour time units. This particular system assumes that all five weekdays are potentially equal for curriculum distribution purposes. It does not readily accommodate swimming only on Friday afternoon, for example, although it can absorb one or two such "out-of-synch" components without too much strain.

Figure 10.3 illustrates the two-day time-×-staff organizational system for classroom 1. Consecutive half-hour time blocks are listed on the left side from top to bottom over a two-day span. Staff members are listed from left to right at the top, with space available at the right for entering unscheduled personnel when appropriate. Students' names are entered in the resulting grid and are written in colors that correspond to instructional environments. Thus, blue indicates instruction in the classroom, green, the playground, red, a nonschool community environment, yellow, the cafeteria, and so on, for all specifiable environments. Teaching staff and others can tell at a glance from this chart who is working with what student at what time and where the instruction is occurring. Reference to the working program plan (Chapter 5) will supply the information needed to determine precisely what is being taught.

Spaces marked in the grid indicate staff breaks, including the teachers' desk time to update data records. Student's names appearing in the column with a blank at the top for staff designation are in free play.

The organizational schedule for classroom 1 is arranged so that the column designations for Teacher, Asst. 1, and Asst. 2 are removable and can be interchanged across columns. This interchange is accomplished, in fact, every two days, so that column 1, which now shows Teacher at the top (on Monday, for example), will become Asst. 1 on Wednesday, and Asst. 2 will moves to the column formerly under Asst. 1. Teacher then assumes the column for Asst. 2 for the first half of the day and then finishes the middle-column specifications in the afternoon, when the second assistant leaves. On Friday, a similar rotation from left to right across column heads occurs and continues every two days indefinitely. Each student thus receives instruction on each objective from each of the three members of the teaching staff, an arrangement that has been found to promote generalization of learned skills (Rogers-Warren and Warren, 1977).

The issue of free time is a hotly contested one in education of the severely handicapped. Many feel that severely handicapped students should be continuously programmed throughout the school day. Indeed, Fredericks, Anderson, and Baldwin (1979) reported a research study that strongly suggested that summative student progress was highly correlated with the amount of time each student spends in direct instruction during the school day. Our feeling is that a structured free-play setting in an elementary classroom can provide a valuable instructional asset if properly designed. We believe that direct instructional time should be *maximized* but also carefully designed to accomplish desired objectives. Some instructional activities, especially of the large-group variety, may not teach anything and, in fact, may work against horizontal (child-to-child) contact. The morning preschool-style circle, for example, is typically age-inappropriate for an elementary class and serves to focus attention toward vertical (child-to-adult) contact.

When a classroom free-time environment contains age-appropriate and stimulating materials and equipment, and the area can provide a break for hard-working students and a chance to practice learned skills in a relaxed environment; it can also stimulate vertical social contact and strengthen social skills. The fact is there are too few teaching staff members to structure a continuous day program for nine students adequately and tightly so that the development of functional life skills will be promoted. The free-time area, when skillfully designed, provides a useful technique for maintaining a high motivation to learn at other times by offering a relaxing, yet stimulating environment in free time.

Another traditional area of concern is the need for teaching staff breaks. Teacher unions have successfully fought for the right of teachers to have a suitable amount of break time available to them during the instructional day. Yet, teachers in programs for severely handicapped students often prefer to eliminate break time in favor of increasing the instructional time available to students. Our opinion is that a break in the morning schedule is advisable for all scheduled teaching staff. Teaching severely handicapped students is a demanding and fatiguing job. As in any such stressful employment, a rest break has restorative properties and can serve in the long run to enhance teaching effectiveness. Time also should be scheduled during the classroom day for the teacher's paperwork. Data must be plotted on charts, decision lines drawn, programs updated on clipboards, and so on. Apart from the small amount of time available to teaching staff after students have departed in the afternoon, the scheduled break time for the teacher may provide the only reasonable period for paperwork and graphics. (Some break!) This function is essential, however, to the success of the educational program and should not be overlooked or eliminated.

What does Figure 10.3, the classroom organizational schedule, tell us about the educational program of classroom 1? Some of the most striking aspects of the program are readily apparent.

1. The program emphasizes group rather than one-to-one interaction.
2. Instruction takes place in at least four separate environments.

3. Morning and afternoon fifteen-minute breaks are provided for teaching assistants, and thirty-minute desk time for paperwork is provided for the teacher.
4. The program permits free time for students but at a low ratio relative to instructional time (thirteen student hours per day free time and ninety-one student hours per day instruction, for an average of about 85 percent of program time devoted to direct measured instruction).
5. The program alternates daily because of the two-day schedule, a situation that promotes a wide spectrum of curriculum applications.
6. Because staff designated by schedule column changes every two days, the program allows all aspects of curriculum for each student to be taught by each staff member.

We know from a glance at Figure 10.3 that a substantial portion of the classroom day is conducted by teaching staff *in the classroom* itself. This is appropriate for an elementary school program where a greater amount of instruction in functional life skills can be delivered in a single, properly equipped classroom for severely handicapped students at the more disabled end of the continuum. Students who are in middle school or secondary programs, however, or who are at the higher functioning end of the continuum would be expected to receive an increasing proportion of their instructional day in nonclassroom environments. This is the case, for example, with classroom 2 (not shown) where the organizational schedule reflects about two-thirds nonclassroom instructional time per day. About 50 percent of the instruction in the classroom 1 is blue-coded in the schedule, reflecting in-class instruction.

CURRICULUM

What sort of skills are being taught to the nine students in classroom 1? The organizational schedule tells us where instruction takes place, when, and by whom, but does not convey the content of the program. To learn the content, let's examine a hypothetical working program plan for Laura, one of the students in classroom 1.

Table 10.3 presents a subsection of the environmental assessment that was conducted for Laura in establishing her working program plan. This assessment procedure is nonstandardized and unpublished, but it is patterned after the procedures suggested by Falvey, Ferrara-Parrish, Johnson, Pumpian, Schroeder, and Brown (1979). The material conveyed in the table shows Laura's abilities to perform certain skills at home and in the free-play area of the classroom – skills that would be self-sustained age-appropriate recreational and leisure activities if learned.

Table 10.4 presents a T-Format from Laura's working program plan, illustrating a long-range goal and one short-term instructional objective

TABLE 10.3

A Portion of an Environmental Assessment Record for Laura

Domain: Recreation/leisure

Environment: Classroom

Subenvironment: Table in free-play area

Activity: Turning on tape recorder (listening to music)

Skills Needed		Comments	Adaptations Needed
1. Scan and locate recorder.	+		1. Student positioned in special chair.
2. Reach to tape recorder.	+		2. Tape recorder placed within 6" of either hand.
3. Touch tape recorder.	−		3. Use adaptor with recorder, so S. required only to press adaptor and music will go on.
4. Turn tape recorder on.	−		
5. Keep recorder on long enough to hear music.	−	5. Must keep adaptor depressed to keep music on — hand slips off or raises up.	

Activity: Manipulate toys/objects

1. Scan, locate object.	+		Object placed within 6" of right hand.
2. Open fingers.	−		
3. Reach towards object.	−	3. Will move hand 3" towards object if object held at shoulder level.	
4. Grasp object.	−		

TABLE 10.3
(Continued)

Skills Needed	Comments	Adaptations Needed
Subenvironment: On mat in play area		
Activity: Tape recorder/toy play		
1. Keep head up.	–	S. placed across bolster to promote relaxation in upper extremity and facilitate looking.
Environment: Home		
Subenvironment: Kitchen		
Activity: Eating/drinking		
1. Sit at table.	+	S. in positioning chair placed at table.
2. Scan, locate food on plate.	–	
3. Scan, locate food on spoon.	+	3. Hold spoon at midline 6" from face.
4. Attempt to eat with spoon.	–	4. Fixation, touch to show preference, not yet established.	4. Fixate on spoon, plate, glass, or touch object.
5. Eat from spoon.	–	5. Fed by parent, sibling.
6. Tongue in mouth.	+	
7. Open mouth at sight of food.	+	
8. Keep food in mouth.	–	8. 50 percent spills out.
9. Chew.	–	9. Use processed food.
10. Swallow.	+	
11. Scan, locate glass.	+	
12. Drink from glass.	–	12. Spills.	12. Fed by parents/sibling.

(Continued)

TABLE 10.3
(Continued)

Skills Needed		Comments	Adaptations Needed
Activity: Wash hands			
1. Scan, locate rag.	+		Place rag 6" from either hand, either on table or slightly below eye level.
2. Open fingers.	−		
3. Reach for rag.	−		
4. Touch rag.	−		
5. Allow hands to be wiped.	+		
Subenvironment: Bedroom/living room			
Activity: Listening to music			
1. Lie on floor or bed in relaxed position.	+		1. Place over bolster to relax arms, legs.
2. Sit in chair.	+		
3. Reach to recorder.	+		3. Use adaptor.
4. Touch recorder.	−		
5. Press recorder.	−		
6. Keep recorder on.	−	Hand slips off.	
7. Turn recorder off.	+		Remove hand from adaptor.

TABLE 10.4
T-Format from Laura's Working Program Plan

Long-range goal: Within one year, the student will reach toward, touch, and grasp objects placed on a table or on the floor within 6 inches of her left hand.

Instructional objective: When given the cue, "touch the toy," S. will reach out with left hand and touch toy when toy is held at student-arm level, at a distance of 3 inches from left hand. Task will be completed across trainers, settings, and objects. Criterion for each step: 80 percent correct trials for three consecutive days.

Task Analysis	*Instructional Procedure*
1. At cue, "touch the toy," S. will open fingers, left palm flat.	*Setting:* 1. S. in positioning chair placed on regular chair at regular table with T. sitting directly across table. 2. S. in positioning chair on floor with T. sitting directly across small teacher-made table. 3. S. lying prone over bolster with T. sitting directly in front of S. on floor.
2. At cue, "touch the toy," S. will reach with flattened left hand toward the toy a distance of 3 inches.	
3. At cue, "touch the toy," S. will reach with flat left hand toward toy (distance of 3 inches) and touch the toy.	*Materials:* Two or three small toys of different textures, bright contrast.
	Procedures: Verbal cue each step: allow 5 sec. latency, repeat cue, allow 5 sec., stop trial. (Serial task analysis: 10 trials per session)
	Step 1: T. rubs palm and back of left hand to prompt open fingers. Fade prompt.
	Step 2: Continuous encouragement/ physical prompt to move hand in right direction.
	Step 3: Reduce encouragement/ physical prompt to move hand in physical prompt.
	Reinforcement: Step 1 2: For correct response, move toy into flat palm, rub against palm, praise. Step 4: For correct response, stroke side of face, increase pressure of hand against object (mold hand around object). All steps: For partial of prompted response, reinforce only if response is improvement over previous trial. For incorrect or no response, no praise, take through appropriate response.
	Measurement: Record frequency of correct responding per session with no physical prompts.
	Generalization: Vary teaching staff and objects.
	Next objective: Move object down toward table.

---

with task analysis and instructional procedure derived, in part, from the environmental assessment shown in Table 10.3. Figure 10.4 presents graphic data showing acquisition by Laura of this objective over a series of eleven sessions of ten trials each.

As Figure 10.4 shows, progress was rapid and steady across the three steps in the forward serial chain. Since teaching sessions occurred once per day over 10 trial blocks (in this case, carried out by a nonscheduled practicum student in the free-play area), data were graphed by frequency of independent, correct responses over each step. The columnar-numerical graph paper also served as the raw data scoring sheet. Looking at session 1 in Figure 10.4, the slashes through the numbers 2, 8, and 9 moving from

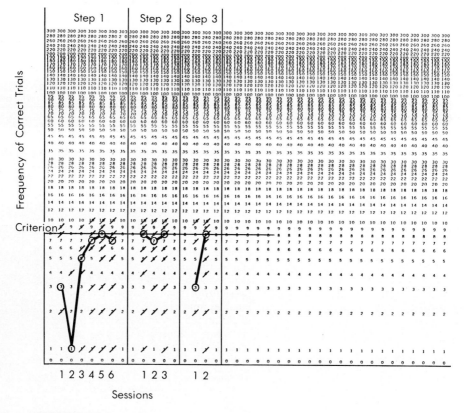

FIGURE 10.4
Laura's progress across the three steps of the objective task-analyzed in Table 10.3

Data are graphed as frequency, the number of correct trials per session.

bottom to top of the graph indicate correct actions for those trials. Three correct trials is a frequency of three for the session, so that number is circled and connected by line graph to corresponding frequencies as we move from left to right within steps of the task-analyzed skill.

Table 10.5 presents a long-range goal, instructional objective, and procedure for Betty, a second student in classroom 1, whose T-Format for clothing removal we examined earlier in Chapter 7. This objective was also derived from analysis of assessment data on Betty's toileting capabilities in different environments. Note the backward serial chain selected for this task-analyzed skill. Note also the next specified objective calls for a fine-motor skill applied to dressing and undressing. It is a reasonable assumption that other instructional objectives being taught at present that involve fine-motor aspects of hand and finger grasp and movement will generalize to zipper and snap manipulation later on when this skill is taught.

Figure 10.5 presents Betty's progress on the first seven steps of this instructional program. Instruction occurs five times per day in conjunction with Betty's toilet-training program. Data are expressed as a percentage of the five trials each session (or day, in this case). Instruction on this skill is carried out by each member of the teaching staff on a rotating basis. The activity occurs between the scheduled half-hour activities shown on the classroom organizational schedule. Within the designated half-hour blocks, about twenty minutes is devoted to instruction. The remaining ten minutes are typically reserved for relocating students for the next activity–getting from one environment to another, toileting, diapering, and so on. Betty's dressing program is carried out during these transfer periods when she is in the school environment and as dictated by her toilet-training program.

Space will not permit a wider sample of the kinds of instructional programs that characterize the total educational approach of classroom 1, but Betty, Laura, and seven other students are receiving instruction in a multiplicity of environments across all the *critical functions* identified in the priority matrix in Chapter 5. Each student is receiving instruction both in small groups and individually, and each student has individual task-analyzed objectives and individualized curriculum sequences as well. Classroom 1 students are instructed in the school cafeteria, bathrooms, hallways, the playground, the classroom itself, and in at least one partial mainstream environment in the school. In addition, they receive instruction in their own homes, in a nearby group home, at a nearby park, at a community swimming pool, during transportation on the school bus, on public streets, and in a neighborhood variety store. They receive instruction in these environments from all members of the teaching staff according to the rotation system of the classroom schedules and sometimes from parents. Data are collected on all objectives in all environments, using the procedures outlined in Chapter 7. The program is dynamic and fluid, and

TABLE 10.5
A T-Format of a Clothing Removal Objective for Betty

Long-range education goal(s): Betty will become independent in her dressing and undressing skills in all environments.

Short-term instructional objective: While toileting, given unsnapped and unzippered pants, Betty will pull her pants up and down at the appropriate time without physical assistance for 80 percent of the trials on two out of three days.

Task Analysis (Pulling pants up and down)	Instructional Procedure
10. Thumbs hook waistband.	*Setting:* Bathroom 1–1.
9. Push down pants – waist to hips.	*Materials:* Betty's pants and panties.
8. Push down pants – hips to midthigh.	*Serial backward chain procedure(s)* (inclusive of cues, actions, schedules, and effects): T. gives cue, "Push *down* pants" and puts S. through #10– #7. After toileting, T. gives cue, "Pull up pants" and puts through step #1 and #2. S. does #1 without assistance. Next step, repeat same procedure of putting through. S. must perform #2 and #1 on own, and so forth. Score + or –. Mark + when S. does all steps from point where T. ceases to motor S. through.
7. Push down pants – midthigh to knees.	
6. Grasp panties.	
5. Pull up panties – knees to midthigh.	
4. Pull up panties – midthigh to hips.	
3. Grasp pants.	
2. Pull up pants – knees to hips.	
1. Pull up pants – hips to waist.	*Correction procedure:* If incorrect or no response, return to missed position in steps. Repeat cue, allowing another chance. If still incorrect or no response, put S. through. Score + only if S. responds correctly on first chance.
	Reinforcement: Praise for independent responses.
	Measurement: Graph progress of each step, 5 × day. 80 percent mastery on two out of three days = criterion for moving to next step.
	Generalization strategies: Betty will independently pull her pants up and down at the appropriate time in all toileting environments (home, restaurant, etc.).
	Next objective (if applicable): While toileting, Betty will unzip and unsnap her pants at the appropriate time, without physical assistance for 80 percent of trials on two out of three days.

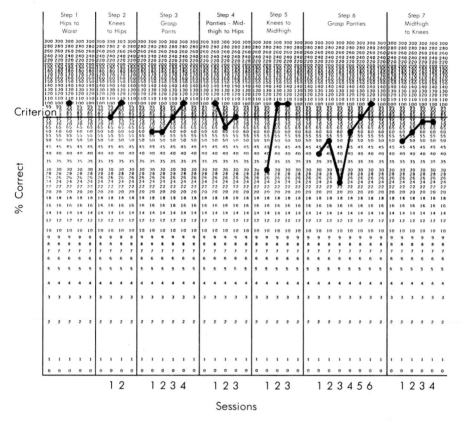

FIGURE 10.5
Betty's progress on the first seven steps of a dressing program

the results are striking. Interactions with mildly disabled students, other severely handicapped students (classroom 2) and, most importantly, with nondisabled age peers are steadily increasing in frequency and in complexity and quality.

ELEMENTS OF AN ELEMENTARY PROGRAM

COMMUNICATION INSTRUCTION

Not long ago, communication instruction with severely handicapped students was primarily restricted to programmed language sessions offered only at fixed points in the classroom schedule. In many cases, students were removed from the classroom context and taken to a speech therapy room located elsewhere in the school. Students were drilled in the early steps of vocabulary acquisition, just as many of us were drilled in our first halting efforts to acquire Spanish, French, or German at the university level. Severely handicapped students got picture cards instead of word flash cards to name. Motivation was often supplied by bits of candy or food rather than through avoidance of a professor's frown, but the techniques of instruction were similar and the results relatively comparable. We, nearly all of us, acquired some rudimentary vocabulary but failed to put it to good use when it would have counted for something.

In the mid 1970s, the authors, together with Donald M. Baer at the University of Kansas, published a comprehensive language development program for severely handicapped students (Sailor, Guess, and Baer, 1973; Guess, Sailor, and Baer, 1974, 1976a, 1976b, 1977a, 1977b, 1978a, 1978b). This program, an outgrowth of nearly a decade of research ,was published in a massed-trial instructional format, with scoring forms acccompanying each of sixty-one linguistic steps calling for up to sixty trials of instruction per session for each step. In the years since publication, the authors have witnessed and, we hope, also contributed to some important ways in which the sequence of steps are taught (cf., Guess, 1980; Warren, Rogers-Warren, Baer, and Guess, 1980). What is recognized now that was not in 1976 is the importance of the *context* in which language is taught. Again, we are struck with the importance of where severely handicapped students are instructed. Horstmeier and MacDonald (1978a, 1978b) were the first to place a strong emphasis on environmental context in the publication of their language program, a system that used parents as agents of instruction whenever possible. Most recently, Musselwhite and St. Louis (1982) discussed the shift of language-training methodology toward inclusion of trials spread across a wider time span, use of multiple trainers, and provision of natural cues and consequences. Guess and Mulligan (1982) have recently presented a rationale and format for teaching communication skills *as part of* the instructional programs for teaching other skill areas. The training program uses the curriculum-sequencing model described in Chapter 8.

The general area of communication development in severely handicapped students has grown to enormous proportions in recent years, relative to parallel developments in other curriculum areas. There are now excellent resources available to the teaching staff for starting functional and durable communicative skills with their severely handicapped students. As a general basis for sequencing linguistic components in a program of ongoing instruction, we would (naturally) continue to recommend Sailor, Guess, and Baer, 1973; Guess, Sailor, and Baer (1974, 1976a, 1976b, 1977a, 1977b, 1978a, 1978b); and also McDonald and Horstmeier (1978a, 1978b). For an extremely useful and comprehensive review and discussion of the issues, methods, and prerequisites to instruction, we recommend the recent text by Musselwhite and St. Louis (1982). These authors, and also Bigge (1982), provide a useful description of the role of eating and drinking skills and their facilitation, as well as instruction in the parallel development of speech skills in physically handicapped students. Bigge (1982) also provides a useful discussion of adaptive equipment and the range of available communication boards of value to severely handicapped students. Koegel, Rincover, and Egel (1982) and Wilcox and Thompson (1980) provided comprehensive reviews of issues and methods in teaching manual sign skills, particularly to autistic children. Rittenhouse and Myers (1982) have provided an excellent well-illustrated manual for initial manual sign instruction. Students interested in research on communication development in severely handicapped students will find the chapter by Guess (1980) a useful summary. Sailor, Guess, Goetz, Schuler, Utley, and Baldwin (1980), Reichle and Yoder (1979), and Shane (1979) have provided comprehensive discussions of the nature of relevant assessment in prelanguage instruction and of the need to match an appropriate communicative system and initial lexicon to the needs of a particular severely handicapped student.

Finally, we would strongly recommend the communication board training manual recently produced by Waldo, Riggs, Davaz, Hirsch, Eye, and Marshall (Note 2). This long-awaited project provides the reader with a step-by-step, individualized approach to functional and motivating nonspeech communication for severely handicapped students.

The chapter by Sailor et al. (1980) suggested a hierarchy of preferred language output modes that specified speech as the most salient and preferred mode. Manual signing ranked next if speech were ruled out during assessment. Ranking last were symbolic systems of the communication board variety for students too impaired in upper extremity use to sign expressively. Since that writing, we have become considerably less satisfied with the manual signing alternative. Signing, we now feel, tends to mitigate against maximally integrated placements for severely handicapped students. It does so by requiring the presence of an interpreter for all those situations of spontaneous language use that occur with persons in the community at large who do not comprehend manual signs. Most persons, even today, do not comprehend signs. For this reason, we now suggest that for those students for whom speech has been ruled out for the initial expressive vocabulary-building effort, the mode of expression be symbolic-graphic. The only exception that we would make to this general rule is to teach signs to those severely handicapped, hearing-impaired students who are being partially mainstreamed, or will be placed, into a hearing-impaired program where most of the significant others in the environment produce and respond to manual signs.

The relative advantages and disadvantages of symbol systems have been thoroughly reviewed and discussed by Musselwhite and St. Louis (1982). These authors have also provided a very useful description of (1) various types of switches that can be adapted for various handicapping conditions to enable use of a communication board (like eye control switches), (2) various response-assist options (like a head-stick), (3) options for presenting expressive content (like direct selecting), (4) various output options (like print, simulated vocal, and so on), and (5) various options for symbol output systems (like Bliss-symbolics) (pp. 149–199). We strongly recommend this book for basic consideration of all aspects of establishing an initial communication program for severely handicapped students. It provides an up-to-date alternative to the earlier landmark work by Vanderheiden and Grilley (1976) and provides a discussion of communication aids that is much more directly useful to very severely handicapped students.

Let's return now for a moment to classroom 1. The communication needs of most of the students in this educational program have been determined to be nonverbal output and speech or speech/symbolic input (cf., Sailor et al., 1980). Although instruction in communication skills takes place at specified times and in small groups for many of the students, the primary basis for instruction is language use in all environments by all staff. Instruction in communication skills, in other words, is continuous throughout the day and is carried on at home by the student's parents or group home staff, when possible.

Of the students in classroom 1, several have communication boards that are portable and collapsible, and can be mounted on the lap tray of their adapted wheelchairs. Several other students who have proficient use of their arms and hands have communication booklets that contain symbol cards for expressive output. The boards as well as the booklets are programmed with various sections (booklet) and overlays (board) that correspond to the respective language requirements and needs of various environments. Thus Ken, a student in classroom 1, has a color-coded booklet that has a special section for the classroom, one for home, one for the recreation and leisure environment, and one for the community, with words he is learning to use in the grocery store, at the swimming pool, and so on. The primary advantage to Ken of having his communcation booklet is that he can show pictured words to store clerks, locker room attendants, police officers, and so on, and make himself readily understood. Each symbol card has the word for the symbol printed on the card for this purpose. When Ken was being taught manual signs in an earlier program, he failed to display his signs in public and for good reason. He now shows no reticence in communicating and is almost always rewarded for his efforts by the community at large.

Waldo et al. (Note 2) provide, as mentioned earlier, a step-by-step program for teaching expressive symbol use to severely handicapped students. These authors recommend the symbols from the *Standard Rebus Glossary* (Clark, Davies, and Woodcock, 1974). Studies that have compared the

Rebus symbols with other symbol systems, such as Blissymbolics, have tended to suggest a greater ease of acquisition for these symbols, probably because of their greater simplicity, iconicity, and phonetic base (Clark, Note 3). Our own limited experience with Rebus symbol cards used in conjunction with the instructional procedure suggested by Waldo et al. leads us to consider the communication board/booklet expressive system to be a major innovative development in the field and a good bet for instilling motivation in severely handicapped students to amass increasingly complex and useful linguistic skills.

There is some suggestion, although it is too early to tell at this writing, that expressive speech in at least some severely handicapped students may be facilitated and thus may develop parallel to instruction focused on symbol output. Finally, we tend to agree, for now, with Schuler (1979) that symbol output may yet prove to be the system of choice for expression with nonverbal autistic children.

SOCIAL DEVELOPMENT

Socialization, like communication, is an area of rapid development in education of the severely handicapped in the past few years. Wehman and Schleien (1981), for example, have recently published a comprehensive review and compendium of recreation and leisure skill equipment and programs available for severely handicapped students. Tremblay, Strain, Henderson, and Shores (1980), Certo and Kohl (in press), and Brown, Ford, Nesbit, Sweet, Donnellan, and Gruenewald (Note 4) have provided up-to-date considerations in promoting interactions between severely handicapped and nonhandicapped children on regular public school campuses.

Additionally, at least three recent projects have yielded published curricula that provide step-by-step instructional procedures for developing increased social skills among severely handicapped students and among severely handicapped students in interactions with nonhandicapped age peers (Wuerch and Voeltz, 1981; Ford, Brown, Pumpian, Baumgart, Nesbit, Schroeder, and Loomis, 1980; Gee, Roger, Graham, Piuma, Halvorsen, Beckstead, Murray, Wallen, and Sailor, Note 5).

The Social Interaction Curriculum (SIC) developed in San Francisco (Gee et al., Note 5) begins with an environmental inventory completed by parents and teaching staff. From this inventory, initial target social responses are identified, and instructional times and places are selected. Transient social responses like greetings are taught first, followed by leisure exchanges or play responses between two or more persons. Peer tutoring is included as a somewhat more advanced instructional procedure later on in the process. Age-appropriate games are taught in the context of developing social skills (for example, Frisbee, Lego Blocks). Both the

Voeltz/Hawaii curriculum and the Gee/San Francisco curriculum stress small-group instruction, using small numbers of training trials, different instructors, and a wide variety of environments in order to promote maximum generalization of social skills.

Severely handicapped students have traditionally been exposed to *vertical* social development patterns—patterns that trap students in primarily one-way interactions involving a single, care-providing adult. The process has resulted in strong institutionalized tendencies to ignore age peers and to compete with them for adult attention, a process that contributes to the developmment of aberrant behavior.

Now, students are strongly encouraged to acquire a *horizontal* process interaction pattern. It promotes the value of interaction among age peers, whether disabled or nondisabled. The horizontal pattern, because it is normal in the broader social context, tends to mitigate against displays of aberrant behavior to gain adult attention. It increases motivation to live in a social context and leads to the development of normal appearance and behavior through the process of imitation. The shift in stress from vertical to horizontal social interaction patterns is one of the most striking and beneficial changes in the field of education of the severely handicapped.

PREVOCATIONAL DEVELOPMENT

Of all the dramatic developments we have witnessed in the past few years in various curriculum areas for severely handicapped elementary programs, the prevocational area is certainly the least well developed. Nearly everyone agrees that some prerequisite instruction should be carried out in the upper-age ranges of the elementary program to prepare a student for significant vocational instruction at the level of the middle and secondary school programs. Few people, however, agree on the form that instruction should take.

In a section entitled "Prevocational Skills," Van Etten, Arkell, and Van Etten (1980, pp. 251–252) point out the dilemma of unknown prerequisites. Do we spend a portion of our school day in an elementary program having our students play workshop? Do we line them up along a bench and have them sort screws, nuts, and bolts, or assemble something like hair curler kits, moving from left to right up the assembly line? If so, what specific skills can we expect to transfer to genuine vocational preparation later on? If we reject the workshop preparation model, what can we do to assist transition to vocational training? Van Etten et al. (1980) suggest that the more traditional prevocational tasks, such as folding clothes, being someplace on time, cleaning tools and the work area, and so on, are useful skills to have *outside* of the strictly vocational arena and thus constitute a useful prevocational curriculum as well.

Our feeling is that there are probably no generally transferable prevocational skills that will directly facilitate later vocational preparation, apart from the range of social, communicative, and functional life skills that comprise the working program plan as developed from the priority matrix presented in Chapter 5. We believe that folding towels is a useful instructional component only as a part of a general instructional plan to increase a student's independent living skills in the present home environment. As an isolated task intended to somehow foster later vocational skill development, we feel it is useless, mundane, and probably of low motivational value.

We clearly favor movement away from educational offerings that reinforce the concept of sheltered, segregated, and otherwise institutionalized future placements. Pumpian, Baumgart, Shiraga, Ford, Nesbit, Loomis, and Brown (1980) recently presented a model for general consideration in the vocational preparation of severely handicapped students at the secondary and postschool age level. Their model calls for a wide, community-based approach to job training that focuses on environmental assessment as the starting point and *individualized* training for specific employment that would be followed up by supervised instruction on site. This is clearly a very different alternative to the traditional segregated, sheltered workshop model.

In the absence of information at the elementary school level of likely future job placement sites for severely handicapped students, we would argue that the best *prevocational* curriculum would be the total functional life skills curriculum generally appropriate to the elementary school special day class. We would relegate towel folding, nut and bolt sorting, and similar activities to the realm of block stacking and bead stringing: meaningless activities that depress students and fail to teach useful skills.

THE FUTURE DIRECTION OF THE ELEMENTARY PROGRAM

We conclude discussion of the elementary school program by pointing to the future of educational services to the elementary school-age population as we can best forecast it. As a field, we have finally moved from the need to pattern our programs after a preschool program for normal children because of the mental age of our students. We have recognized the importance of functional life skill instruction and the corresponding uselessness of preacademic instruction on developmental tasks. What remains is to *integrate* our educational service models more fully with other community resources, including the home.

The future of elementary programs for the severely handicapped will clearly lie in a school-without-walls concept (cf., Brown et al., Note 4), which, although based on the elementary school campus, will focus increasing amounts of time off-campus in a multiplicity of environments. This will include the place of residence, where increasing competence and mobility is needed in order to become more independent and to enjoy a higher quality of life.

To accomplish this transition fully will require an unprecedented degree of interagency cooperation. Ultimately, educators will need to combine instructional plans with group care staff, recreation personnel, vocational and rehabilitation personnel, and, more completely, parents.

Many school districts presently treat the parents of severely handicapped children as no more than bodies who must show up when called and sign an IEP. The future for meaningful elementary programs calls for much more than that. We recognize that not all parents, for a variety of reasons, have the time and/or capability to become active participants in their child's instructional program. But for those parents who have the wherewithal and the desire to participate, the need for their involvement is great. Although resources must be committed to their training and to supply them with information, it is well worth the increased investment.

When instructional programs are conducted and monitored at home as well as in school and community, the progress observed is striking. We look forward to the day when parents who express a desire to assist in the process are *scheduled* on an organizational plan that they helped to develop and that spans a twelve-hour day, not just a six-hour school day. That day, we suspect, is not far off.

SUMMARY

We began this chapter with a discussion of various approaches to the structure of elementary programs for severely handicapped students since passage of PL 94–142. We then presented an outline of what we consider to be model programs for this age group using two hypothetical severely handicapped classes as examples. Sample formats were presented and discussed to illustrate the instructional model, and a classroom organizational chart was presented to illustrate the overall staff pattern. Classroom diagrams were used to illustrate the physical layout of the model classes, and lists of minimal furnishings and supplies were presented. Finally, particular attention was devoted to communication, social and prevocational development as elements in an elementary program. We concluded the chapter with an overview of likely future objectives of elementary level, severely handicapped programs.

CHAPTER 11 _____

The Secondary Program

Parents of handicapped adolescents are fully aware of the rapid changes that take place during the secondary school years. This is a period of transition, as peer and community values start to replace or modify parental standards, expectations, and lifestyles. Growing independence in adolescents is directed toward achieving the skills that will allow them to eventually leave the home and establish an independent life in the community. This is a period often filled with uncertainty, conflict, and sometimes fear. It is a time in which parents may have a tendency to overprotect their child, and the child, in turn, may frequently openly rebel against authority in the home.

All these problems, and many more, are likely to be magnified in the case of severely handicapped adolescents. Their parents become increasingly concerned about the time when public school services will no longer be available and they will not be able to provide their children with food, shelter, and protection. Many questions arise: "Where will my child live?" "Who will provide the money to support him?" "Will she have to be placed in an institution?" "Are nursing homes available?" Other equally important parental concerns relate to their children's sexual behavior, their personal safety, and their acceptance into community settings and activities. Many of these questions asked by parents of older severely handicapped children have not been adequately addressed by educators and other service providers in our society.

Efforts have thus far been primarily directed toward procuring and maintaining educational opportunities for severely handicapped children, especially those of a younger age. Many severely handicapped adults who remain in institutional settings have, for the time, been written off. Deinstitutionalization, for the most part, has been directed at younger children, and public school programs have been geared toward preschool and especially elementary classes. However, as these children grow older, they must move on to secondary-level classes. The nature and ultimate success of these classes are important elements in our efforts to provide services to severely handicapped students. These classes and related secondary-level services must provide for a successful transition from home to community, thus preparing the severely handicapped person for adaptive living in postschool environments.

TRANSITION FROM HOME TO COMMUNITY

Community living arrangements of various types for severely handicapped adults are discussed in detail in Chapter 12. In this chapter, we will suggest that secondary-level educational programs must also play a major role in preparing severely handicapped persons for community living. Certo, Brown, Belmore, and Crowner (1977) and Certo and Kohl (in press) have emphasized the importance of combining classroom instruction with community-skill training at the secondary level. Important adaptive behavior and vocational skills are taught concurrently in classroom and community settings or, where possible, exclusively in community settings (Brown, Nisbet, Ford, Sweet, Shiraga, and Loomis, Note 1). The community-school service delivery model described by these writers is congruent with the transition model presented in this chapter. Also of "special" importance in this model are secondary-level classes in regular public junior and senior high schools. The public school is perceived as the environment in which the severely handicapped young adult is prepared for eventual community living through three major channels: school to home, school to community, and home to community.

SCHOOL TO HOME

The infant and elementary program models presented earlier emphasized the importance of teaching functional skills that enable severely handicapped children to better adapt to living conditions at home, that is, skills that make it easier for parents or primary caregivers to maintain their children in a home and community environment. As part of this process, we have stressed the importance of teaching both general skills and specific adaptive behavior skills that might well be unique to a particular household.

The secondary-level program necessarily places more emphasis on the general independent living skills required for successful maintenance in settings other than the original home. In this transition model, the classroom teacher and parents jointly, where possible, identify home-living-skill deficiencies that require additional training programs. This additional training is then coordinated between the school and home. Training programs might, for example, be needed in cooking and shopping skills, using a vacuum sweeper, washing clothes, developing leisure activities, and possibly learning appropriate sexual conduct and hygienic precautions. These and numerous other areas of training and development are primarily oriented toward adult domestic living arrangements.

Finally, Freagon (1982) has provided a review of the issues and a set of specific tactics that pertain to joint efforts of residential caregivers and public school teachers of severely handicapped students. Included in this paper is a sample schedule that illustrates a combined school-group home instructional approach to teaching domestic living skills.

SCHOOL TO COMMUNITY

The interaction model for transition from home to community living includes an extension of the classroom to representative urban or rural community settings. These ideally include vocational training and opportunities for work. The community thus becomes a part of the secondary-level program. Certo et al. (1977) have underscored the importance of teaching community living skills both in the classroom and in various community settings where the behaviors are expected to occur. They underscore the fact that many living skills can best be taught in the actual community settings, rather than in the more artificial environment of the school classroom. These writers have also examined the difficult decision of which skills can best be taught in the classroom and which can best be taught in natural community environments. Brown et al. have extended the argument for community-based instruction by calling for a total nonschool instructional model, which will be discussed in some detail later in this chapter.

A survey of secondary special education programs in Vermont indicated that 86 percent of the respondents felt that teaching the use of community services to handicapped persons was necessary for postschool adjustment (Williams, Friedl, and Vogelsberg, Note 2). This finding is probably typical of other states and accentuates the need for teaching community living skills during the secondary-level school years.

HOME TO COMMUNITY

The third component of the transition model indirectly involves the secondary-level school program. The interaction between school and home expands the development of domestic living skills. The interaction of school and community teaches appropriate vocational and community living skills. The design of the secondary-level program includes provisions for skill training in both the home and community. Parents, for example, are encouraged to support the development of community living skills by pro-

viding occasions in the community where the behavior can occur and by helping to identify skill areas where new or additional training is necessary. Parents or parent surrogates are thus essential components in the successful transition from home to community.

On the other hand, the secondary public school program can also serve as a catalyst to help bring appropriate community services to the home in preparation for eventual community living. The school serves both to initiate and to follow up on services that can help prepare the severely handicapped person for the community. The program would ensure, for example, initial contact between group homes and parents during the school year, contact with the public health nurse if continued medical assistance were required, contact with community social services to help prepare parents emotionally for the possible movement of their child from the family home to a group home, and so on. In each of these examples, the public school plays a major role in helping to bring together the service providers with the parents.

The secondary program model presented thus actively interrelates classroom instruction with training in community living skills, vocational preparation, and domestic living. The classroom is a provider and an integrator of services, as well as a facilitator of interactions among the school, the home, and the community. Each component is essential for successful transition from home to community living in the postschool years.

A TRANSITION MODEL

ROLE OF THE TEACHER

In this transition model, the teacher of the secondary-level program for the severely handicapped has a number of important roles and responsibilities, many of which are not within traditional teaching assignments and expectations. The home-to-community-living transition model requires the teacher to extend the instructional environment beyond the immediate school setting. It requires much more than occasional visits to selected community settings and periodic parent-teacher conferences. The model requires that the teacher assume at least the following roles.

Instructor.   The teacher is responsible for providing direct instruction to students in a variety of content areas, including vocational training, self-help skill development, community living, and the appropriate use of leisure time. The teacher must interrelate these training activities in a functional manner and identify in each student the specific areas where instructional programming is most needed. The responsibility includes the supervision and scheduling of teaching assistants who also must share major teaching roles.

Integrator of Training Activities.   The teacher assumes a facilitative role that integrates other community service agencies into a total habilitation program. These additional agencies might include, for example, state and local vocational training programs, local businesses and industries that provide on-site work experiences, and any other agencies in the community that may potentially provide direct training and instruction to severely handicapped persons. Parent training activities in the home comprise a major component of these integrated services, just as they have in the previous classroom models. The teacher's role as a facilitator requires that all these training programs and activities be planned and implemented in an organized manner that allows for maximum transfer of skill acquisition across persons and settings.

Integrator of Community Services.   The teacher helps identify and elicit the support of various community services for severely handicapped students at the secondary level. In this role, the classroom teacher serves as both a resource person and an initiator of requests for services. Teachers must have sources available to them for contact with vital services relating directly or indirectly to eventual community living accommodations. These services and agencies might include the identification of potential group homes, foster homes, or boarding homes; information on various transportation systems; and essential medical and health services. This identification of needed services is an important component of the transition from home to community living. The teacher should have available a list of resource agencies in the community for parents to contact during the secondary-level school years so that sound planning can take place for that time when public school services are no longer available.

In summary, our transition model requires a teacher to identify areas of instruction for community living skills, coordinate an array of essential training personnel, integrate training programs in the school, the community, and the home, and identify and procure additional services and information necessary to start up and sustain semi-independent living in the community.

CLASSROOM DESIGN

It is difficult to describe or even identify any one type of secondary design for severely handicapped students. The physical arrangement of the classroom, for example, is totally dependent upon the availability of other areas for training in the public school and in the community where the school is located. Certainly, elementary schools are *not* recommended for secondary-level classrooms. The elementary school provides neither opportunities for age-appropriate peer interactions nor, typically, the ancillary training areas needed for secondary-level classes. Elementary schools do not, for example, have home living areas where domestic skills can be taught nor vocational training areas nor lounge and recreational areas appropriate for older students.

If we are to take seriously the goal of providing public education to severely handicapped students, then equal responsibility must be taken to ensure that education classes are placed in those public school buildings that can accommodate the chronological age level of the students involved. For this reason, *secondary-level classes for the severely handicapped should be located in secondary-level public school facilities.*

Within these facilities, opportunities for the use of important training areas are necessary. Access to particular training areas will ultimately determine the design of the secondary-level classroom program. The classroom design is obviously not a single space where all education and training activities take place. Instead, the classroom is essentially a homeroom where various training activities and services are coordinated both within the school building and beyond the school to the community and home settings. The home-to-community transition model emphasizes training in those community settings where the behaviors or skills must ultimately occur.

Thus, the first issues in program design revolve around what specific skills can best be taught in formal training areas and what components or dimensions of those skills should be trained in real-life situations (see Certo et al., 1977 for further discussion of this issue).

Vocational Training Areas. Vocational training should, whenever possible, take place in real-life work settings. The vocational training areas within the public schools are utilized only for those students who need to develop the most basic work habits and skills

Domestic Living Training Areas. Many of the domestic skills required for independent living can be taught in the public schools, provided that various types of equipment and materials are made available within several instructional areas. Students should have access to kitchen equipment for learning food preparation and cooking skills and to laundry equipment for learning washing and drying skills. Unfortunately, many of the areas for teaching advanced domestic skills in the public schools are not adapted to the needs of students in wheelchairs. Cabinets, for example, may be placed too high on the walls, electrical outlets may be difficult to reach from a wheelchair, and so on. The physical design of a classroom for severely handicapped students at the secondary level should take into consideration the special adaptations required for physical disabilities.

Other types of domestic skills can be taught in areas without permanent equipment, provided adequate space is available. Teaching students to use record players, TVs, radios, vacuum sweepers, and similar small appliances require only the space that can be found in a typical classroom setting. Other domestic skills can and should be taught as they occur in the natural environment of the school building, for example, the use of vending machines, lockers, light switches, fire exits, telephones, and water fountains. The school program should extend, wherever possible, to those locations and situations in the community where relevant skills can be taught in the most natural and functional manner. Group homes in the vicinity of a school program, for example, are usually empty during the day and provide excellent training environments for domestic living skills.

CURRICULUM

Location-Specific Training Activities. All aspects of the curriculum at the secondary level are directed toward preparing the students to live in the particular community environments in which they are likely to reside upon completion of the public school program. Brown, Nietupski, and Hamre-Nietupski (1976) have discussed the *criterion of ultimate functioning* as an important concept in public school education for the severely handicapped. This concept refers to the need to provide students with those skills necessary to future adaptive functioning in postschool environments. Where the student is likely to be located at some future time is predicted at the outset. Then the student is prepared to adapt to the demands and expectations of that environment. The criterion of ultimate functioning concept and the home-to-community-living transition model both require that instruction be oriented toward the unique living conditions found in each community.

There are distinct differences in the community-living requirements and lifestyles of urban and rural areas. For example, public bus systems are usually not found in small communities, and students there must rely on independent methods of mobility like a local taxi service or private transportation. Smaller communities have fewer specialized shopping stores, fewer public recreational services, and, of course, fewer options for employment. All these conditions, and more, influence important dimensions of the curriculum content. Vocational training in smaller communities is more likely to be oriented toward sheltered employment. In urban areas, more opportunities tend to exist for training in competitive employment situations.

On a more personal and social level, previous environmental studies have shown quite distinct differences between small and urban communities in the frequency and quality of interactions (Barker, 1973). For example, in smaller communities, the likelihood of contacts with the same persons across multiple settings is greater than in larger cities. This indicates the need for differential social skill training. An instructional objective in a small community might, for example, emphasize learning names of selected persons in the community who might be encountered across settings. In larger communities, the objective might center on how to interact initially with strangers.

Teaching Age-Appropriate Skills.   Brown, Branston, Hamre-Nietupski, Pumpian, Certo, and Gruenewald (1978) have noted that

> since severely handicapped students manifest significant skill deficits, they frequently receive instruction only on curriculum objectives characteristically offered to and mastered by infants or very young children. As severely handicapped students become adolescents or young adults, the outcome of such curricular strategies often results in the delivery of instruction which is nonfunctional, artificial, and inappropriate for their chronological age. (p. 7)

These authors emphasize the importance of teaching functional, age-appropriate skills in secondary level programs, skills that are appropriate to the natural environment. Brown et al. (1978) and Brown, Branston-McLean, Baumgart, Vincent, Falvey, and Schroeder (1979) have presented a workable strategy for developing chronological-age-appropriate curricular content for severely handicapped adolescents and young adults. Their strategy consists of six sequential phases.

Phase I: Delineate curriculum domains. In this initial phase, four curriculum content areas are considered important. These include domestic skills, vocational training, use of leisure and recreational activities and skills necessary for community living.

Phase II: Delineate the variety of natural environments in which severely handicapped students function or might function. For each of the content areas in Phase I, it is next necessary to identify in the community the various settings where the behavior would be expected to occur presently or at some future time. In Phase II, a listing is made of those environments in the community that would require the use of domestic skills, vocational training, leisure time, and community living skills.

Phase III: Delineate and inventory the subenvironments in which severely handicapped students function or might function. Smaller environments and settings within each larger environment are next identified and listed. For example, a home might be divided into subenvironments, such as a bedroom, bathroom, and dining room.

Phase IV: Delineate and inventory the activities that occur in the subenvironments. This phase requires that an inventory be made of appropriate age-related activities that would be expected to occur in the various subenvironments. Activities appropriate to a bathroom might include, for example, toileting, cleaning the sink, folding towels, and bathing. Haas and Hanline (Note 3) and Freagon (Note 4) have recently developed prototypes of some generally usable check lists for this purpose.

Phase V: Delineate the skills needed in order to engage in the activities. The next phase in this curriculum design strategy requires the delineation of behavioral skills that will allow the severely handicapped individual to participate to at least some degree in the various activities identified in Phase IV. This might include, for example, a listing of the specific responses necessary for taking a bath. A procedure for delineating these skills has been described by Belmore and Brown (1978).

Phase VI: Design and implement the instructional programs necessary to ensure the performance of the delineated skills in the natural environment. This final phase entails the teaching of the appropriate skills that have been targeted for remedial training in Phase V. This, of course, includes use of many of the various instructional programs to be discussed later in this chapter.

The most significant contribution of the curriculum development strategy summarized by Brown et al. (1978) is the emphasis placed on teaching functional, chronological-age-related skills that are necessary for successful interactions in domestic, community, and vocational settings. The inventories of the various environments and subenvironments should reflect types of location-specific training activities indigenous to individual communities that vary in population density and lifestyles.

Teaching Skill Clusters. In the discussion of teaching strategies in Chapter 8, emphasis was placed on teaching skill clusters or potential response classes. This strategy was further detailed in Chapters 9 and 10, describing educational approaches for younger severely handicapped students. The same principle holds true for secondary-level training programs for severely handicapped students. A number of individual programs are available for remedial training in various skill areas. However, a total curricular strategy would include combining these programs into functional behavioral sequences that provide optimal generalization across and within the content areas. Further development of communication skills, for example, can be most efficiently programmed when teaching students domestic self-help, community living, or vocational skills. Various types of motor manipulation responses important to self-help training might well be included as part of the students' vocational program. Social skills are taught across all components of the students' daily curriculum.

Within the social context, variation in cues are included as an integral component of the curriculum. Proper social greetings, for example, are taught for various persons, settings, and situations; proper eating manners are taught in the home, in restaurants, cafeterias, and fast-food establishments. In all instances, *the curriculum should be specifically designed for promoting maximum generalization across actions and across the various cue conditions that signal when and where the behavior should occur.*

TRAINING PROGRAMS FOR SECONDARY-LEVEL STUDENTS

COMMUNICATION

By the time students reach the age of secondary-level classes, a particular communication mode should have been identified and minimally established; this could include speech, manual signing, communication boards, or a combination of any two modes. For this age group, however, quite severe communication deficits will still be present for many, if not most, severely handicapped students. Many will be very limited in their ability to express themselves and will not be able to understand much of what is communicated to them. Many will have developed (or will continue to demonstrate) innappropriate speech patterns. Many severely handicapped adolescents will lack a basic communication system for interacting in even the most common types of social encounters. There remains, accordingly, much to be done in further developing and refining the communication skills for secondary-level severely handicapped students. This effort should include expanding the student's present communication skill level; reducing, in some cases, inappropriate speech patterns; and, for some students, upgrading nonspeech modes.

Expanding Communication Skills.   Primary objectives for training at the secondary level include increasing the students' communication in a variety of settings and conditions, and providing the vocabulary necessary for domestic and community living in postschool environments.

There are, at present, very few language training curricula for handicapped secondary-level students. Most language training programs have been specifically designed for children, so that the content of these programs reflects activities more appropriate to younger age levels. The Guess, Sailor, and Baer program (1976a, 1976b, 1977, 1978) has been used with older (and even adult) severely handicapped persons. Use of this program for older students does require, however, fairly extensive adaptations of the training activities and materials to render them age-appropriate.

The late-intermediate (Phase III) section of the Waryas and Stremel-Campbell (1978) language training program is appropriate to secondary-level severely handicapped students. This phase of the program continues to build grammar and more complicated forms of syntax. In fact, for some older severely handicapped students, the early-intermediate (Phase II) section of the Waryas and Stremel program may be appropriate. This phase focuses on expanding the students' use of basic grammatical repertoires and teaching the productive and receptive use of auxiliary verbs, negatives, and possessives.

For the most part, however, communication training programs for severely handicapped students at the secondary level are not recommended. Attention should be directed, instead, toward teaching communication skills, and expanding these skills within the context of other ongoing programs and natural communication opportunities. This offers the opportunity to relate communication content directly to functional skill training in a more natural manner. Hamre-Nietupski and Williams (1977) have, for example, included basic vocabulary training in their programs for teaching sex education and social skills at the secondary level. In these programs, the necessary vocabulary content is taught in conjunction with other skill-training areas. In a similar fashion, communication skills should be expanded within vocational training, domestic skill training, and community living instruction. Teaching students, for example, to identify (expressively and receptively) the names of various appliances during domestic skill training provides a much more functional opportunity for their vocabulary to be expanded. Teaching appropriate social greetings in real-life community settings is another example of functional communication training at the secondary level.

As a word of caution, however, this type of communication training should not be done in a haphazard fashion. Specific communication training objectives and programs should be developed for each setting or situation where skill expansion is desired. Appropriate instructional procedures (like modeling or prompting) should be systematically followed by the teaching staff, and provisions for prompting generalization should be built into the training effort (see Chapter 4).

In some cases, specific programs to develop conversational and social communication may be needed for groups of students. Garcia (1974) conducted a study in which three verbal responses were trained separately and then together to form a rudimentary conversational unit in two severely retarded adolescents who were imitative and who also exhibited a small repertoire of words. Generalization was systematically trained across settings and adults. This study illustrates procedures for both establishing rudimentary conversational speech and extending the skill to other persons and environments.

One of the problems associated with the training of conversational speech in handicapped individuals is the observation that they might have very little to talk about. A study by Keilitz, Tucker, and Horner (1973) serves as an excellent example of developing appropriate conversational speech around a common physical property, a television set. Specifically, their procedures sought to increase verbalization among mildly and moderately retarded adolescents about news events appearing on television. This study investigated both cues and consequent effects as variables influencing verbalization. The two event cues were massed and distributed news presentations. *Massed news* was defined as uninterrupted presentations. *Distributed news* presentations were temporally spaced according to content with interspersed opportunities for verbalizations between news items. The effects (or reinforcers) for verbalization included tokens (exchangeable for money) and verbal praise. Verbal responses were scored for accuracy of information, and accuracy was scored according to subject (for example, "horses"), action ("paraded"), object ("in county fair horse show"), and additional information ("Lawrence, Kansas"). Results showed the accuracy of verbal statements about the news was higher in the distributed news format, and news reporting accuracy was higher under reinforcement procedures. Although the study was not conducted with severely handicapped students, the procedures used would seem to be applicable to this population.

Wildgen (Note 5) reported on a procedure to teach spontaneous speech to severely handicapped adolescents, using picture cards as stimuli. In the first part of the study, the students were taught to tell stories for each picture card, using past, present, and future tenses. Modeling and differential reinforcement procedures were used in the training sessions. In the second part of the study, two of the students participated in conversational speech training. Sessions were held in a lounge area where the trainer conversed with the students about their past experiences, current activities, and future plans. Again, modeling and differential reinforcement procedures were used to teach appropriate tense usage in the conversational speech training.

Hamre-Nietupski and Williams (1977) have described an instructional program to teach verbal interaction skills for making small talk. These skills were taught with modeling and verbal prompting procedures. The program, described in four phases, moved from the classroom to appropriate community settings, like stores, public libraries, and school dances. A unique feature of the program used role playing for teaching appropriate verbal interactions when students were called names, teased, or egged-on by others to act inappropriately. Similarly, Certo and Kohl (1982) presented a series of tactics for promoting communicative social interactions among severely handicapped students and their age peers.

Environmental Manipulations.   Instructional programs designed to develop or enhance specific communication skills among severely handicapped students at the secondary level are important components of the curriculum. There are, however, many opportunities for developing age-appropriate communication interactions through more global manipulations of events or conditions in the environment (Rogers-Warren and Warren, 1977). This approach involves manipulating physical properties of settings to increase the opportunities for communication to occur.

In an example of such an "ecobehavioral" approach, Van Biervliet (Note 6) demonstrated that more conversation occurred among severely and moderately retarded adolescents when meals were served family style, as compared to food served cafeteria style. Family-style serving required that food be placed in bowls and on platters which were passed around the table during mealtimes. The family-style serving procedures produced different effects among the students, which were generally related to the degree and complexity of the students' speaking abilities. A larger increase in peer-directed speech was observed among the more verbally skilled participants. A real advantage offered by this procedure was the increase in conversational speech attained through this rather simple manipulation of how students were served their meals. This type of alteration in the dining room setting required little formal staff training.

The ecobehavioral approach would seem to have a great deal of promise for developing functional communication skills among severely handicapped students in secondary-level classes. It requires an initial analysis of existing situations in which students are together in one location followed by manipulations of conditions in those situations to increase the likelihood of appropriate communication interactions.

Reducing Deviant Speech. A large number of atypical speech patterns exist among severely handicapped students in secondary-level classrooms. These range from deviant speech to abusive language and profanity. Not surprisingly, a survey of vocational teachers in sheltered workshops found that irritating verbal manners were more likely to result in the firing of retarded workers than were poor communication skills (Malgady, Barcher, Towner, and David, 1979). Certainly, reducing inappropriate speech among severely handicapped students at the secondary level is important for successful interactions in community settings and domestic living arrangements.

Common deviant speech patterns found among secondary-level students include echolalia, perseveration, voice intensity problems, and inappropriate situational content. All of these problems may, of course, be found at earlier age levels. *Echolalia,* as previously discussed, is common among young severely handicapped children, especially autistic children.

Speech perseveration is present when the same response (often quite appropriate) is repeated over and over again. The authors are familiar, for example, with an adolescent girl who could not terminate a greeting response ("Hi"). She would appropriately say "Hi" when other persons approached her. The problem occurred, however, when the same responses would be repeated until the other persons were well beyond hearing distance. An earlier study reported by Butz and Hasazi (1973) reported the successful reduction of perseverative speech in a nine-year-old mildly retarded boy through the use of differential positive reinforcement procedures.

Voice intensity problems occur when the speech his transmitted at a volume level that is either too loud or too soft. Speaking in voice levels that are too loud has been typically associated with older retarded residents who grew up in institutional settings. Likely excessive noise levels in many institutional environments are responsible for gradually "shaping" louder speaking voices over the years. In some cases, the lack of voice loudness is the problem. Jackson and Wallace (1974) reported on a study to increase voice intensity in a 14-year-old severely handicapped boy who attended a public school classroom. The procedure consisted of reinforcing speech at increasingly greater distances between the student and teacher. Results were reported to be quite successful.

Inappropriate speech constitutes the most common type of deviant verbal behavior among severely handicapped adolescents. Typically, this is a problem in discriminating the appropriate situational cues for speech as they relate to context and time. Barton (1970), for example, reported a study in which a severely handicapped boy would frequently answer questions with jingles or advertising slogans. Sanders (1971) reported on an adolescent retarded girl whose main topic of conversation centered on supplies needed by the institution in which she resided. Excessive profanity might also be included under inappropriate speech patterns. The authors are familiar with a severely handicapped adolescent who uses a four-letter word to respond verbally to almost any type of question or command.

It is likely that the deviant speech patterns described above are maintained by occasional effects in the form of attention from other persons. Extinction of the inappropriate behavior, combined with differential positive effects for appropriate speech, have been the most commonly used remediation procedures. Procedures to reduce speech patterns should be built into the instructional program for adolescent students across persons and settings for maximum results. This requires an awareness by attending teachers, therapists, and parents of the need to ignore the identified speech deviation and to systematically reinforce more acceptable verbalizations when they occur. It is also necessary to monitor progress with accurate data collection procedures. The data analysis is also important in identifying situations in which the deviant speech is most likely to be evidenced, thus providing the opportunity for more concentrated intervention procedures.

Improving Non-speech Modes.   The previous chapter on classroom designs for elementary-level severely handicapped students discussed fundamental communication aids. These aids involve no electronic or moving parts, and a second person is required to determine the message being sent by the student. At the secondary classroom level, it is important to consider communication aids that are more independent for students using this type of system.

Independent communication aids allow the student to produce entire messages in the correctly assembled form without assistance from a second person. Most independent aids produce a printed copy of the message, that is, letters or words selected by the student from a display board are printed out. The second person is needed only to respond to the student in the same manner as one would respond to a verbal question or comment. The Auto-Com, described by Harris-Vanderheiden (1976), exemplifies an independent communication aid that can be obtained for either portable or nonportable use. The Auto-Com is an electronically operated communication device that prints out letters and words. This eliminates the need for a second person to monitor elements of a message as is required by more standard communication boards. Bliss symbols have also been incorporated into the Auto-Com system (Harris-Vanderheiden, 1976).

The use of independent communication aids, such as Auto-Com, would be especially important for those students at the secondary class level who are preparing for semi-independent living in the community. These aids allow the receivers to independently receive and interpret messages sent by the student, thus avoiding one of the major problems associated with the more basic communication aids described in earlier chapters.

For those students using signing at the secondary level, major emphasis should be placed on the types of expansions commonly recommended for speech. This includes functional vocabulary training and conversational speech. A major problem with signing remains, of course, in community interactions where the audience is generally not familiar with sign systems. Some effort should be made to acquaint persons in the community who have considerable contact with severely handicapped students with some basic and highly functional signs they might encounter. These community persons might include, for example, employment supervisors, bus drivers who consistently transport students who sign, and house parents or staff members in semi-independent living arrangements.

DEVELOPING SELF-HELP SKILLS FOR DOMESTIC LIVING ENVIRONMENTS

The strategy presented earlier by Brown, Branston-McClean, Baumgart, Vincent, Falvey, and Schroeder (1979) offers a viable plan of action for identifying the types of domestic living skills that are important for severely handicapped students at the secondary level. This strategy recommended that an inventory be made of appropriate age-related activities that could be expected to occur in various subenvironments. These might include, for example, semi-independent living accommodations in the community. Additionally, a list of self-care skills for semi-independent and independent functioning has been prepared by Hamre-Nietupski and Williams (1977). It includes basic grooming, dressing, domestic maintenance, and cooking skills.

Programs for teaching specific domestic living skills to secondary-level students are somewhat limited at this time. Many of the programs that are available have not included profoundly retarded persons in the validation sample, and many have not been empirically investigated. Nevertheless, available instructional materials in the domestic living area can provide a teacher with the framework of a training program so that adaptations can be made for the more severely handicapped students at the secondary level. Table 11.1 presents, for example, some selected programs that appear to be applicable to a severely handicapped population. Some, in fact, have been developed and validated with severely handicapped students.

TABLE 11.1
Domestic Skill Training Programs Appropriate
to Secondary-Level Students

Area of of Training	Author(s)	Source
Self-medication	M. Brickey	*Mental Retardation,* 1978, Vol. 16 pp. 29–33.
Dressing/ undressing	N. Azrin, R. Schaeffer, and M. Wesolowski	*Mental Retardation,* 1976, Vol. 16 pp. 29–33.
Complexion care	I. Keilitz, R. D. Horner, and K. Brown	*Project MORE:* Bellvue, Wash., Edmark Associates, 1975.
Hair washing	P. Lewis, C. Ferneti, and I. Keilitz.	*Project MORE:* Bellvue, Wash., Edmark Associates, 1975.
Use of deodorant	P. Lewis, C. Ferneti, and I. Keilitz.	*Project MORE:* Bellvue, Wash., Edmark Associates, 1975.
Toothbrushing	H. Bouter, and P. Smeets.	*International Journal of Rehabilitation Research,* 1979, Vol. 2, pp. 61–69.
Cooking	M. Robinson-Wilson	In G. T. Bellamy (ed.), *Habilitation of Severely and Profoundly Retarded Adults.* College of Education, Center on Human Development, University of Oregon, Eugene, Oregon, 1976.
Cooking	C. Spellman, T. Debriere, D. Jarboe, S. Campbell, and C. Harris.	In M. Snell (ed.), *Systematic Instruction of the Moderately and Severely Handicapped.* Charles E. Merrill Publishing Co., 1978, pp. 391–411.
Clothing selection	D. Nutter, and D. Reid.	*Journal of Applied Behavior Analysis,* 1978, Vol. 11, pp. 475–487.
Premenstrual care	P. Dedrick	In L. Brown, W. Williams, and T. Crowner, (eds.), *A Collection of Papers and Programs Related to Public School Services for Severely Handicapped Students.* Vol. IV, Specialized Education Services, Madison (Wisconsin) Public Schools, 1974, pp. 448–465.
Use of mouthwash	R. Nietupski	In L. Brown, W. Williams, and T. Crowner (eds.), *A Collection of Papers and Programs Related to Public School Services for Severely Handicapped Students.* Vol. IV, Specialized Education Services, Madison (Wisconsin) Public Schools, 1974, pp. 446–448.

(Continued)

TABLE 11.1
(Continued)

Use of telephone	J. Nietupski	In L. Brown, W. Williams, and T. Crowner (eds.), *A Collection of Papers and Programs Related to Public School Servicces for Severely Handicapped Students.* Vol. IV, Specialized Education Services, Madison (Wisconsin) Public Schools, 1974, pp. 507–560.
Folding towels	C. Fish	In D. Anderson, G. Hodson, and W. Jones (eds.), *Instructional Programming for the Handicapped Student.* Springfield, IL.: Charles C Thomas, 1975, pp. 526–528.
Folding washcloths	C. Fish	In D. Anderson, G. Hodson, and W. Jones (eds.), *Instructional Programming for the Handicapped Student.* Springfield, IL.: Charles C Thomas, 1975, pp. 529–531.
Making beds	R. Holt	In D. Anderson, G. Hodson, and W. Jones (eds.), *Instructional Programming for the Handicapped Student.* Springfield, IL.: Charles C Thomas, 1975, pp. 546–549.
Setting tables	B. Rowder	In D. Anderson, G. Hodson, and W. Jones (eds.), *Instructional Programming for the Handicapped Student.* Springfield, IL.: Charles C Thomas, 1975, pp. 563–565.
Sorting clothes		In D. Anderson, G. Hodson, and W. Jones (eds.), *Instructional Programming for the Handicapped Student.* Springfield, IL.: Charles C Thomas, 1975, pp. 567–569.
Sweeping floors		In D. Anderson, G. Hodson, and W. Jones (eds.), *Instructional Programming for the Handicapped Student.* Springfield, IL.: Charles C Thomas, 1975, pp. 570–571.
Washing clothes		In D. Anderson, G. Hodson, and W. Jones (eds.), *Instructional Programming for the Handicapped Student.* Springfield, IL.: Charles C Thomas, 1975, pp. 573–575.

Cuvo (1978) has presented a framework for teachers who wish to design their own instructional programs for teaching domestic (or community) living skills. Cuvo suggests that first a content task analysis should be made in conjunction with persons whose performance already meets acceptable standards. A janitor, for example, might be asked to model skills necessary for sweeping or mopping tasks. An experienced cook might be asked to model food preparation skills. Task analyses of these skills are then made and used as an initial component in developing a training program.

The second step in the model proposed by Cuvo is to have the task analysis examined by persons in the rehabilitation field who are familiar with rearranging cues to meet particular sensory or physical problems associated with severely handicapped conditions. In this way, the procedures are made more suitable for the students to be trained. Cuvo suggests that handicapped persons who already have the particular skill be asked to go through the training procedures to further validate content of the program.

Another more recent paper by Cuvo and Davis (1980) provides a review of various types of instructional techniques used in teaching home living skills to handicapped persons, focusing on antecedent cues. These include verbal instructions, visual cues, modeling, role playing, and physical prompts. Advantages and disadvantages of these various techniques are discussed with appropriate illustrations from the literature on domestic and community living skill training.

Pictorial Instruction.   The use of pictoral instruction to teach daily living skills has been described by Spellman, Debriere, Jarboe, Campbell, and Harris (1978) and by Freagon, Gillin, McDonnell, Hasley, Dolan, Williams, Woodyall, Cisco, Brankin, Costello, and Peters (1981). Various types of domestic skills are taught by picture books, in which the pictures show the sequential order in which certain tasks are completed. The picture books are used to teach meal preparation, food preparation, housekeeping tasks, shopping skills, and so on.

Figure 11.1 provides an illustration of a picture recipe book for preparing a hot dog. According to Spellman et al. (1978), "since persons with severe handicaps cannot use many of the existing symbol systems to obtain new information, picture books were developed as an instructional format" (p. 393).

The use of pictorial instruction does require the ability to understand the reference to the object or action that is symbolized by the picture. For some students, explicit instruction is required to learn this process. Additionally, most of the programs described by Spellman et al. have been used with moderately and mildly retarded students. Nevertheless, this particular

FIGURE 11.1
Hot dog recipe book

Reprinted from M. Snell (ed.), *Systematic Instruction of the Moderately and Severely Handicapped* (Columbus, Ohio: Charles E. Merrill, 1978), p. 401. Used by permission.

type of instructional format does hold promise for severely handicapped students, especially when the pictures are combined with other prompting and fading procedures. As suggested by Spellman et al., the development of generic skills via pictorial instruction has numerous advantages in teaching a variety of domestic living tasks. Johnson (Note 7) has designed a manual for teaching persons how to develop pictorial instruction workbooks for domestic living skills.

Freagon, Pajon, Brankin, Galloway, Rich, Karel, Wilson, Costello, Peters, and Hurd (1981) developed a pictorial aid program for shopping skills in a supermarket. Each shopper-student carries a workbook through the aisles of the market. On the left-hand side of the book are labels from the cans, bottles, or boxes to be selected. The student scans the shelves until an item is located that matches the label in the workbook. The item is then placed in the cart, the price is entered in a hand-held electronic calculator (another program), and the label is shifted in the workbook from the left side ("To select") to the right side ("Purchased"). In this case, the picture book uses a simple match-to-sample technique to develop selection skills in a shopping context.

Training Extended to the Home.   The transition model in this chapter emphasizes as one aspect the coordination of training between the school and home. This coordination is especially important when teaching domestic skills necessary for eventual semi-independent living in the community. Parents should be fully informed of the procedures and techniques for each of the domestic living skills being taught at school. Ideally, parents should also be following the same procedures in the home. If this is not possible, at least parent participation might be enlisted to set occasions in the home where newly learned domestic living skills could be maintained over time. The important thing is not to allow domestic skill instruction to become isolated to the school, but rather to structure continuity of teaching in the student's home environment.

DEVELOPING LEISURE TIME AND RECREATIONAL SKILLS

A major component of the secondary-level curriculum for severely handicapped students involves instruction in a variety of leisure time activities. Leisure time instruction is assuming increasing importance in the national effort to provide community-based living environments for severely handicapped individuals. Additionally, as the number of work hours decreases in our highly technological society, the use of spare time assumes even more prominence. Educational efforts should be expended to teach severely handicapped students a variety of skills that will enable them to lead happier lives through hobbies and recreational opportunities, just as non-handicapped persons do. There are many potential areas of instruction for severely handicapped students, including activities that can be engaged in by oneself, group participation activities, and sporting events. Leisure time and recreational skills range from activities involving little physical prowess to skills providing much needed exercise and physical fitness training. Some activities can be carried out in a home environment and some involve access to community-based facilities.

Wehman, Renzaglia, Berry, Schutz, and Karan (1978) have pointed out that there exist few leisure time programs that include specific procedures for teaching severely handicapped students and that there are relatively few recreation programs available for severely handicapped adolescents and adults. They reported one study, for example, that taught both physical fitness and table games to severely handicapped adolescents and adults. Another publication by Wehman (1979) has outlined some major components that classroom teachers should consider in recreation skill development for severely handicapped students. Two more recent works, Wehman and Schleien (1979a and 1979b) and Woerch and Voeltz (1981), have provided comprehensive leisure skill curricula for severely handicapped individuals.

One of the manuals produced by Wehman and Schleien (1979a) provides task-analyzed procedures for teaching a variety of hobby skills, including program categories for camping, cooking, cycling, kite flying, leisure walking, playing musical and rhythmical instruments, nature activities, needlework, painting, pet care, photography, table games, woodworking, spectator participation in home and community events, and others. All the individual programs within each major category provide a list of the materials needed for teaching the skill, specific procedures of instruction, and criterion levels for successful performance. Additionally, for each program category, there is a listing of core skills that are necessary for performance in each of the training activities within that category.

Table 11.2, for example, provides a listing of individual activities included under the program category of "needlework" and the motor sensory/motor skills that are essential for each activity.

A second manual produced by Wehman and Schleien (1979b) pertains to teaching sport skills. This manual is arranged in a manner similar to the one for hobbies and includes major program categories, individual activities within each category, and a listing of core motor and sensory motor skills appropriate to each training activity. The program categories in this manual include badminton, basketball, bowling, croquet, field hockey, fishing, football, golf, gymnastics, handball, horseshoes, playground equipment, shuffleboard, soccer, softball, swimming, tennis, track and field,

TABLE 11.2
Needlework

Name of Activity/ Leisure Skill	Core Skills											
	HEAD CONTROL	ATTENDING/FOCUSING	VISUAL/AUDITORY TRACKING	OBJECT PERMANENCE	MEANS/ENDS	PALMAR GRASP	PINCER GRASP	ARM/LEG EXTENSION (REACHING, PUSHING)	ARM/LEG FLEXION (PULLING)	CONTROLLED HAND RELEASE	SITTING UNSUPPORTED	STANDING UNSUPPORTED
Hold needle	X	X					X	X	X			
Thread needle	X	X					X	X	X	X		
Cut thread	X	X					X	X	X	X		
Tie knot at end of thread	X	X					X	X	X	X		
Push and pull needle through material	X	X				X	X	X	X	X		
Weave thread over and under yarn	X	X				X	X	X	X			
Make hook rug	X	X					X	X	X	X		
Connect dots, needle, and yarn pattern	X	X				X	X	X	X			
Make pot holder	X	X				X	X	X	X	X		
Operate sewing machine	X	X	X	X	X			X	X	X	X	

SOURCE: P. Wehman and S. Schleien, *Leisure Skills Curriculum for Developmentally Disabled Persons: Virginia Model, Book III,* "Hobbies" (Richmond, Vir.: School of Education, Virginia Commonwealth University, 1979) p. 90. Used by permission.

volleyball, weight training, and winter sports activities. Table 11.3 illustrates one of the training activities ("Entering swimming pool") that is included under the swimming program category in the manual.

One final consideration addressed by Wehman and Schleien (1980) pertains to the assessment and selection of leisure skills for severely handicapped individuals. In this article, the authors discussed several assessment procedures that include evaluating the preference of the individual for particular activities, the duration of time spent in leisure activities, the fre-

TABLE 11.3
Leisure Skills Curriculum for Developmentally Disabled Persons: Virginia Model
Subprogram Activity Category: Swimming

Instructional Objective: Given a swimming pool with a water depth of 3′, the participant will enter the pool and stand in the waist-high water for 1 minute, 100 percent of the time.
Materials: Swimming pool (3′ water depth)
Verbal Cue: "Billy, get into the water."

Task Analysis	Correction Procedures, Activity Guidelines, and Special Adaptations
1. Walk to ladder of swimming pool.	1. Teacher gives verbal cue to participant; if participant responds correctly, teacher provides reinforcement immediately.
2. Extend dominant arm outward toward ladder railing, palm faced down.	
3. Lower arm until palm makes contact with railing.	2. If participant does not respond correctly, then teacher repeats verbal cue and models correct response.
4. Curl fingers around top of railing.	3. If participant still does not respond correctly, then teacher repeats verbal cue and physically guides participant through correct response.
5. Wrap thumb around opposite side of top of railing.	
6. Apply inward pressure to grasp railing firmly.	4. This instructional sequence is repeated several times in each training session with participant.
7. Bend knee of right leg, raising foot 3″ off step.	
8. Lower foot to next by extending knee.	5. Because of the inherent dangers involved in any swimming program, it is highly recommended that a one-to-one instructional basis be used.
9. Step down to same step with right foot.	
10. Step down to next step with right foot.	6. A slight elevation around the pool provides safety against accidentally falling in while walking around the deck. A safety precaution that is always helpful is the use of the "buddy system."
11. Step down to same step with left foot.	
12. Step down to pool floor with right foot.	7. Steps with handrails leading into the water should be built with short tiers and a wide step to provide for easy entrance and exit. In some cases, rails are fixed across pool to permit participants to hold on and gain a feeling of security.
13. Step down to pool floor with left foot.	
14. Stand in water for 5 seconds.	
15. Stand in water for 10 seconds.	
16. Stand in water for 15 seconds.	8. Pool steps should be widely spaced and have smooth edges with handrails available.
17. Stand in water for 30 seconds.	
18. Stand in water for 1 minute.	9. Floating cork ropes can be used to divide pool into deep and shallow ends and may be used to help find way to ladder.

SOURCE: P. Wehman and S. Schleien, *Leisure Skills Curriculum for Developmentally Disabled Persons: Virginia Model,* Book IV, "Sports" (Richmond, Vir.: School of Education, Virginia Commonwealth University, 1979), p. 112. Used by permission.

quency and direction of the social interactions that occur during the activities, and the appropriateness of the activities. Importantly, Wehman and Schleien also presented a model for classroom teachers to use in selecting leisure skills for training. Criteria in that model include the level of functioning and physical characteristics of the students, the age-appropriateness of the skill to be taught, preference of the students, and considerations of access to materials and living environments. The authors pointed to the importance of evaluating the home and community environments in selecting leisure skills for severely handicapped students.

Another manual for teaching recreational activities, Sliney and Geelen (1977), includes specific training programs for simple individual recreational skills such as throwing, bouncing, rolling, catching, striking, kicking, moving, and balancing and for cooperative game activities such as basketball. The procedures are based on task analyses for each skill. Included for teachers are specific instructions derived from learning principles. This manual is well done and provides another resource for the leisure time and recreational skill area.

DEVELOPING SKILLS FOR APPROPRIATE SEXUAL BEHAVIOR

Historically, controversies have persisted concerning the public school's role in offering sex education courses to nonhandicapped students. Various groups have insisted that the home is the place to convey information concerning sexual conduct, reproduction, and personal hygiene. This controversy will likely have some ramifications for severely handicapped classes at the secondary level. There will undoubtedly be schools and school districts that adhere to the belief that sex education is not appropriate to a curriculum for either handicapped or nonhandicapped students. There will likely be individual teachers who would not feel comfortable in teaching some of the more anatomical and biological components of sexuality to older students in severely handicapped classrooms.

Yet it is most important that sex education be included in a combined school and home program for severely handicapped adolescent students. Because appropriate sexual conduct is necessary for eventual community living, a comprehensive instructional program in this area is needed. The program should cover many of the types of social skills related to interaction between members of the opposite sexes. It should include the teaching of the reproduction process and should contain, as far as possible, the teaching of skills for the prevention of venereal diseases, proper menstrual care for women, and the responsibilities of marriage and child bearing.

All this may seem abstract for a severely handicapped population, but there is no reason that appropriate training programs cannot be designed in the same manner as in other areas of skill development. Specific skills for sexual behavior and conduct can be task-analyzed and arranged in sequential steps, using training procedures and techniques common to other teaching areas.

A good starting point for developing a sex education curriculum for severely handicapped students is a program designed by Hamre-Nietupski and Williams (1977) for students who are somewhat higher functioning. This curriculum is divided into two phases.

Phase I includes training for the discrimination of body parts, sex distinctions, discrimination between sexes as a function of growth (age), and premenstrual identification and menstrual hygiene for adolescent girls. This phase also includes training for appropriate social and physical interactions between female and male students. Training procedures for the curriculum include modeling and verbal prompts. The curriculum was developed in cooperation with parents for three classrooms containing twenty adolescent students.

Phase II of the curriculum includes content for reproduction, prenatal growth, and intercourse. The program provides numerous suggestions and procedures for appropriate materials and reading matter accompanying the teaching sequence. Especially useful is a large reference section of recommended readings for professionals, parents, and students. These references cover many of the legal issues and concerns relative to sex education for the handicapped as well as information on marriage, parenthood, physical and biological aspects of reproduction, working with parents, and other topical areas. The program described by Hamre-Nietupski and Williams provides a good content outline for a sex education curriculum appropriate to a higher functioning, severely handicapped population of students. At present, however, the area of sex education remains one in which the available instructional programs are grossly underdeveloped in proportion to instructional needs.

COMMUNITY LIVING SKILLS

We have witnessed over the last decade a successful beginning attempt to provide educational opportunities to severely handicapped students in our public schools. Certainly, most persons would agree that public schools represent an important community setting. However, paradoxes occur. A teacher of secondary-level students in a public school once related the story of how her principal refused permission for students in the class to attend a play being given in a community auditorium. The refusal was based on the reason that other persons attending the play would not be accustomed to "seeing that type of child." The ill-conceived logic in this anecdote is even more apparent because the severely handicapped students have been well accepted by nonhandicapped students in the principal's own school.

Secondary-level classes for severely handicapped students in public rather than private or otherwise segregated schools may indeed provide the best opportunity for teaching the skills necessary for successful integration into other community settings.

Many of the content areas for developing community living skills overlap with areas discussed earlier pertaining to home living and leisure time. Semi-independent living in the community should include skills reflecting the interchange that takes place between the home and a variety of community services and activities, including vocational training and job placement. Fig. 11.2 lists some major content areas that should be considered at the secondary level. Specific, though not exhaustive lists of examples of individual skill areas are included under the four major content headings.

BASIC COMMUNITY INTERACTION SKILLS

There are certain almost generic skills that should be taught to severely handicapped students who will interact in community settings, either in procuring essential services and goods or as participants in community activities and programs.

Public Transportation. Certo, Schwartz, and Brown (1977) have described a detailed program for teaching severely handicapped students to

BASIC COMMUNITY INTERACTION SKILLS
Public Transportation
Telephone
Money Exhange
Social Behavior
Emergency Procedures

PROCUREMENT OF ESSENTIAL GOODS
Groceries
Clothes
Personal Items
Household Items

PARTICIPATION IN COMMUNITY ACTIVITIES
Movies
Sporting Events
Community Activity Centers
    Handicapped
    Nonhandicapped
Church
Eating in Restaurants

PROCUREMENT OF ESSENTIAL SERVICES
Haircuts
Medical Care
Dental Care
Banking
Budget Counseling

FIGURE 11.2
An outline of curriculum content areas for developing community
interaction skills among severely handicapped students at the secondary
class level

use a public bus system. At one skill level, students were taught to use a
public bus to arrive at specific destinations identified by the classroom
teacher. A second, more advanced skill level taught students to solve problems in working out complex travel routes appropriate to individual needs
and circumstances.

A study by Neef, Iwata, and Page (1978), with moderately retarded
adolescents, suggested that classroom instruction using simulated bus
riding skills was more time efficient in teaching these skills than actual
training in the community. Training procedures used in the classroom consisted of role playing, manipulating a doll on a simulated model, and responding to questions about slide sequences. Another study by Page, Iwata, and
Neef (1976), again using moderately retarded students, suggested that
classroom instruction was effective in teaching pedestrian skills in city traffic conditions. Freagon, Pajon, Brankin, Galloway, Rich, Karel, Wilson,
Costello, Peters, and Hurd (1981) and Brown, Branston, Hamre-Nietupski,
Pumpian, Certo, and Gruenewald (1979) have argued that simulated in-

struction for community living skills seems to function best only as a rehearsal strategy before actual instruction in a community situation. They argue that without the actual conditions present in community settings, the changeability of the settings, and the chance contingencies, students cannot generalize the learned skills and adapt to subtle differences in situations over time.

Use of Telephone.   Teaching severely handicapped students how and when to use a telephone is an important component of the secondary-level classroom curriculum. It is an example of a skill that can be taught in the classroom setting with few problems in generalization to other settings. Nietupski and Williams (1974) have provided a detailed program to teach severely handicapped students how to use the telephone when initiating selected recreational activities (like going for a walk, eating dinner, watching TV). A teletrainer, borrowed from the telephone company, was used in the instructional program in the classroom setting. Risley and Cuvo (1980) described a program to teach moderately retarded adults to make emergency telephone calls to the police, fire department, and physician. Training was conducted in a sheltered workship where the adults were employed.

Money Exchange.   The ability to use money in exchange for commodities and services represents another important, although very complex, community living skill that should be taught to severely handicapped students. At a basic level, it is necessary to teach them at least that money is required for the procurement of essential services and goods. On a more complex level, attempts should be made to teach the value and equivalences of money as exchange for services and commodities. To date, most programs to teach counting money (Bellamy and Buttars, 1975) and coin summation (Borakove and Cuvo, 1976; Lowe and Cuvo, 1976) have involved moderately and mildly handicapped students. The procedures described in these studies, however, might with appropriate modifications have application to severely handicapped students.

Certo and Swetlik (1976) have described a program in which ten severely handicapped students were taught the skill of using money to make purchases in a simulated classroom store and in community stores. This program, however, reported only the purchase of items with pennies, which itself is not realistic in our present-day economy. A desirable aspect of the program was the teaching of functional money exchange wherein actual purchases were made to emphasize the importance of the concept.

Freagon, Pajon, Brankin, Galloway, Rich, Karel, Wilson, Costello, Peters, and Hurd (1981) reported a shopping program, discussed earlier, that included a component for monetary exchange. The student learns to add prices of grocery items into an electronic calculator as she or he progresses through the supermarket. If the student has begun with, for example, a ten-dollar bill, items are selected until the calculator reads ten dollars or more. The student at that point returns the last item selected to the shelf and proceeds to the check-out stand. Later instructional programs teach the student to count back the correct amount of change and to recognize and count various denominations of bills and coins. The important aspect of these programs is that they begin with functional use in a community context, where the contingencies of daily life are free to motivate the student to adapt and succeed.

Social Behavior.   Appropriate and successful interactions in community settings require the teaching of social skills to severely handicapped students. These range from the reduction or elimination of inappropriate behaviors to the development of personal skills that generally conform with accepted community standards. In essence, severely handicapped students can be taught to behave in a manner that reduces the extent to which they might be identified as retarded by members of the community. This chapter earlier mentioned the need to reduce bizarre and inappropriate speech patterns and the need to teach verbal interaction skills for making small talk. Nonverbal interaction skills would include basic manners in public places and conduct appropriate to different types of settings or activities. Standing up and cheering, for example, is an acceptable behavior at a football game but not at a movie.

Carney, Clobuciar, Corley, Wilcox, Bigler, Fleisher, Pany, and Turner (1977) and Gee, Roger, Graham, Piuma, Beckstead, Halvorsen, Murray, Wallen, and Sailor (Note 8) have suggested the importance of establishing behaviors that are appropriate to appearance, movement, and proximity to other persons in various school and community settings. The two studies identified a number of target behaviors for social-skill training among severely handicapped students. Hamre-Nietupski and Williams (1974) have also described procedures for social-skill training, especially in reference to sexual conduct in public settings.

Emergency Procedures.   This is an area that has not received much attention in published training programs or procedures. It would seem, however, extremely important to teach severely handicapped students some basic emergency procedures when interacting in community settings. The need to identify and locate a policeman, for example, or to locate and use a pay telephone is important to know when a person is lost. Teaching severely handicapped students how to communicate their need for assistance when they become ill in community settings is another example. Teaching students to show identification cards containing information about where they live and who can be contacted in emergency situations is an appropriate area for skill training.

Many of the emergency procedures would be specific to a particular community, because communities vary in size. Importantly, the classroom teacher should work with parents in developing emergency procedures. Additional benefits could be gained by providing information to local law enforcement agencies and other helping groups on the special needs that severely handicapped persons have in interacting in community settings.

In summary, the skills included in this section are important for community interactions across a number of settings. These skills vary in complexity and, logically, the time involved in systematic instruction. Many severely handicapped students will not acquire all the skills and behaviors, but that does not imply that they cannot or should not participate in community activities or in the procurement of goods and services. We agree, for example, with the *principle of partial participation* espoused by Brown, Branston-McClean, Baumgart, Vincent, Falvey, and Schroeder (1979) wherein each student is taught to participate to the maximum extent possible in all normal community activities, even though that may mean only a partial involvement in some activities. This means that some students will be less successful in some community interactions and will have fewer opportunities available to them for independent living. For these individuals, more supervision and direction will likely be required in order for them to engage in community settings where goods and services are provided and where other types of desirable activities are available to them.

PROCUREMENT OF ESSENTIAL GOODS

This type of community interaction and skill development includes a large number of behaviors. Essentially, they involve instruction on how to become a consumer of goods ranging from essential commodities to items related to personal interests and pleasures. A large part of our life entails the identification of products needed for our lifestyle (and survival), the ability to identify where the products can be obtained, the ability to know what we can afford to purchase, and the actual process of buying something. For severely handicapped individuals, those skills represent a major avenue to more independent living. As such, they constitute important target behaviors for instruction at the secondary level.

It is important to note that teaching severely handicapped students what to purchase and when to purchase is just as essential as teaching them how to make purchases. An instructional program developed by Nietupski, Certo, Pumpian, and Belmore (1976) serves to illustrate this point. In this program, shopping skills at a grocery store were directly related to meal preparation and the replenishment of essential food items. A prosthetic shopping aid was devised for each student. This aid included the preferred foods for the student and a method whereby removable tapes attached to the items were placed on a shopping list as the items were used. The instructional program also included specific details on making food purchases at the store. In essence, the program effectively combined meal preparation skills with shopping skills in a functional manner appropriate to students who could not read labels. A similar type of shopping aid could be developed for other essential items consumed by severely handicapped students. This would include clothing, toiletry items, household supplies, and so on.

Spellman et al. (1978) have discussed the use of picture cards as prosthetic aids for grocery shopping. The cards are similar to those previously described in this chapter for teaching cooking and food preparation skills. Freagon, Gillin, McDonnell, Hasley, Dolan, Williams, Woodyatt, Cisco, Brankin, Costello, and Peters (1981) have utilized a similar program, discussed earlier.

The procedures described by Nietupski et al. (1976), Spellman et al. (1978), and Freagon et al. (1981) are similar in that each provides prosthetic aids for assisting handicapped students in making purchases at stores. These types of procedures are important for instruction at the secondary level. Obviously, the most effective plan would involve a combination of school and home instruction in teaching students how to generate shopping lists and then procure the goods in community stores. For optimal generalization, the procedures for identifying needed commodities should include all types of goods and products essential for community living.

PROCUREMENT OF ESSENTIAL SERVICES

There are a number of services provided by the community that severely handicapped persons should at least be aware of. They need to know, for example, that haircuts and hair styling can be obtained at a barbershop or hair salon and that medical and dental services are provided in offices and clinics. Students capable of money management may need to know about savings accounts, or they may need assistance in monitoring their budgets. For essential services that might be used frequently by severely handicapped students (such as barbershops), skill training would be required to teach the behaviors appropriate to these settings. The procurement of essential services in community settings is another example of an area in which further program development is needed, because its curriculum content is important for severely handicapped students.

PARTICIPATION IN COMMUNITY ACTIVITIES

Many of the activities available to severely handicapped students could also be included under the leisure/recreational skills that were discussed earlier. Certainly, many of the instructional programs described by Wehman and

Schleien (1979a and 1979b) are directly or indirectly related to participation in community activities. We want to re-emphasize the importance of teaching severely handicapped students how to interact in community activities, for the integration of the students into community life will likely fail if they are restricted to home and work settings in the postschool years. The following chapter will discuss in more detail the integration of severely handicapped adults into community activities.

The classroom teacher is the logical person to identify settings within the community that are accessible to severely handicapped students and to provide instruction on the behaviors expected in these settings. Movies, sporting events, restaurants, and churches are examples of settings available in almost all communities. Some communities do have special activities and programs for handicapped persons. These include settings where individual hobbies can be pursued under appropriate instruction. Summer recreational programs often have special courses for handicapped individuals. Other community activity centers, such as the YWCA and YMCA, also provide a variety of activities appropriate to severely handicapped students.

VOCATIONAL SKILL TRAINING

The development of vocational skills must constitute the primary emphasis in secondary-level classrooms for severely handicapped students. The extent to which students are prepared for sheltered or competitive employment beyond the school-age years will, in great part, reflect our success in bringing these individuals into the mainstream of community life. There are several options available for incorporating vocational training into the secondary-level instructional program. These options will depend greatly on the skill level of the student, available job-training placement options in the community for severely handicapped persons, and vocational training resources within the public school setting.

The vocational training options to be discussed for students in secondary-level classrooms are listed in Figure 11.3. These include school-based simulated work settings, sheltered workshop placement, and competitive employment.

SCHOOL-BASED SIMULATED WORK SETTINGS

In the previous chapter, attention was directed toward the importance of including prevocational training in the curriculum content for elementary/intermediate-level classrooms for severely handicapped students. This discussion included teaching a number of generic skills that are prerequisite

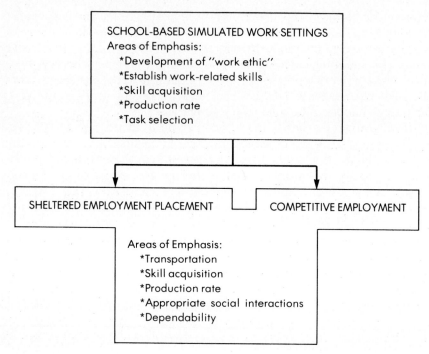

FIGURE 11.3
Vocational training options and areas of instructional emphasis at the
secondary level

to vocational tasks. School-based simulated work settings extend this vocational preparedness sequence to include more intense and specific work
conditions and tasks. This type of setting is designed to provide a solid basis
for preparing secondary-level students for either sheltered employment
placement or competitive employment. At the least, all students in
secondary-level programs should be included in some type of work training
for half of the school day.

In some school settings, simulated work can be coordinated with existing
vocational training classes offered to nonhandicapped students, a situation
that requires a vocational trainer or other person who has been prepared
to train severely handicapped students. In this arrangement, students
would attend vocational training activities in the appropriate location in the
school setting. These students would probably be accompanied by a
teaching assistant or vocational training assistant who is familiar with the
techniques and procedures necessary for the acquisition of vocational skills.

In many situations, the secondary teacher may have to assume major
responsibility for establishing and implementing school-based work settings. This will likely be necessary in schools that have not yet accepted,

in principle, the inclusion of severely handicapped students into existing vocational training areas. In these situations, the teacher will most likely need additional consultations from vocational training personnel, if available. Additionally, secondary-level teachers for severely handicapped students should have some formalized instruction in the area of vocational training. This type of training is necessary whether the teacher is to assume major responsibility in this area or is to serve as a liaison to other vocational training areas, sheltered workshops in the community, or sites for competitive employment opportunities.

Opportunities for school-based vocational instruction will vary from school to school but, in general, we are opposed to a model of exclusive simulation of work environments in a classroom setting. Sorting nuts and bolts and quasi-assembly tasks tend to be too removed from any real-life vocational opportunities to be useful for generalized training. It would be better to identify work areas on campus, such as the food preparation area, physical plant maintenance, janitorial area, and so on, that would impart a realistic flavor to job-prerequisite training experiences. Listed below are five areas of emphasis that should be included in school-based work settings.

Development of a Work Ethic.   A basic concept important to the vocational preparation of severely handicapped students pertains to the development of a work ethic. Martin, Flexer, and Newberry (1979) have pointed out that in many cases severely handicapped workers do poorly in job placements, not because they are inadequately trained, but because they just do not realize what work is all about. They go on to say "that a person (client) must have a concept of remunerative work as a viable means to an end" (p. 147). Martin et al. feel that handicapped persons will develop the work ethic if they are reinforced for work during childhood years, if money is used as a secondary reinforcer, if they are taught that the work effort is a means to money, and if other conditions, such as competitive work environments, family and societal expectations, and so on, lead in that direction. Studies conducted by Martin et al. to develop a work ethic have attempted to establish money as a strong reinforcer, with monetary goal-setting procedures used to motivate severely retarded clients to maintain production levels over time.

Thus, an effort to establish a work ethic among severely handicapped students would seem to be a primary objective in school-based simulated work settings. The earning of money for production could be established as a motivator through students being required to pay for goods and for recreational activities in the community. This arrangement could be functionally related to other community-preparedness training programs in relevant school areas, such as money exchange and the procurement of essential goods and services, which were discussed earlier. Parents or parent surrogates should be extensively involved in a program to establish money as a secondary reinforcer for work-related activities.

Establishing Work-Related Social Skills.   School-based settings provide excellent opportunities for teaching the types of social skills necessary for successful employment in community settings. Mithaug and Haring (1977) have pointed out that productivity, as well as social patterns and work habits, are important factors effecting job success among workers who are severely handicapped. Gold (1975) has examined the literature on job placement of retarded persons. He found that virtually all studies indicate that failure on the job is due not to task performance but to the social interactions in the work settings.

School-based work settings provide opportunities to either increase or decrease the varied and often idiosyncratic social behavior that would detrimentally effect future employment success among severely handicapped students. They may be taught important work-related social skills, such as social interchanges with co-workers and supervisors, the productive use of break time, appropriate clothing for the job, personal cleanliness, the ability to understand and use work-related jargon, and importantly, dependability in getting to work on time and not leaving the work area at inappropriate times. Another work-related behavior to be taught in the school-based work setting for higher functioning students might be the development of job interview skills similar to the instructional program described by Hill, Wehman, and Pentecost (1979).

Skill Acquisition.   An obviously important component of school-based work settings is the teaching of vocational skills that are appropriate to the physical, sensory, social, and intellectual capabilities of the individual student. The pioneer work of Marc Gold serves to remind us of the potential many severely handicapped persons have for work-related skill acquisitions when given the opportunity for a technically sound instructional program.

School-based work settings afford the opportunity to expose severely handicapped students to a number of vocational tasks that vary extensively in both content and complexity. Each student should be given the chance to demonstrate his or her potential via training in functional work skill areas. Important to this process is the selection of techniques and procedures for skill acquisition. The increasing amount of available literature in this area relies heavily on the types of teaching procedures and techniques that have been discussed in earlier chapters. These include task analysis, reinforcement, and systematic changes in stimuli. (See Bellamy, Inman, and Schwarz, 1978; Bellamy, Sowers, and Bourbeau, Note 9; and Rusch, in press, for a review of techniques and procedures as they relate to vocational training for severely handicapped students.)

One of the most detailed and empirically based skill acquisition training programs for the vocational habilitation of severely handicapped persons may be found in a book by Bellamy, Horner, and Inman (1979). Their instructional program is based on the premise that vocational training is a process designed to develop new response topographies in a worker's behavioral repertoire. The format suggested for vocational training involves providing individual instruction through the use of a forward chaining procedure in all steps of the task. Four separate training strategies are described to provide guidelines for the teacher in the instructional setting. These include step training, teaching difficult steps, chain training, and setting training.

A more global approach to vocational skill acquisition for severely handicapped persons has been described by Wehman, Renzaglia, and Schutz (1977). These authors provide a logically arranged hierarchy of behavioral procedures that can be used for different types of problems encountered by a severely handicapped population. Identified skill acquisition problems include discrimination deficits and sensory/motor deficits. For discrimination deficits during skill acquisition, the hierarchy suggested by Wehman et al. is: (1) give verbal instruction, (2) model and give verbal instruction, (3) give verbal and physical guidance, (4) break task down into simpler steps (easy-to-hard sequence) and repeat 1 through 3, (5) use cue redundancy or stimulus fading, and (6) always accompany any strategy with positive reinforcement for correct responding. For acquisition problems that are due to sensory/motor deficits, they add the following suggestions: (1) use prosthetic devices or physical arrangement of the materials, (2) use gestural instructions, and (3) use tactile cue redundancy.

A review and understanding of the procedures presented by Bellamy et al. (1979) and Wehman et al. (1978) should provide the classroom teacher or vocational teacher with a systematic and efficient approach to instruction leading to vocational skill acquisition in school-based work settings.

Production Rate.   Increasing the production rate, or work output, during vocational training in school-based work settings is another important objective for future vocational success. Once a task has been learned by a severely handicapped person, the individual rate of production is critical for remuneration in sheltered or competitive employment settings. Bellamy et al. (1978) pointed out that, with few exceptions, research on productivity has been limited to mildly or moderately handicapped individuals. Bellamy et al. (1979) regard low productivity among severely handicapped individuals as something that can be improved by changing the antecedent and consequent events of work-related behavior. In improving productivity, the supervisor should function as a contingency arranger and manager. Procedures suggested by Bellamy et al. for increasing and maintaining work rate are designed to (1) help the supervisor utilize information about worker performance, and (2) provide a systematic approach to developing supervision strategies that may be effective in specific situations.

Wehman, Renzaglia, and Schutz (1977) have provided specific procedures for improving the production of severely handicapped persons who have impaired motor abilities or who engage in interfering behavior.

For school-based work settings, attempts to increase production rates could be interfaced efficiently with the establishment of a work ethic. The work ethic implies establishing money as a motivator for task performance. Increased productivity and consequently more money provides even more functional learning toward the attainment of this goal. Certainly, the use of real money is perceived as a more realistic orientation to work than other less functional consequences for increased production, such as tokens for special privileges, avoidance techniques, and so on.

Task Selection.   Discussion thus far has centered on four areas important to school-based work settings for severely handicapped students in secondary-level programs. A major problem (and controversy) that directly affects the attainment of these goals is the selection of skills or tasks for training.

Mithaug, Hagmeier, and Haring (1977) have focused upon the functional relationship between vocational training and job placement of the severely handicapped worker. They feel that the development of a successful prevocational training program for this population is contingent upon the precise specification of a long-term objective—job placement. Rather than providing a flexible and general training program that could potentially lead anywhere (and as a consequence would probably lead nowhere), this approach specifies the client's next most probable placement as the basis for training.

Rusch (1979; in press) suggests that there are social/vocational behaviors that, when acquired, may contribute to long-term maintenance of employment for the handicapped. The persons responsible for placement should list those skills that potential employers in various occupations identify as important for entry into the labor force and then have the employers rank the identified behaviors as to their importance in each of their particular work settings.

All this implies a career education program for handicapped students in the public schools. Clark (1979) has emphasized the importance of starting such a program for handicapped students in the elementary classroom.

For severely handicapped students, it would appear even more important to identify and design vocational programs in school-based work settings that are, in fact, functionally related to postschool vocational opportunities in the community. The tasks to be used in school-based work settings should be directly related to potential employment opportunities. This, of course, also indicates a need for the secondary-level program and, possibly later on, the community college program (see Chapter 12) to be interrelated with existing sheltered or competitive employment opportunities in the community and to community vocational placement personnel who can provide a liaison to potential competitive employment settings.

SHELTERED EMPLOYMENT TRAINING

The school-based work setting in the public school is perceived as the initial level at which to incorporate vocational training in secondary programs for severely handicapped students. It, in effect, serves as a controlled training site for preparing them for work in the community during the latter years of their public school education. The school-based work setting should, in fact, be one part of a total vocational training program. Another component involves the actual training and placement of students in work sites in the community during an increasingly longer period of the school day. Two viable options for on-the-job training in the community include sheltered and competitive employment.

For many severely handicapped individuals, sheltered employment will remain the most realistic source of work training during the postschool years. For this reason, it is important that appropriate steps toward success in these settings be taken while the students are still in school. This type of transition, if properly executed, should increase the chances of successful vocational production in the adult years.

The identification of skills and production expectations in sheltered work training settings can assist the teacher and other vocational personnel to prepare students for the transition to sheltered employment placement in the community. Many of these skills could be trained in school-based work settings before the student begins part-time sheltered employment. Additionally, many of the social behaviors expected of clients in these settings could also be taught before the student begins the transition.

As can be observed in Figure 11.2 presented earlier, the areas of emphasis for both sheltered and competitive employment opportunities are similar to the areas of emphasis advocated for the school-based work settings, that is, skill acquisition, production rate, and appropriate social interactions. Additional areas of emphasis would include transportation and dependability on the job.

The ability to use public transportation has already been addressed in the section on community living skills. Within the context of sheltered employment, severely handicapped students would need specific instruction on using a public transportation system to go to and from the school and the sheltered employment training site. This again affords the teacher an opportunity to teach a functional, work-appropriate community living skill while students are still in public school settings.

A second area of emphasis for vocational training that includes part-time work in a sheltered or competitive employment site is job dependability. This includes such factors as getting to work on time, remaining in the work area during production periods, and avoiding excessive absenteeism from work. A cooperative effort between the teacher and personnel in the sheltered employment training site can expedite the teaching of a dependable work attitude and can provide remedial instruction to correct deficiencies during the secondary school years.

The model we advocate here is not the traditional sheltered workshop. Too often, sheltered workshops have become terminal placement options for severely handicapped persons, and new learning has ceased to take place. Rather our view of sheltered employment training calls for placement in community-based work settings that are defined as *training* environments. The student as a "volunteer" is taught productive work skills in these settings. While instruction continues, the settings can become training stations, with students rotated from station to station in order to develop a variety of generalized work skills. Brown, Nisbet, Ford, Sweet, Shiraga, and Loomis (Note 1), for example, have found hospital supply areas in the basements of Madison, Wisconsin, hospitals to be excellent sheltered employment training areas.

COMPETITIVE EMPLOYMENT

The ideal vocational training program for severely handicapped students in secondary-level classes is the actual training of a specific job for competitive employment in the community. Within this framework, public school personnel assist in training severely handicapped students for a particular work setting. Models for training severely handicapped adults for competitive employment have been described by Mithaug et al. (1977) and Wehman (1979). However, a model proposed by Belmore and Brown (1978) provides earlier instruction for competitive employment, starting while students are still attending public schools. Belmore and Brown maintain that public schools must develop service delivery models that provide for the career education needs of persons with severely handicapping conditions. Their model is based on a job skill inventory that allows school personnel to first identify, and then instruct, important skills necessary for a specific competitive job in the community. This comprehensive inventory gathers the information necessary for successful job performance, including, for example, reasons for severely handicapped students being considered for the job, a description of the work setting, a general description of the social environment, specific work skills required, language skills required, needed academic skills, and a specific task analysis of the job. This strategy was highly successful in the hospital supply area training program described by Brown et al. (Note 1) and has actually led to the hiring, by sheltered work-training sites of the severely handicapped trainees, into regular competitive employment in some instances.

The inventory outlined by Belmore and Brown provides an opportunity to select students that are potentially capable for a job and then to provide direct on-the-job training once employment has started. This arrangement obviously involves a close working relationship between school personnel and supervisors at the competitive employment site. It also involves support from the parents of the severely handicapped students. It represents overall the most advanced type of vocational preparation available to school personnel.

It is apparent that many of the job skills necessary for competitive employment could be taught in simulated school-based work settings. Nevertheless, actual on-the-job training coordinated with the school provides the most functional and realistic model for preparing severely handicapped students for postschool life in the community.

Clearly, vocational preparation of severely handicapped students is a broad area and is itself the topic of many textbooks in our field. We have, in this chapter, attempted only to provide a conceptual frame of reference from which to approach the area. For further reading, we would suggest the paper by Brown et al. (Note 1); a recent chapter by Bellamy and Wilcox (1982); a text that contains this chapter (Lynch, Kiemon, and Stark, 1982); and a recent chapter by Rusch (in press). For a comprehensive review of the literature on current secondary instructional models for severely handicapped students, the reader is referred to Meyers-Winton (Note 10).

TOWARD A TOTAL NONSCHOOL INSTRUCTIONAL MODEL

At this writing, educational service delivery systems for severely handicapped students are in a state of rapid transition. In various parts of the country, one can observe a range of instructional models for secondary students. There are quasi-assembly-line tasks in classrooms within segregated (handicapped only) institutions or "special" schools and in special day classes in regular public schools. There is also community-based instruction operating for part of the day out of classes in regular schools. And finally, there is the nonschool instructional model recently espoused by Brown et al. (Note 1).

The nonschool instructional design, although posing some severe challenges to the traditional organization of school district services, is a nearly ideal instructional model for this age group. Under this system, teachers are based at sheltered work training sites (like hospital basement supply areas, industrial plants, fast-food franchises, and so on), and students from different homerooms (or schools) are rotated across these sites for generalized work skill development. They learn to use public transportation to get from site to site and from work site to group home for domestic skill training, and so on. Teachers, in turn, rotate across community training sites from time to time in order to provide generalized training experience for students across *persons*. Communication and motor-movement therapists work with students at the various training sites, thus incorporating useful, functional, therapeutic tactics into real-life settings. Because each student encounters a variety of work-training experiences, a natural kind of *vocational assessment* becomes possible. Certain students will match with certain kinds of vocational activity. When high motivation is apparent and productivity rates are observed to increase in certain job-student combinations, then intensified instruction can begin that will likely lead to future competitive employment in situations containing the identified job-skill clusters.

Nonschool instruction is in its early developmental period. It represents a large step for most school districts that are only now coming to accept severely handicapped classes on regular high school campuses. In our opinion, however, the model is completely realistic and worthy of large-scale research efforts in the hopes that it will provide an eventual solution to the miasma of postschool, dead-end placements for our severely handicapped young adults.

SUMMARY

This chapter has presented a model for secondary classes for severely handicapped students that is based on the transition from home to community living. We have suggested a framework to assist the classroom teacher in structuring content areas for this level of student. More importantly, we have tried to provide a philosophy of how the secondary-level programs for severely handicapped students can better meet their needs as they near the end of their formal public school education. Underpinning this philosophy is the necessity of using the secondary school site as a point of departure for successful living as adults in the community—a success that one hopes will continue, with community support, throughout the life span of severely handicapped individuals.

CHAPTER 12

Postschool Living
and the Community

THE CASE FOR COMMUNITY SERVICES

> In Jack's case not only the home environment failed to provide the support services he needed, but (so did) almost every other agency he was referred to. The deaf community was approached for help and advocacy for Jack. They sent a representative on several occasions to see him. This soon stopped because they could not communicate with Jack since he was retarded. The medical community could not communicate with Jack, and would not treat apparent symptoms. His commitment to a state hospital was recommended because of the doctor's opinion about Jack's lack of communication skills. The group home staff recommended Jack be evicted from the home because of his behavior. Instead of attempting to change the unacceptable behaviors, it was easier to evict the client.
>
> Jack's case is one of a *lack of coordination of services*. If all the agencies worked together to provide for the whole client, for the entire day, they would surely be more successful. Everyone needs to be working toward the same goal of a successful placement in the community with meaningful work activities for each client. Individual differences and problems should not interfere with this goal. (Kochany and Keller, 1980; p. 66; emphasis added)

We have discussed in previous chapters a longitudinal progression of educational programs for severely handicapped children from birth through the secondary-level program. With the exception of infant and some preschool programs, we have considered the public schools to be the major integrative system for preparing severely handicapped persons for eventual postschool living in community settings. It is important to note that all this effort, time, and expense might come to nothing if community support systems are not available or are inadequate to maintain and enrich the lives of severely handicapped adults subsequent to their departure from the public school system. Indeed, the prospects of institutionalization or placement in other similarly restrictive environments may become a reality for many severely handicapped adults in the absence of appropriate community support systems. At present, we have a long way to go in providing these services – a journey that will require intensive cooperation between agencies and advocate groups at the local, state, and federal levels.

There are many issues and controversies pertaining to the assimilation of severely handicapped children and adults into the normal community. The most compelling arguments for community placement evolve around fundamental moral and constitutional rights available to all citizens in our society.

One major principle to emerge during the past decade was that of *normalization,* discussed by Nirje (1970) and Wolfensberger (1972). Under this principle, those conditions of everyday life that typify the norms and cultural patterns of the society at large would be made available to handicapped persons. The normalization principle, and all that it implies, has been central to a national trend to return institutionalized individuals of all ages to the community and to prevent long-term institutionalization of any member of our society. This effort is especially important to the severely handicapped population, which constitutes approximately 71 percent (Scheerenberger, 1976) of all people in residential institutions.

In addition to the normalization principle, several advocate groups have recently called for renewed efforts to include severely handicapped persons in community-based living environments. A resolution passed by The Association for the Severely Handicapped (TASH) in 1979 stated that this organization "will work toward the rapid termination of living environments and educational/vocational/recreational services that segregate, regiment and isolate persons from the individualized attention and sustained normalized community interactions necessary for maximal growth, development and the enjoyment of life" (Note 1).

The universities of Wisconsin and Illinois, with the public school districts of Madison and Milwaukee, Wisconsin, have presented cogent arguments refuting the familiar justifications used to limit interactions between severely handicapped students and their normal peers (Brown, Branston, Hamre-Nietupski, Johnson, Wilcox, and Gruenewald, 1979). These authors, for example, challenged the assertions that segregated centralized delivery presents the most efficient model for providing needed therapy or individualized education to the handicapped student. Direct therapy, formerly restricted to the isolated setting, can be organized just as efficiently within the regular school, with the added benefit of access to "significant others" in the student's environment. Therapists have new opportunities to train relatives and staff who have consistent contact with the student.

In addition to the new opportunities for skill generalization, the authors say, this increased contact can result as well in advantages for non-handicapped peers, teachers, and special education personnel by altering attitudes through positive experiences. Regular education teachers may acquire new skills in individualizing programs for their own students. Special education teachers, no longer isolated, will benefit from an awareness of chronologically age-appropriate activities and objectives for their students through observation of their normal peers.

The Center on Human Policy at Syracuse University has presented arguments for maintaining persons with retardation in community settings (Note 2) and has issued a declaration of the constitutional right of all persons to live in community settings (Figure 12.1).

Given the goal to maintain severely handicapped adults in community settings, what type of coordinated effort is required? Where will severely handicapped adults live? What types of support services are needed? What type of community organization is required to interrelate the efforts of public and private service providers, government agencies, and advocacy groups to serve severely handicapped adults in the community? These are

---

THE COMMUNITY IMPERATIVE:
A REFUTATION OF ALL ARGUMENTS
IN SUPPORT OF
INSTITUTIONALIZING ANYBODY
BECAUSE OF MENTAL RETARDATION

In the domain of Human Rights:
   All people have fundamental moral and constitutional rights.
   These rights must not be abrogated *merely* because a person has a
      mental or physical disability.
   Among these fundamental rights is the right to community living.

In the domain of Educational Programming and Human Service:
   All people, as human beings, are inherently valuable.
   All people can grow and develop.
   All people are entitled to conditions which foster their development.
   Such conditions are optimally provided in community settings.

Therefore:
   In fulfillment of fundamental human rights and
   In securing optimum developmental opportunities,
   all people, regardless of the severity of their disabilities, are entitled
      to community living.

FIGURE 12.1
Declaration of the constitutional right of all persons to live in community settings

SOURCE: © Center on Human Policy, Syracuse University, 1979. Used by permission.

not easy questions, and at present, there are no universal answers. For example, a selected sample of ninety-two severely, multiply handicapped residents surveyed in Alameda County, California, (Note 3), in 1980 showed that 25 percent were unserved by the communities and 47 percent were inappropriately served in school. These figures, although discouraging, probably exemplify the present level of commitment to severely handicapped adults in most communities and most states.

COMMUNITY LIVING ARRANGEMENTS

A number of options are possible for providing living arrangements for severely handicapped adults in community settings. These living arrangements are presented in Figure 12.2 in a hierarchy that reflects, for the most part, the degree of environmental restriction associated with each option. This hierarchy should be viewed with considerable caution since the degree of possible community interaction associated with each option would likely show a wide variance, depending on the particular settings.

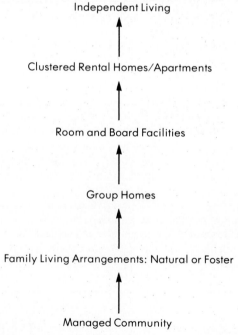

FIGURE 12.2
Range of community living options for severely handicapped adults

Family living arrangements (natural or foster) might, for example, afford more opportunities for interaction in the community than some group homes or room and board facilities. Indeed, the level of social and physical isolation associated with an independent living arrangement might be more restrictive than in a group home where extensive efforts are made to provide frequent community interactions for severely handicapped residents. Unfortunately, for each of the living options included in the figure, we really have insufficient data to empirically assess or evaluate the extent to which these living arrangements support the desired normalized interactions. This lack of information is directly related to the relatively recent trend toward providing community living arrangements for severely handicapped adults. A 1977 survey conducted by Bruininks, Hauber, and Kudla (1980) showed, for example, that about one-third of mentally retarded persons living in community residential facilities were classified as severely and profoundly retarded.

FAMILY LIVING ARRANGEMENTS: NATURAL OR FOSTER

Maintaining a severely handicapped adult in the natural or foster home is an option that requires careful consideration. A major risk is that the person may become isolated from more normalized community interaction by overprotective parents or foster parents. Keeping severely handicapped adults at home may be more convenient than making a concerted effort to include them in vocational, social, and recreational opportunities in the community. Kochany and Keller (1980) identified problem areas in which parental reluctance and/or interference led to termination of competitive employment for severely handicapped persons involved in Virginia's Project Employability. They pointed out that parents frequently fail to realize the extent to which their son or daughter's working may affect not only the child but the entire family structure. Parents of a newly employed severely handicapped adult will require support and information in a number of areas: understanding of Supplemental Social Security Income benefits and their termination with employment, transportation or travel training arrangements, and their own insecurity about the work environment. The authors presented a case study that demonstrates the difficulties and eventual job failure of one severely handicapped individual, where parental interference on the job was a major contributor. The need for parental support systems is clearly indicated. Certainly, consideration should be given to the time when parents may no longer be physically capable of caring for their child in the home.

Foster home placement at its best offers the potential for a caring, nurturant home environment that can provide a healthy support and growth system for the severely handicapped adult, just as rooming house arrangements have always provided a home away from home for young people seeking their first employment in large cities. Foster placements, however, have been abused by individuals more interested in profits accruing from social welfare payments than in the well-being of their clients. Some states have very restrictive licensing policies for the operation of foster homes, whereas others are quite lax in this regard. Parents and advocates for severely handicapped adults should evaluate the foster care living option carefully in terms of its potential to continue the persons' progress toward independent living in the normal community, while at the same time offering a comfortable alternative to more restrictive placements.

If family living arrangements for severely handicapped adults are decided upon, a service system is needed to provide parents with specialized assistance in day-to-day management. *Respite care* for parents needs to be provided, and importantly, parents should be helped to locate vocational, social, and recreational services for their child. If parents do decide to maintain the adult severely handicapped person in the home, then service agencies and advocate groups in the community are responsible for providing as much assistance as possible to the family.

GROUP HOMES

Group homes provide an arrangement whereby a small number of handicapped persons live together in the community under supervision. The supervision can be provided by live-in houseparents or through a manager system wherein one person coordinates care staff personnel who work in shifts.

Group homes have long constituted a major living arrangement for handicapped persons. A large survey of group home facilities conducted by O'Connor (1976) in 1974 indicated, however, that fewer than 20 percent of residents in these homes were severely handicapped. A more recent survey of group homes in Florida indicated that 40 percent of the residents were severely or profoundly retarded (Polivka, Marvin, Brown, and Polivka, 1979). This latter (but smaller) survey possibly indicates an increasing use of group homes to serve handicapped persons in the community.

Advantages of Group Homes. Group homes offer several advantages. First, they provide living accommodations that are accessible to a variety of community vocational, social, and recreational settings. Second, group homes offer the opportunity for continued training of severely handicapped adults in self-help and community living skills. Bergman (1975) reported that severely retarded adults in a program in San Francisco have done very well in group homes that provided such training. Close (1977) reported a group home study of fifteen severely and profoundly retarded adults ranging in age from twenty-one to thirty-nine years. All residents entered the group home from a state institution for the mentally retarded. Systematic training in self-care and community living skills was carried out by staff members in the home. A manager staffing system was used with supplementary assistance from college students and volunteers. Results of the study showed residents in the group home made significantly greater improvement in self-care and social skill development than did a control group of adults who remained in the institution.

Problems of Group Homes.   Other persons have indicated problems with group homes as a community living option. After several years of attempting to provide group homes for retarded children and adults in eastern Nebraska, Skarnulis (1976) concluded,

> As permanent residences the group homes can never fulfill their original objective of serving *all* of the people from state institutions who need to be served in the community plus the people there waiting to be served. It takes too many of them, they are too costly to operate, they are less normalizing than they need be, they take too long to set up, there is too much community opposition, they are not easily integrated into community, etc., etc., etc. (p. 59)

Supporting the observations of Skarnulis is a survey by Berkiansky and Parker (1977) who reported major concerns from persons in neighborhoods where group homes were to be developed, and a survey by O'Conner (1976) who found only 69 percent of community facilities to be normalized.

In terms of cost, a study by Intagliata, Wilder, and Cooley (1979) reported group homes were significantly higher than either family care or natural family placement. Nevertheless, group home costs were still well below those for institutional care.

Placed in perspective, group homes do appear to offer a viable community living alternative for severely handicapped adults. Many of the problems associated with them are probably more directly related to generic deficiencies in the total community network of services for severely handicapped persons. The few systematic studies of severely handicapped adults placed in group homes indicate positive results when staff members are well trained. Schalock and Harper (1978), in examining the factors contributing to the return of mentally retarded clients from a community-based living program to a training program, found that maintenance and generalization of specific social and self-management skills were directly related to the success of individuals in community placements. This points to the need to formally train and place group home supervisors. Such a training effort would seem appropriate for community colleges that already provide human service programs.

Another factor that has mitigated against group homes in the past has been the high burn-out rate of group home managers or houseparents. In the early years of group home development, house managers were usually young couples with an interest in working with disabled people, who also found it helpful to have a rent-free living alternative as well as a small salary. Usually one or both members of the management couple worked outside the home or went to college in addition to their employment in the home. The turnover rate in this arrangement was costly. Young couples found that the demands of group home management far exceeded their expectations, and the disruption of their own normal lifestyle was often more than they could tolerate. The inception of a management model that employs different persons working at the home in shifts has helped reduce the burn-out problem in many communities, but at some cost to a normalized and homelike living arrangement.

Another impetus toward higher-quality group homes would be combined state and local efforts to provide needed funds. This would certainly require a reallocation of monies presently funneled into state institutions so that support funds for deinstitutionalization activities followed the resident out of the hospital into community placement. Taylor, McCord, and Searly (1981) have argued that states should use Title XIX funds (part of the Federal Medicaid program) to establish and maintain small community-based, intermediate-care facilities for severely handicapped persons.

Community Attitudes and Group Homes. The success of group homes must eventually rest with community attitudes concerning placement of handicapped persons in residential neighborhoods. In this context, group homes face issues and problems similar to neighborhood integration of minority groups. Holmes (1979) provided an analysis of five urban community living arrangements in Pennsylvania serving adults whose primary disability was mental retardation. The author examined three apartment clusters and two group homes. Holmes's study concluded that community reactions were more positive toward apartment clusters. Group home development was impeded by negative community reactions. The report went on to place the responsibility for the problems on the group home management personnel. The data revealed, according to Holmes, a lack of use of normalization principles. Although the homes were located in minority communities, there was little or no minority representation among either the group home staff or clients. The residents had little or no input into the operation of their group home programs, and finally, little or no community preparation had taken place.

In some communities, the effort to establish group homes for severely handicapped persons has met with a warm, facilitative, and constructive reaction from the neighborhoods in which they developed. Singer, Stemm, and Close (Note 4), for example, reported the development of a group home in Shasta City, a small community in the shadow of Mt. Shasta in sparsely populated Northern California. This home was established to enable severely handicapped young people to return to their community from a large state hospital hundreds of miles away. These young school-age adults were thus able to attend school at the regular public high school in town and live in a normalized environment. Singer and his staff worked with all levels of the community and the neighborhood from the inception of the group home idea. They explained to neighbors, the police, school officials, and others what they might realistically expect, and what the placement would mean to these formerly hospitalized persons. The result of the groundwork was striking. People in the community asked questions, expressed fears, and in various ways *got involved* in the issue. When the license for the home was granted, the neighbors actually came over to assist in the renovation of the house. The spirit in that community was not unlike the "barn-raising" sense of community that pervaded the American West in earlier years.

Late in 1980, on the other hand, CBS's popular television program "60 Minutes" aired a case study of another group home in a suburban community. This group home was developed with much less community preparation; from the neighbors' point of view, it just appeared one day in a house that had been up for sale. The reaction of the neighbors in this case study was to "sandbag" and even to write letters in opposition to the home. Severely handicapped persons have been hidden in America, in a sense, and their appearance in communities for the first time can be threatening and frightening to individuals who are not acquainted with them. Much of the success of the group home movement and other community alternatives to institutionalization will rest on adequate community preparation and public information. Unfortunately, in many communities, solutions may still involve following the path of litigation. A precedent has already been set in one court decision that ruled in favor of a group home for preschool, multiply handicapped children faced with a single-family zoning limitation. In this case, it was ruled that the zoning ordinance violated due process by being unreasonably restrictive in delineating permissible occupants (*Berger* vs. *State of New Jersey, Mental Disability Law Reporter,* 1976, 1, 214–219). Similarly, the state of New York has ruled that group homes with a limited number of dependents have the same status as single-family dwellings for zoning purposes.

The zoning issue is a complex one, for although many state codes (for example, California and New York) now reflect the specific recognition of small group homes as single-family residences, local ordinances may conflict. For example, municipal authorities have used the argument that state licensing and support of a home signifies a commercial use of the property, which should then be restricted to business zones. Less subtle defenders of local codes have argued that mentally retarded residents pose a "danger" or "nuisance" to the surrounding neighborhood, or that constant medical supervision would be required, making a residential use permit inappropriate (for example, *Defoe* vs. *San Francisco City Planning Commission*, District Court of Appeals, California, May 30, 1973). These municipal challenges to normalization have been extensive and varied, as well as successful on more than a few occasions. It becomes clear that, although state laws like California's A.B. 1856 (which provides that a group home serving six or fewer handicapped persons constitutes residential use of property) are necessary and useful first steps, the legal and social challenges must be waged within the local communities themselves. Local restrictive ordinances must be changed or invalidated on the basis that state law pre-empts them (Chandler and Ross, 1976).

OTHER COMMUNITY-BASED LIVING ARRANGEMENTS FOR ADULTS

Room and board homes and clustered apartments are sometimes used as semi-independent arrangements for adults. In these cases, minimal supervision is provided to residents who usually are also employed in some type of sheltered or competitive working situation. In the clustered apartment arrangement, an attending adult is available to assist residents in problems associated with community living. One-to-three-person foster homes are also used to serve handicapped adults in the community. Foster homes are especially desirable for severely handicapped adults who may require more intensive day-to-day supervision. Independent living in apartments, rental homes, and duplexes is likely to be a less realistic option for severely handicapped adults.

Even nursing homes have been considered as alternative residential placements for severely handicapped students. The nursing home, however, because of its convalescent identity and its concentration of and primary existence for senior adults is a wholly inappropriate placement for severely handicapped persons who are not themselves also members of the geriatric population. In our opinion, nursing homes should not be considered as alternative community living arrangements for severely handicapped persons.

There have recently been important strides made in the area of apartment living as a type of supervised community living arrangement. Vogelsberg, Anderson, Berger, Haselden, Mitwell, Schmidt, Skowran, Ulett, and Wilcox (1980) reported the development of an independent skills inventory that was specifically designed to assist in the transition from a restrictive environment to apartment living.

Skarnulis (1976) has pointed out the need to consider nearly all *alternate living units* as models for serving adults in the community. These alternatives would include group homes, staffed apartments, clustered apartments, duplexes, foster homes, and so on. According to Skarnulis, the concept of alternative living units opens the door to development of more creative small living situations. As stated by the author, "It is merely a construct and idea. It is a way of telling people to stop limiting themselves by developing their whole system of residential services according to any one model (such as group homes, foster homes, etc.) and to building in the flexibility for new 'mixes' " (p. 68).

Finally, what trends can we discern for the future that hold promise for eventual independent community living for severely handicapped persons for whom a group home is presently being considered?

Sitkei (1980) reported the results of a two-year survey that followed up group home placements in terms of later mobility. The author examined follow-up data for the number of persons moving to a more independent status, the number transferring to a parallel facility, and the number returning to live with a relative or the family. Of 611 facilities meeting the criteria for inclusion, the data indicated 23 percent of residents had changed residence in the first year and 17 percent in the second. The largest number of transfers were in the younger age group (twenty-one to thirty), and far more transfers were made from publicly supported facilities than from profit-making facilities. Sixty-three percent of the transfers were to a more independent facility (less restrictive). Eighteen percent moved to a less independent living status. Ten percent of the sample returned to state institutions over the two-year period, with the reason given being the lack of community support services.

A SUPPORT SYSTEM FOR COMMUNITY LIVING

It is doubtful that many severely handicapped adults can be maintained in the community without a formalized support system to identify and coordinate the variety of needed services. It is likely that most communities do have already available most of the generic and specialized services necessary for supporting severely handicapped adults in community living. The problem is how to devise a system to make these services more accommodating to the special needs of these adults and how to bring the services together in a comprehensive plan of action.

A recent series of surveys conducted by Vogelsberg, Williams, and Friedl (1980) examined the shortcomings of existing service delivery within a rural northeastern state. These investigators emphasized the importance of survey data as an initial step in systems change at state and local levels. They found that many agency providers considered existing services adequate; others who recognized problem areas felt that a comprehensive assessment was required prior to new resource development. The dominant theme in the recommendations resulting from the data collected was the need for *coordination* and *cooperation* among those agencies providing services. The authors suggested the use of intra-agency agreements, for example, between a special and vocational education agency and a vocational rehabilitation agency, which would specify responsibility for all services and detail how they would be coordinated.

The problem of making services available to the severely handicapped population is underscored by a survey conducted in Seattle by Kenowitz, Gallagher, and Edgar (1977). This survey identified generic community services that were accessible to severely handicapped persons and their families. *Generic services* were defined as the typical services that families either received outright (like use of public transportation or freedom to eat in a restaurant) or were able to purchase for a standard fee (like a dental examination or life insurance). Results from the survey indicated that in general, severely handicapped persons had fewer services available to them, and in many cases, the services were available only at a significantly higher cost than for nonhandicapped persons. Another important finding was the much lesser extent to which severely handicapped persons were involved in community social and recreational activities. The authors stated the need for developing a process for the sensitization of community generic services to make them more accessible to severely handicapped persons and their families. They suggested the development of community action networks to assist in this process.

> These networks would exist in every community and might be coordinated at a local association for Retarded Citizens Center, University hospital, fraternal organization, parent group counseling center, or public school. The primary responsibility of this network would be to bring together families of the severely handicapped and all agencies responsible for delivering some type of service. (p. 38)

This type of community network for serving the severely handicapped is similar in philosophy to the community support system model to be presented. This model, shown in Figure 12.3, provides for a *community coordinating group* composed of representatives of various advocacy groups for the handicapped, generic service providers, and specialized service agencies for the severely handicapped. At the core of the community coordinating group is an *activator* whose various roles and responsibilities will be described later.

There are a number of groups, agencies, and services that can be listed under the three major headings shown in Figure 12.3. The availability of one or more of these agencies and services would vary from community to community. Larger communities, for example, would have more possible

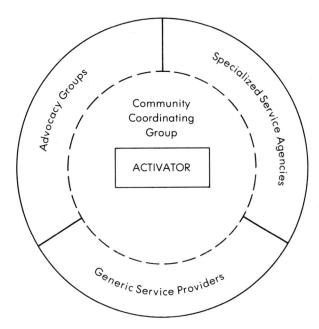

FIGURE 12.3
Community support system model for serving severely handicapped persons

contacts for a community coordinating group serving the severely handicapped adult (as well as children). Smaller communities might need to form a coordinating group on a regional basis similar to cooperative school districts that merge educational services in more sparsely populated regions.

Additionally, the possibilities for active involvement in a community coordinating group might differ from similar types of agencies and services between communities or regions. Certainly the degree of involvement for a particular agency or service provider might vary over time. Nevertheless, it is important that major agencies and service providers be identified in each of the areas shown in the figure, since each area has an important but distinct type of input necessary for a viable community support system serving severely handicapped adults.

ADVOCACY GROUPS

Advocacy groups for the handicapped are important to a community coordinating group, since they provide avenues for improving and obtaining needed services. Such groups as the Association for Retarded Citizens, The Association for the Severely Handicapped, United Cerebral Palsy Association, National Easter Seal Society, National Society for Autistic Citizens, and so on, have all played a vital role in the development and procurement of services for handicapped children and adults. These groups have lobbied for important legislation at state and national levels, and they have worked with local governments for improving the living conditions of the handicapped. They have influenced in a positive way the serving of handicapped students in public schools, and they have worked to make the general public more aware of problems facing handicapped individuals.

One of the difficulties is that these groups have often pursued the same goals and objectives along different paths. A coordinating group for the severely handicapped would offer an important opportunity for groups to combine their resources to assist severely handicapped adults in community settings, to lobby for needed changes, and to activate on a broader level a community awareness and social change program. The fact that the advocacy groups would be interacting with both generic service providers in the community and specialized services for the handicapped would further strengthen their attempts to promote positive changes at the community level.

GENERIC SERVICE PROVIDERS

The inclusion of generic service providers in the community coordinating group for the severely handicapped is essential to the support system model. These service providers offer the best opportunity for sustained community interactions among severely handicapped adults. On the other hand, they are likely to be represented by individuals who are less familiar with problems facing severely handicapped individuals in the community. By including generic service providers in the community coordinating group, the opportunity arises for first making the service providers more aware of existing problems and then eliciting their active support and participation in solving the problems. Below are listed some possible generic service providers in the community who might be contacted for participation in the group. Also discussed briefly are reasons why these service providers might be important contributors to a community coordinating group.

Community or county *public health services* often provide ongoing medical assistance or maintenance to persons with chronic health problems. This type of service would be important to severely handicapped adults who need ongoing medical treatment that does not require visits to a physician's office or medical clinic. Examples include the monitoring of seizure control medication, special diets, personal hygiene, chronic abrasions resulting from confinement to wheelchairs, periodic monitoring of high blood pressure or heart conditions, and so on. Public health nurses could play an important role by providing periodic home checks to severely handicapped adults living in semi-independent living arrangements who have minor but continuing medical care needs.

Medical problems have been cited as a major reason for readmitting individuals to institutional settings (Keys, Boroskin, and Ross, 1973; Pagel and Whitling, 1978). Numerous anecdotal reports have indicated that physicians, dentists, and other professionals are often reluctant to attend to the health problems of severely handicapped persons. This points to the need to involve medical personnel in community efforts to provide services for the severely handicapped adult. Inclusion of representatives from the local *medical associations* in the coordinating group might assist in locating physicians willing to treat severely handicapped persons and also serve to sensitize medical personnel to their needs.

Vincent and Broome (1977), for example, outlined strategies they used for gaining the support of the medical community in their preschool service delivery project. These principles are applicable to adults as well. Initial contact was made with a physician known to be supportive of services for the handicapped, and meetings were arranged through the physician with local nursing and family practice groups. These meetings, where needed services and referrals were discussed, were followed by ongoing acknowledgement and reinforcement of those physicians who remained involved. Biannual summary reports containing information relevant to physicians' recommendations and prescriptions for patients were considered important factors in dispelling the feeling that "referring a child to an educational system is like sending him into a big vacuum that never sends information back" (p. 178). The necessity for the exchange and coordination of information is, again, quite clear.

The same problems also exist for dental services, which means that the same rationale holds for including a representative from the local *dental association* in the community coordinating group.

Typically, most *community mental health clinics and community guidance and counseling services* have not been actively involved in serving mentally handicapped persons, especially severely handicapped adults; yet they have the potential for providing needed assistance to the severely handicapped adult and other community support persons (like foster parents or group home parents).

Mental health and guidance services might provide direct intervention for behavioral problems and deficiencies or they can provide vocational counseling and assessment, and guidance and consultation on community living problems. They can also serve an advocacy function for severely handicapped adults living in semi-independent settings.

These agencies can be consulted by parents and surrogate parents for information pertaining to intervention and training programs for some severely handicapped adults. Their services in this capacity would be similar to those previously provided by public school programs. An additional service of the mental health and guidance agencies might involve counseling parents who are coping with anxieties and concerns about having their severely handicapped son or daughter living away from home.

Many communities, large and small, now have *structured recreational programs* for their citizens. This represents a most important element in a community support system serving the severely handicapped adult. The system should include recreational programs planned specifically for disabled persons as well as the identification of programs and activities accessible to the handicapped adult. The previous chapter on secondary programs for the severely handicapped student discussed the importance of teaching recreational skills and identified training programs to teach these skills. Involvement of community recreational agencies in the support system model provides opportunities and settings for these skills to be applied and enhanced during the postschool years.

Representation from a local or state *vocational rehabilitation agency* is another vital component of the support system model. A representative from this agency is needed to assist in locating potential employers of the severely handicapped and to provide additional vocational training when necessary. This agency might also be able to locate supplemental funds for on-the-job training and provide counseling for specific employment problems encountered by the severely handicapped adult working in the community. Ideally, the vocational rehabilitation agencies in the community should be assisting school personnel to prepare severely handicapped persons for employment in the community while they are still in school (as discussed in the previous chapter). These services should logically be extended to the postschool years as part of a community support system.

Many communities have established *housing authority agencies* to monitor problems associated with rental properties and the sale of homes. A representative of this agency serving a community support group for the severely handicapped adult would be advantageous in view of the fact that negative public attitudes exist toward handicapped persons seeking rental property (or those seeking rental properties in behalf of the handicapped). A recent survey by Trippi, Michael, Colao, and Alvarez (1978) found that only one of one hundred potential landlords was willing to rent property to a mentally retarded person. It was also found that the severity of the handicapping situation was not an important factor in the decisions.

Input from a representative of a local housing authority might help identify possible rentors for severely handicapped adults and might help reduce discrimination toward handicapped persons seeking rental property.

Another likely representative for a support group would be a member of the Office of Civil Rights or of the local *human rights committee or agency*. These committees have been instrumental in reducing discrimination practices effecting minority groups and handicapped persons. In many cases, the committees have actively supported local efforts to provide barrier-free building entrances and sidewalks in public and private sectors of the community. These committees have also frequently assisted efforts to provide public transportation for handicapped persons, a source of major concern for severely handicapped persons residing in community settings.

A representative from the *local religious council,* available in most communities, would provide another source of support. Religious groups in the community can be one of the most direct influences in changing public attitudes toward persons with handicapped conditions. These groups are a likely source of volunteers to help severely handicapped adults maintain themselves in the community. Churches and synagogues too, are an important area where severely handicapped persons can participate in community facilities and recreational activities.

A potentially important organization for a community support system is the *local council on aging* found in many communities. In many cases, the objectives and goals of this council are similar to those of groups working with the severely handicapped. These include, for example, public transportation needs, recreation facilities, and assistance in maintaining independent living in the home. Inclusion of a representative from a council on aging can be useful for severely handicapped adults during their senior citizen years, when quality nursing homes, group living arrangements, and other types of living accommodations for elderly persons become important.

SPECIALIZED SERVICES

Persons and agencies in the community who work directly with severely handicapped individuals should be included as active members of the community coordinating group. Representatives of specialized services, such as physical or rehabilitative therapy, can supply information pertaining to the real-life problems facing severely handicapped adults who are being maintained in the community. They can identify areas where services are not available or where services are inadequate to the needs of the severely handicapped adult.

The *secondary-level classroom teacher for severely handicapped students* serves as a desirable link between public school education programs and postschool living in community settings. The transition-from-home-to-community-living model presented in the previous chapter outlined areas in which the classroom teacher should provide direct instruction to prepare severely handicapped students for life in the community. As a member of the coordinating committee, the secondary-level classroom teacher would have the opportunity to assist in identifying further training needs and in procuring programs and materials to help in the training. The secondary-level classroom teacher would be a good source of information on the competencies and skills of severely handicapped adults which would be available for locating settings in the community where they might function successfully. Additionally, the secondary classroom teacher could receive feedback from other agencies and service providers, indicating where more public school education and training is required to meet the needs of severely handicapped adults after they leave the public school system. This is most important in revising and updating the curriculum offered at the secondary level, a point well illustrated by the progress report of Project Employability, where "development of work skills which are generalizable across a variety of specific jobs and settings" was found to be the major factor in competitive placement of the severely handicapped person (Wehman, 1980; p. 15).

For severely handicapped adults working in competitive employment sites, the *job supervisor* (or designate) would be a valuable representative to the community coordinating group for reasons similar to those given for a representative from sheltered workshops.

Representatives from the various community living options discussed earlier in this chapter would be essential to the coordinating committee. *Persons working in the community living facilities* have the most contact with severely handicapped adults, and they are more likely to be aware of problems relating to interactions in community settings.

The overall coordinating group would thus provide opportunities for home living personnel to interact with essential generic service representatives as well as other specialized service providers in order to provide an integrated community support program for the severely handicapped adult.

THE COMMUNITY ACTIVATOR

Scheerenberger (1976) pointed out that one important component of a functional continuum of care for severely handicapped persons in the community is a central point of referral that includes a person or agency who is knowledgeable about community services and the criteria for their use. He further stated that "without such a point of referral, programs may either not be used or not used in a timely matter" (p. 144). Although Scheerenberger was discussing all mentally retarded persons in the community and not just severely handicapped persons, the concept is applicable to the support system model described in this chapter. The community support model shown earlier in Figure 12.3 depicts an *activator* at the center of the system—a person who coordinates the services and goals of the advocacy groups, the generic service providers, and the specialized services.

The activator is essential to the community support model. This person may, indeed, be attached to a certain group or agency, such as the local association for retarded citizens or, as in California, for example, the community regional center; or the activator may be attached to a local branch of city government, a university, or any type of private, nonprofit service organization.

The activator should be a knowledgeable professional person who has been formally trained in the area of the severely handicapped. This person would have a number of roles and responsibilities that would vary from community to community. The activator should, however, assume the following responsibilities regardless of location.

Referral Source. In this capacity, the activator must be the one person in the community support system who is familiar with the various services and agencies serving the needs of severely handicapped adults. This would include employment opportunities, community living options, recreational opportunities and, in general, all types of generic and specialized services. The activator should maintain an up-to-date file of each service and a listing of appropriate persons to contact when specific services are needed or problems arise.

Community Awareness. Another function of the activator involves taking steps to make the needs of severely handicapped adults known to the community at large and especially to those agencies and services that can help support these individuals in successful community living. In this role, the activator must be an advocate for all severely handicapped adults in the community, serving as a public relations person in their behalf.

Tracking System. The activator should maintain a system that identifies each severely handicapped adult in the community with respect to the services they need and the services that are being provided to them. This would include up-to-date information on employment, vocational training, living arrangement, needed medical assistance, and so on. This information is needed, not only to assist individual severely handicapped adults in the community, but also to provide overall demographic data when additional services are requested.

Lobbyist. The activator may need to serve as a lobbyist (an advocate) for severely handicapped adults at both the local and state levels to help safeguard their rights and the existing laws. Within this context, the activator would need to work closely with various community advocate and parent groups to determine objectives and courses of action to be taken.

Coordinator of Support System Committee.   Another responsibility of the activator would be to elicit the participation of advocacy groups, generic service providers, and specialized services in the community support system group. The activator should assume a major role in bringing these groups together to help identify objectives for action and to implement recommendations from the coordinating group.

A CONTINUING EDUCATIONAL MODEL

It is clear from the preceding discussion that a number of agencies and individuals can be convened and coordinated to ensure the continuation of functional life skills development of severely handicapped individuals when they reach the end of their public school years. What is missing in most locations, at this writing, is an interagency system or service model that would form the basis and funding vehicle for such a coordinated activity. In many states, the continuing education model may meet this need in a realistic fashion.

In California, for example, there exists a highly developed network of community colleges, many with excellent blue-collar training facilities located on modern, well-maintained campuses. California also has a network of developmental disabilities *regional centers* that coordinate expenditure of state funds and procure needed services for identified developmentally disabled clients.

San Francisco State University's Department of Special Education was awarded a large grant by the State Department of Development Services for the 1982–1983 school year to pilot a continuing education model in that state which would bring together community colleges and regional centers in a manner that would provide just such a coordinated postschool effort (Lindsay, Rosenberg, and Sailor, Note 5). Under this model, classes for severely handicapped adults are established on local community college campuses. The campus itself becomes a vocational and community living skill training environment that extends into and encompasses the community in the same manner that was discussed in Chapter 11 for the secondary school program. Clients in this model are identified as recipients of service by the local regional center whose representative (an advocate) is a member of the community coordinating group. Because it is an educational model, the teacher of each community college class is the program facilitator for each student in his or her class.

It is anticipated that this "over 21" project model will enable even the *most* severely handicapped, multiply disabled adult to have a normalized, meaningful, community-based alternative to the dead-end experience that has come to characterize many sheltered workshop and activity center programs. The continuing educational model has no upper age limit and thus can serve as a basis for continuing instruction for a severely handicapped adult until such time that the student has attained competitive employment and independent living status. It can provide lifelong services for students who will always be in need of an umbrella of sheltered services.

SUMMARY

This chapter has presented the need for a support system for maintaining severely handicapped adults in community settings during the postschool years. The model stresses including advocacy groups, generic service providers, and specialized services as part of the community support system. An activator is also recommended for the support system model to guide and coordinate efforts across agencies and services who must be modeled in a community commitment to serve severely handicapped adults. A support system is vital to the successful integration of severely handicapped adults in the community, and it provides for optimal assistance in helping them achieve this fundamental human right.

BIBLIOGRAPHY

ALLEN, E. Early intervention. In M. A. Thomas (ed.), *Hey, don't forget about me!* Reston, Va.: Council for Exceptional Children, 1976.

ALLEN, E. Early intervention for young severely and profoundly handicapped children: The preschool imperative. *AAESPH Review,* 1978, *3,* 30–41.

ANDERSON, D. R., HODSON, G. D., and JONES, W. G. (eds.) *Instructional programming for the handicapped student.* Springfield, Ill.: Charles C Thomas, 1975.

APPELL, M. Early education for the severely handicapped/hearing impaired child. In B. Campbell and V. Baldwin (eds.), *Severely handicapped/hearing impaired students: Strengthening service delivery.* Baltimore: Paul H. Brookes, 1982, 181–197.

AXELROD, S. *Behavior modification for the classroom teacher.* New York: McGraw-Hill, 1977.

AXELROD, S., BRANTNER, J. P., and MEDDOCK, T. D. Overcorrection: A review and critical analysis. *Journal of Special Education,* 1978, *12*(4), 367–391.

AYRES, A. J. Improving academic scores through sensory integration. *Journal of Learning Disabilities,* 1972, *5,* 338.

AZRIN, N. H., and HOLZ, W. C. Punishment. In W. K. Honig (ed.), *Operant behavior: Areas of research and application.* New York: Appleton–Century–Crofts, 1966.

BAILEY, J., and MEYERSON, L. Vibration as a reinforcer with a profoundly retarded child. *Journal of Applied Behavior Analysis,* 1969, *1,* 91–97.

BALTHAZAR, E. E. *Balthazar scales of adaptive behavior, part one: Handbook for the professional supervisor.* Champaign, Ill.: Research Press, 1971a.

BALTHAZAR, E. E. *Balthazar scales of adaptive behavior, part two: Handbook for the rater technician.* Champaign, Ill.: Research Press, 1971b.

BARKER, R. G. *Qualities of community life.* San Francisco: Jossey–Bass, 1973.

BARTON, E. Inappropriate speech in a severely retarded child: A case in language conditioning and generalization. *Journal of Applied Behavior Analysis,* 1970, *3,* 209–307.

BAUMEISTER, A., and FOREHAND, R. Effects of contingent shock and verbal command on body rocking of retardates. *Journal of Clinical Psychology,* 1972, *16,* 586–590.

BAYLEY, N. *Bayley scales of infant development.* Atlanta: The Psychological Corporation, 1969

Behavioral Characteristics Progression. Palo Alto, Calif.: Vort Corporation, 1973.

BELLAMY, G. T., and BUTTARS, K. Teaching trainable retarded students to count money: Toward personalized independence through academic instruction. *Education and Training of the Mentally Retarded,* 1975, *10,* 18–26.

BELLAMY, G. T., HORNER, R. H., and INMAN, D. P. *Vocational habilitation of severely retarded adults.* Baltimore: University Park Press, 1979.

BELLAMY, G. T., INMAN, D. P., and SCHWARZ, R. H. Vocational training and production supervision: A review of habilitation techniques for the severely and profoundly retarded. In N. Haring and D. Bricker (eds.), *Teaching the severely handicapped (Vol. 3).* Seattle: AAESPH, 1978.

BELLAMY, G. T., and WILCOX, B. Secondary education for severely handicapped students: Guidelines for quality services. In K. Lynch, W. Kiemon, and J. Stark (eds.), *Prevocational and vocational education for special needs youth: A blueprint for the 1980's.* Baltimore: Paul H. Brookes, 1982.

BELMORE, K., and BROWN, L. A job inventory strategy designed for severely handicapped potential workers. In N. Haring and D. Bricker (eds.), *Teaching the severely handicapped (Vol. 3).* Seattle: AAESPH, 1978.

BERGMAN, J. *Community homes for the retarded.* Lexington, Mass.: D. C. Heath, 1975.

BERKIANSKY, H., and PARKER, R. Establishing a group home. *Mental Retardation,* 1977, *15,* 8–11.

BERKSON, G., and DAVENPORT, R. K. Stereotyped movements in mental defectives: I. Initial survey. *American Journal of Mental Deficiency,* 1962, *66,* 849–852.

BERKSON, G., and MASON, W. Stereotyped movements of mental defectives: III. Situation effects. *American Journal of Mental Deficiency,* 1963, *68,* 409–412.

BETTELHEIM, B. *The empty fortress.* New York: The Free Press, 1967.

BIGGE, J. *Teaching individuals with physical and multiple disabilities* (2nd ed.). Columbus, Ohio: Charles E. Merrill, 1982.

BIJOU, S. W. Behavioral teaching of young handicapped children: Problems of application and implementation. In S. W. Bijou and R. Ruiz (eds.), *Contributions of behavior modification to education.* Hillsdale, N.J.: Erblaum Associates, 1980.

BIJOU, S. W., and BAER, D. M. *Child development II: Universal stage of infancy.* New York: Appleton–Century–Crofts, 1965.

BLECK, E. E., and NAGEL, D. A. (eds.), *Physically handicapped children: A medical atlas for children.* New York: Grune and Stratton, 1975.

BOBATH, B., and BOBATH, K. *Motor development in the different types of cerebral palsy.* London: Wm. Heinemann, 1975.

BORAKOVE, L., and CUVO, A. Facilitative effects of coin displacement on teaching coin summation to mentally retarded adolescents. *American Journal of Mental Deficiency,* 1976, *81,* 350–356.

BRACKMAN, B., FUNDAKOWSKI, G., FILLER, J., and PETERSON, C. The Chicago early childhood education project. In B. Wilcox, F. Kohl, and T. Vogelsberg (eds.), *The severely and profoundly handicapped child.* Proceedings from the Statewide Institute for Education of the Severely and Profoundly Handicapped, State Board of Education, Illinois Office of Education, 1977.

BRICKER, D. Education synthesizer. In M. A. Thomas (ed.), *Hey, don't forget about me!* Reston, Va.: The Council for Exceptional Children, 1976, 84–97.

BRICKER, D., BRICKER, W. A., IACINO, R., and DENNISON, L. Intervention strategies for the severely and profoundly handicapped child. In N. G. Haring and L. J. Brown (eds.), *Teaching the severely handicapped (Vol. 1),* New York: Grune and Stratton, 1976.

BRICKER, D., and IACINO, R. Early intervention with severely/profoundly handicapped children. In E. Sontag (ed.), *Educational programming for the severely and profoundly handicapped.* Reston, Va.: Council for Exceptional Children, 1977.

BRICKER, D., SEIBERT, J., and CASUSO, V. Early intervention. In J. Hogg and P. Mittler (eds.), *Advances in mental handicap research.* New York: John Wiley and Sons, 1980.

BRICKER, D., VINCENT-SMITH, L., and BRICKER, W. A. Receptive vocabulary: Performance and selection strategies of delayed and nondelayed toddlers. *American Journal of Mental Deficiency,* 1973, *77,* 579–584.

BRICKER, W. A., and BRICKER, D. D. An early language training strategy. In R. L. Schiefelbusch and L. L. Lloyd (eds.), *Language perspectives: Acquisition, retardation, and intervention.* Baltimore: University Park Press, 1974.

BRICKER, W. A., and CAMPBELL, P. H. Interdisciplinary assessment and programming for multihandicapped students. In W. Sailor, B. Wilcox, and L. Brown (eds.), *Methods of instruction for severely handicapped students.* Baltimore: Paul H. Brookes, 1980.

BRODY, J. F., BUMFERD, M., CONELY, M., HALL, C., McGLINCHEY, M., MITALA, R., and ROEBUCK, R. (eds.), *APT: A resource book for use with citizens who show severely/profoundly retarded behavior.* Spring City, Pa.: Pennhurst State School, 1975.

Brown v. *board of education,* 347 U.S. 483 (1954).

BROWN, F., HOLVOET, J., GUESS, D., and MULLIGAN, M. The individualized curriculum sequencing model (III): Small group instruction. *Journal of the Association for the Severely Handicapped,* 1980, *5,* 352–367.

BROWN, L., BRANSTON-McCLEAN, M. B., BAUMGART, D., VINCENT, L., FALVEY, M., and SCHROEDER, J. Utilizing the characteristics of current and subsequent least restrictive environments in the development of curricular content for severely handicapped students. *AAESPH Review,* 1979, *4,* 407–424.

BROWN, L., BRANSTON, M. B., HAMRE–NIETUPSKI, S., JOHNSON, F., WILCOX, B., and GRUENEWALD, L. A rationale for comprehensive longitudinal interactions between severely handicapped students and nonhandicapped students and other citizens. *AAESPH Review,* 1979, *4* (1), 3–14.

BROWN, L., BRANSTON, M., HAMRE–NIETUPSKI, S., PUMPIAN, I., CERTO, N., and GRUENEWALD, L. A strategy for developing chronological age-appropriate and functional curricular content for severely handicapped adolescents and young adults. *The Journal of Special Education,* 1978, *13,* 81–90.

BROWN, L., FALVEY, M., PUMPIAN, I., BAUMGART, D., NISBET, J., FORD, A., SCHROEDER, J., and LOOMIS, R. *Curricular strategies for teaching severely handicapped students functional skills in school and nonschool environments (Vol. 10).* University of Wisconsin–Madison and Madison Metropolitan School District, 1980.

BROWN, L., FALVEY, M., VINCENT, B., KAYE, N., JOHNSON, F., FERRARA–PARRISH, P., and GRUENEWALD, L. Strategies for generating comprehensive, longitudinal and chronological age–appropriate individual educational plans for adolescent and young adult severely handicapped students. In L. Brown, M. Falvey, D. Baumgart, I. Pumpian, J. Schroeder, and L. Gruenewald (eds.), *Strategies for teaching chronological age–appropriate functional skills to adolescent and young adult severely handicapped students.* Madison, Wis.: Madison Metropolitan School District, 1979.

BROWN, L., NIETUPSKI, J., and HAMRE–NIETUPSKI, S. The criterion of ultimate functioning and public school services for severely handicapped children. In M. A. Thomas (ed.), *Hey, don't forget about me!* Reston, Va.: Council for Exceptional Children, 1976, 2–15.

BROWN, L., WILCOX, B., SONTAG, E., VINCENT, B., DODD, N., and GRUENEWALD, L. Toward the realization of the least restrictive environments for severely handicapped students. *AAESPH Review,* 1977, *2,* 195–201.

BROWN, S. L., and DONOVAN, C. M. Stimulation activities (Vol. 3). In D. S. Schafer and M. S. Moersch (eds.), *Developmental programming for infants and young children.* Ann Arbor, Mich.: The University of Michigan Press, 1977.

BROWNING, R. M., and STOVER, D. O. *Behavior modification in child treatment.* Chicago, Ill.: Aldine, 1971.

BRUININKS, R., HAUBER, F., and KUDLA, M. National survey of community residential facilities: A profile of facilities and residents in 1977. *American Journal of Mental Deficiency,* 1980, *84,* 470–478.

BURTON, T. A., and HIRSHOREN, A. The education of severely and profoundly retarded children: Are we sacrificing the child to the concept? *Exceptional Children,* 1979, *45,* 598–602.

BUTZ, R., and HASAZI, J. The effects of reinforcement on perseverative speech in a mildly retarded boy. *Journal of Behavior Therapy and Experimental Psychiatry,* 1973, *4,* 167–170.

CAMPBELL, P. H. Individualized team programming with infants and young handicapped children. In D. P. McClowry, A. M. Guildord, and S. Richardson (eds.), *Infant communication: Development, assessment, and intervention.* New York: Grune and Stratton, in press (1982).

CARNEY, I., CLUBUCIAR, A., CORLEY, E., WILCOX, B., BIGLER, J., FLEISHER, L., PANY, D., and TURNER, P. Social interaction in severely handicapped students. In *The severely and profoundly handicapped child.* Springfield, Ill.: State Department of Education, 1977.

CERTO, N., BROWN, L., BELMORE, K., and CROWNER, T. A review of secondary level educational service delivery models for severely handicapped students in the Madison Public Schools. In E. Sontag (ed.), *Educational programming for the severely and profoundly handicapped.* Reston, Va.: The Council for Exceptional Children, 1977.

CERTO, N., and KOHL, F. L. A strategy for developing interpersonal interactior. and instructional content for severely handicapped students. In N. Certo, N. Haring, and R. York (eds.), *Public school integration of severely handicapped students: Rational issues of progressive alternatives.* Baltimore: Paul H. Brookes, in press.

CERTO, N., SCHWARTZ, R., and BROWN, L. Community transportation: Teaching severely handicapped students to ride a public bus system. In N. Haring and L. Brown (eds.), *Teaching the severely handicapped.* New York: Grune and Stratton, 1977.

CERTO, N., and SWETLIK, B. Making purchases: A functional money–use program for severely handicapped students. In L. Brown, N. Certo, K. Belmore, and T. Crowner (eds.), *Madison's alternative for zero exclusion: Papers and programs related to public school services for secondary age severely handicapped students (Vol. 6, Part 1).* Madison, Wis.: Special Education Services, 1976.

CHAMBERS, D. Right to the least restrictive alternative setting for treatment. In B. J. Ennis and P. R. Friedman (eds.), *Legal rights of the mentally handicapped (Vol. 2).* New York: Practicing Law Institute, 1976, 991–1014.

CHANDLER, J., and ROSS, S., JR. Zoning restrictions and the right to live in the community. In *The mentally retarded citizen and the law,* The President's Committee on Mental Retardation, New York: The Free Press, 1976, 305–343.

CLARK, G. M. *Career education for the handicapped child in the elementary classroom.* Denver: Love, 1979.

CLARK, DAVIES, and WOODCOCK. *Standard rebus glossary.* Circle Pines, Minn.: American Guidance Services, 1974.

CLOSE, D. Community living for severely and profoundly retarded adults: A group home study. *Education and Training of the Mentally Retarded,* 1977, *12,* 256–262.

COHEN, M. A., and GROSS, P. J. *Developmental resource, behavior sequences in assessment and program planning (Vol. 1).* New York: Grune and Stratton, 1979a.

COHEN, M. A., and GROSS, P. J. *Developmental resource, behavior sequences in assessment and program planning (Vol. 2)*. New York: Grune and Stratton, 1979b.

COHEN, S., SEMMES, M., and GURALNICK, M. Public Law 94–142 and the education of preschool handicapped children. *Exceptional Children*, 1979, *45*, 279–285.

CONNOR, F. P., WILLIAMSON, G. G., and SIEPP, J. M. *Program guide for infants and toddlers with neuromotor and other developmental disabilities*. New York: Teachers College Press, 1975.

Consortium on Adaptive Performance Evaluation (CAPE), final report (G00772139) to the United States Department of Education, U.S. Office of Special Education, Washington, D.C., 1980.

CORBETT, J. Aversion for the treatment of self–injurious behavior. *Journal of Mental Deficiency Research*, 1975, *19*, 79–95.

CRESS, P. J., SPELLMAN, C. R., DeBRIERE, T. J., SIZEMORE, A. C., NORTHAM, J. K., and JOHNSON, J. L. Vision screening for persons with severe handicaps. *Journal of the Association for the Severely Handicapped*, 1982, *6*(3), 41–50.

CUVO, A. Validity task analyses of community living skills. *Vocational Evaluation and Work Adjustment Bulletin*, 1978, *11*, 13–21.

CUVO, A., and DAVIS, P. Teaching community living skills to mentally retarded persons: An examination of discriminative stimuli. *Gedrag*, 1980, *8*(1), 14–33.

DuBOSE, R. Identification. In M. E. Snell (ed.), *Systematic instruction of the moderately and severely handicapped*. Columbus, Ohio: Charles E. Merrill, 1978.

FALVEY, M., FERRARA–PARRISH, P., JOHNSON, F., PUMPIAN, I., SCHROEDER, J., and BROWN, L. Curricular strategies for generating comprehensive, longitudinal and chronological age–appropriate functional individual *vocational* plans for severely handicapped adolescents and young adults. In L. Brown, M. Falvey, D. Baumgart, I. Pumpian, J. Schroeder, and L. Gruenewald (eds.), *Strategies for teaching chronological age–appropriate functional skills to adolescent and young adult severely handicapped students, (Vol. 9, Part 1)*. Madison, Wis.: Madison Metropolitan School District, 1979, 102–161.

FAVELL, J., FAVELL, J., and McGIMSEY, J. Relative effectiveness and efficiency of group vs. individual training of severely retarded persons. *American Journal of Mental Deficiency*, 1978, *83*, 73–84.

Federal Register. Washington, D.C.: U.S. Government Printing Office, August 23, 1977.

FILLER, J. W. Service models for handicapped infants. In R. Dubose and S. G. Garwood (eds.), *Educating handicapped infants*. In press.

FILLER, J., ROBINSON, C., SMITH, R., VINCENT-SMITH, L., BRICKER, D., and BRICKER, W. Mental retardation. In N. Hobbs (ed.), *Issues in the classification of children (Vol. 2)*. San Francisco: Jossey-Bass, 1975.

FINNIE, N. *Handling the young cerebral palsied child at home.* New York: E. P. Dutton, 1975.

FORD, A., BROWN, L., PUMPIAN, I., BAUMGART, D., NISBET, J., SCHROEDER, J., and LOOMIS, R. Strategies for developing individualized recreation/leisure plans for adolescent and young adult severely handicapped students. In L. Brown, M. Falvey, I. Pumpian, D. Baummgart, J. Nisbet, and A. Ford, *Curricular strategies for teaching severely handicapped students functional skills in school and nonschool environments (Vol. 10).* University of Wisconsin–Madison and Madison Metropolitan School District, 1980.

FOSTER, R. W. *Camelot behavioral checklist.* Bellevue, Wash.: Edmark Associates, 1974.

FOWLER, H. The implication of sensory reinforcement. In R. Glaser (ed.), *The nature of reinforcement,* New York: Academic Press, 1971.

FOXX, R. M., and AZRIN, N. H. Restitution: A method of eliminating aggressive–disruptive behavior of retarded and brain damaged patients. *Behavior Research and Therapy,* 1972, *10,* 15–27.

FOXX, R. M., and AZRIN, N. H. The elimination of autistic self–stimulatory behavior by overcorrection. *Journal of Applied Behavior Analysis,* 1973, *6,* 1–14.

FRANKEL, F., and GRAHAM, V. Systematic observation of classroom behavior of retarded and autistic children. *American Journal of Mental Deficiency,* 1976, *83,* 73–84.

FRANKEL, F., and SIMMONS, J. Q. Self–injurious behavior in schizophrenic and retarded children. *American Journal of Mental Deficiency,* 1976, *80,* 512–522.

FREAGON, S. Residential caregivers and public school teachers of severely handicapped children and youth. In C. L. Hansen (ed.), *Severely handicapped students in the community.* Seattle: University of Washington, Program Development Assistance System, 1982.

FREAGON, S., GILLIN, M., MCDONALD, K., HASLEY, G., DOLAN, S., WILLIAMS, M., WOODYATT, D., CISCO, M., BRANKIN, G., COSTELLO, D., and PETERS, W. M. Teacher–made materials for severely handicapped students that are curriculum domain related, functional, local community referenced, chronologically age–appropriate, individualized and allow participation in activities. *Journal of Special Education Technology,* 1981, *4*(2), 52–65.

FREAGON, S., PAJON, M., BRANKIN, G., GALLOWAY, A., RICH, D., KAREL, P., WILSON, M., COSTELLO, D., PETERS, W. M., and HURD, D. *Teaching severely handicapped children in the community: Processes and procedures.* Dekalb, Ill.: Northern Illinois University, 1981.

FREDERICKS, B., ANDERSON, R., and BALDWIN, V. The identification of competency indicators of teachers of the severely handicapped. *AAESPH Review,* 1979, *4,* 81–95.

FREEMAN, B. J., and RITVO, E. R. Parents as paraprofessionals. In E. R. Ritvo (ed.), *Autism: Diagnosis, current research and management.* New York: Spectrum Publications, 1976.

FRITH, G. H. "Advocate" vs. "professional employee": A question of priorities for special educators. *Exceptional Children,* 1981, *47*(7), 486–492.

GAINER, W. L., ZWEIG, R. L., DOLE, P. W., and WATT, S. A. (eds.), *Observation guide for the Santa Clara inventory of developmental tasks.* Santa Clara Unified School District, Santa Clara, Calif.: Richard L. Zweig Associates, 1974.

GALLAGHER, J. J. The special education contract for mildly handicapped children. *Exceptional Children,* 1972, *38,* 527–535.

GARCIA, E. The training and generalization of a conversation speech form in nonverbal retardates. *Journal of Applied Behavior Analysis,* 1974, *7,* 137–151.

GARCIA, E., BAER, D. M., and FIRESTONE, I. The development of generalized imitation within topographically determined boundaries. *Journal of Applied Behavior Analysis,* 1971, *4,* 101–112.

GARDNER, W. I. *Behavior modification in mental retardation.* Chicago, Ill.: Aldine, 1971.

GAYLORD-ROSS, R. Task analysis and the severely handicapped. In S. Savage (ed.), *Individualized critical skills model.* Training and Resource Group, California State Department of Education, Personnel Development Unit, Alameda, Calif., 1982.

GAYLORD-ROSS, R. A decision model for the treatment of aberrant behavior in applied settings. In W. Sailor, B. Wilcox, and L. Brown (eds.), *Methods of instruction for severely handicapped students.* Baltimore: Paul H. Brookes, 1980.

GENTRY, D., and ADAMS, G. A curriculum–based direct intervention approach to the education of handicapped infants. In N. G. Haring and D. D. Bricker (eds.), *Teaching the severely handicapped (Vol. 3),* Seattle: AAESPH, 1978.

GENTRY, N. D., ADAMS, G. B., ANDREWS, M., CHANDLER, L., FREEDMAN, P., KELLY, J., LIVINGSTON, S., ROBINSON, R., RUSCH, J., SOLTMAN, S., STADE, E., and VANDERVEER, B. *Infant learning program: Behavior repertoire for handicapped infants* (3rd rev.). Experimental Educational Unit, Child Development and Mental Retardation Center, University of Washington, 1977.

GILHOOL, T. K. Education: An inalienable right. *Exceptional Children,* 1973, *39,* 597–609.

GOLD, M. W. Task analysis of a complex assembly task by the retarded blind. *Exceptional Children,* 1976, *43*(2), 78–85.

GOLD, M. W. Vocational training. In J. Wortis (ed.), *Mental retardation and developmental disabilities: An annual review (Vol. 7).* New York: Brunner/Mazel, 1975.

GOLD, M. W., and POMERANTZ, E. J. Issues in prevocational training. In M. E. Snell (ed.), *Systematic instruction of the moderately and severely handicapped.* Columbus, Ohio: Charles E. Merrill, 1978.

GOLDBERG, I. I. Human rights for the mentally retarded in the school system. *Mental Retardation,* December, 1971. 3–7.

GRIFFIN, P., SANFORD, A., and WILSON, D. *Learning accomplishment profile* (Diagnostic ed.). Winston–Salem, N.C.: Kaplan School Supply, 1975.

GUESS, D. Methods in communication instruction for severely handicapped persons. In W. Sailor, B. Wilcox, and L. Brown (eds.), *Methods of instruction for severely handicapped students.* Baltimore: Paul H. Brookes, 1980.

GUESS, D., and BAER, D. M. Some experimental analyses of linguistic development in institutionalized retarded children. In B. Lahey (ed.), *The modification of language behavior.* Springfield, Ill.: Charles C Thomas, 1973, 3–60.

GUESS, D., BAER, D. M., and SAILOR, W. Remedial behavioral approach to teaching speech deficient children. *Human Communication,* 1978, *3,* 55–69.

GUESS, D., HORNER, D., UTLEY, B., HOLVOET, J., MAXON, D., TUCKER, D., and WARREN, S. A functional curriculum sequencing model for teaching the severely handicapped. *AAESPH Review,* 1978, *3,* 202–215.

GUESS, D., and MULLIGAN, M. The severely and profoundly handicapped. In E. L. Meyen (ed.), *Exceptional children and youth: An introduction* (2nd ed.). Denver: Love, 1982.

GUESS, D., and NOONAN, M. J. Curricula and instructional procedures for severely handicapped students. *Focus on Exceptional Children,* 1982, *14*(5), 1–12.

GUESS, D., SAILOR, W., and BAER, D. To teach language to retarded children. In R. Schiefelbusch and L. Lloyd (eds.), *Language perspectives: Acquisition, retardation, and intervention.* Baltimore: University Park Press, 1974, 529–563.

GUESS, D., SAILOR, W., and BAER, D. M. *Functional speech and language training for the severely handicapped. Part 1: Persons and things.* Lawrence, Kans.: H and H Enterprises, 1976a.

GUESS, D., SAILOR, W., and BAER, D. M. *Functional speech and language training for the severely handicapped. Part 2: Actions with persons and things.* Lawrence, Kans.: H and H Enterprises, 1976b.

GUESS, D., SAILOR, W., and BAER, D. M. *Functional speech and language training for the severely handicapped. Part 3: Possession and color.* Lawrence, Kans.: H and H Enterprises, 1977a.

GUESS, D., SAILOR, W., and BAER, D. M. *Functional speech and language training for the severely handicapped. Part 4: Size, relation and location.* Lawrence, Kans.: H and H Enterprises, 1978a.

GUESS, D., SAILOR, W., and BAER, D. M. A behavioral–remedial approach to language training for the severely handicapped. In E. Sontag (ed.), *Educational programming for the severely and profoundly handicapped.* Reston, Va.: The Council for Exceptional Children, 1977b.

GUESS, D., SAILOR, W., and BAER, D. M. Children with limited language. In R. Schiefelbusch (ed.), *Language intervention strategies.* Baltimore: University Park Press, 1978b, 101–144.

HAMRE–NIETUPSKI, S. and WILLIAMS, W. Implementation of selected sex education and social skills programs with severely handicapped students. *Education and Training of the Mentally Retarded,* 1977, *12,* 364–372.

HANSON, M. J. A model for early intervention with culturally diverse single and multi–parent families. *Topics in Early Childhood Education,* 1981, *1,* 37–44.

HANSON, M. J. *Teaching your Down's syndrome infant: A guide for parents.* Baltimore: University Park Press, 1977.

HARING, N. Infant identification. In M. A. Thomas (ed.), *Hey, don't forget about me!* Reston, Va.: The Council for Exceptional Children, 1976, 16–35.

HARING, N. G. Measurement and evaluation procedures for programming with the severely andd profoundly handicapped. In E. Sontag, N. Certo, and J. Smith (eds.), *Educational programming for the severely and profoundly handicapped.* Reston, Va.: Council for Exceptional Children, 1977.

HARING, N. G. (ed.), *The behavior of exceptional children.* Columbus, Ohio: Charles E. Merrill, 1979.

HARING, N. G., and BRICKER, D. Overview of comprehensive services for the severely/profoundly handicapped. In N. G. Haring and L. J. Brown (eds.), *Teaching the severely handicapped (Vol. 1).* New York: Grune and Stratton, 1976.

HARING, N. G., LIBERTY, K. A., and WHITE, O. R. Rules for data-based strategy decisions in instructional programs: current research and instructional implications. In W. Sailor, B. Wilcox, and L. Brown (eds.), *Methods of instruction for severely handicapped students.* Baltimore: Paul H. Brookes, 1980.

HARRIS–VANDERHEIDEN, D. Field evaluation of the auto–con. In G. Vanderheiden and K. Grilley (eds.), *Non–vocal communication techniques and aides for the severely physically handicapped.* Baltimore: University Park Press, 1976.

HAYDEN, A. H. Handicapped children, birth to age 3. *Exceptional Children,* 1979, *45,* 510–516.

HAYDEN, A. H., and DMITRIEV, V. Early developmental and educational problems for the child with Down's syndrome. In B. Z. Friedlander, G. Kirk, and G. Sterritt (eds.), *The exceptional infant (Vol. 3).* New York: Brunner/Mazel, 1975.

HAYDEN, A. H., and HARING, N. G. Programs for Down's syndrome children at the University of Washington. In T. Tjossem (ed.), *Intervention strategies for high risk infants and young children.* Baltimore: University Park Press, 1976.

HAYDEN, A. H., MCGINNES, G., and DMITRIEV, V. Early and continuous intervention strategies for severely handicapped infants and very young children. In N. G. Haring and L. J. Brown (eds.), *Teaching the severely handicapped (Vol. 1).* New York: Grune and Stratton, 1976.

HAYNES, U., PATTERSON, G., D'WOLF, N., HUTCHISON, D., LOWRY, W., SCHILLING, M., and SIEPP, J. *Staff development handbook: A resource for the transdisciplinary process.* New York: United Cerebral Palsy Association, 1976.

HEWETT, F. M. Teaching speech to autistic children through operant conditioning. *American Journal of Orthopsychiatry*, 1965, *17*, 927–936.

HILL, J. W., WEHMAN, P., and PENTECOST, J. H. Developing job interview skills in severely developmentally disabled clients. In P. Wehman and J. Hill (eds.), *Vocational training and placement of severely handicapped persons (Project employability - Vol. 1)*. Richmond, Va.: Virginia Commonwealth University, 1979, 184–207.

HOBBS, N. *The futures of children: Categories, labels, and their consequences.* San Francisco: Jossey–Bass, 1975.

HOLMES, R. F. Characteristics of five community living arrangements serving mentally retarded adults in southwestern urban Pennsylvania. *Mental Retardation*, 1979, *17*, 181–183.

HOLVOET, J., GUESS, D., MULLIGAN, M., and BROWN, F. The individualized curriculum sequencing model (II): A teaching strategy for severely handicapped students. *Journal of the Association for the Severely Handicapped*, 1980, 5, 325–336.

HOMME, L. *How to use contingency contracting in the classroom.* Champaign, Ill.: Research Press, 1970.

HORSTMEIER, D. S., and MACDONALD, J. D. *Environmental prelanguage battery.* Columbus, Ohio: Charles E. Merrill, 1978a.

HORSTMEIER, D. S., and MACDONALD, J. D. *Ready, set, go; talk to me.* Columbus, Ohio: Charles E. Merrill, 1978b.

INTAGLIATA, J., WILDER, B., and COOLEY, F. Cost comparison of institutional and community based alternatives for mentally retarded persons. *Mental Retardation*, 1979, *17*, 154–156.

JACKSON, D., and WALLACE, R. The modification and generalization of voice loudness in a fifteen year old girl. *Journal of Applied Behavior Analysis*, 1974, *1*, 461–472.

JUSTEN, J., and BROWN, G. Definitions of severely handicapped: A survey of state departments of education. *AAESPH Review*, 1977, *2*(1), 8–14.

KAZDIN, A. E. *Behavior modification in applied settings.* Homewood, Ill.: The Dorsey Press, 1975.

KEILITZ, I., TUCKER, D., and HORNER, R. Increasing mentally retarded adolescents' verbalizations about current events. *Journal of Applied Behavioral Analysis*, 1973, *6*, 621–630.

KELLEHER, R. T., and GOLLUB, L. R. A review of positive conditioned reinforcement. *Journal of the Experimental Analysis of Behavior*, 1962, *5*, 543–597.

KENOWITZ, L., GALLAGHER, J., and EDGAR, E. Generic services for the severely handicapped and their families: What's available? In E. Sontag, J. Smith, and N.

Certo (eds.), *Educational programming for the severely and profoundly hand-icapped*. Reston, Va.: The Council for Exceptional Children, 1977, 53–57.

KEYS, V., BOROSKING, A., and ROSS, R. The revolving door in a mentally retarded hospital: A study of returns from leave. *Mental Retardation*, 1973, *11*, 55–56.

KISH, G. B. Studies of sensory reinforcement. In W. K. Honig (ed.), *Operant behavior: Areas of research and application*. New York: Appleton–Century–Crofts, 1966.

KOCHANY, L., and KELLER, J. An analysis and evaluation of the failures of severely disabled individuals in competitive employment. In P. Wehman and M. Hill (eds.), *Vocational training and placement of severely disabled persons: Project employability*. Richmond, Va.: Virginia Commonwealth University, 1980, 47–72.

KOEGEL, R. L., EGEL, A. L., and DUNLAP, G. Learning characteristics of autistic children. In W. Sailor, B. Wilcox, and L. Brown (eds.), *Methods of instruction for severely handicapped students*. Baltimore: Paul H. Brookes, 1980.

KOEGEL, R. L., and RINCOVER, A. Some research on the difference between generalization and maintenance in extra–therapy settings. *Journal of Applied Behavior Analysis*, 1977, *10*, 1–16.

KOEGEL, R. L., RINCOVER, A., and EGEL, A. L. *Educating and understanding autistic children*. San Diego: College–Hill Press, 1982.

KOEGEL, R. L., and SCHREIBMAN, L. Teaching autistic children to respond to simultaneous multiple cues. *Journal of Experimental Child Psychology*, 1977, *24*, 299–311.

KOEGEL, R. L., and WILHELM, H. Selective responding to the components of multiple visual cues by autistic children. *Journal of Experimental Child Psychology*, 1973, *15*, 442–453.

LAMBERT, N., WINDMILLER, M., COLE, L., and FIGUEROA, R. *AAMD adaptive behavior scale, public school version* (1974 rev.). Washington, D.C.: American Association on Mental Deficiency, 1975.

LANGLEY, B., and DUBOSE, R. Functional vision screening for severely hand-icapped children. *The New Outlook for the Blind*, 1976, *8*, 346–350.

LEBLANC, J. M., ETZEL, B. C., and DOMASH, M. A. A functional curriculum for early intervention. In K. E. Allen, V. A. Holm, and R. L. Schiefelbusch (eds.), *Early intervention–A team approach*. Baltimore: University Park Press, 1978.

LIBERTY, K. A. *Decide for progress: Dynamic aims and data decisions*. Working paper, Regional Resource Center. Eugene, Oreg.: University of Oregon, 1972.

LILLY, M. S. A training based model for special education. *Exceptional Children*, summer 1971, 745–749.

LINDSLEY, O. R. Direct measurement and prosthesis of retarded behavior. *Journal of Education*, 1964, *147*, 60–82.

LIPPMAN, L., and GOLDBERG, I. I. *Right to education.* New York: Teachers College Press, 1973.

LOVAAS, O. I. A behavior therapy approach to treatment of childhood schizophrenia. In J. Hill (ed.), *Symposia on child development (Vol. 1),* Minneapolis: University of Minnesota Press, 1967, 108–159.

LOVAAS, O. I. *The autistic child: Language development through behavior modification.* New York: Irvington, 1977.

LOVAAS, O. I., KOEGEL, R. L., SIMMONS, J. Q., and LONG, J. S. Some generalization and follow–up measures on autistic children in behavior therapy. *Journal of Applied Behavior Analysis,* 1973, *6,* 131–166.

LOVAAS, O. I., SCHAEFFER, B., and SIMMONS, J. Q. Experimental studies in childhood schizophrenia: Building social behaviors by use of electric shock. *Journal of Expermental Research in Personality,* 1965, *1,* 99–109.

LOVAAS, O. I., and SCHREIBMAN, L. Stimulus overselectivity of autistic children in a two-stimulus situation. *Behavior Research and Therapy,* 1972, *9,* 305–310.

LOVAAS, O. I., SCHREIBMAN, L., KOEGEL, R. L., and REHM, R. Selective responding by autistic children to multiple sensory input. *Journal of Abnormal Psychology,* 1971, *77,* 211–222.

LOWE, M., and CUVO, A. Teaching coin summation to the mentally retarded. *Journal of Applied Behavior Analysis,* 1976, *9,* 483–489.

LOWELL, E. L., and ROUIN, C. C. (eds.), *State of the art: Perspectives on serving deaf–blind children.* California State Department of Education: Southwestern Region Deaf/Blind Center, 1977.

LYNCH, K., KIEMON, W., and STARK, J. *Prevocational and vocational education for special needs youth: A blueprint for the 1980's.* Baltimore: Paul H. Brookes, 1982.

LYON, S., and LYON, G. Team functioning and staff development: A role release approach to providing integrated educational services to severely handicapped students. *Journal of the Association for the Severely Handicapped,* 1980, *5,* 250–263.

McCORMICK, L., and GOLDMAN, R. The transdisciplinary model: Implications for service delivery and personnel preparation for the severely and profoundly handicapped. *AAESPH Review,* 1979, *4,* 152–161.

MACDONALD, J., and HORSTMEIER, D. *Environmental language intervention program.* Columbus, Ohio: Charles E. Merrill, 1978.

MAGER, R. F. *Preparing instructional objectives* (2nd ed.). Belmont, Calif.: Fearon, 1975.

MALGADY, R., BARCHER, P., TOWNER, G., and DAVIS, J. Language factors in vocational evaluation of mentally retarded workers. *American Journal of Mental Deficiency,* 1979, *83,* 432–438.

MARTIN, A. S., FLEXER, R. W., and NEWBERRY, J. F. The development of a work ethic in the severely retarded. In T. Bellamy, G. O'Conner, and O. Karan (eds.), *Vocational rehabilitation of severely handicapped persons.* Baltimore: University Park Press, 1979.

MILLER, J. G., and YODER, D. E. Language intervention for the mentally retarded. In R. L. Schiefelbusch and L. L. Lloyd (eds.), *Language perspectives: Acquisition, retardation, and intervention.* Baltimore: University Park Press, 1974.

Mills v. *board of education of the District of Columbua,* 348, F. Supp. 866 (D. D. C. 1972).

MITHAUG, D. E., HAGMEIER, L. D., and HARING, N. G. The relationship between training activities and job placement in vocational education of the severely and profoundly handicapped. *AAESPH Review,* 1977, *2,* 89–110.

MITHAUG, D. E., and HARING, N. G. Community vocational and workshop placement. In N. Haring and L. Brown (eds.), *Teaching the severely handicapped (Vol. 2).* New York: Grune and Stratton, 1977, 257–284.

MULLIGAN, M., GUESS, D., HOLVOET, J., and BROWN, F. The individualized curriculum sequencing Model (I): Implications from research on massed, distributed or spaced trial training. *Journal of the Association for the Severely Handicapped,* 1980, *5,* 325–336.

MURPHY, R. J., and DOUGHTY, N. R. Establishment of controlled arm movements in profoundly retarded students using response contingent vibratory stimulation. *American Journal of Mental Deficiency,* 1977, *82*(2), 212–216.

MURPHY, R. J., NUNES, D. L., and HUTCHINGS-RUPRECHT, M. Reduction of stereotyped behavior in profoundly retarded individuals. *American Journal of Mental Deficiency,* 1977, *82*(3), 238–245.

MUSSELWHITE, C. R., and ST. LOUIS, K. W. *Communication programming for the severely handicapped: Vocal and non–vocal strategies.* Houston, Tex.: College–Hill Press, 1982.

NEEF, N., IWATA, B., and PAGE, T. Public transportation training: In vivo versus classroom instruction. *Journal of Applied Behavior Analysis,* 1978, *11,* 331–344.

NIETUPSKI, J., and WILLIAMS, W. Teaching severely handicapped students to use the telephone to initiate selected recreational activities and to respond appropriately to telephone requests to engage in selected recreational activities. In L. Brown, W. Williams, and T. Crowner (eds.), *A collection of papers and programs related to public school services for severely handicapped students (Vol. 4).* Madison, Wis.: Special Education Services, 1974.

NIETUPSKI, R., CERTO, N., PUMPIAN, I., and BELMORE, K. Supermarket shopping: Teaching severely handicapped students to generate a shopping list and make purchases functionally linked with meal preparation. In L. Brown, N. Certo, K. Belmore, and T. Crowner (eds.), *Madison's alternative for zero exclusion: Papers and programs related to public school services for secondary age severely handicapped students (Vol. 6, Part 1).* Madison, Wis.: Special Education Services, 1976.

NIRJE, B. Symposium on normalization. The normalization principle: Implications and comments. *Journal of Mental Subnormality*, 1970, *16*, 62–70.

O'CONNER, G. *Home is a good place: A national perspective of community residential facilities for developmentally disabled persons.* Monograph on Mental Deficiency. Washington, D.C., 1976.

PAGE, T., IWATA, B., and NEEF, N. Teaching pedestrian skills to retarded persons: Generalization from the classroom to the natural environment. *Journal of Applied Behavior Analysis*, 1976, *9*, 433–444.

PAGEL, S., and WHITLING, C. Readmissions to a state hospital for mentally retarded persons: Reasons for community placement failure. *Mental Retardation*, 1978, *16*, 164–166.

PANYAN, M., and HALL, V. Effects of serial *versus* concurrent task sequencing on acquisition, maintenance, and generalization. *Journal of Applied Behavior Analysis*, 1978, *11*, 67–74.

Pennsylvania association for retarded children v. *commonwealth of Pennsylvania*, 343, F. Supp. 279 (E. D. Pa. 1972).

PIAGET, J. *The origins of intelligence in children.* New York: International Universities Press, 1952.

PIAGET, J. *The construction of reality in the child.* New York: Ballentine Books, 1954.

PIAGET, J. *Plays, dreams and imitations in childhood.* New York: Norton, 1962.

POLIVKA, C., MARVIN, W., BROWN, J., and POLIVKA, L. Selected characteristics, services and movement of group home residents. *Mental Retardation*, 1979, *17*, 227–230.

PREMACK, D. Catching up with common sense, or two sides of a generalization: Reinforcement and punishment. In R. Glasser (ed.), *The nature of reinforcement.* New York: Academic Press, 1971.

PREMACK, D. Reinforcement theory. In D. Levine (ed.), *Nebraska symposium on motivation.* Lincoln, Nebr.: University of Nebraska Press, 1965.

PUMPIAN, I., BAUMGART, D., SHIRAGA, B., FORD, A., NISBET, J., LOOMIS, R., and BROWN, L. Vocational training programs for severely handicapped students in the Madison Metropolitan School District. In L. Brown, M. Falvey, I. Pumpian, D. Baumgart, J. Nisbet, and A. Ford. *Curricular strategies for teaching severely handicapped students functional skills in school and nonschool environments (Vol. 10).* University of Wisconsin–Madison and Madison Metropolitan School District, 1980.

REICHLE, J. E., and YODER, D. E. Assessment and early stimulation of communication in the severely and profoundly mentally retarded. In R. L. York and E. Edgar (eds.), *Teaching the severely handicapped (Vol. 4).* Seattle: AAESPH, 1979.

REYNOLDS, B. S., NEWSOM, C. D., and LOVAAS, O. I. Auditory overselectivity in autistic children. *Journal of Abnormal Child Psychology,* 1974, *2,* 253–263.

RIMLAND, B. The differentiation of childhood psychoses: An analysis of checklists for 2,218 psychotic children. *Journal of Autism and Childhood Schizophrenia,* 1971, *1,* 161–174.

RINCOVER, A., and KOEGEL, R. L. Research on the education of autistic children: Recent advances and future directions. In B. B. Lahey and A. E. Kazdin (eds.), *Advances in clinical child psychology (Vol. 1).* New York: Plenum Press, 1977.

RINCOVER, A., NEWSOM, C. D., LOVAAS, O. I., and KOEGEL, R. L. Some motivational properties of sensory stimulation in psychotic children. *Journal of Experimental Child Psychology,* 1977, *24,* 312–323.

RISLEY, R., and CUVO, A. Training mentally retarded adults to make emergency telephone calls. *Behavior Modification,* 1980, *4,* 513–525.

RITTENHOUSE, R. K., and MYERS, J. J. *Teaching sign language: The first vocabulary.* Normal, Ill.: Illinois Associates, 1982.

ROGERS, S. J., and D'EUGENIO, D. B., Assessment and application (Vol. 1). In D. S. Schafer and M. S. Moersch (eds.), *Developmental programming for infants and young children.* Ann Arbor, Mich.: The University of Michigan Press, 1977.

ROGERS, S. J., D'EUGENIO, D. G., BROWN, S. L., DONOVAN, C. M., and LYNCH, E. W. Early intervention developmental profile (Vol. 2). In D. S. Schafer and M. S. Moersch (eds.), *Developmental programming for infants and young children.* Ann Arbor, Mich.: The University of Michigan Press, 1977.

ROGERS-WARREN, A., and WARREN, S. F. *Ecological perspectives in behavior analysis.* Baltimore: University Park Press, 1977.

RUSCH, F. R. Competitive employment. In M. E. Snell (ed.), *Systematic instruction of the moderately and severely handicapped* (2nd Ed.). Columbus, Ohio: Charles E. Merrill, in press.

RUSCH, F. R. Toward the validation of social/vocational survival skills. *Mental Retardation,* 1979, *17,* 143–145.

SAILOR, W., GUESS, D., and BAER, D. M. An experimental program for teaching functional language to verbally deficient children. *Mental Retardation,* 1973, *11,* 27–35.

SAILOR, W., GUESS, D., GOETZ, L., SCHULER, A., UTLEY, B., and BALDWIN, M. Language and severely handicapped persons: Deciding what to teach to whom. In W. Sailor, B. Wilcox, and L. Brown (eds.), *Methods of instruction for severely handicapped students.* Baltimore: Paul H. Brookes, 1980.

SAILOR, W., and HARING, N. Some current directions in education of the severely/multiply handicapped. *AAESPH Review,* 1977, *2,* 3–23.

SAILOR, W., and HORNER, R. D. Educational and assessment strategies for the severely handicapped. In N. Haring and L. Brown (eds.), *Teaching the severely handicapped (Vol. 1).* New York: Grune and Stratton, 1976.

SAILOR, W., and MIX, B. J. *The TARC assessment system.* Lawrence, Kans.: H and H Enterprises, 1975.

SAILOR, W., and TAMAN, T. Stimulus factors in the training of prepositional usage in three autistic children. *Journal of Applied Behavior Analysis,* 1972, *5,* 183–192.

SAILOR, W., WILCOX, B., and BROWN, L. *Methods of instruction for severely handicapped students.* Baltimore: Paul H. Brookes, 1980.

SANDERS, R. A time–out procedure for the modification of speech content: A case study. *Journal of Behavioral Therapy and Experimental Psychiatry,* 1971, *2,* 199–202.

SCHAFER, D. S., and MOERSCH, M. S. (eds.), *Developmental programming for infants and young children.* Ann Arbor, Mich.: The University of Michigan Press, 1977.

SCHALOCK, R. L., and HARPER, R. S. Placement from community–based mental retardation programs: how well do clients do? *American Journal of Mental Deficiency,* 1978, *83,* 240–247.

SCHEERENBERGER, R. C. *Deinstitutionalization and institutional reform.* Springfield, Ill.: Charles C Thomas, 1976.

SCHREIBMAN, L. Effects of within–stimulus and extra–stimulus prompting on discrimination learning in autistic children. *Journal of Applied Behavior Analysis,* 1975, *8,* 91–112.

SCHROEDER, G., and BAER, D. M. Effects of concurrent *versus* serial training on generalized vocal imitation in retarded children. *Developmental Psychology,* 1972, *6,* 293–301.

SCHULER, A. L. *An experimental analysis of conceptual and representational abilities in a mute autistic adolescent: A serial vs. a simultaneous mode of processing.* Unpublished doctoral dissertation, University of California, 1979.

SEGAL, S. S. *No child is uneducable.* Oxford: Pergamon Press, 1972.

SHANE, H. C. Approaches to communication training with the severely handicapped. In R. L. York and E. Edgar (eds.), *Teaching the severely handicapped (Vol. 4).* Seattle: AAESPH, 1979.

SHEARER, D. *The Portage guide to early education.* Portage, Wis.: Cooperative Educational Service Agency No. 12, 1972.

SITKEI, E. G. After group home living – what alternatives? Results of a two year mobility follow–up study. *Mental Retardation,* 1980, *18,* 9–13.

SKARNULIS, E. Less restrictive alternatives in residential services. *AAESPH Review,* 1976, *1,* 40–84.

SLINEY, M., and GEELEN, K. *Manual of alternative procedures: Recreational activities.* Medford, Mass.: Massachusetts Center for Program Development and Evaluation, 1977.

SMITH, B. J. *Policy options related to the provision of appropriate early intervention services for very young children and their families.* A Publication of the Policy Options Project. Reston, Va.: The Council for Exceptional Children, 190.

SMITH, D. D., and SNELL, M. E. Classroom management and instructional planning. In M. Snell (ed.), *Systematic instruction of the moderately and severely handicapped.* Columbus, Ohio: Charles E. Merrill, 1978.

SOMERTON, M. E., and TURNER, K. D. *Pennsylvania training model individual assessment guide.* Harrisburg, Pa.: Pennsylvania Department of Education, 1975.

SONTAG, E., BURKE, P. J., and YORK, R. Considerations for the severely handicapped in public schools. *Education and Training of the Mentally Retarded,* 1973, *8,* 20–26.

SONTAG, E., SMITH, J., and SAILOR, W. The severely handicapped. Who are they? Where are we? *Journal of Special Education,* 1977, *11,* 5–11.

SPELLMAN, C., DEBRIERE, T., JARBOE, D., CAMPBELL, S., and HARRIS, C. Pictorial instruction: Training daily living skills. In M. Snell (ed.), *Systematic instruction of the moderately and severely handicapped.* Columbus, Ohio: Charles E. Merrill, 1978.

SPRADLIN, J. E., and GIRARDEAU, F. L. The behavior of moderately and severely retarded persons. In N. R. Ellis (ed.), *International review of research in mental retardation (Vol. 1).* New York: Academic Press, 1966, 257–298.

The STEP system, sequential tasks for educational planning (Vol. 1). Santa Cruz, Calif.: Cajon Valley Union School District, Special Education Department of the Santa Cruz County Office of Education, 1977.

STERNAT, J., MESSINA, R., NIETUPSKI, J., LYON, S., and BROWN, L. Occupational and physical therapy services for severely handicapped students: Toward a naturalized public school service delivery model. In E. Sontag (ed.), *Educational programming for the severely and profoundly handicapped.* Reston, Va.: The Council for Exceptional Children, 1977.

STILLMAN, R. D. *Assessment of deaf–blind children: The Callier–Azusa scale.* Reston, Va.: The Council for Exceptional Children, 1975.

STOKES, T. R., and BAER, D. M. An implicit technology of generalization. *Journal of Applied Behavior Analysis,* 1977, *10,* 341–367.

STORM, R., and WILLIS, J. Small group training as an alternative to individual programs for profoundly retarded persons. *American Journal of Mental Deficiency,* 1978, *83,* 283–288.

SUMNER, J. G., MUESER, S. T., HSU, L., and MORALES, R. G. Overcorrection treatment for radical reduction of aggressive disruptive behavior in institutionalized mental patients. *Psychological Reports,* 1974, *15,* 655–662.

TAYLOR, S., McCORD, W., and SEARLY, S. Medicaid dollars and community homes: The community ICF/MR controversy. *The Journal of the Association for the Severely Handicapped,* 1981, *6,* 59–64.

THOMPSON, T., and GRABOWSKI, J. (eds.). *Behavior modification of the mentally retarded.* New York: Oxford University Press, 1972.

TOUCHETTE, P. E. Transfer of stimulus control: Measuring the moment of transfer. *Journal of the Experimental Analysis of Behavior,* 1971, *15,* 347–354.

TREMBLAY, A., STRAIN, P., HENDERSON, J., and SHORES, R. The activity context of preschool children's social interaction: A comparison of high and low social interactors. *Psychology in the Schools,* 1980, *17,* 380–385.

TRIPPI, J., MICHAEL, R., COLAO, A., and ALVAREZ, A. Housing discrimination toward mentally retarded persons. *Exceptional Children,* 1978, *44,* 430–433.

USOE/BEH, 1974, Request for Proposal 74–10: Programs for Severely Handicapped Children and Youth.

UZGIRIS, I., and HUNT, J. *Instrument for assessing infant psychological development.* Urbana, Ill.: The University of Illinois, 1966.

UZGIRIS, I., and HUNT, J. *Assessment in infancy: Ordinal scales of psychological development.* Urbana, Ill.: University of Illinois Press, 1975.

VANDERHEIDEN, G. C., and GRILLEY, K. *Non–vocal communication techniques and aids for the severely physically handicapped.* Baltimore: University Park Press, 1976.

VAN ETTEN, G., ARKELL, C., and VAN ETTEN, C. *The severely and profoundly handicapped: Programs, methods, and materials.* St. Louis: C. V. Mosby, 1980.

VAUGHN, C., and ASBURY, D. Nerve–ophthalmology. *General ophthalmology,* Los Altos, Calif.: Lange Medical, 1974.

VINCENT, L., and BROOME, K. A public school service delivery model for handicapped children between birth and five years of age. In E. Sontag, J. Smith, and N. Certo (eds.), *Educational programming for the severely and profoundly handicapped.* Reston, Va.: The Council for Exceptional Children, 1977, 177–188.

VINCENT, L. J., SALISBURY, C., WALTER, G., BROWN, P., GRUENEWALD, L. J., and POWERS, M. Program evaluation and curriculum development in early childhood/special education. In W. Sailor, B. Wilcox, and L. Brown (eds.), *Methods of instruction for severely handicapped students.* Baltimore: Paul H. Brookes, 1980.

VOELTZ, L. M. Children's attitudes toward handicapped peers. *American Journal of Mental Deficiency,* 1980, *84,* 455–464.

VOGELSBERG, R. T., ANDERSON, J., BERGER, P., HASELDEN, T., MITWELL, S., SCHMIDT, C., SKOWRON, A., ULETT, D., and WILCOX, B. Programming for apartment living: A description and rationale of an independent living skills inventory. *Journal of the Association for the Severely Handicapped,* 1980, *5*(1), 38–54.

VOGELSBERG, R. T., WILLIAMS, W., and FRIEDL, M. Facilitating systems change for the severely handicapped: Secondary and adult services. *Journal of the Association for the Severely Handicapped,* 1980, *5,* 73–85.

WALDO, L., BARNES, L., and BERRY, G. *Total communication checklist and assessment.* Kansas Neurological Institute, 1979.

WARREN, S. F., ROGERS-WARREN, A., BAER, D. M., and GUESS, D. Assessment and facilitation of language generalization. In W. Sailor, B. Wilcox, and L. Brown (eds.), *Methods of instruction for severely handicapped students.* Baltimore: Paul H. Brookes, 1980.

WARYAS, C., and STREMEL-CAMPBELL, K. Grammatical training for the language-delayed child. In R. L. Schiefelbusch (ed.), *Language intervention strategies.* Baltimore: University Park Press, 1978, 145–192.

WEHMAN, P. Project employability: Toward competitive employment for severely disabled individuals. In P. Wehman and J. Hill (eds.), *Vocational training and placement of severely disabled persons (Project employability – Vol. 1).* Richmond, Va.: Virginia Commonwealth University, 1979, 1–23.

WEHMAN, P. Training and advocacy in job placement of severely handicapped workers. In P. Wehman and Mark Hill (eds.), *Vocational training and placement of severely disabled persons: Project employability.* Richmond, Va.: Virginia Commonwealth University, 1980, 12–27.

WEHMAN, P., RENZAGILA, A., BERRY, G., SCHUTZ, R., and KARAN, O. Developing a leisure skill repertoire in severely and profoundly handicapped persons. *AAESPH Review,* 1978, *3,* 162–172.

WEHMAN, P., RENZAGILA, A., and SCHUTZ, R. Behavioral training strategies in sheltered workshops for the severely developmentally disabled. *AAESPH Review,* 1977, *2,* 24–36.

WEHMAN, P., and SCHLEIEN, S. Assessment and selection of leisure skills for severely handicapped individuals. *Education and Training of the Mentally Retarded,* 1980, *15,* 50–57.

WEHMAN, P., and SCHLEIEN, S. *Leisure skills curriculum for developmentally disabled persons: Virginia model (Book III: Hobbies).* Richmond, Va.: Virginia Commonwealth University, 1979a.

WEHMAN, P., and SCHLEIEN, S. *Leisure skills curriculum for developmentally disabled persons: Virginia model (Book IV: Sports).* Richmond, Va.: Virginia Commonwealth University, 1979b.

WEHMAN, P., and SCHLEIEN, S. *Leisure programs for handicapped persons: Adaptations, techniques, and curriculum.* Baltimore: University Park Press, 1981.

WHEELER, A. H., and FOX, W. L. *Managing behavior, part V: Behavior modification: A teacher's guide to writing instructional objectives.* Lawrence, Kans.: H and H Enterprises, 1972.

WHITE, O. R. Adaptive performance objectives: Form versus function. In W. Sailor, B. Wilcox, and L. Brown (eds.), *Methods of instruction for severely handicapped students.* Baltimore: Paul H. Brookes, 1980.

WHITE, O. R., and HARING, N. G. *Exceptional teaching: A multimedia training package.* Columbus, Ohio: Charles E. Merrill, 1976.

WHITE, O. R., HARING, N. G., EDGAR, E., and BENDERSKY, J. *Uniform performance assessment system (UPAS).* Seattle: College of Education, Experimental

Education Unit, Child Development and Mental Retardation Center, University of Washington, 1978.

WILCOX, B., and THOMPSON, A. *Critical issues in educating autistic children and youth.* U.S. Department of Education, Office of Special Education, November 1980.

WILHELM, H., and LOVAAS, O. I. Stimulus overselectivity: A common feature in autism and mental retardation. *American Journal of Mental Deficiency,* 1976, *81,* 227–241.

WILLIAMS, W. Procedures of task analysis as related to developing instructional programs for the severely handicapped. In L. Brown, T. Crowner, W. Williams, and R. York (eds.), *Madison's alternative for zero exclusion: A book of readings.* Madison, Wis.: University of Wisconsin, 1975.

WING, L. *Autistic children: A guide for parents and professionals.* New York: Brunner/Mazel, 1972.

WOLFENSBERGER, W. *The principle of normalization in human services.* Downsview, Toronto, Canada: National Institute on Mental Retardation, York University Campus, 1972.

WUERCH, B. B., and VOELTZ, L. M. *The Ho'onanea program: A leisure curriculum component for severely handicapped children and youth.* Honolulu, Hawaii: University of Hawaii at Manoa, United States Office of Special Education contract #300-78-0343, 1981.

——— REFERENCE NOTES ———

Chapter 1

1. UTLEY, B., GOETZ, L., GEE, K., BALDWIN, M., SAILOR, W., and PETERSON, J. *Vision assessment and program manual for severely handicapped and/or deaf–blind students.* Bay Area Severely Handicapped Deaf–Blind Project, contract #300–78–0038, U.S. Department of Education, Bureau of Education for the Handicapped, 1981.

Chapter 2

1. BROWN, L., FORD, A., NISBET, J., SWEET, M., DONNELLAN, A., and GRUENEWALD, L. *Opportunities available when severely handicapped students attend chronological age–appropriate regular schools in accordance with the natural proportion.* Unpublished manuscript. University of Wisconsin–Madison and Madison Metropolitan School District, contract #G008102099, U.S. Office of Special Education, 1982.

2. GILHOOL, T., and STUTMAN, E. *Integration of severely handicapped students: Toward criteria for implementing and enforcing the integration imperative of P.L. 94–142 and section 504 (P.L. 93–112).* Paper presented at BEH National Conference on the Concept of the Least Restrictive Environment, Washington, D.C., 1978.

Chapter 3

1. AZRIN, N. H. *Toilet training and mealtime behavior.* Paper presented at the Annual Atlanta Behavior Modification Workshop, March 1973.

Chapter 4

1. GEE, K. J. *Assessment, analysis, and training of generalization in the usage of two manual signs with three non–verbal severely retarded students.* Unpublished Master's Thesis, San Francisco State University, 1978.

Chapter 5

1. HAAS, R., and HANLINE, M. F. *Ecological inventory for domestic environments.* Unpublished manuscript, Department of Special Education, San Francisco State University, October, 1979.

2. BROWN, L., FORD, A., NISBET, J., SWEET, M., DONNELLAN, A., and GRUENEWALD, L. *Opportunities available when severely handicapped students attend chronological age–appropriate regular schools in accordance with the natural proportion.* Unpublished manuscript, University of Wisconsin–Madison and Madison Metropolitan School District, contract #G008102099, U.S. Office of Special Education, 1982.

Chapter 7

1. WHITE, O. R. *Making daily classroom decisions.* Paper prepared for presentation at the 1981 national conference of the American Educational Research Association in Los Angeles, California, as part of a symposium enntitled "Issues in the Assessment of Handicapped Infants and Preschool Children", chaired by Walter Hodges, April 15, 1981.

2. WHITE, O. R. Personal communication, March, 1982.

Chapter 8

1. MULLIGAN, M., and GUESS, D. Using an individualized curriculum sequencing model for teaching communication skills. In L. McCormick and R. L. Schiefelbusch (eds.), *Language and Communication Disorders: An Introduction.* In press.

2. GOLDSTEIN, D., and ALBERTO, P. *Matching appropriate instructional strategies to number of students and task.* Paper presented at the Sixth Annual Conference of the American Association for the Education of the Severely Profoundly Handicapped, Chicago, October, 1979.

Chapter 9

1. HUTCHISON, D. J. *A model for transdisciplinary staff development.* New York: United Cerebral Palsy Association, 1974.

2. GUESS, D., JONES, C., and LYON, S. *Developing an intervention program for severely/multiply handicapped preschool children: A transdisciplinary approach.* University of Kansas, 1981.

3. MALONEY, T., and MURPHY, M. (eds.), *The project LEARN handbook: Environmental considerations for the severely multiply handicapped/orthopedically impaired's educational setting.* The University of Kansas, Bureau of Child Research, 1978.

4. JONES, C., and TAYLOR, M. *Organizing the classroom.* In D. Guess, C. Jones, and S. Lyon (eds.), *Developing an intervention program for severely/multiply handicapped preschool children: A transdisciplinary approach.* University of Kansas, 1981.

Health Information Form for preschool classroom serving severely handicapped children was developed by Diane Josephesen, R.N., M.S.N., F.N.P., of the Mailman Center for Child Development at the University of Miami and adapted by C. Jones and M. Taylor.

5. JONES, C., and RUES, J. Identification, referral, screening, assessment, and IEP development. In D. Guess, C. Jones, and S. Lyon (eds.), *Developing an intervention program for severely/multiply handicapped preschool children: A transdisciplinary approach*. University of Kansas, 1981.

6. LOWRY, J. *Critical characteristics inventory for early intervention services*. Executive summary. Developmental Disabilities Program, Texas, 1981.

7. BRICKER, D., DENNISON, L., and BRICKER, W. A. *A language intervention program for developmentally young children*. Mailman Center for Child Development Monograph Series, No. 1, 1976.

8. WOOLMAN, M. *The concept of program lattice*. Washington, D.C.: Institute of Educational Research, 1962.

9. BRONICKI, M., HOLVOET, J., and GUESS, D. The individualized curriculum sequence. In D. Guess, C. Jones, and S. Lyon (eds.), *Developing an intervention program for severely/multiply handicapped preschool children: A transdisciplinary approach*. University of Kansas, 1981.

Chapter 10

1. FILLER, J. In a personal communication to the authors (March 1982), John Filler at California State University, Hayward, suggested the following general formula for computing staff ratios for severely handicapped classes:

Start with the assumption that an SH classroom may have *no less* than a staff–student ratio of 1–6. So it is possible to have a class of 12 with one teacher and one aide. *However, none of those students may exhibit any significant behavior problems, all are completely ambulatory without assistance and none have significant medical problems requiring assistance during school.* For each violation of the above condition, an additional .20 of instructional staff time per day is added to the base 1–6 ratio. Using such a formula one would then figure the needed staff–student ratio for classroom one as follows:

1. Total students in classroom one = 9. Given base of 1–6 and adjusting, the actual base ratio for classroom of 9 SH would be 1.5–9.

2.
Behavior problems	= 2
Non toilet trained	= 0
Ambulation problems	= 7
Medical problems	= 0

Total = 9

3. Additional staff needed over the 1.5 base is 9 × .20 = 1.8.

4. Actual minimal staff ratio for classroom one should be 3.3–9 not the 2.5–9 recommended by the authors (Sailor & Guess).

On the other hand, for classroom two:

1. Base = 1.5–9.

2.   Behavior problems   = 0
      Non toilet trained   = 0
      Ambulation problems   = 6
      Medical problems   = 0
                        Total = 6

3. Additional staff needed is 6 × .20 or 1.2.

4. Therefore, actual minimal instruction staff needed for the 9 students in classroom two is 1.5 + 1.2 or 2.7, a figure much closer to the author's 2.5 but still more than what the rigid adherence to a 1–4 would suggest. The advantage to such a system is simply that we determine staff–student ratios on the basis of *actual student* needs, not on an expectancy which arises as a result of the SH terminology with no real data or justification.

2. WALDO, L., RIGGS, P., DAVAZ, K., HIRSCH, M., EYE, R., and MARSHALL, A. *Functional communication board training for the severely handicapped.* Kansas Neurological Institute, n.d. (probably 1982).

3. CLARK, C. R. *Research report 107: A comparative study of young children's ease of learning words represented in the graphic systems of Rebus, Bliss, Carrier–Peak and traditional orthography.* Unpublished paper, Minneapolis, Minn.: Research, Development and Demonstration Center in Education of Handicapped Children, 1977.

4. BROWN, L., FORD, A., NISBET, J., SWEET, M., DONNELLAN, A., and GRUENEWALD, L. *Opportunities available when severely handicapped students attend chronological age–appropriate regular schools in accordance with the natural proportion.* Unpublished manuscript, University of Wisconsin–Madison and Madison School District, contract #G008102099, U.S. Office of Special Education, 1982.

5. GEE, K., ROGER, B., GRAHAM, N., PIUMA, C., BECKSTEAD, S., HALVORSEN, A., MURRAY, C., WALLEN, N., and SAILOR, W. *The social interaction curriculum.* Unpublished manuscript, Project REACH, San Francisco State University, contract #300-80-0745, U.S. Office of Special Education, 1982.

Chapter 11

1. BROWN, L., NISBET, N., FORD, A., SWEET, M., SHIRAGA, B., and LOOMIS, R. *The critical need for nonschool instruction in educational programs for severely handicapped students.* Unpublished manuscript, University of Wisconsin–Madison and Madison Metropolitan School District, contract #G008102099, U.S. Office of Special Education, 1982.

2. WILLIAMS, W., FREIDL, M., and VOGELSBERG, T. *Training needs of prevocational service providers in a small rural state.* Unpublished paper, University of Vermont, 1979.

3. HAAS, R., and HANLINE, M. F. *Ecological inventory for domestic environments.* Unpublished manuscript, Department of Special Education, San Francisco State University, October, 1979.

4. FREAGON, S. Unpublished manuscript, Northern Illinois University, Department of Special Education, Dekalb, Illinois, 1982.

5. WILDGEN, J. *"Once upon a time... " or how to teach retarded children to tell stories–toward conversational speech.* Doctoral dissertation, University of Kansas, 1974.

6. VAN BIERVLEIT, A. *The effects of family dining on the verbal behavior of institutionalized children.* Doctoral dissertation, University of Kansas, 1979.

7. JOHNSON, J. *How to produce picture books.* Unpublished paper, Bureau of Child Research, University of Kansas, 1977.

8. GEE, K., ROGER, B., GRAHAM, N., PIUMA, C., BECKSTEAD, S., HALVORSEN, A., MURRAY, C., WALLEN, N., and SAILOR, W. *The social interaction curriculum.* Unpublished manuscript, Project REACH, San Francisco State University, contract #300-80-0745, U.S. Office of Special Education, 1982.

9. BELLAMY, G. T., SOWERS, J. and BOURBEAU, P. E. *Work and work–related services: Post school options for students with severe handicaps.* Unpublished manuscript, University of Oregon, n.d.

10. MEYERS–WINTON, S. *Models for the education of secondary severely handicapped students.* Unpublished manuscript, University of California, Berkeley/San Francisco State University, 1981.

Chapter 12

1. The Association for the Severely Handicapped. *Newsletter, 6*(1), January, 1980.

2. *The community imperative: A refutation of all arguments in support of institutionalizing anybody because of mental retardation.* Unpublished paper, Center on Human Policy, Syracuse University, 1979.

3. *The severely and multiply developmentally disabled adult. A special report on the need for program services.* Regional Center of the East Bay, Oakland, Calif., 1979.

4. SINGER, G. H., STEMM, H., and CLOSE, D. W. Increasing the social interactions of severely handicapped and nonhandicapped children in an integrated setting. *Journal of the Association for the Severely Handicapped,* in press.

5. LINDSAY, W., ROSENBERG, W., and SAILOR, W. *Over 21: A program for severely disabled adults.* State of California, Health and Welfare Agency, Department of Developmental Services contract #81-68120, awarded May, 1982.

AUTHOR INDEX

SUBJECT INDEX

—— READER RESPONSE FORM ——

We would like to find out what your reactions are to *Severely Handicapped Students: An Instructional Design.* Your evaluation of the book will help us respond to the interests and needs of the readers of future editions. Please complete the form and mail it to College Marketing, Houghton Mifflin Company, One Beacon Street, Boston, MA 02108.

1. We would like to know how you rate our textbook in each of the following areas:

	Excellent	Good	Adequate	Poor
a. Selection of topics	———	———	———	———
b. Detail of Coverage	———	———	———	———
c. Order of topics	———	———	———	———
d. Writing style/readability	———	———	———	———
e. Explanation of concepts	———	———	———	———
f. Illustrations	———	———	———	———

2. Please cite specific examples that illustrate any of the above ratings.

_____

_____

_____

3. Describe the strongest feature(s) of the book.

_____

_____

_____

4. Describe the weakest feature(s) of the book.

_____

_____

_____

5. What other topics should be included in this text?

_____

_____

_____

6. What recommendations can you make for improving this book?

_____

_____

_____